ACCA

13 TERRITORY INSPECTION DEPARTMENT

NATSUME ONO

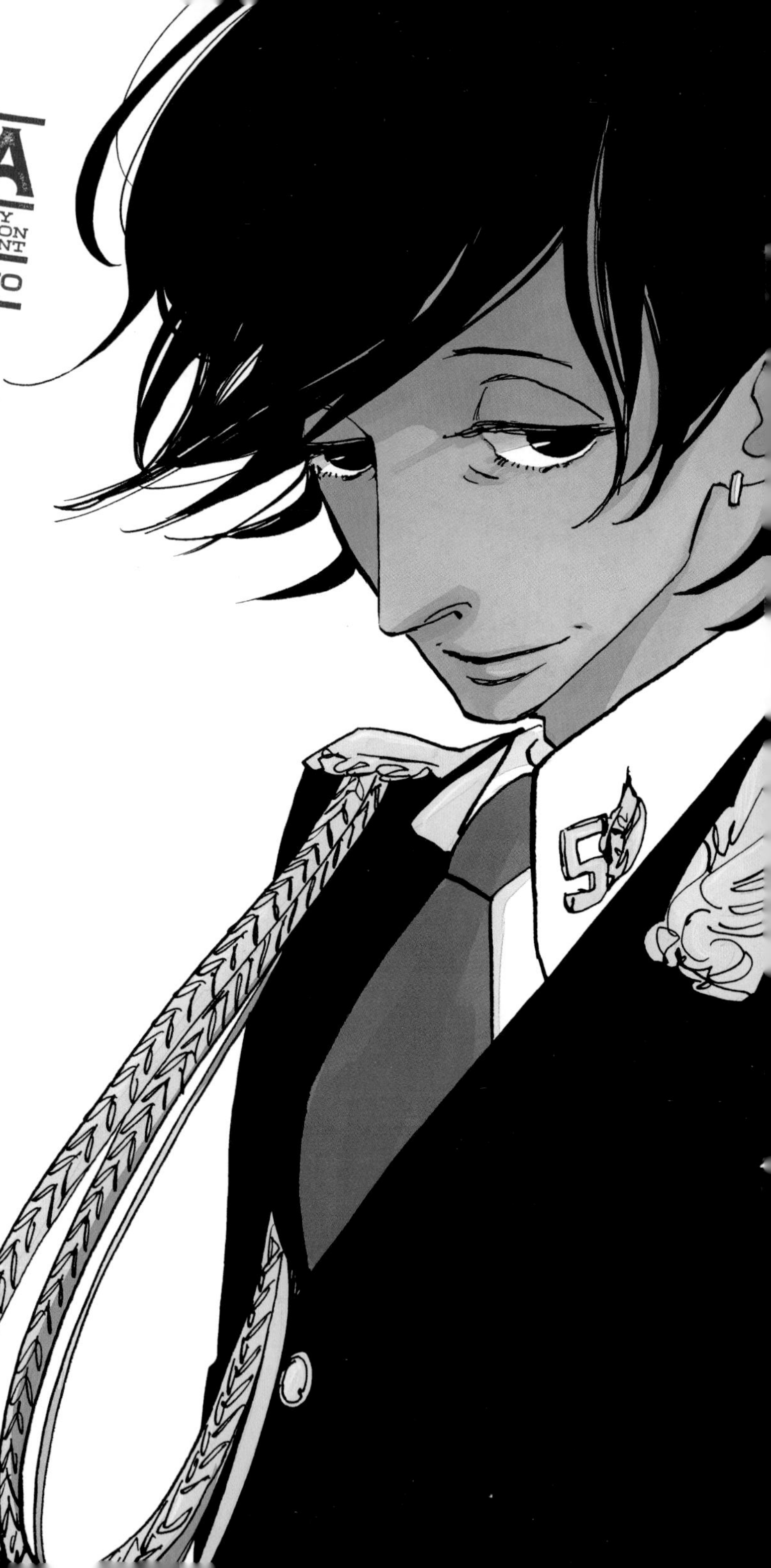

5

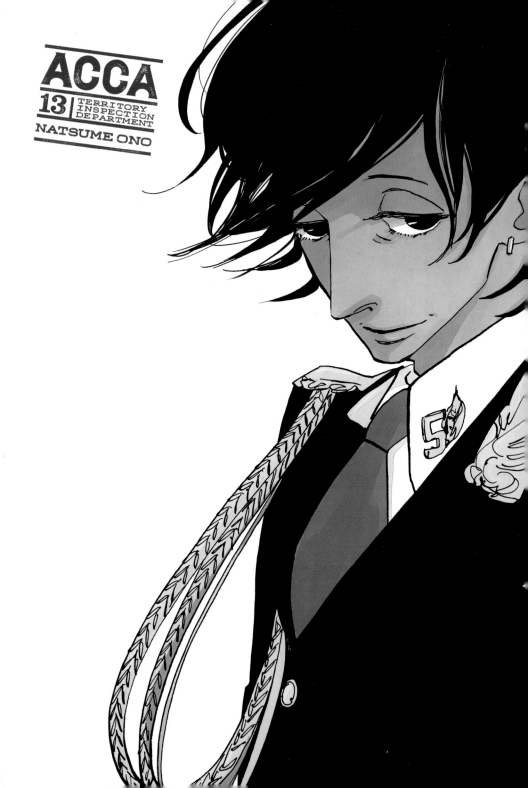

ACCA
13 TERRITORY INSPECTION DEPARTMENT
CONTENTS

5

A C C A
13 Terr Insp Dept
Natsume Ono

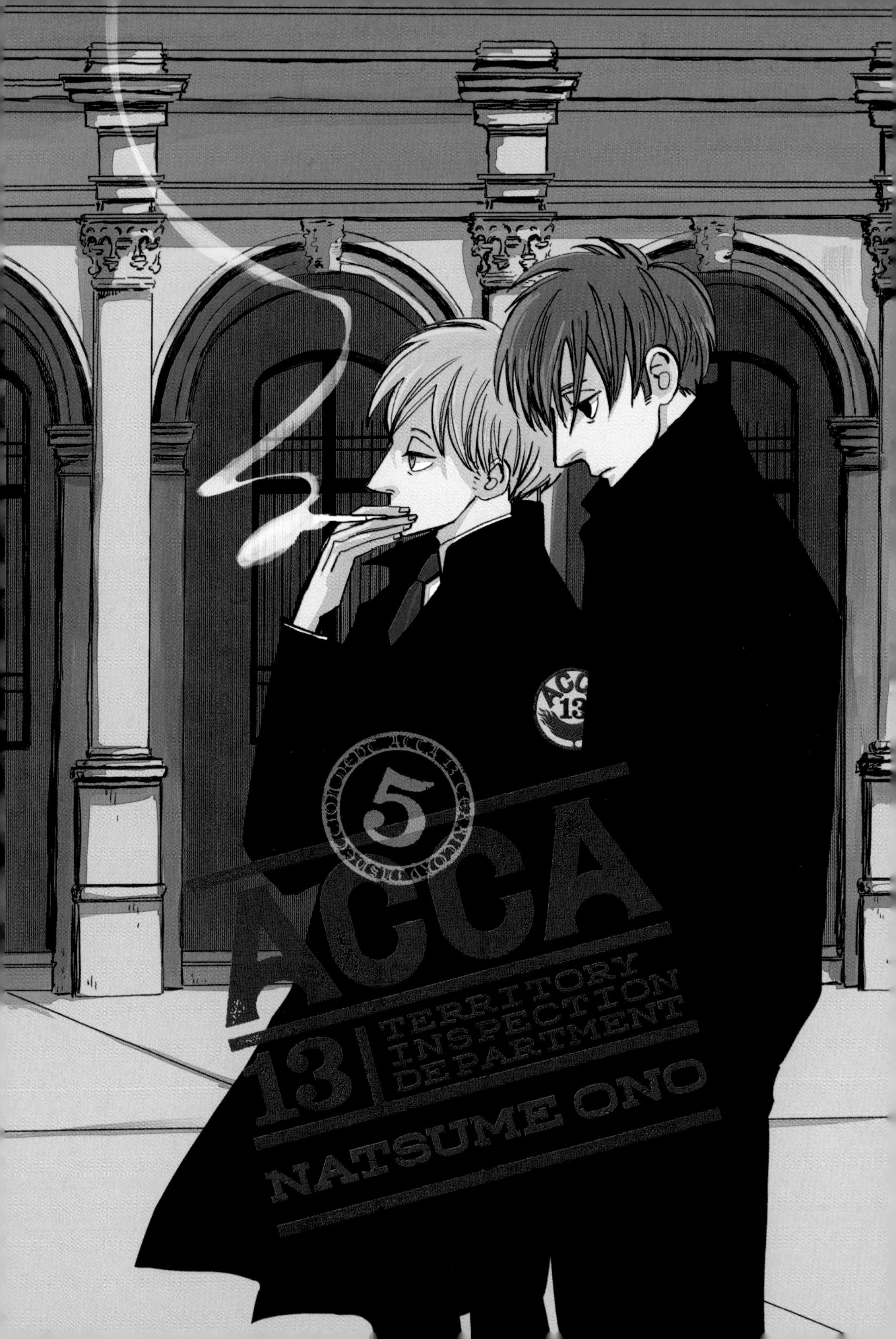
5
ACCA
13
TERRITORY
INSPECTION
DEPARTMENT
NATSUME ONO

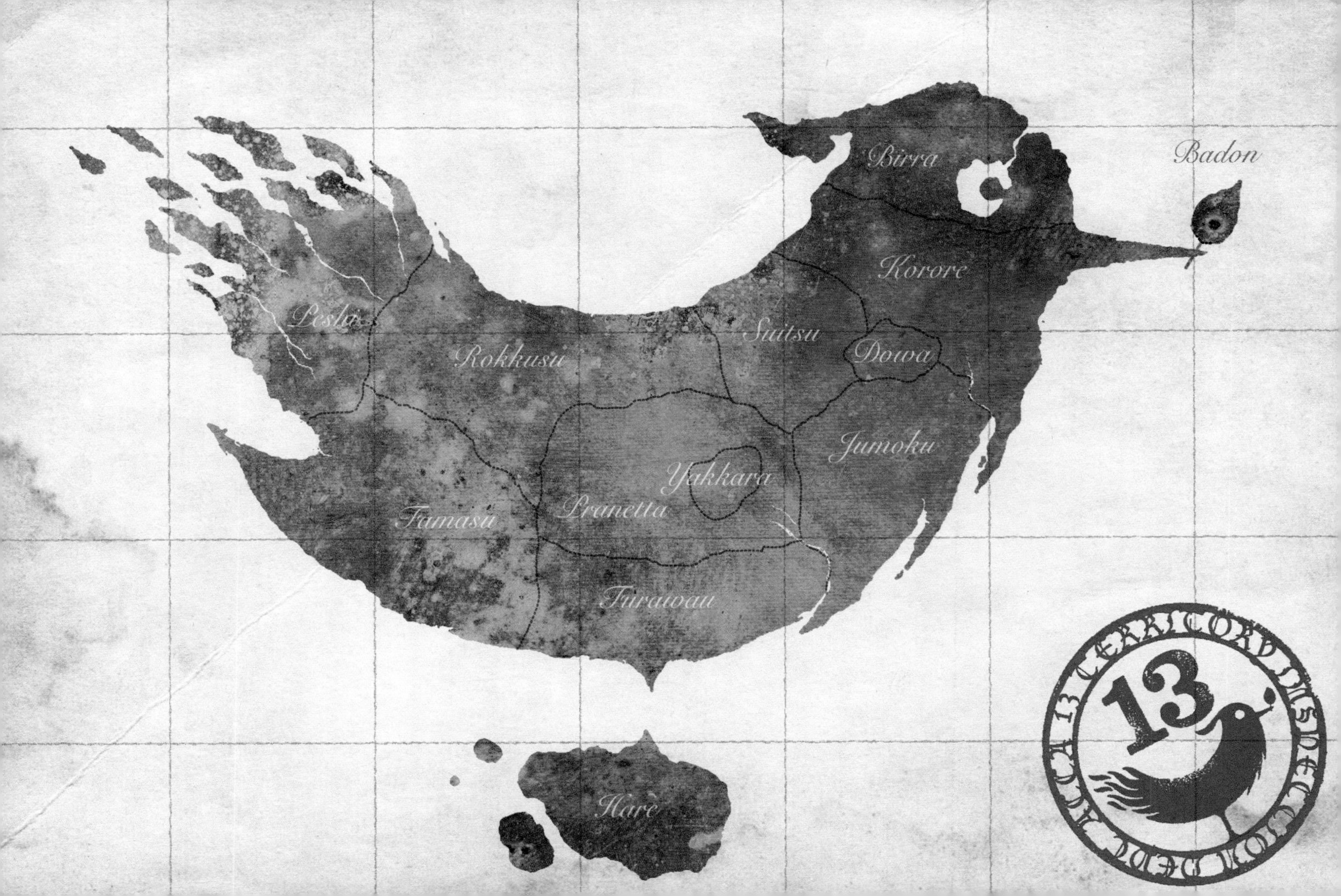
Badon
Birra
Korore
Pesla
Suitsu
Dowa
Rokkusu
Jumoku
Yakkara
Famasu
Pranetta
Furawau
Hare
13

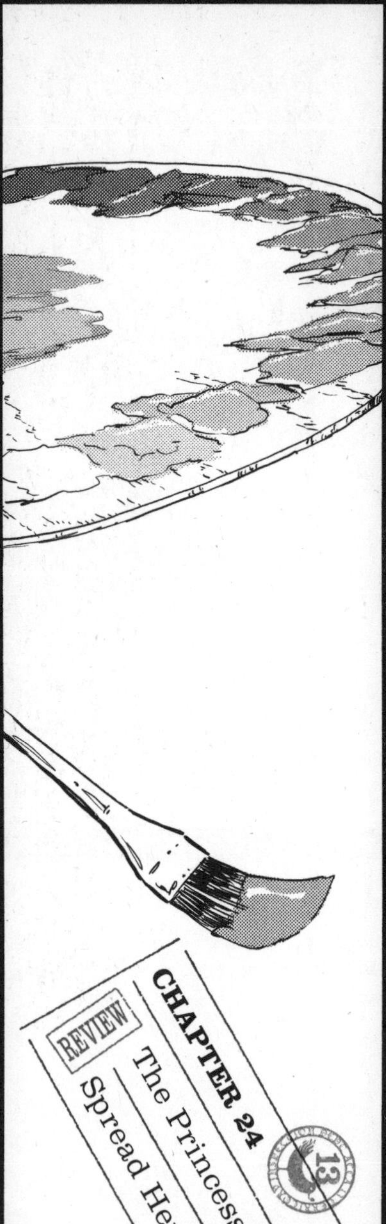
REVIEW
CHAPTER 24
The Princess Who
Spread Her Wings
13

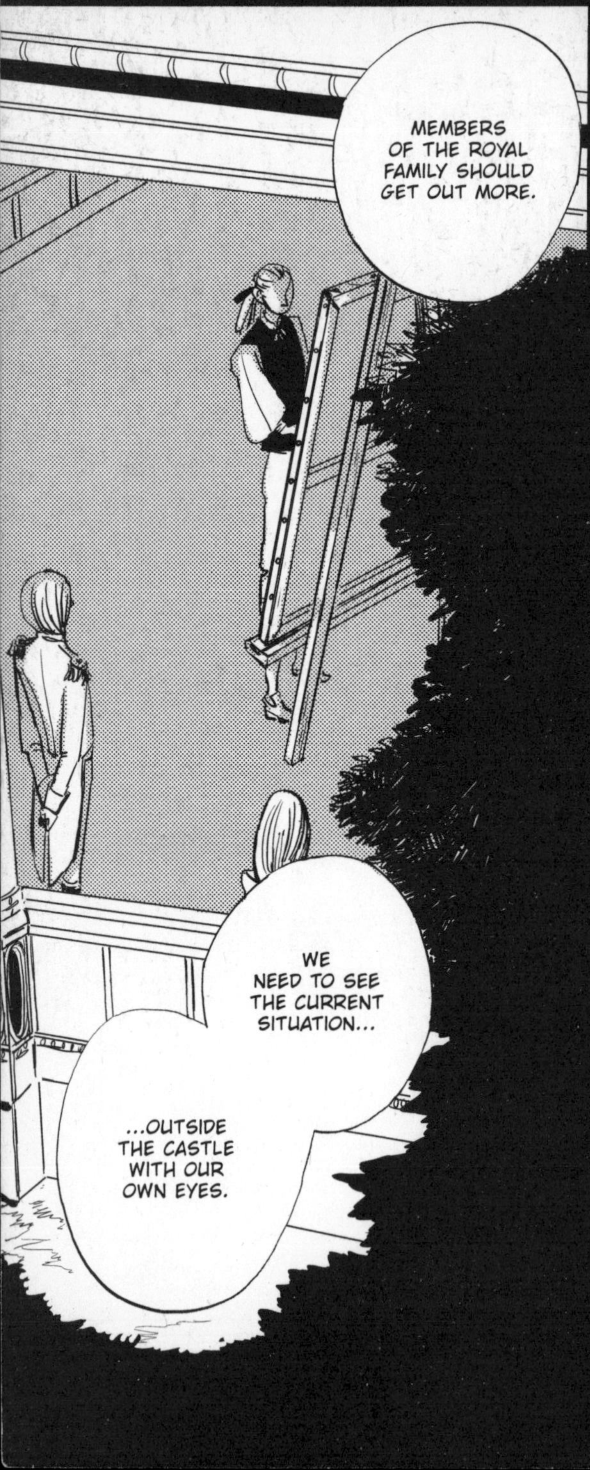
MEMBERS OF THE ROYAL FAMILY SHOULD GET OUT MORE.
WE NEED TO SEE THE CURRENT SITUATION...
...OUTSIDE THE CASTLE WITH OUR OWN EYES.

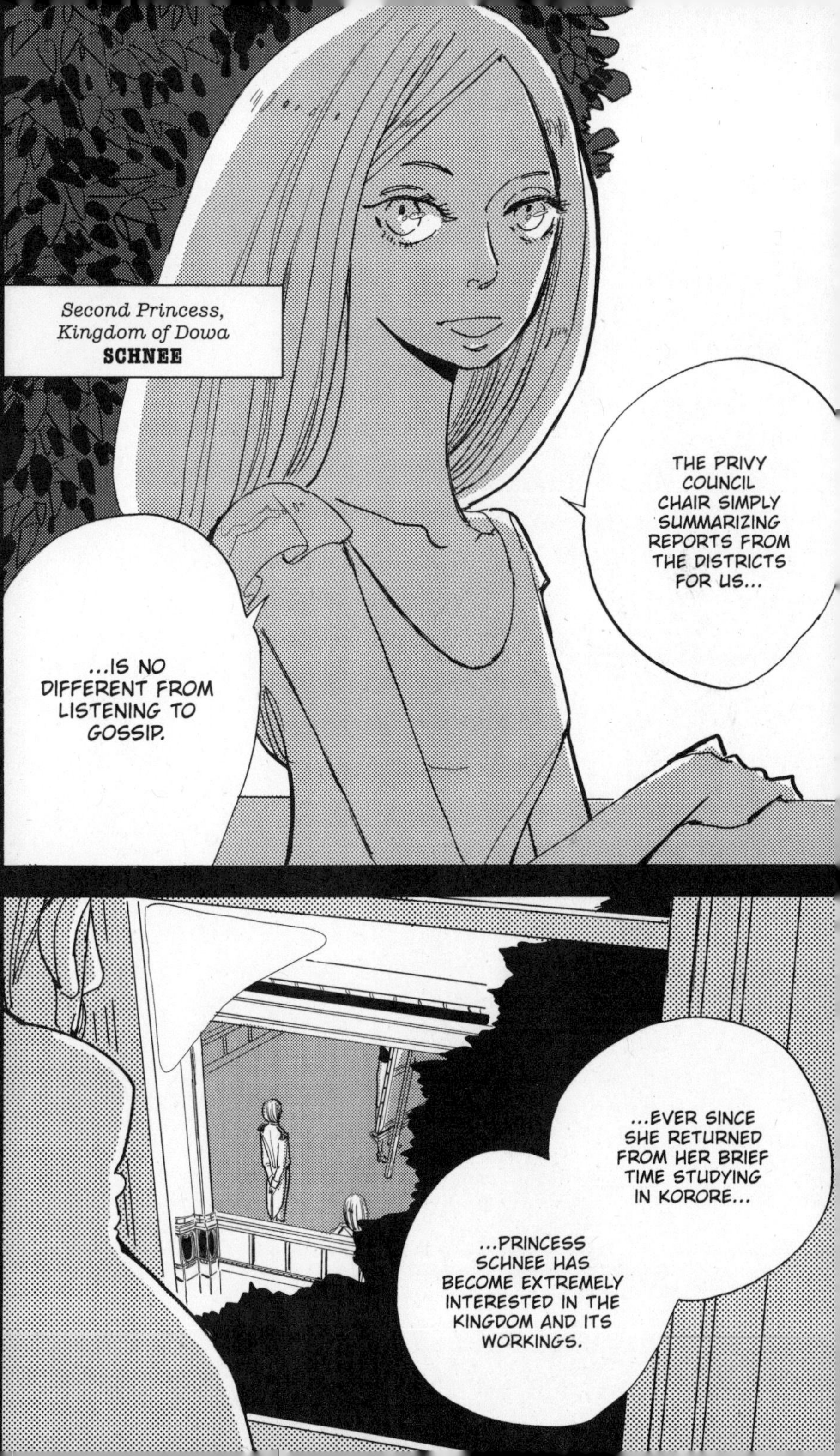
Second Princess, Kingdom of Dowa SCHNEE
THE PRIVY COUNCIL CHAIR SIMPLY SUMMARIZING REPORTS FROM THE DISTRICTS FOR US...
...IS NO DIFFERENT FROM LISTENING TO GOSSIP.
...EVER SINCE SHE RETURNED FROM HER BRIEF TIME STUDYING IN KORORE...
...PRINCESS SCHNEE HAS BECOME EXTREMELY INTERESTED IN THE KINGDOM AND ITS WORKINGS.

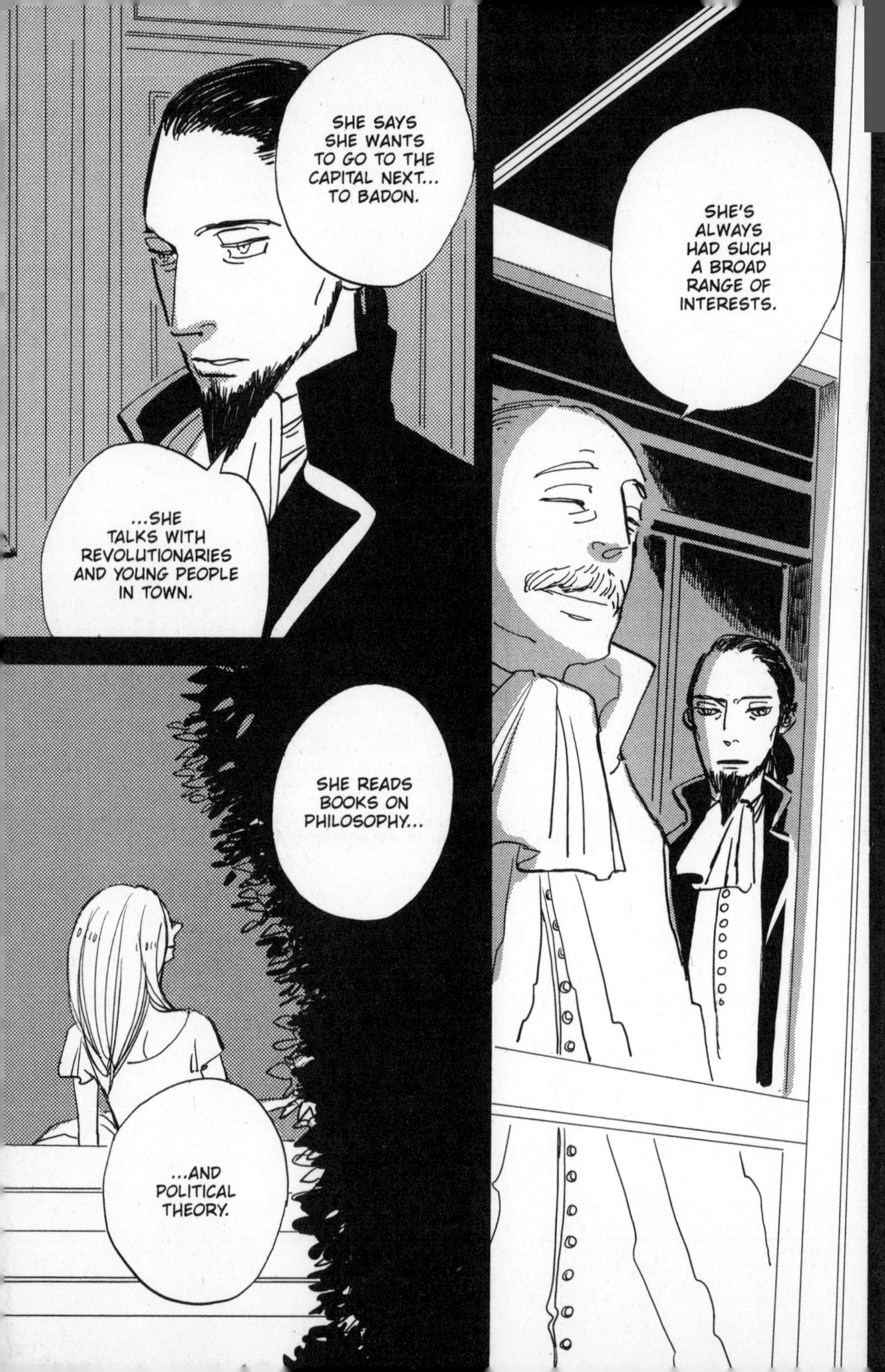
SHE'S ALWAYS HAD SUCH A BROAD RANGE OF INTERESTS.
SHE SAYS SHE WANTS TO GO TO THE CAPITAL NEXT... TO BADON.
...SHE TALKS WITH REVOLUTIONARIES AND YOUNG PEOPLE IN TOWN.
SHE READS BOOKS ON PHILOSOPHY...
...AND POLITICAL THEORY.

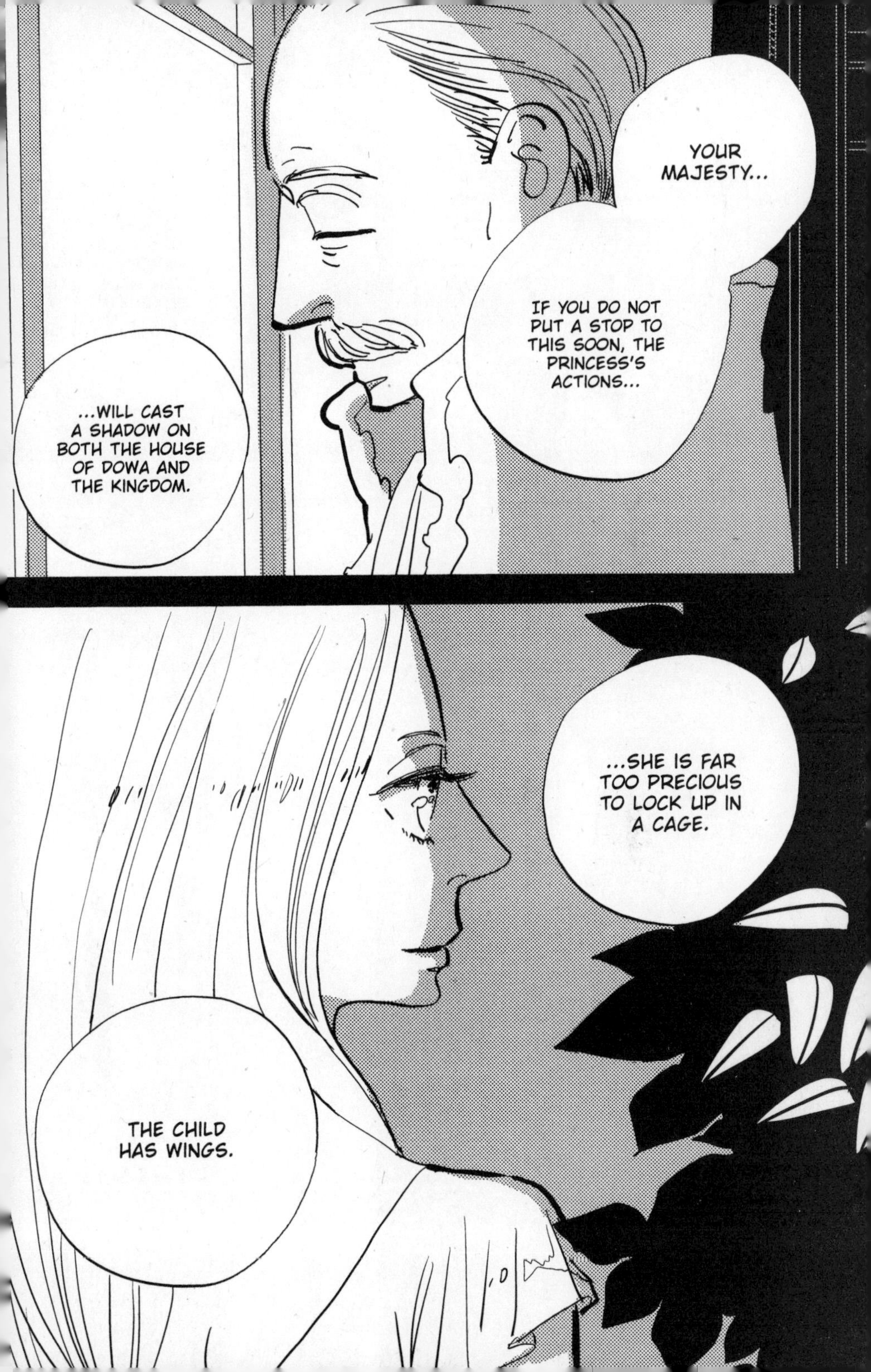
YOUR MAJESTY...
IF YOU DO NOT PUT A STOP TO THIS SOON, THE PRINCESS'S ACTIONS...
...WILL CAST A SHADOW ON BOTH THE HOUSE OF DOWA AND THE KINGDOM.
...SHE IS FAR TOO PRECIOUS TO LOCK UP IN A CAGE.
THE CHILD HAS WINGS.

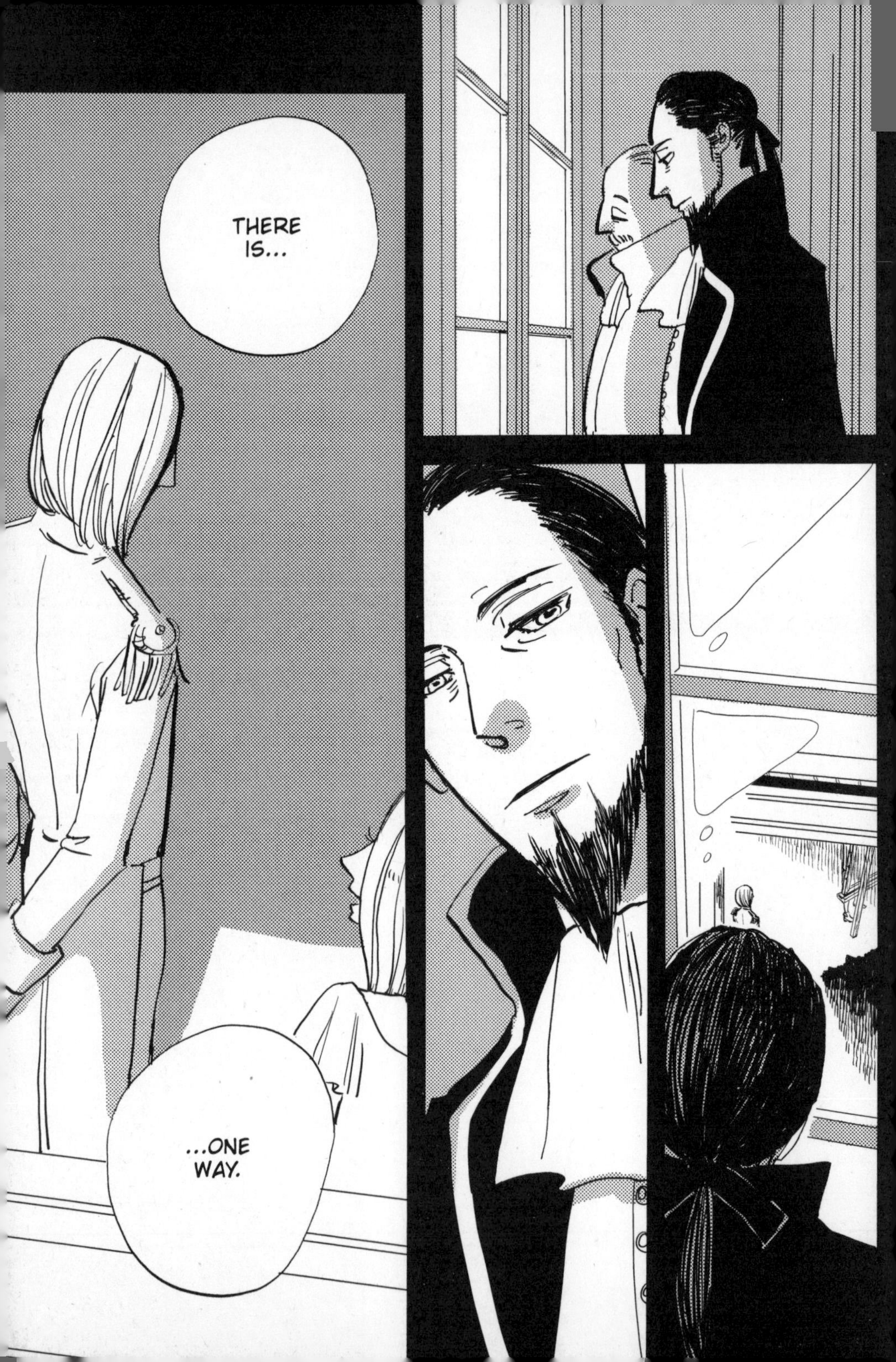
THERE IS...
...ONE WAY.

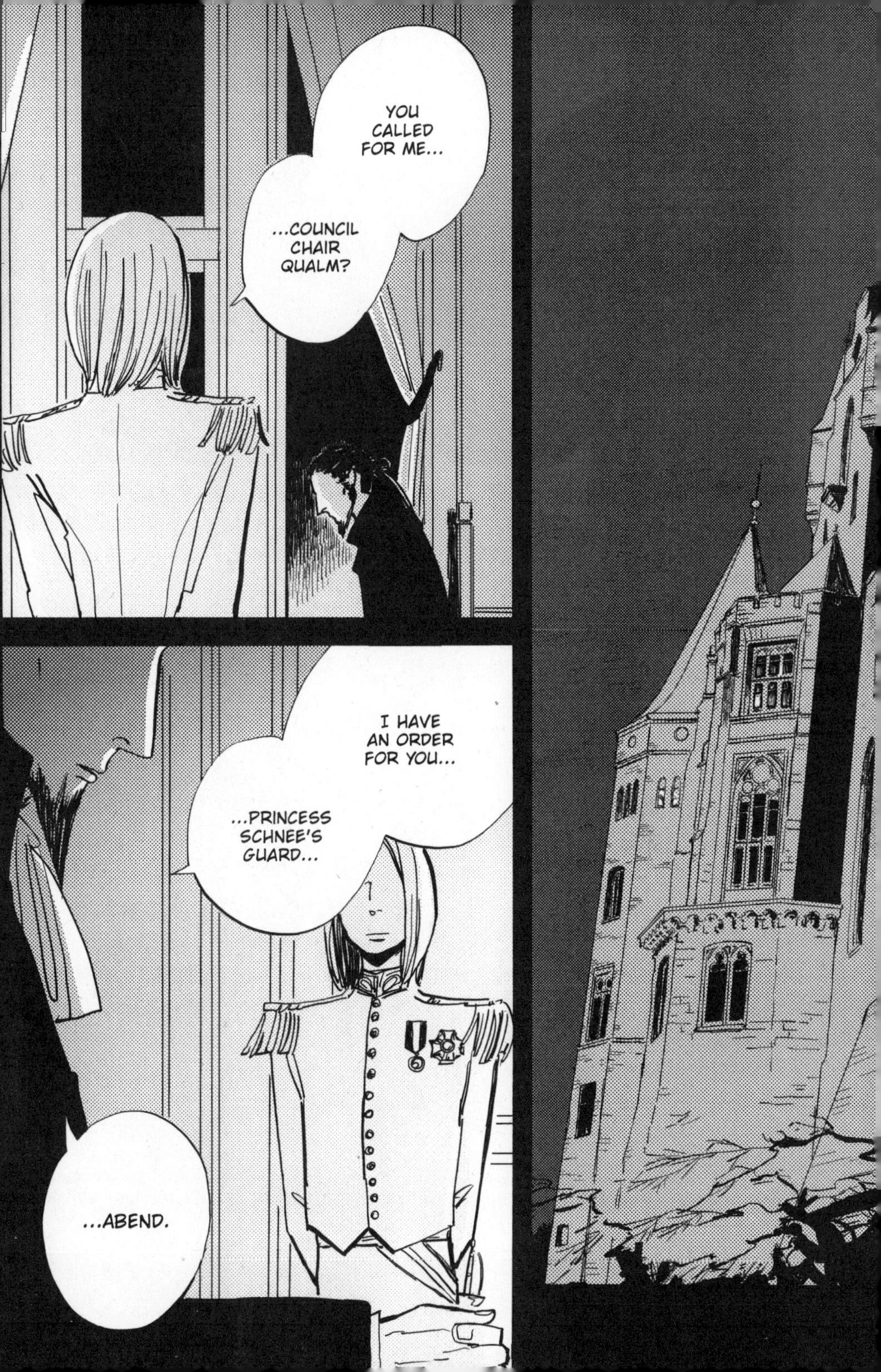
YOU CALLED FOR ME...
...COUNCIL CHAIR QUALM?
I HAVE AN ORDER FOR YOU...
...PRINCESS SCHNEE'S GUARD...
...ABEND.

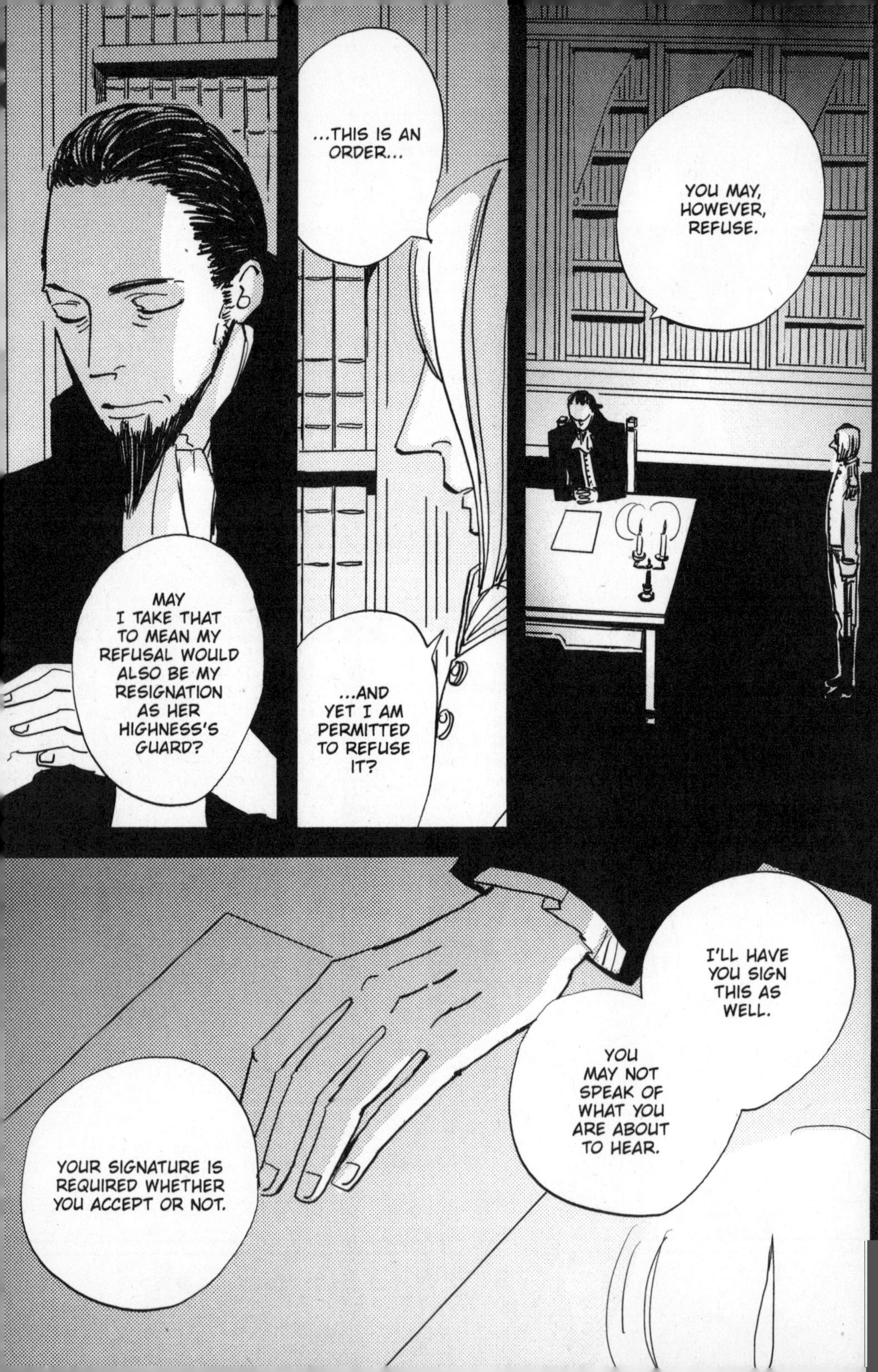
YOU MAY, HOWEVER, REFUSE.
...THIS IS AN ORDER...
...AND YET I AM PERMITTED TO REFUSE IT?
MAY I TAKE THAT TO MEAN MY REFUSAL WOULD ALSO BE MY RESIGNATION AS HER HIGHNESS'S GUARD?
I'LL HAVE YOU SIGN THIS AS WELL.
YOU MAY NOT SPEAK OF WHAT YOU ARE ABOUT TO HEAR.
YOUR SIGNATURE IS REQUIRED WHETHER YOU ACCEPT OR NOT.

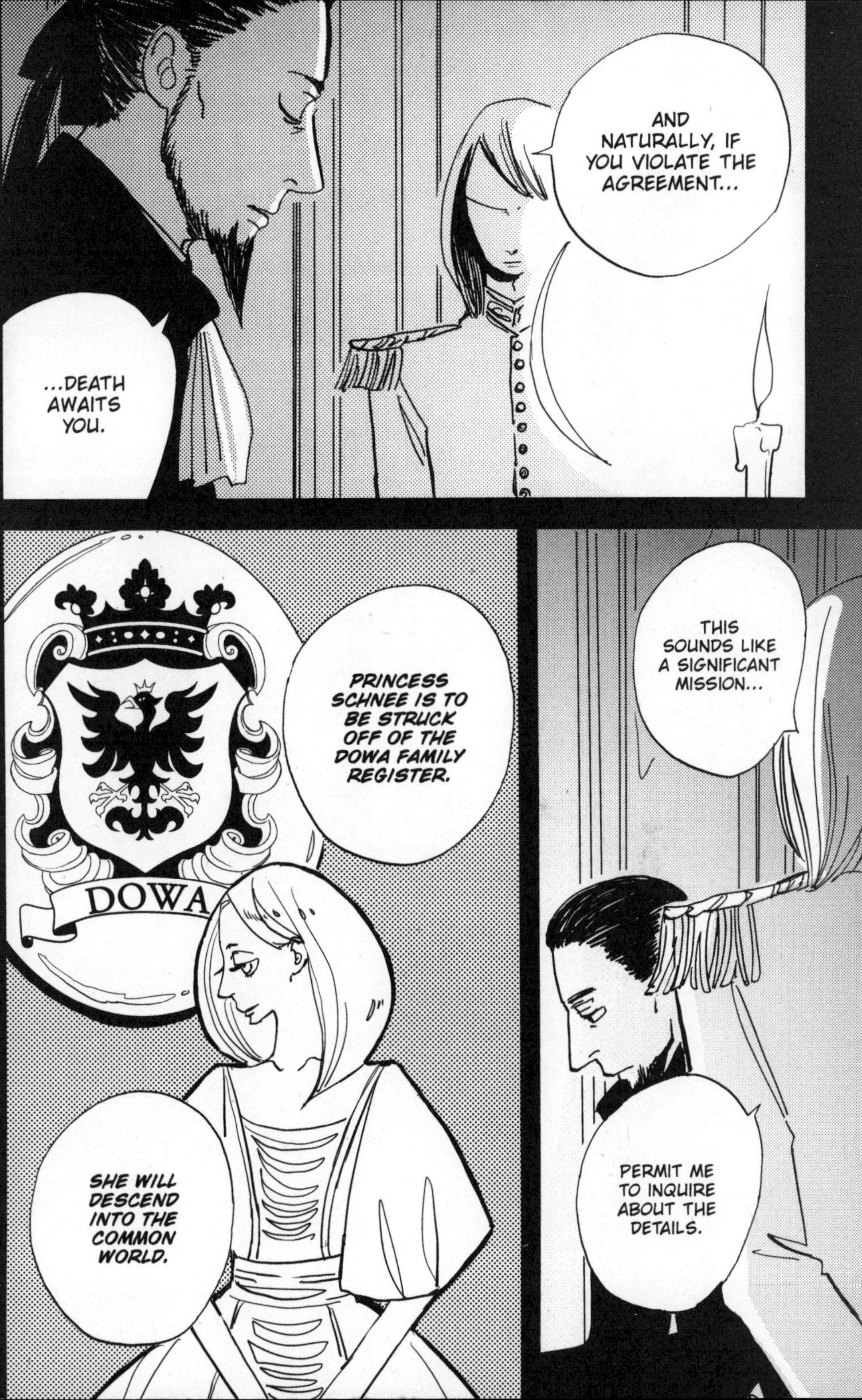
AND NATURALLY, IF YOU VIOLATE THE AGREEMENT...
...DEATH AWAITS YOU.
THIS SOUNDS LIKE A SIGNIFICANT MISSION...
PERMIT ME TO INQUIRE ABOUT THE DETAILS.
PRINCESS SCHNEE IS TO BE STRUCK OFF OF THE DOWA FAMILY REGISTER.
DOWA
SHE WILL DESCEND INTO THE COMMON WORLD.

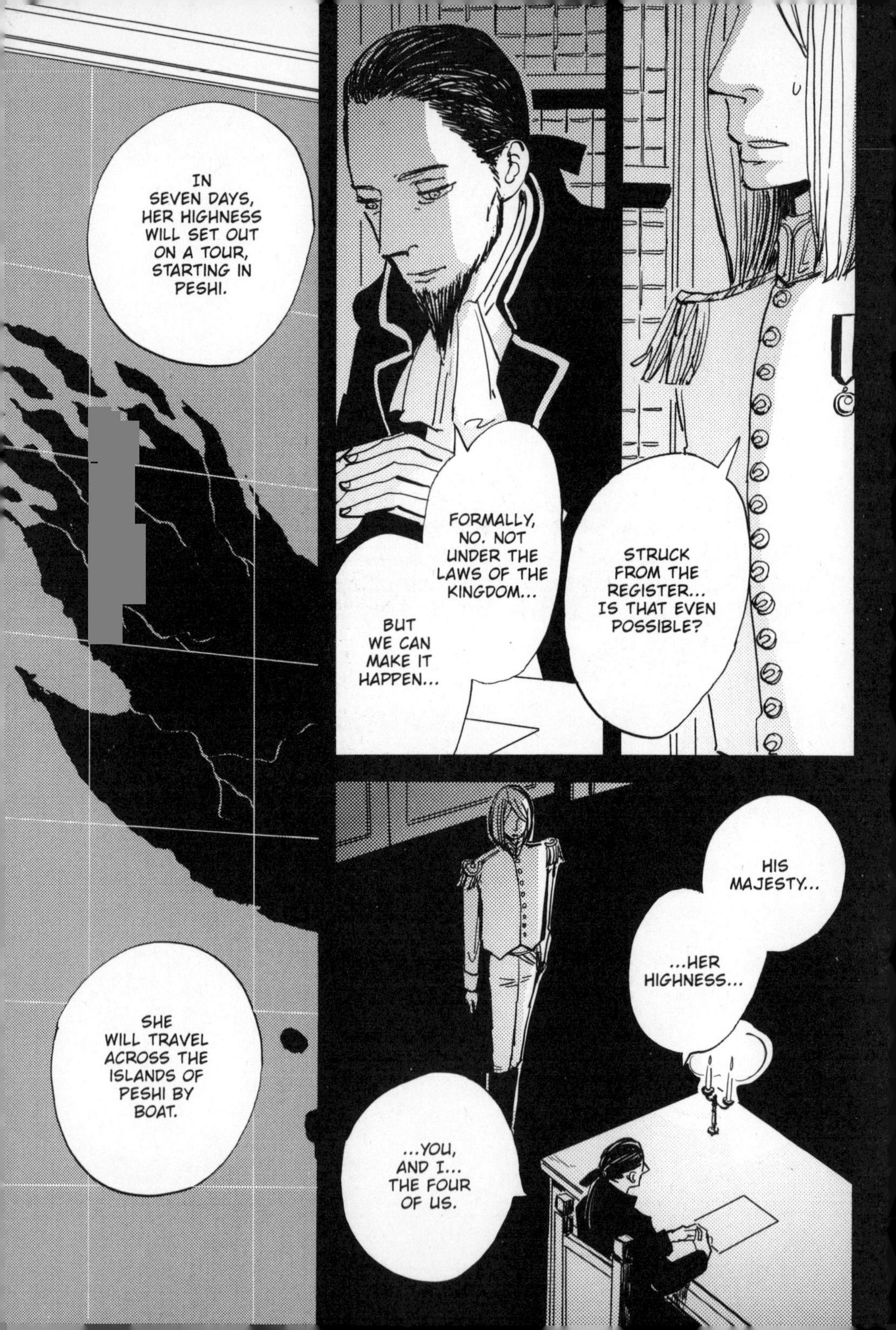
STRUCK FROM THE REGISTER... IS THAT EVEN POSSIBLE?
FORMALLY, NO. NOT UNDER THE LAWS OF THE KINGDOM...
BUT WE CAN MAKE IT HAPPEN...
HIS MAJESTY...
...HER HIGHNESS...
...YOU, AND I... THE FOUR OF US.
IN SEVEN DAYS, HER HIGHNESS WILL SET OUT ON A TOUR, STARTING IN PESHI.
SHE WILL TRAVEL ACROSS THE ISLANDS OF PESHI BY BOAT.

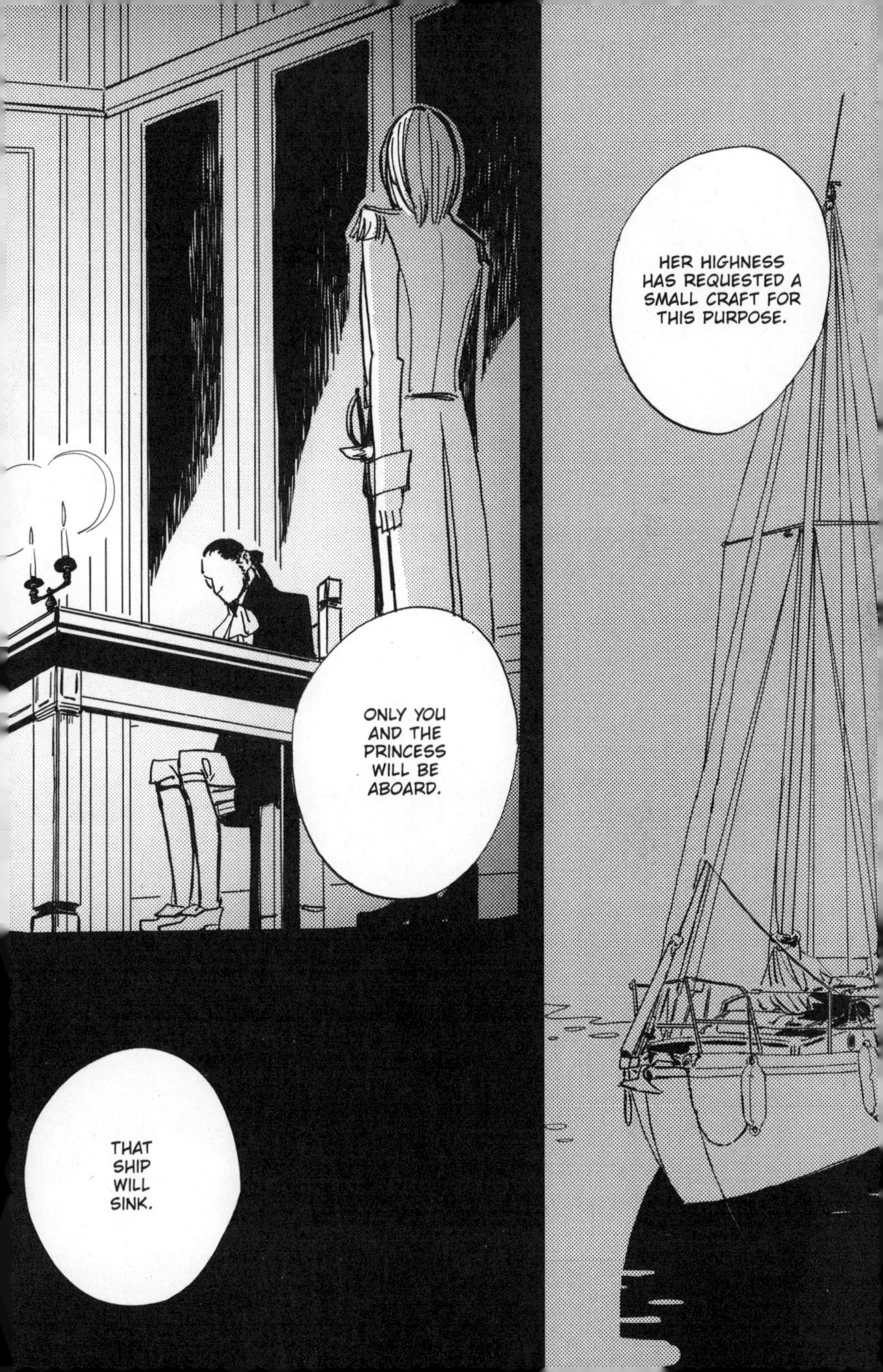
HER HIGHNESS HAS REQUESTED A SMALL CRAFT FOR THIS PURPOSE.
ONLY YOU AND THE PRINCESS WILL BE ABOARD.
THAT SHIP WILL SINK.

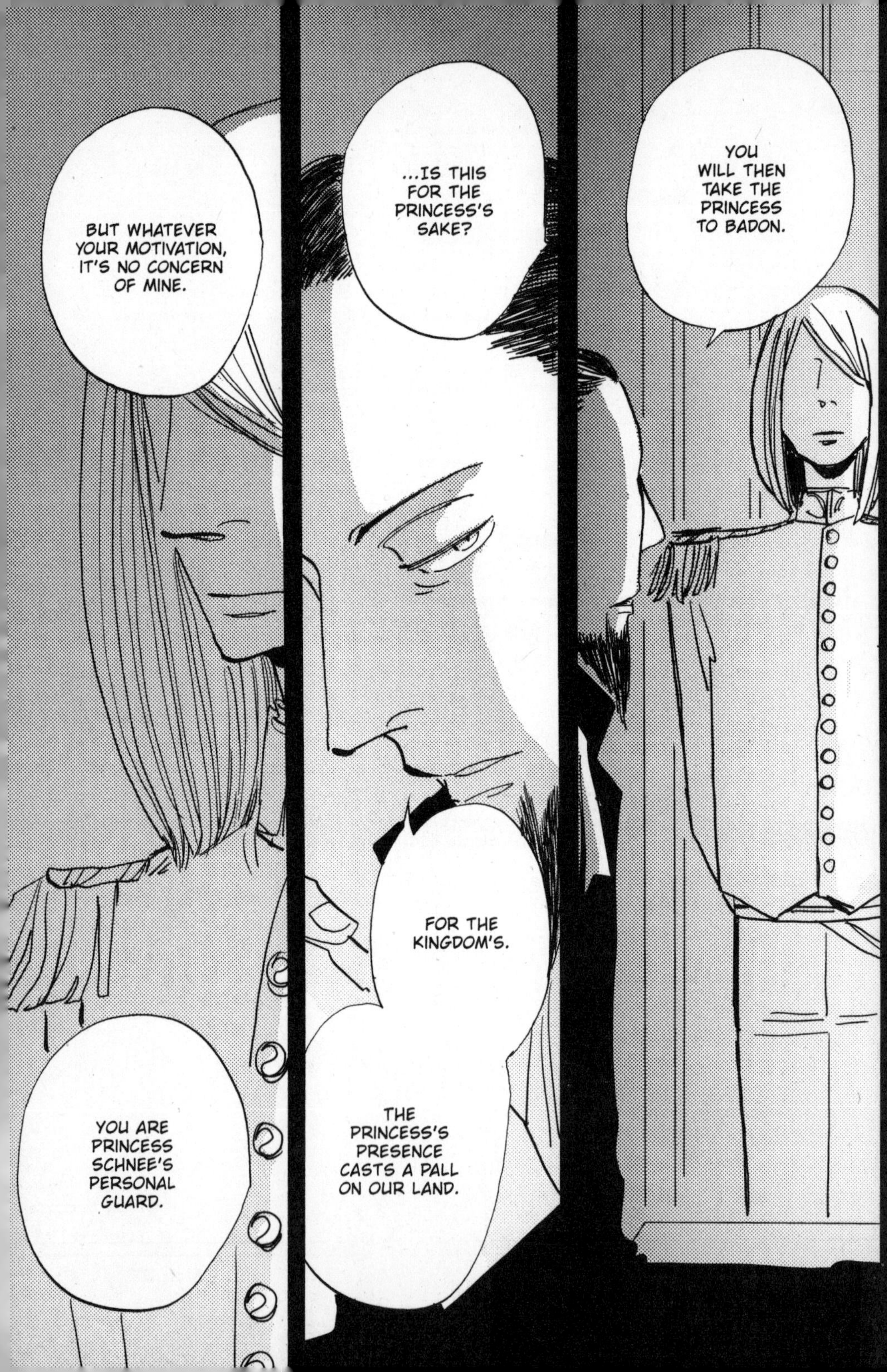
YOU WILL THEN TAKE THE PRINCESS TO BADON.
...IS THIS FOR THE PRINCESS'S SAKE?
FOR THE KINGDOM'S.
THE PRINCESS'S PRESENCE CASTS A PALL ON OUR LAND.
BUT WHATEVER YOUR MOTIVATION, IT'S NO CONCERN OF MINE.
YOU ARE PRINCESS SCHNEE'S PERSONAL GUARD.

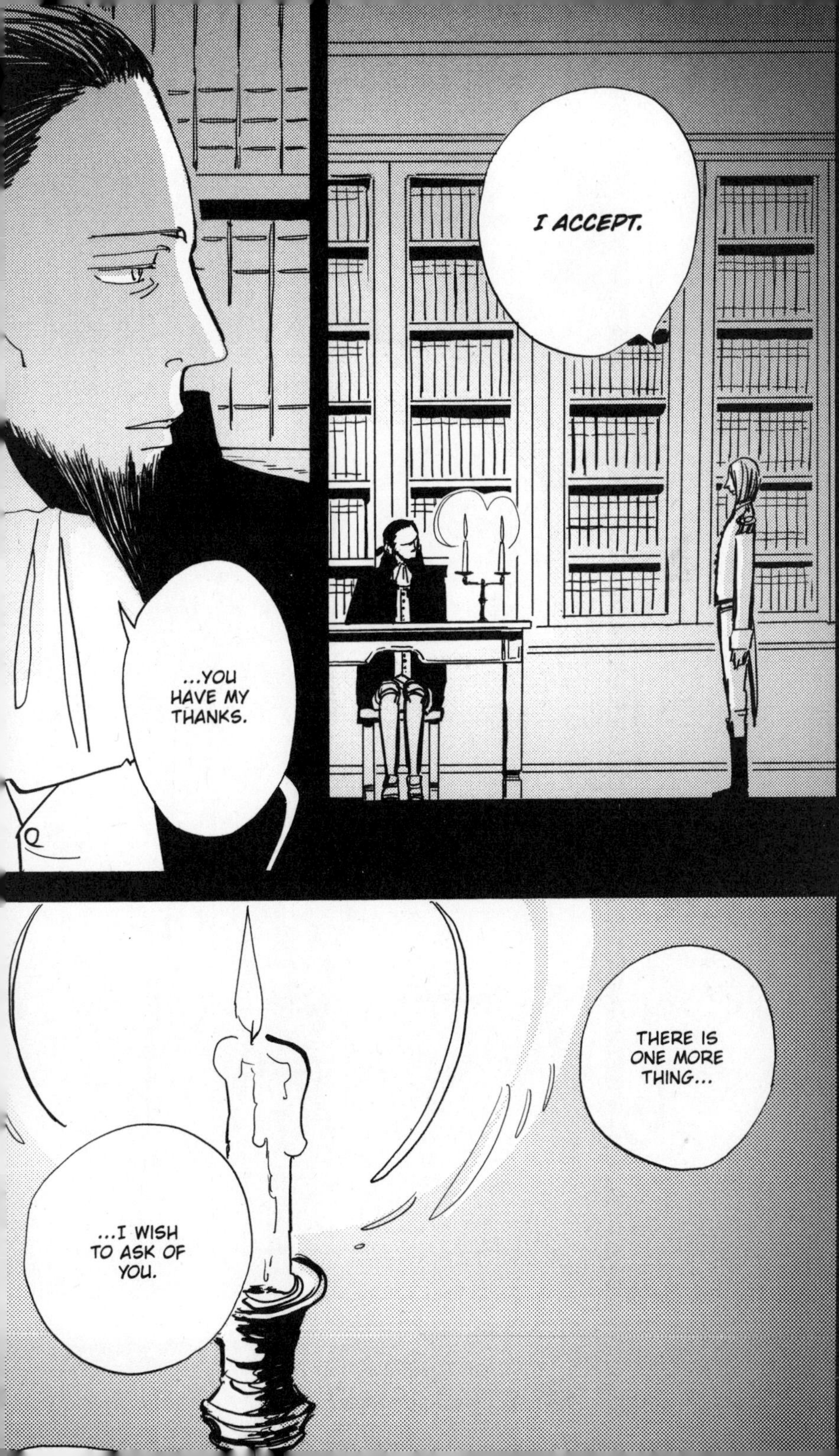
I ACCEPT.
...YOU HAVE MY THANKS.
THERE IS ONE MORE THING...
...I WISH TO ASK OF YOU.

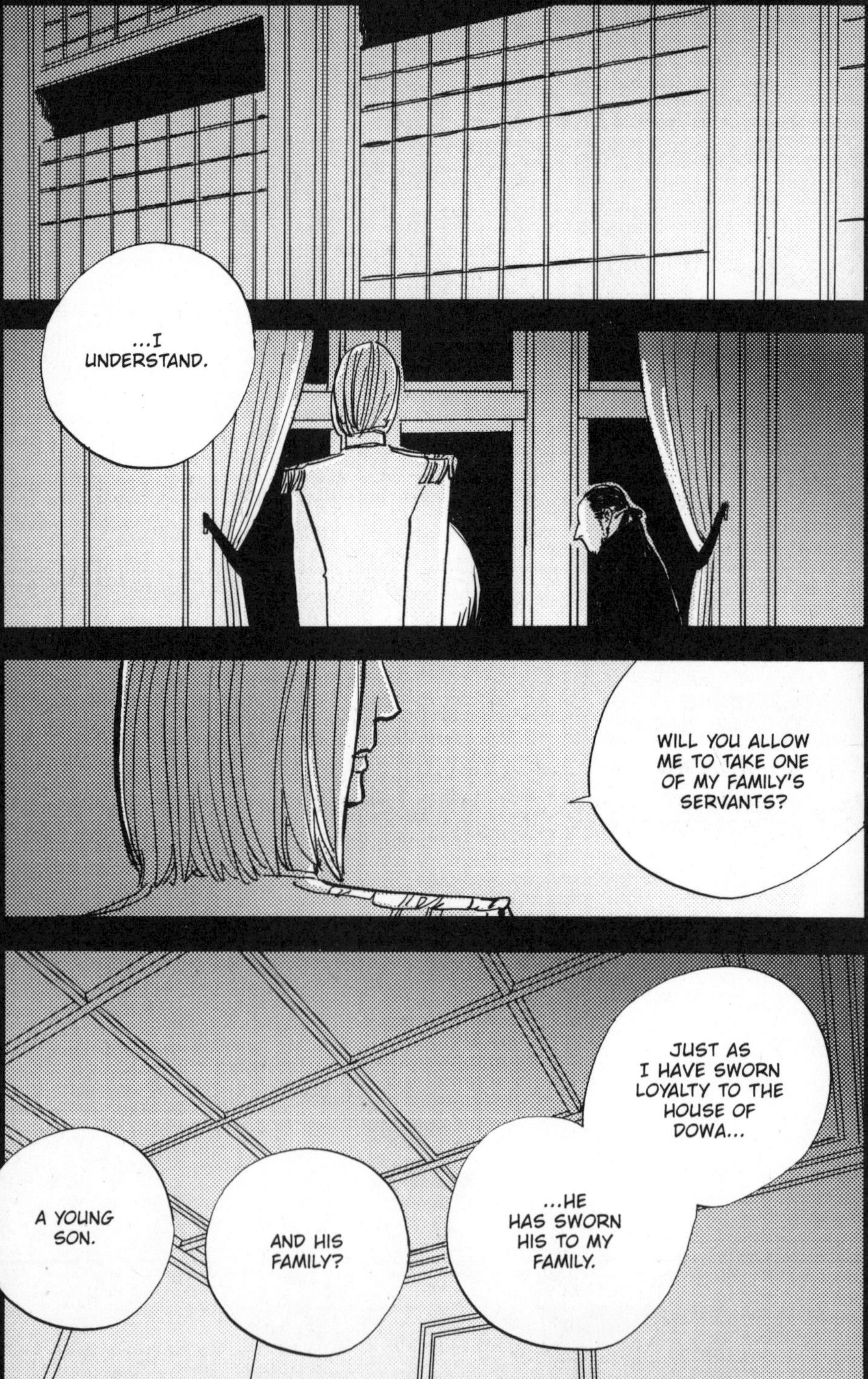
...I UNDERSTAND.
WILL YOU ALLOW ME TO TAKE ONE OF MY FAMILY'S SERVANTS?
JUST AS I HAVE SWORN LOYALTY TO THE HOUSE OF DOWA...
...HE HAS SWORN HIS TO MY FAMILY.
AND HIS FAMILY?
A YOUNG SON.

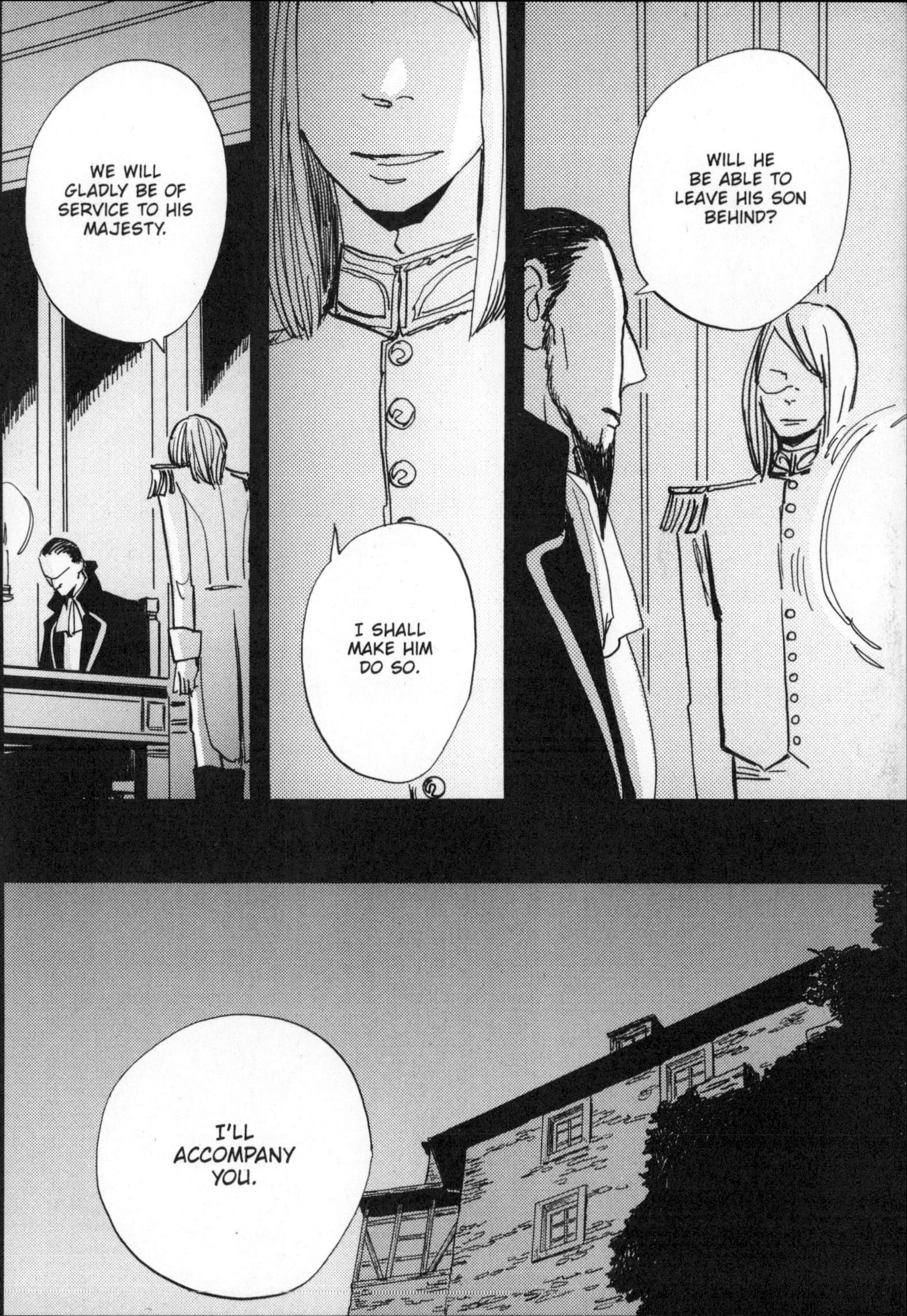
WILL HE BE ABLE TO LEAVE HIS SON BEHIND?
I SHALL MAKE HIM DO SO.
WE WILL GLADLY BE OF SERVICE TO HIS MAJESTY.
I'LL ACCOMPANY YOU.

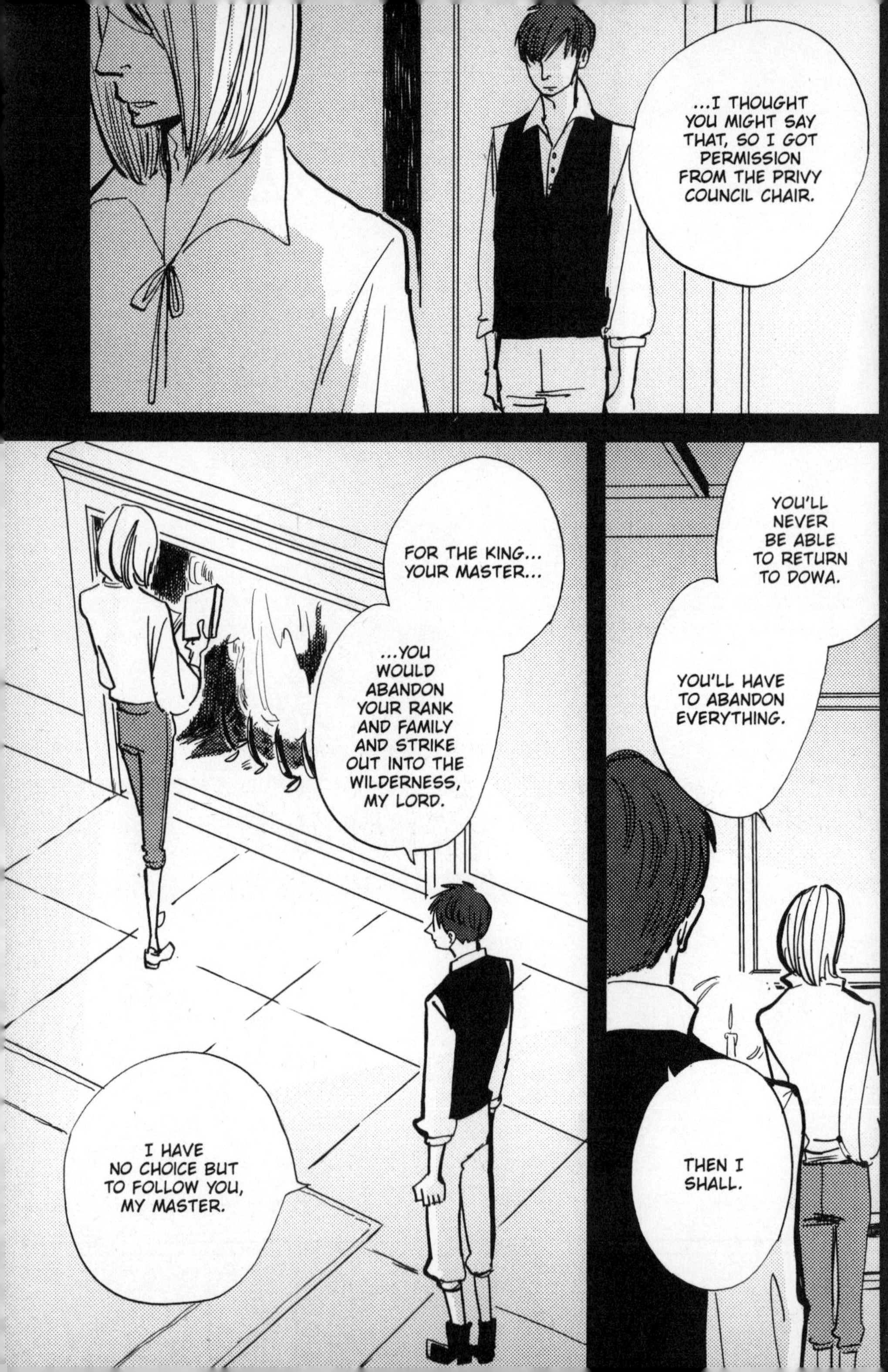
...I THOUGHT YOU MIGHT SAY THAT, SO I GOT PERMISSION FROM THE PRIVY COUNCIL CHAIR.
YOU'LL NEVER BE ABLE TO RETURN TO DOWA.
YOU'LL HAVE TO ABANDON EVERYTHING.
THEN I SHALL.
FOR THE KING... YOUR MASTER...
...YOU WOULD ABANDON YOUR RANK AND FAMILY AND STRIKE OUT INTO THE WILDERNESS, MY LORD.
I HAVE NO CHOICE BUT TO FOLLOW YOU, MY MASTER.

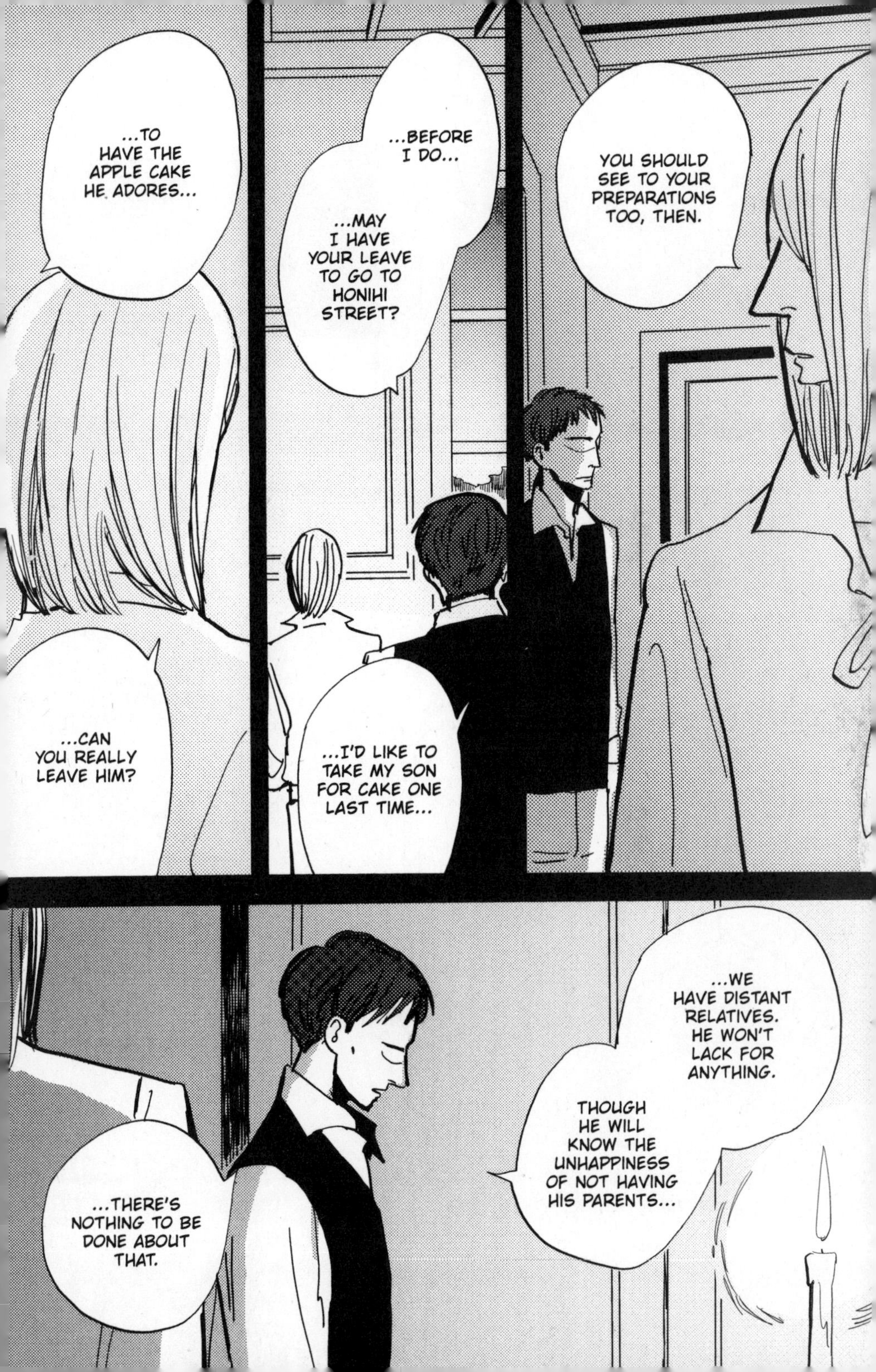
YOU SHOULD SEE TO YOUR PREPARATIONS TOO, THEN.
...BEFORE I DO...
...MAY I HAVE YOUR LEAVE TO GO TO HONIHI STREET?
...I'D LIKE TO TAKE MY SON FOR CAKE ONE LAST TIME...
...TO HAVE THE APPLE CAKE HE ADORES...
...CAN YOU REALLY LEAVE HIM?
...WE HAVE DISTANT RELATIVES. HE WON'T LACK FOR ANYTHING.
THOUGH HE WILL KNOW THE UNHAPPINESS OF NOT HAVING HIS PARENTS...
...THERE'S NOTHING TO BE DONE ABOUT THAT.

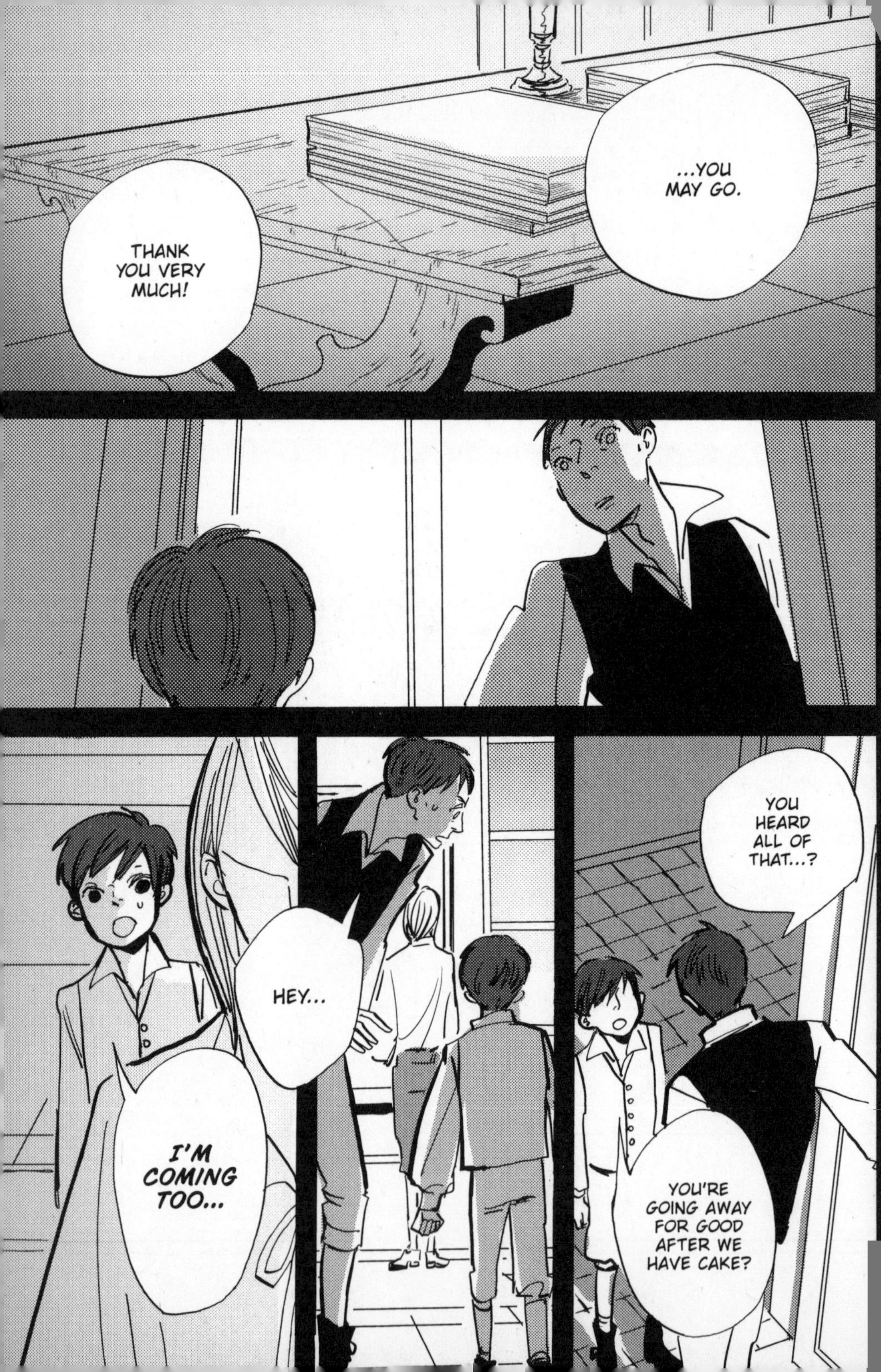
...YOU MAY GO.
THANK YOU VERY MUCH!
YOU HEARD ALL OF THAT...?
YOU'RE GOING AWAY FOR GOOD AFTER WE HAVE CAKE?
HEY...
I'M COMING TOO...

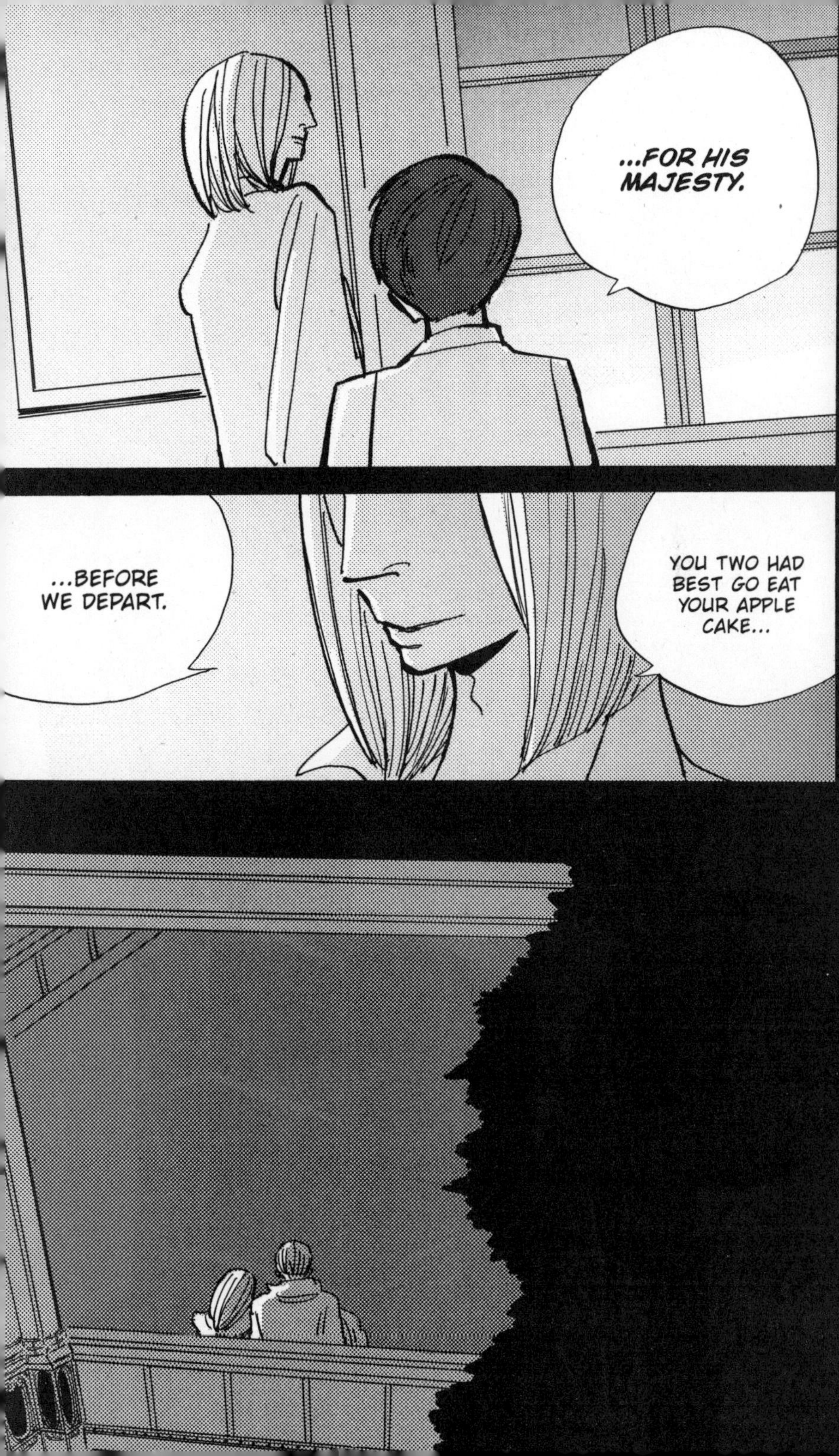
...FOR HIS MAJESTY.
YOU TWO HAD BEST GO EAT YOUR APPLE CAKE...
...BEFORE WE DEPART.

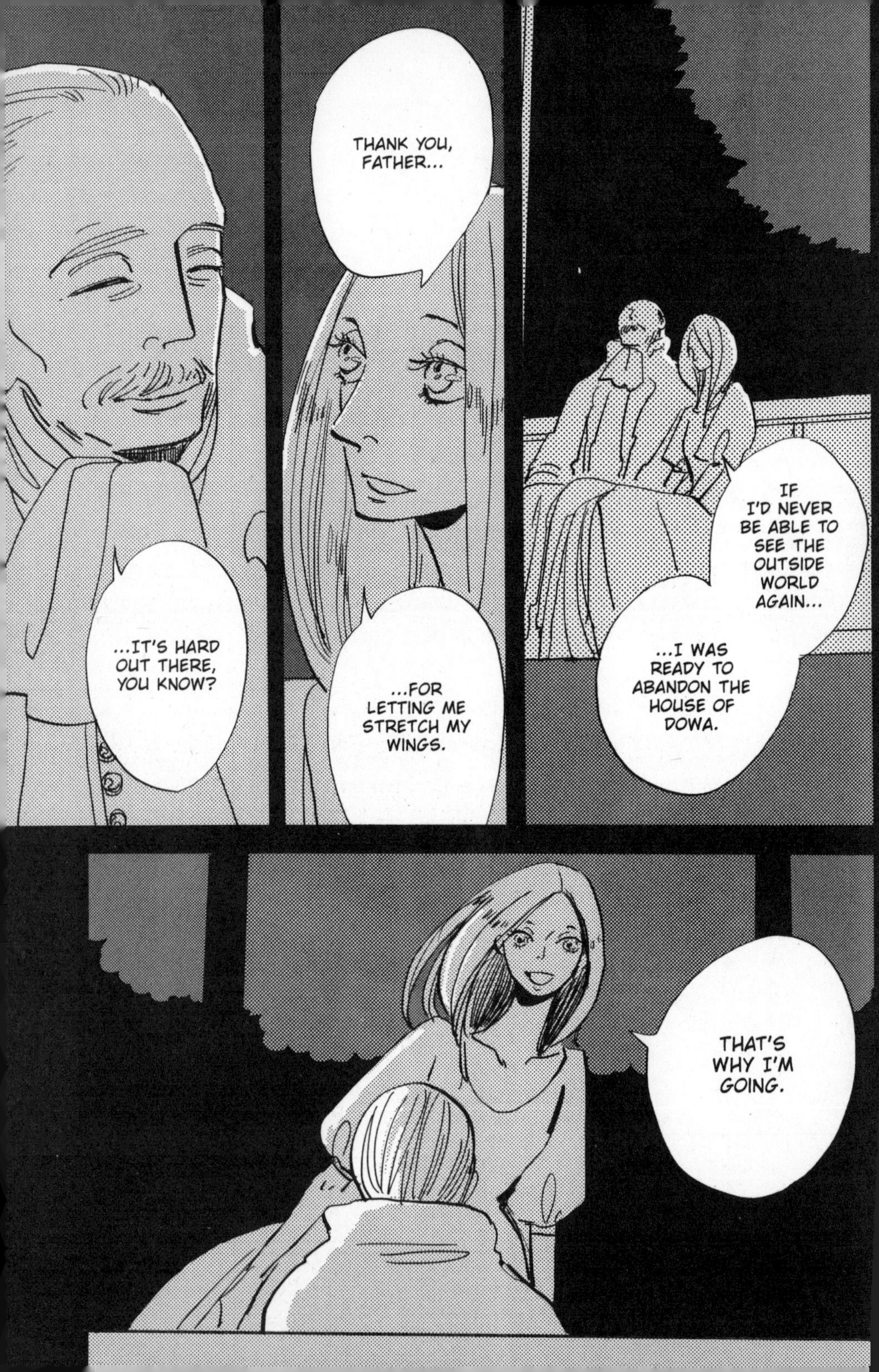
IF I'D NEVER BE ABLE TO SEE THE OUTSIDE WORLD AGAIN...
...I WAS READY TO ABANDON THE HOUSE OF DOWA.
THANK YOU, FATHER...
...FOR LETTING ME STRETCH MY WINGS.
...IT'S HARD OUT THERE, YOU KNOW?
THAT'S WHY I'M GOING.

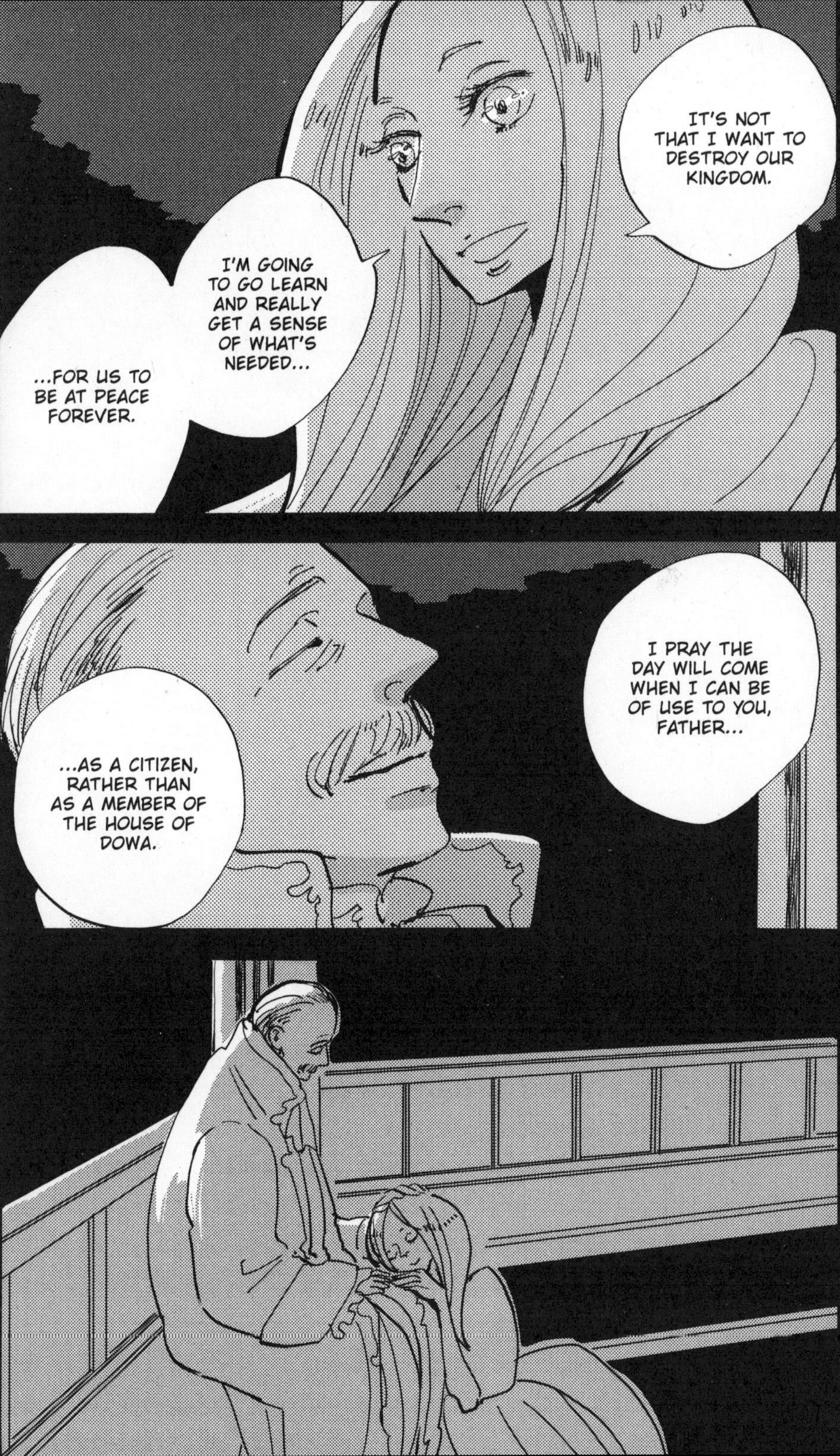

IT'S NOT THAT I WANT TO DESTROY OUR KINGDOM.
I'M GOING TO GO LEARN AND REALLY GET A SENSE OF WHAT'S NEEDED...
...FOR US TO BE AT PEACE FOREVER.
I PRAY THE DAY WILL COME WHEN I CAN BE OF USE TO YOU, FATHER...
...AS A CITIZEN, RATHER THAN AS A MEMBER OF THE HOUSE OF DOWA.

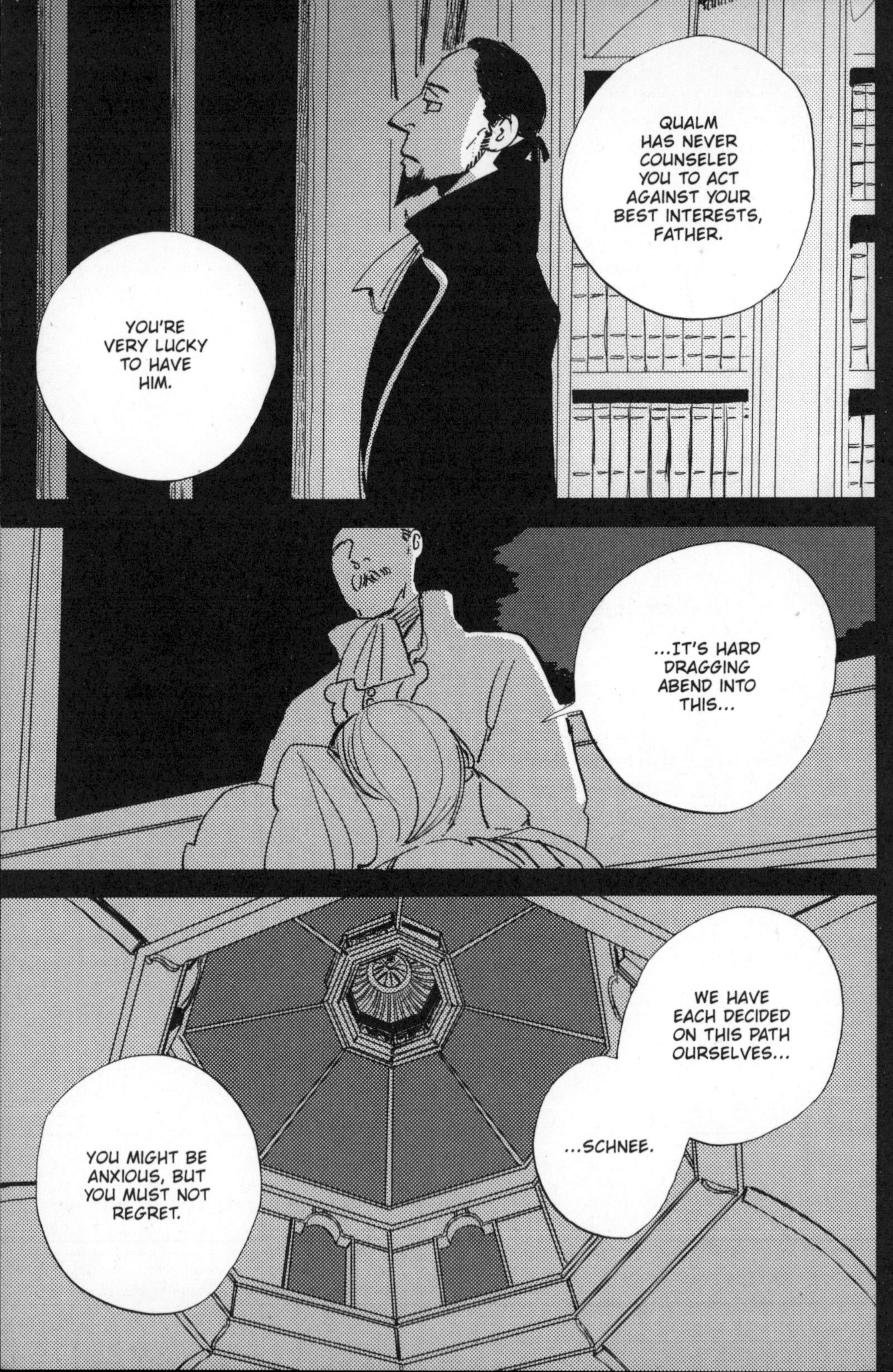
QUALM HAS NEVER COUNSELED YOU TO ACT AGAINST YOUR BEST INTERESTS, FATHER.
YOU'RE VERY LUCKY TO HAVE HIM.
...IT'S HARD DRAGGING ABEND INTO THIS...
WE HAVE EACH DECIDED ON THIS PATH OURSELVES...
...SCHNEE.
YOU MIGHT BE ANXIOUS, BUT YOU MUST NOT REGRET.

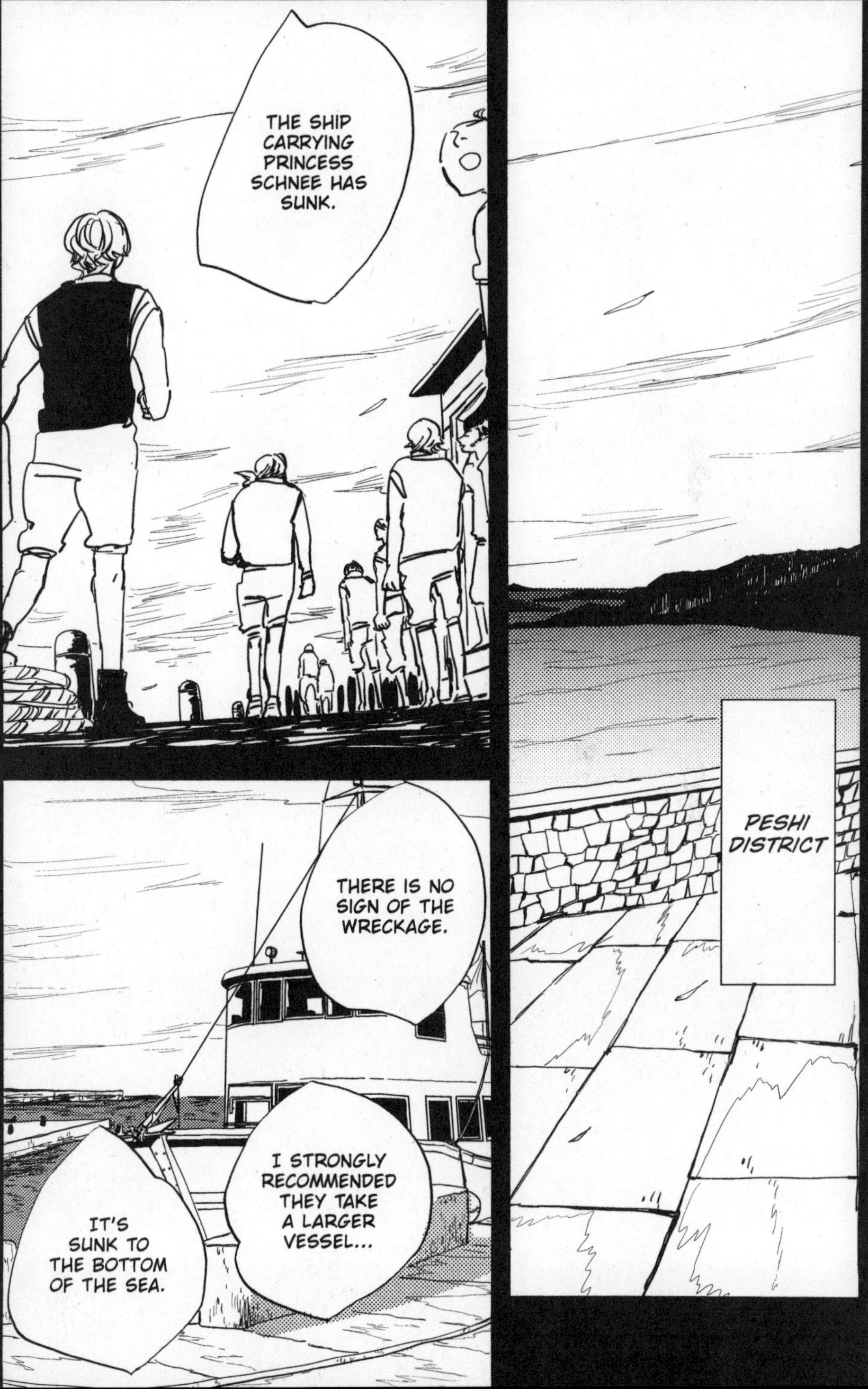
PESHI DISTRICT
THE SHIP CARRYING PRINCESS SCHNEE HAS SUNK.
THERE IS NO SIGN OF THE WRECKAGE.
I STRONGLY RECOMMENDED THEY TAKE A LARGER VESSEL...
IT'S SUNK TO THE BOTTOM OF THE SEA.

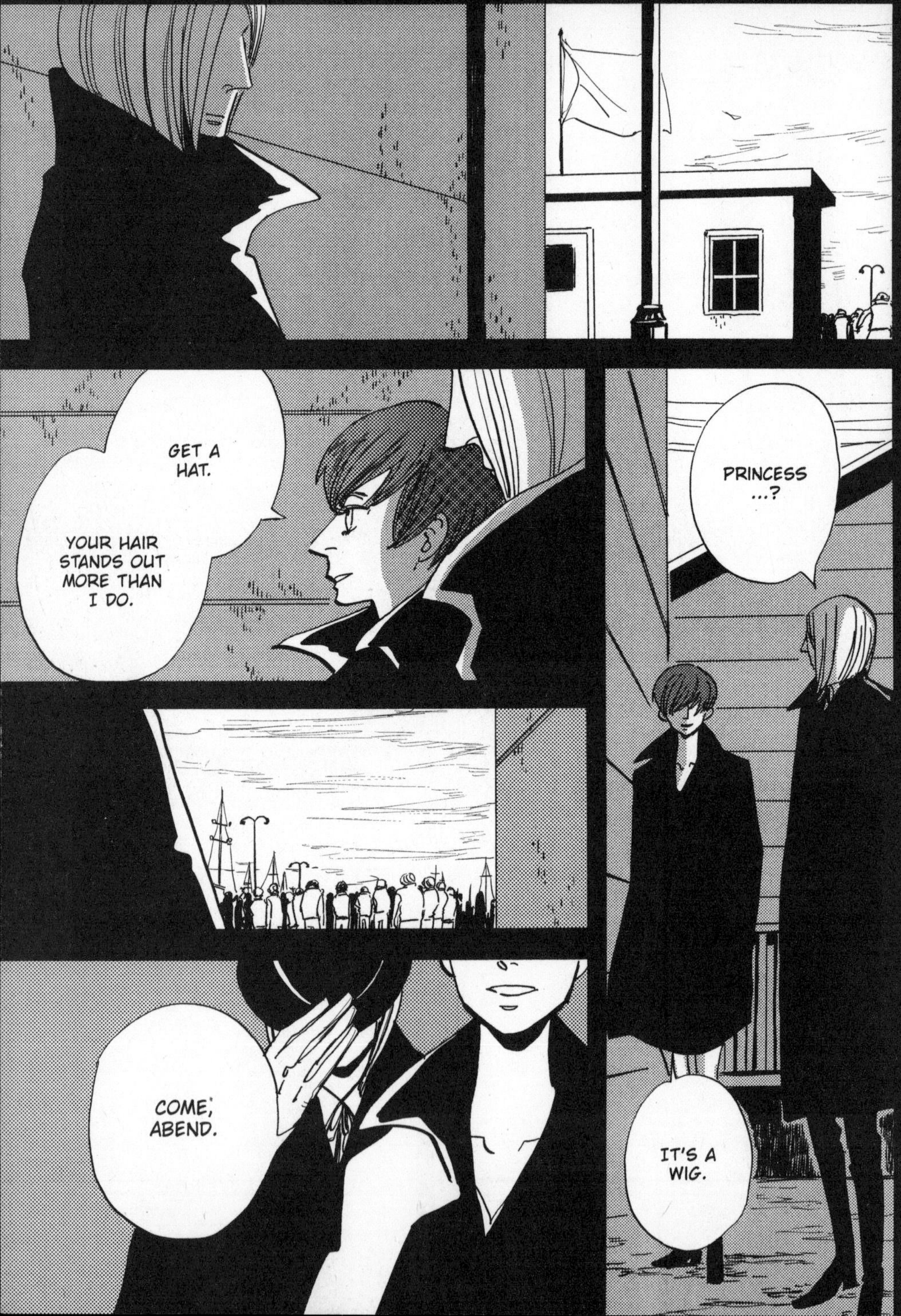
PRINCESS ...?
IT'S A WIG.
GET A HAT.
YOUR HAIR STANDS OUT MORE THAN I DO.
COME, ABEND.

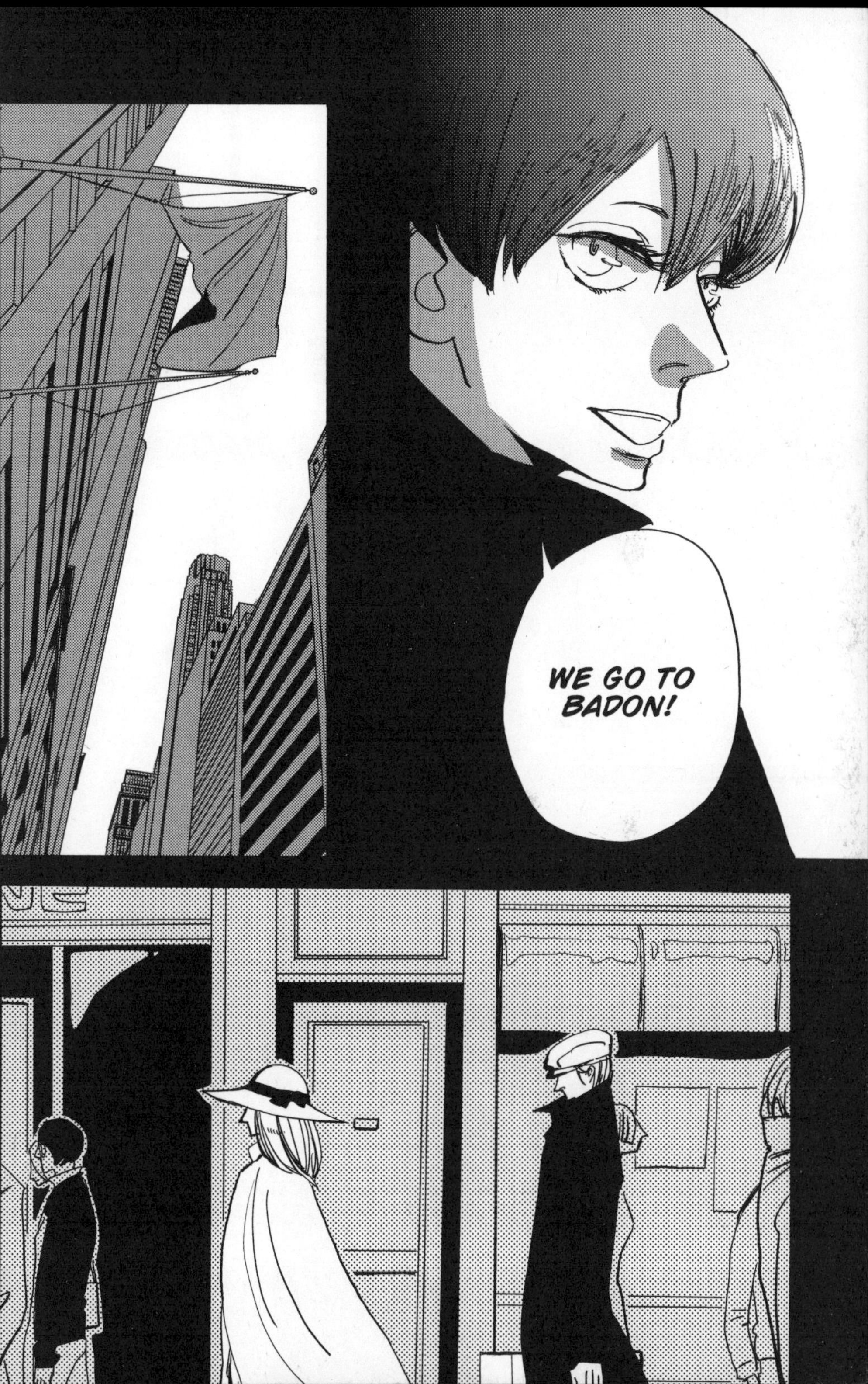
WE GO TO BADON!

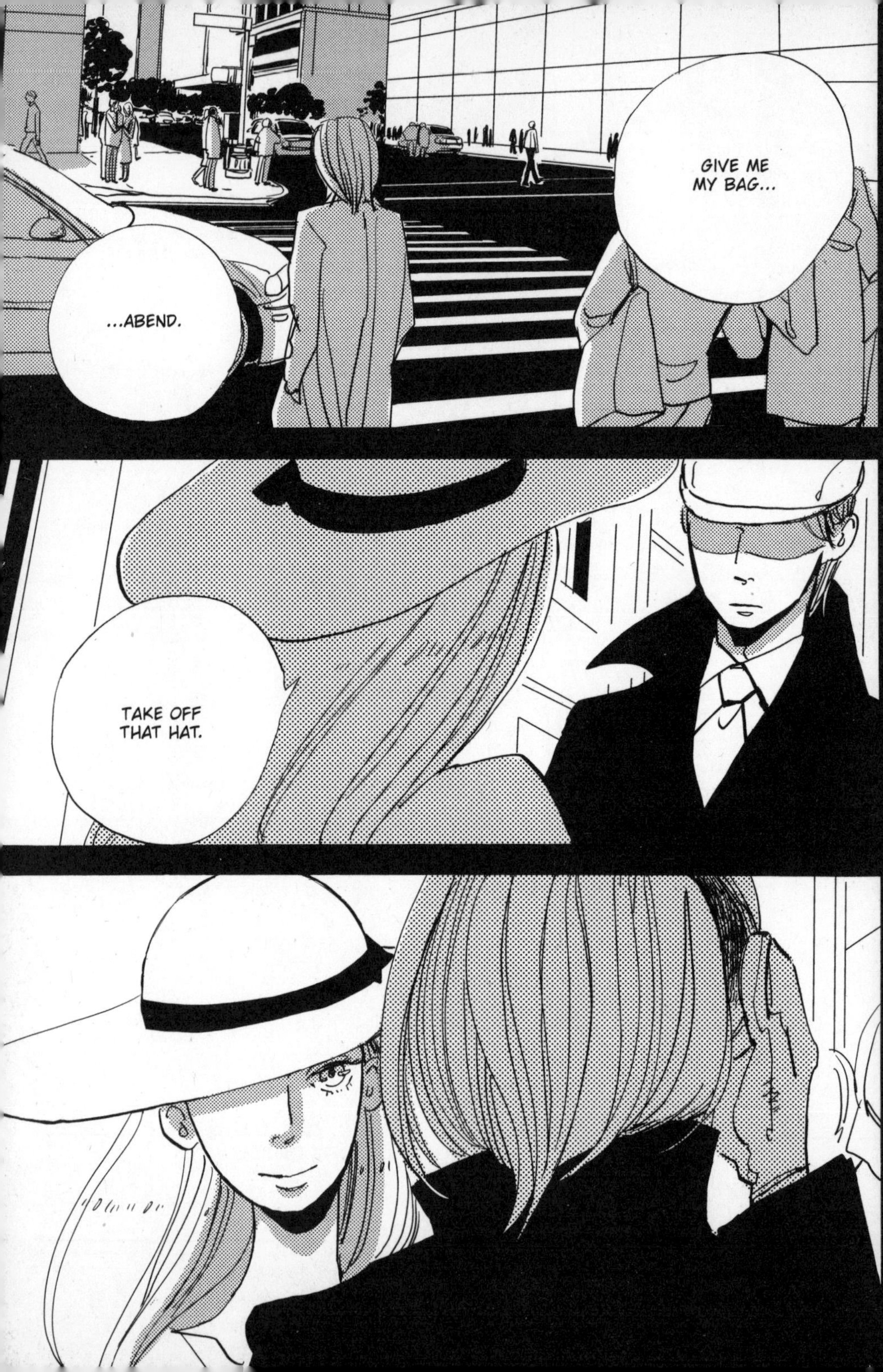
GIVE ME MY BAG...
...ABEND.
TAKE OFF THAT HAT.

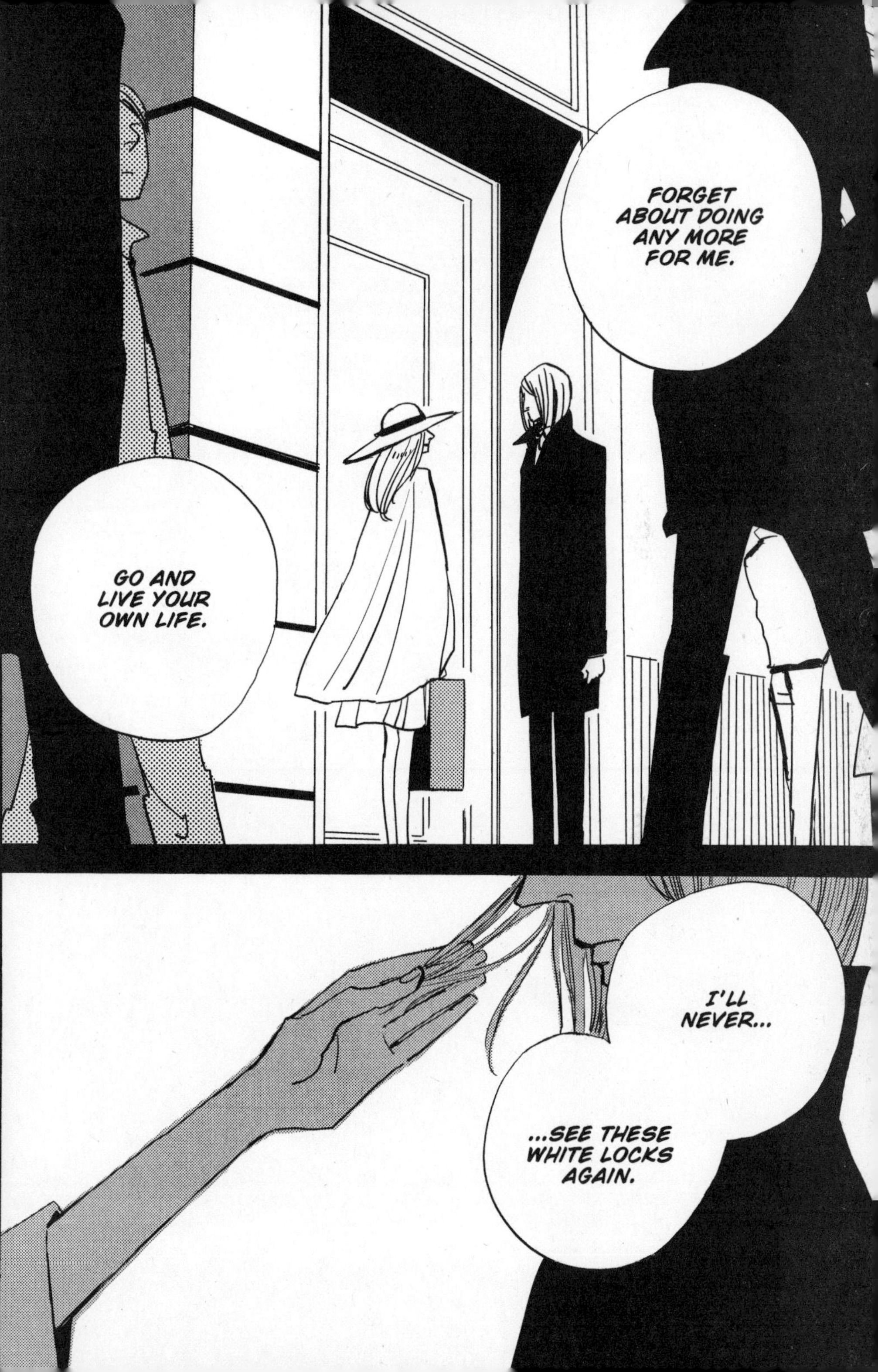
FORGET ABOUT DOING ANY MORE FOR ME.
GO AND LIVE YOUR OWN LIFE.
I'LL NEVER...
...SEE THESE WHITE LOCKS AGAIN.

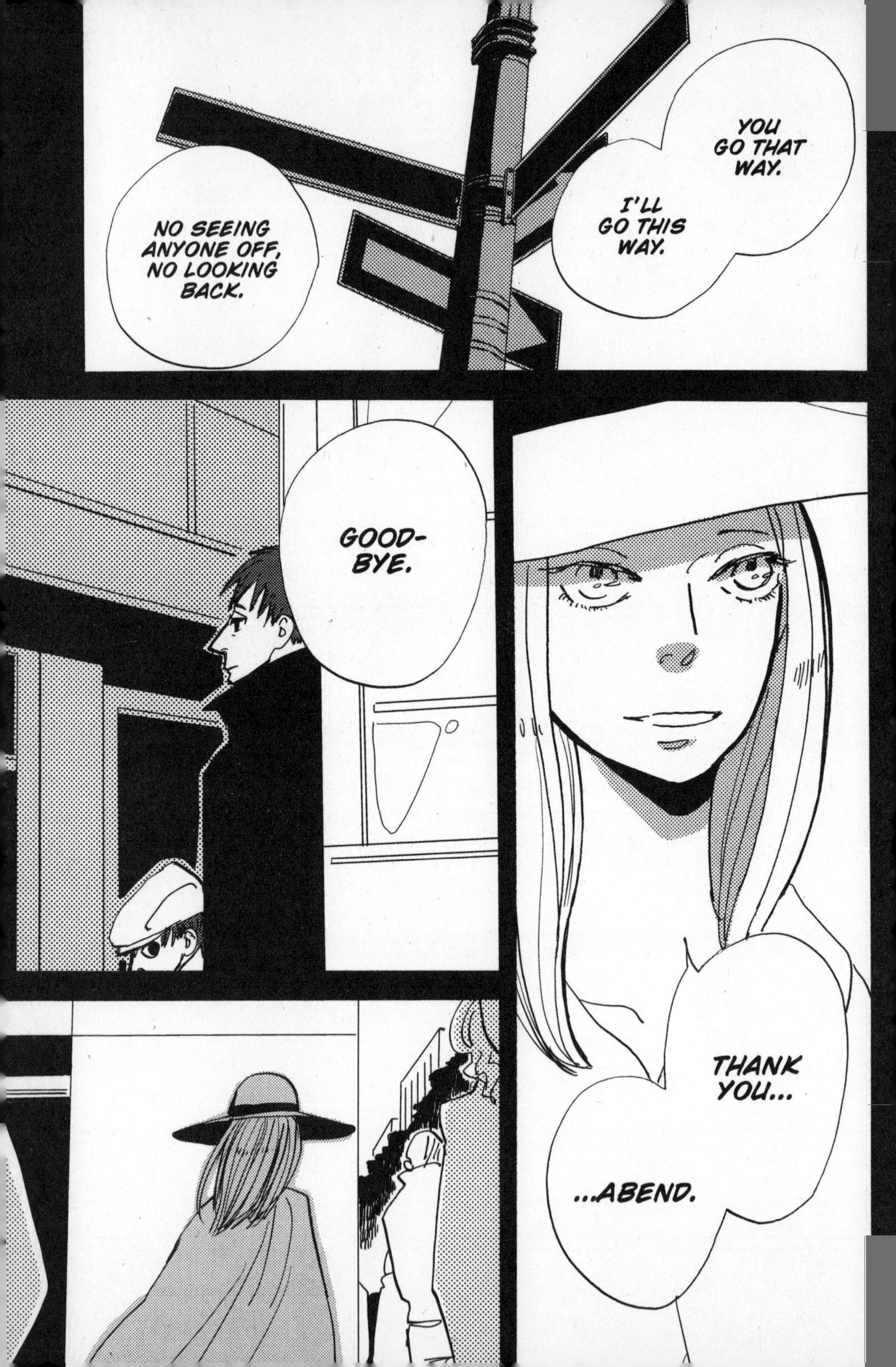
YOU GO THAT WAY.
I'LL GO THIS WAY.
NO SEEING ANYONE OFF, NO LOOKING BACK.
THANK YOU...
...ABEND.
GOOD-BYE.

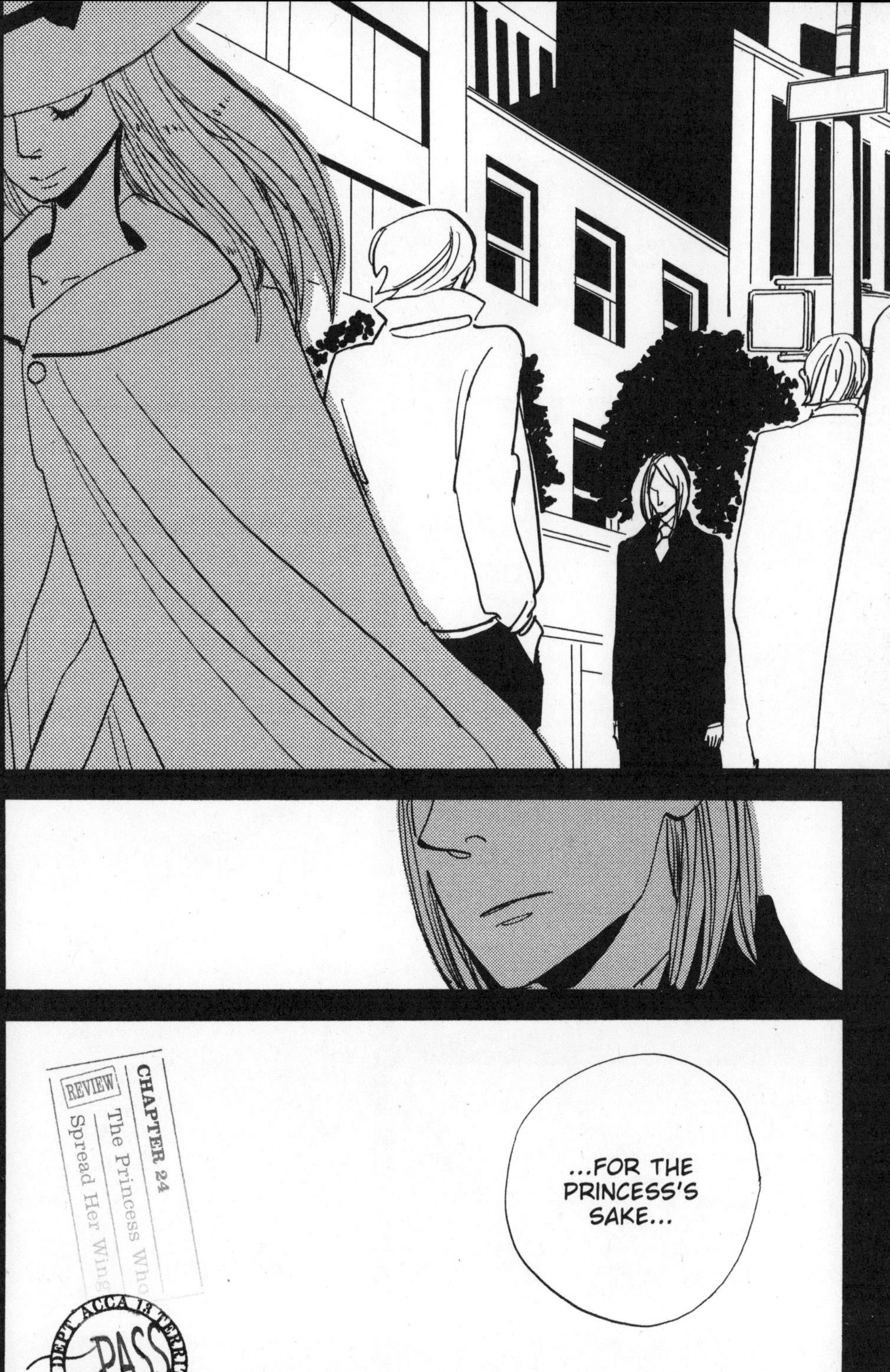
...FOR THE PRINCESS'S SAKE...
REVIEW
CHAPTER 24
The Princess Who
Spread Her Wing
ACCA 13 TERRITORY INSPECTION DEPT.
PASS

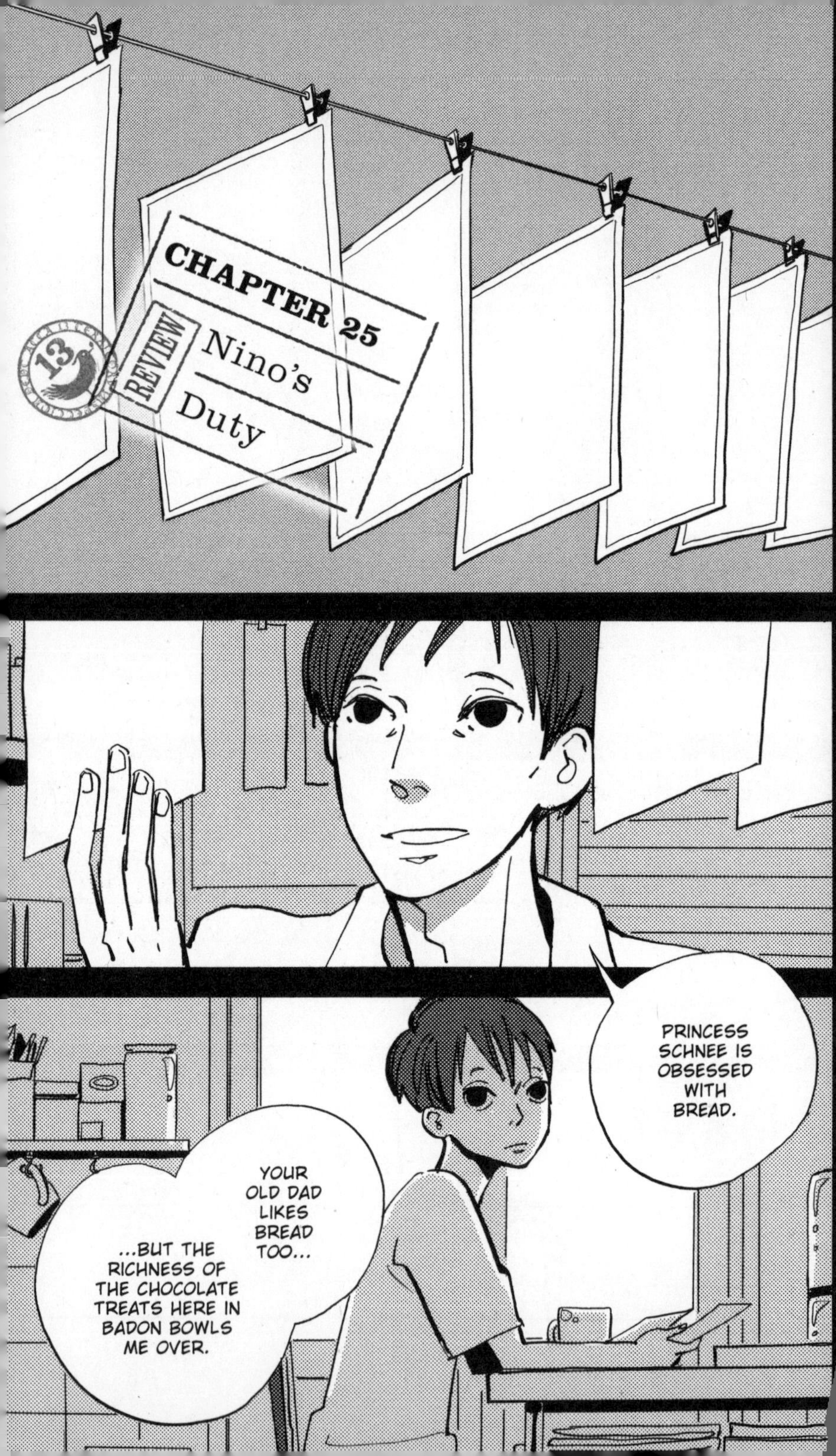
CHAPTER 25
REVIEW
Nino's Duty
PRINCESS SCHNEE IS OBSESSED WITH BREAD.
YOUR OLD DAD LIKES BREAD TOO...
...BUT THE RICHNESS OF THE CHOCOLATE TREATS HERE IN BADON BOWLS ME OVER.

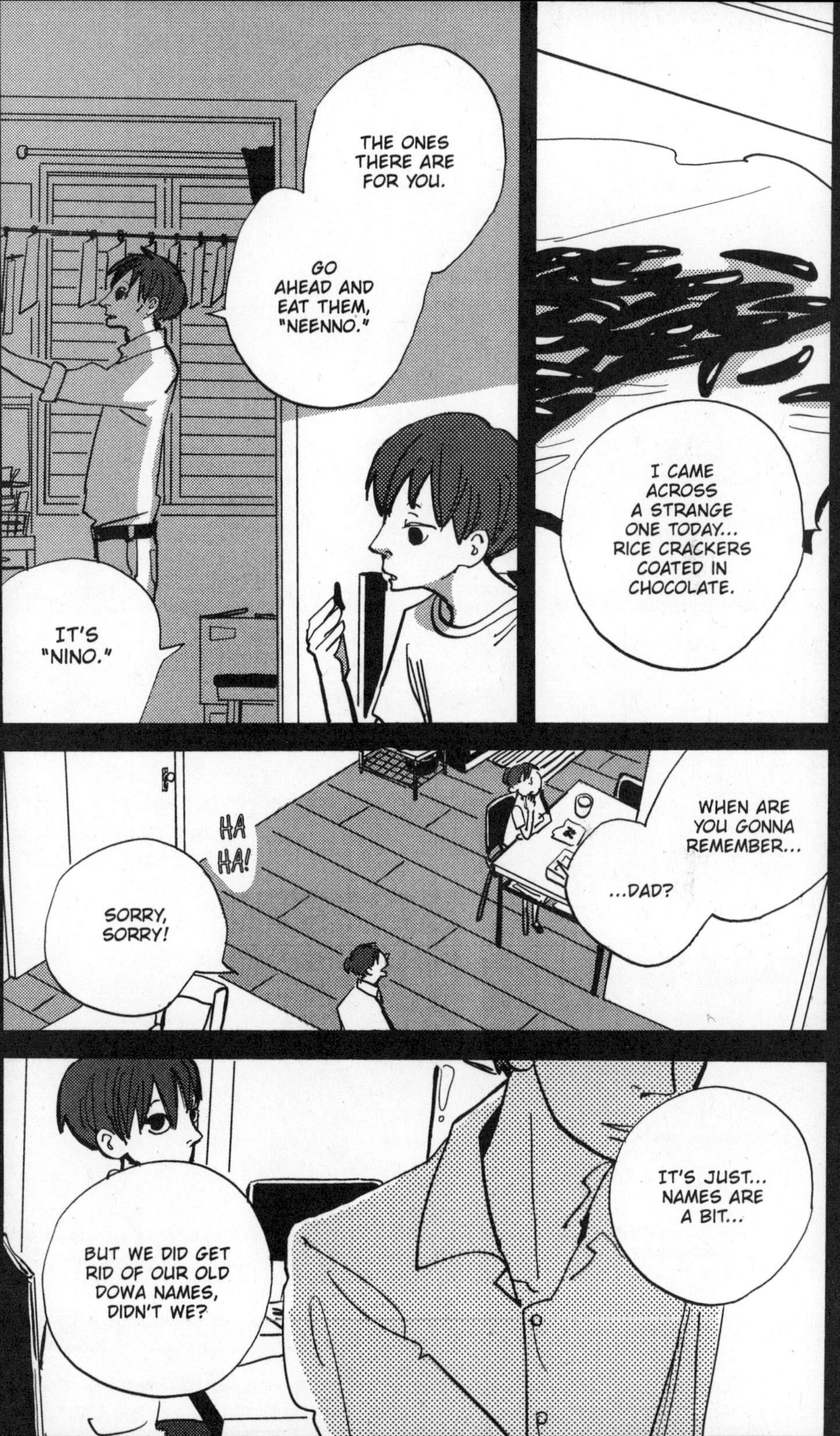
I CAME ACROSS A STRANGE ONE TODAY... RICE CRACKERS COATED IN CHOCOLATE.
THE ONES THERE ARE FOR YOU.
GO AHEAD AND EAT THEM, "NEENNO."
IT'S "NINO."
WHEN ARE YOU GONNA REMEMBER...
...DAD?
HA HA!
SORRY, SORRY!
IT'S JUST... NAMES ARE A BIT...
BUT WE DID GET RID OF OUR OLD DOWA NAMES, DIDN'T WE?

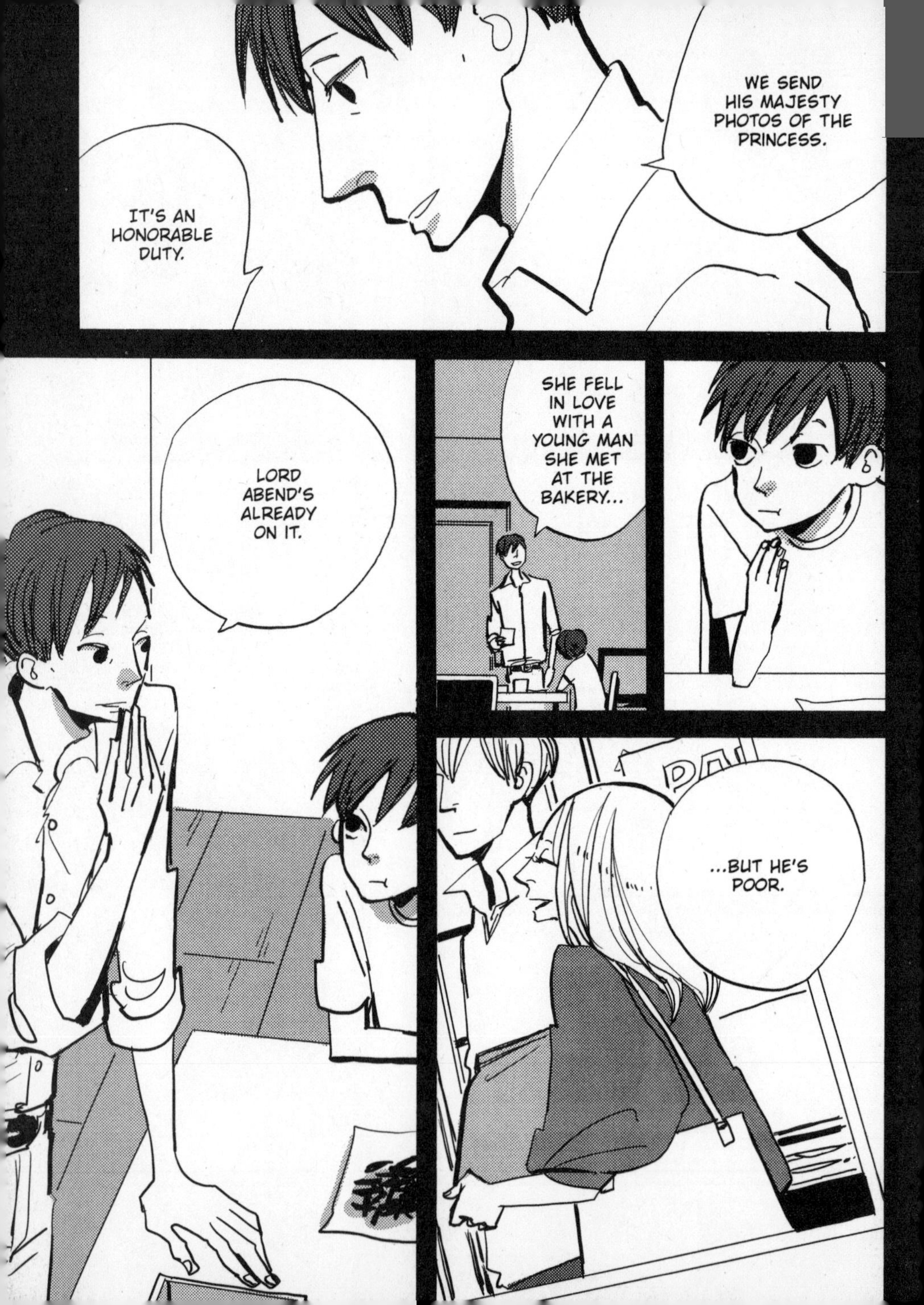
WE SEND HIS MAJESTY PHOTOS OF THE PRINCESS.
IT'S AN HONORABLE DUTY.
SHE FELL IN LOVE WITH A YOUNG MAN SHE MET AT THE BAKERY...
...BUT HE'S POOR.
LORD ABEND'S ALREADY ON IT.

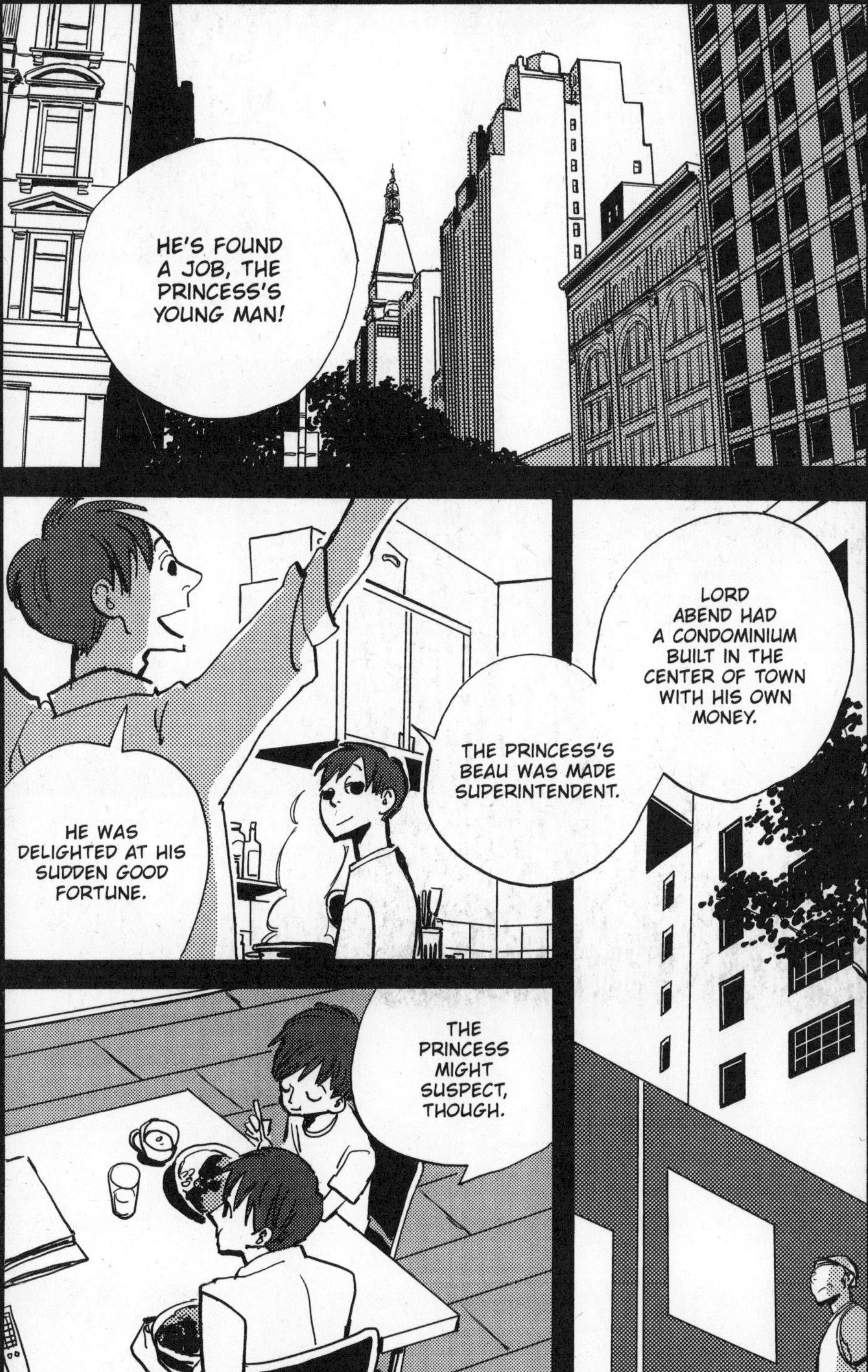
HE'S FOUND A JOB, THE PRINCESS'S YOUNG MAN!
LORD ABEND HAD A CONDOMINIUM BUILT IN THE CENTER OF TOWN WITH HIS OWN MONEY.
THE PRINCESS'S BEAU WAS MADE SUPERINTENDENT.
HE WAS DELIGHTED AT HIS SUDDEN GOOD FORTUNE.
THE PRINCESS MIGHT SUSPECT, THOUGH.

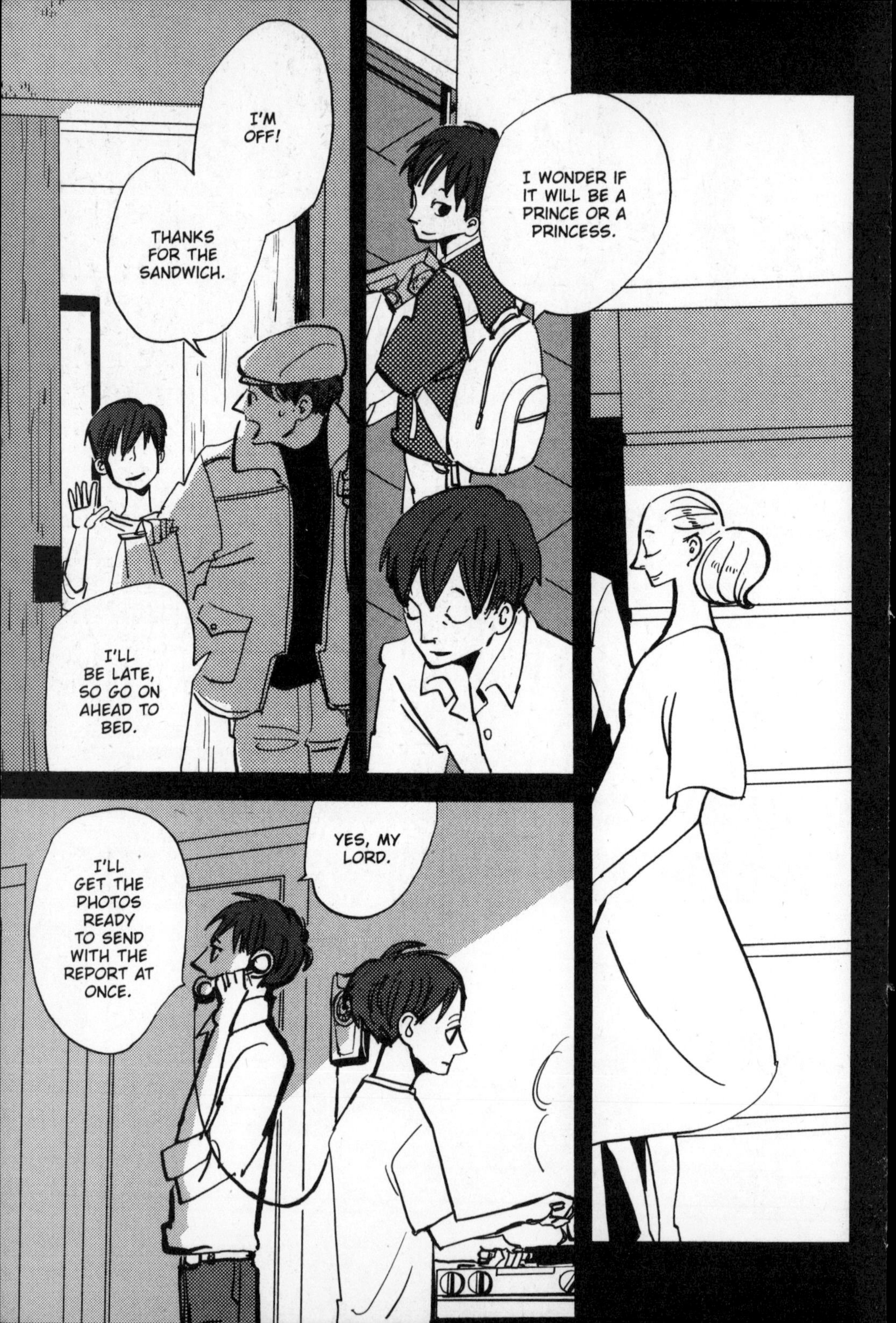
I WONDER IF IT WILL BE A PRINCE OR A PRINCESS.
I'M OFF!
THANKS FOR THE SANDWICH.
I'LL BE LATE, SO GO ON AHEAD TO BED.
YES, MY LORD.
I'LL GET THE PHOTOS READY TO SEND WITH THE REPORT AT ONCE.

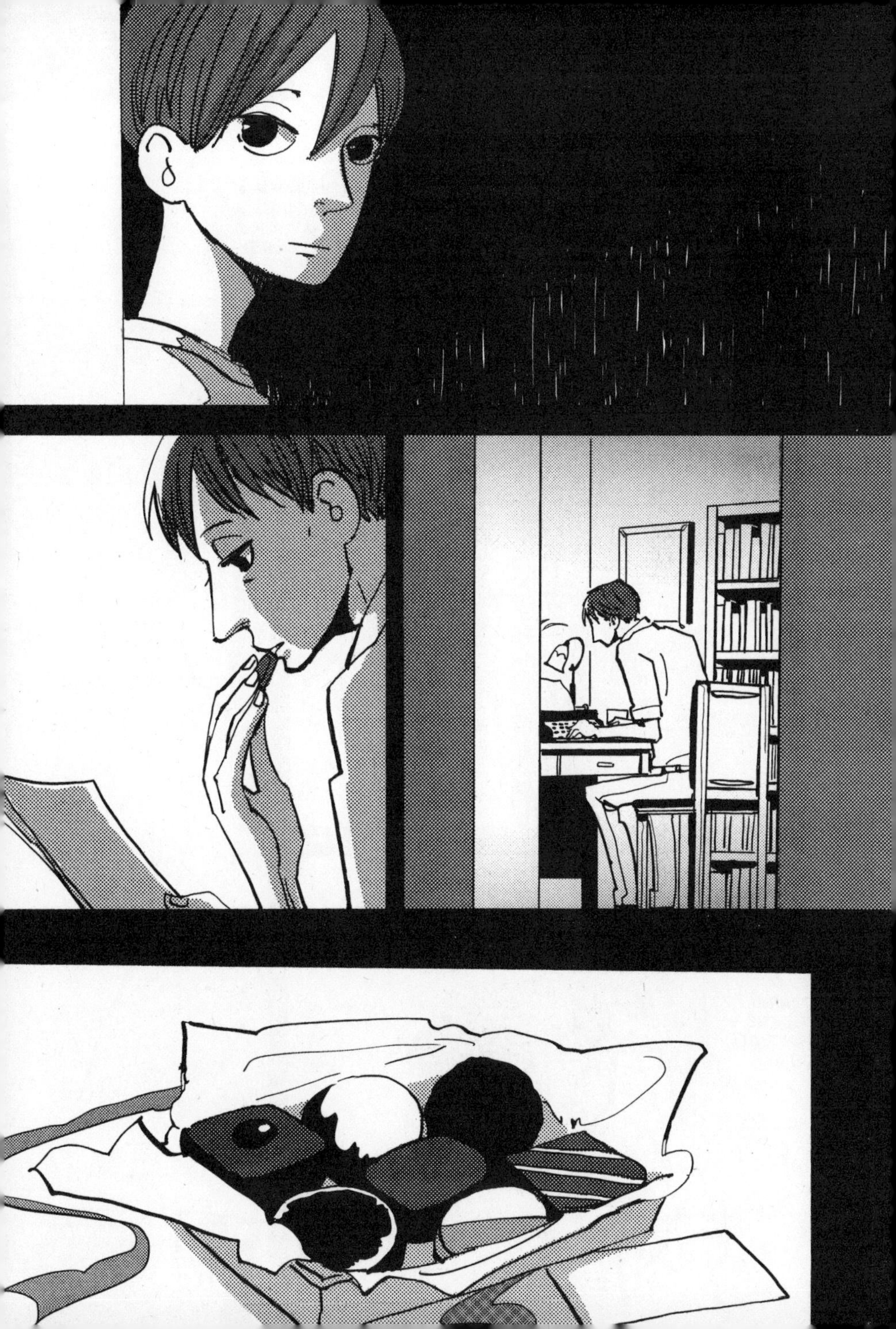

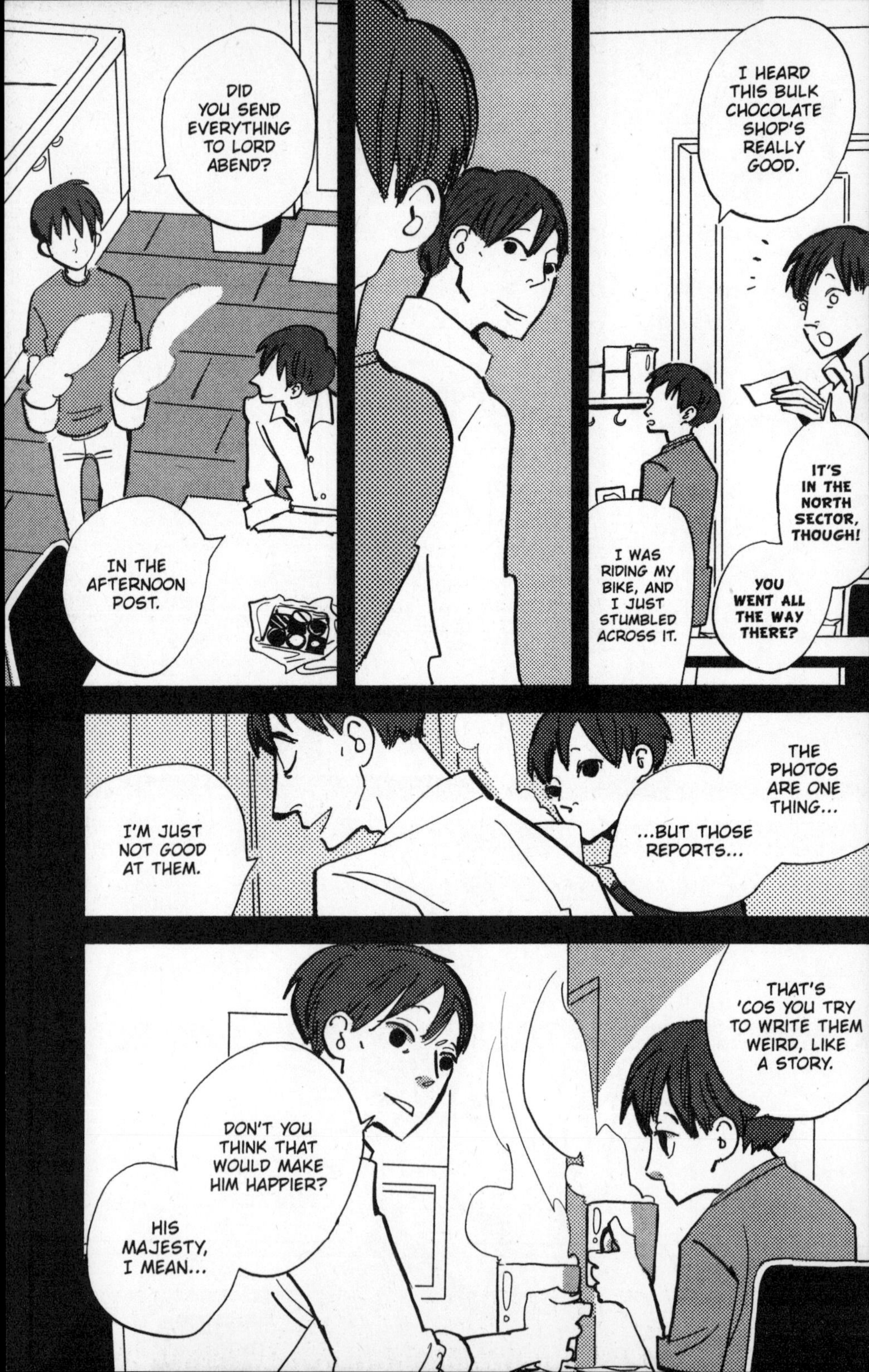
I HEARD THIS BULK CHOCOLATE SHOP'S REALLY GOOD.
IT'S IN THE NORTH SECTOR, THOUGH!
YOU WENT ALL THE WAY THERE?
I WAS RIDING MY BIKE, AND I JUST STUMBLED ACROSS IT.
DID YOU SEND EVERYTHING TO LORD ABEND?
IN THE AFTERNOON POST.
THE PHOTOS ARE ONE THING...
...BUT THOSE REPORTS...
I'M JUST NOT GOOD AT THEM.
THAT'S 'COS YOU TRY TO WRITE THEM WEIRD, LIKE A STORY.
DON'T YOU THINK THAT WOULD MAKE HIM HAPPIER?
HIS MAJESTY, I MEAN...

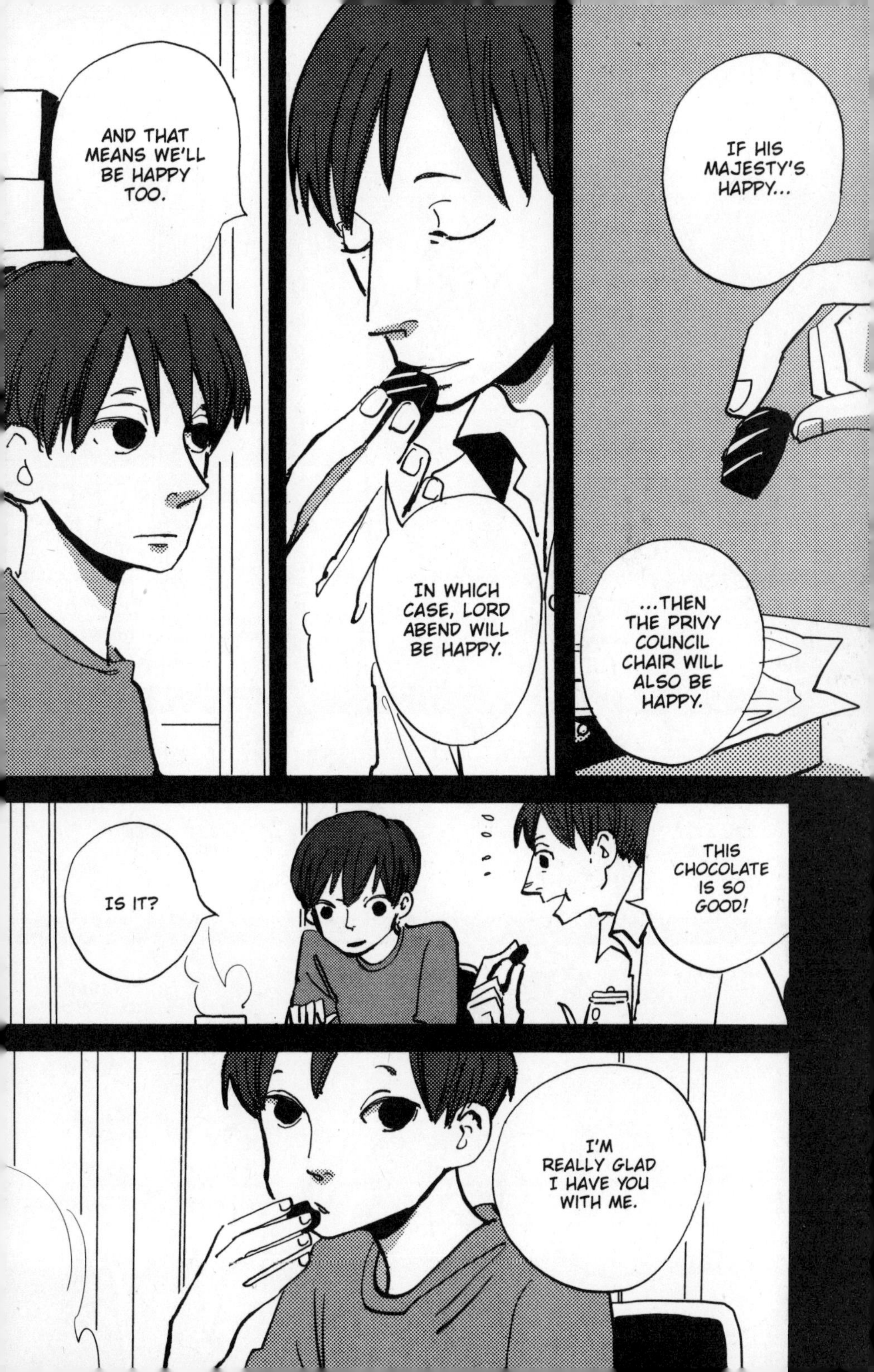
IF HIS MAJESTY'S HAPPY...
...THEN THE PRIVY COUNCIL CHAIR WILL ALSO BE HAPPY.
IN WHICH CASE, LORD ABEND WILL BE HAPPY.
AND THAT MEANS WE'LL BE HAPPY TOO.
THIS CHOCOLATE IS SO GOOD!
IS IT?
I'M REALLY GLAD I HAVE YOU WITH ME.

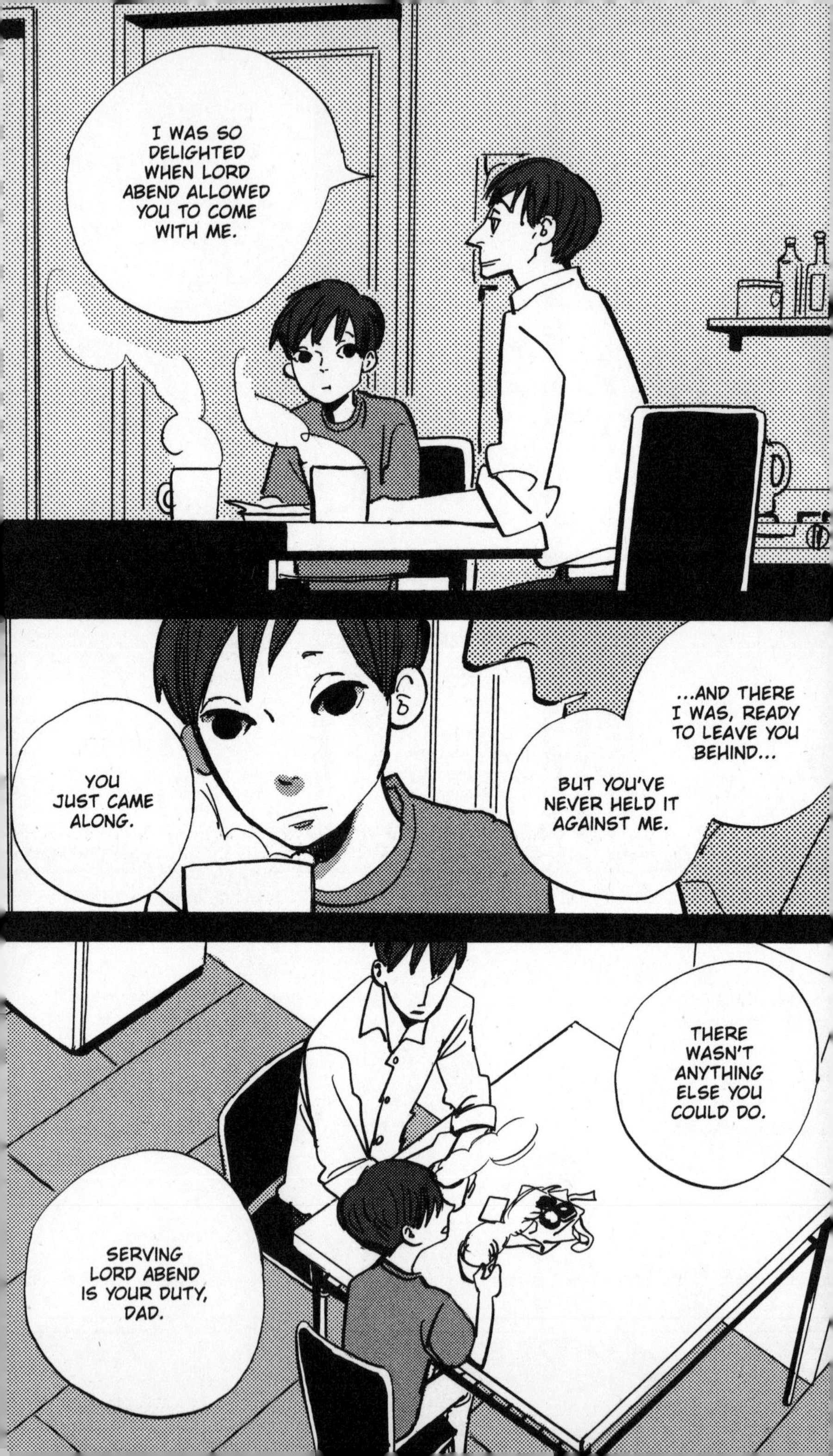
I WAS SO DELIGHTED WHEN LORD ABEND ALLOWED YOU TO COME WITH ME.
...AND THERE I WAS, READY TO LEAVE YOU BEHIND...
BUT YOU'VE NEVER HELD IT AGAINST ME.
YOU JUST CAME ALONG.
THERE WASN'T ANYTHING ELSE YOU COULD DO.
SERVING LORD ABEND IS YOUR DUTY, DAD.

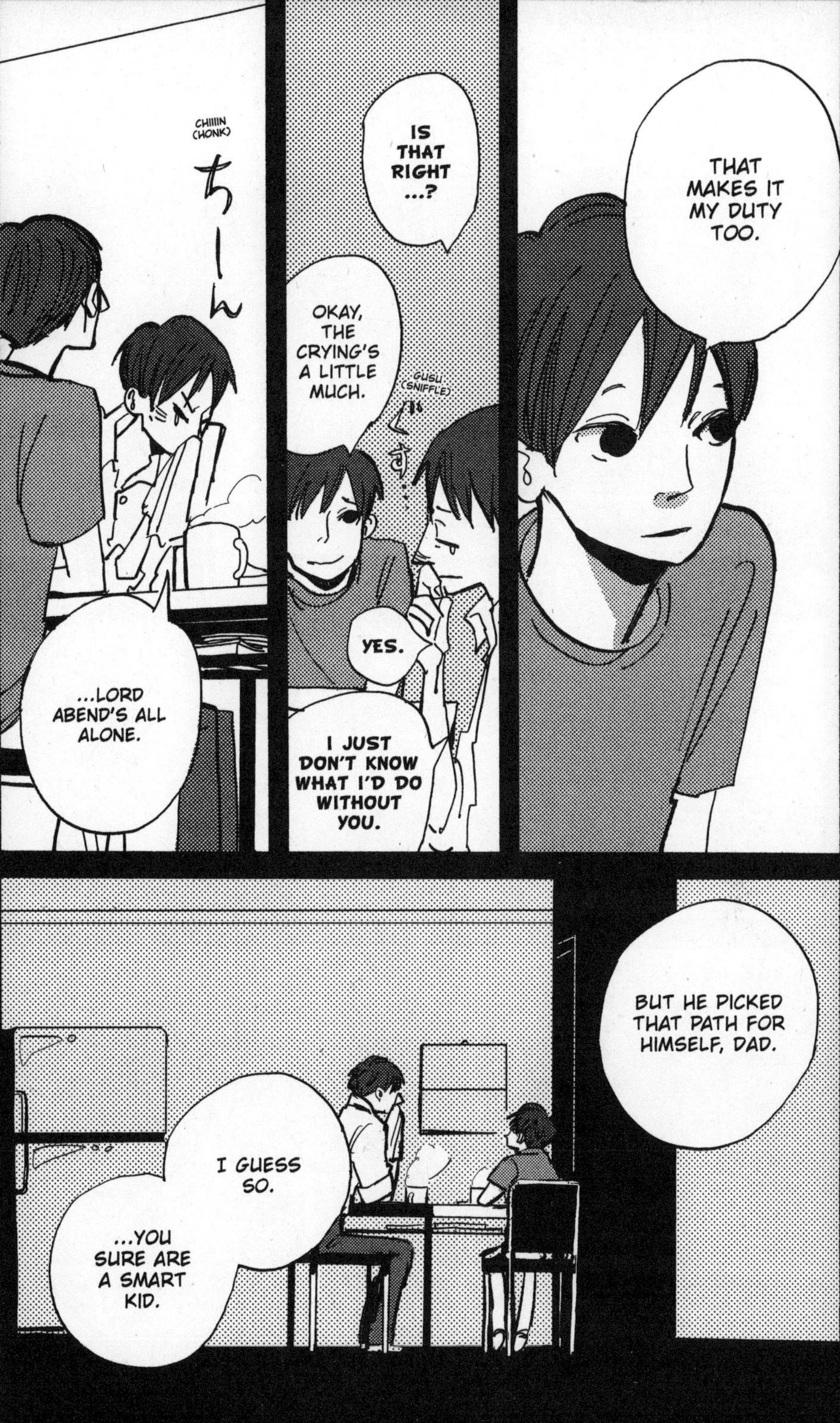
THAT MAKES IT MY DUTY TOO.
IS THAT RIGHT ...?
GUSU (SNIFFLE)
OKAY, THE CRYING'S A LITTLE MUCH.
YES.
I JUST DON'T KNOW WHAT I'D DO WITHOUT YOU.
CHIIIIN (HONK)
...LORD ABEND'S ALL ALONE.
BUT HE PICKED THAT PATH FOR HIMSELF, DAD.
I GUESS SO.
...YOU SURE ARE A SMART KID.

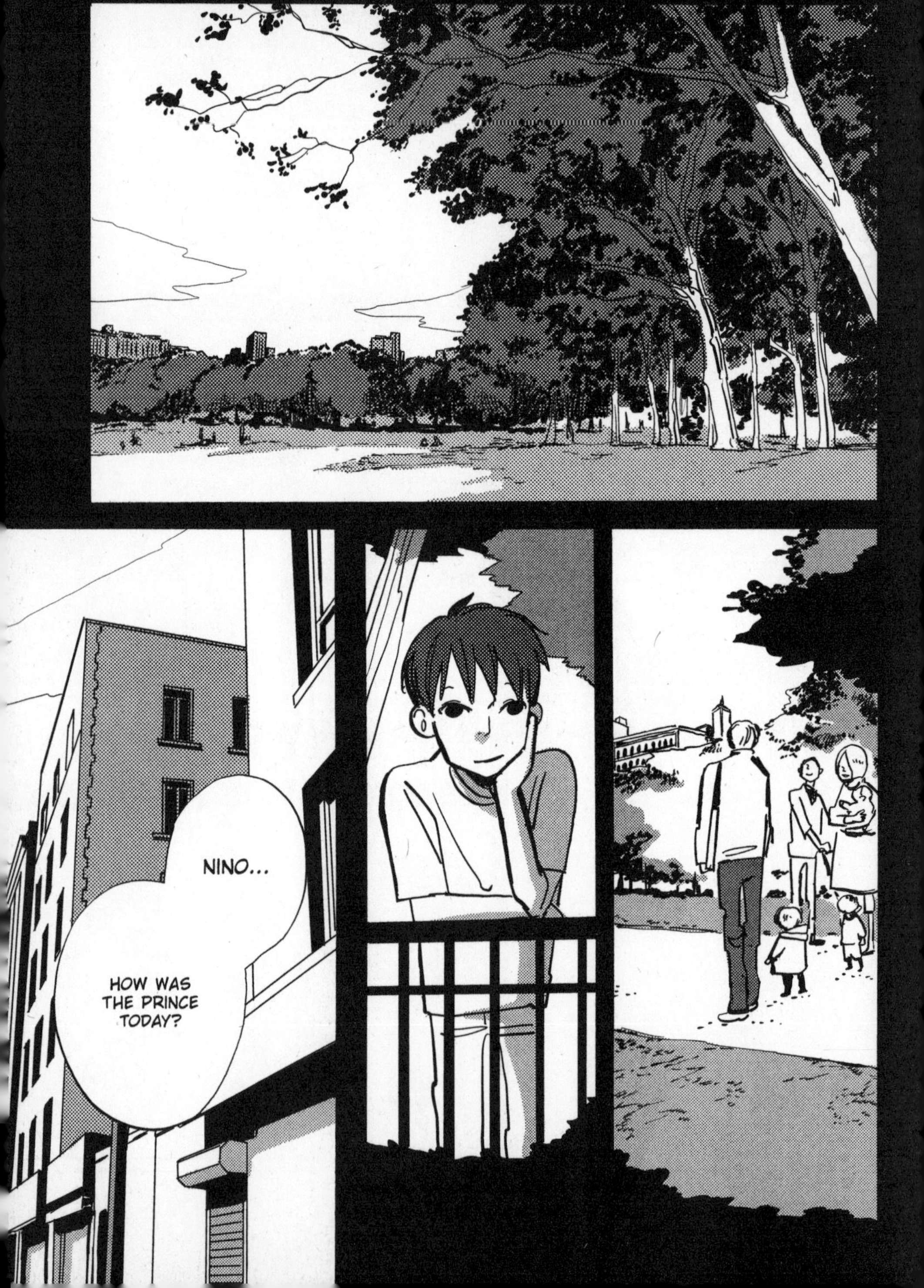
NINO...
HOW WAS THE PRINCE TODAY?

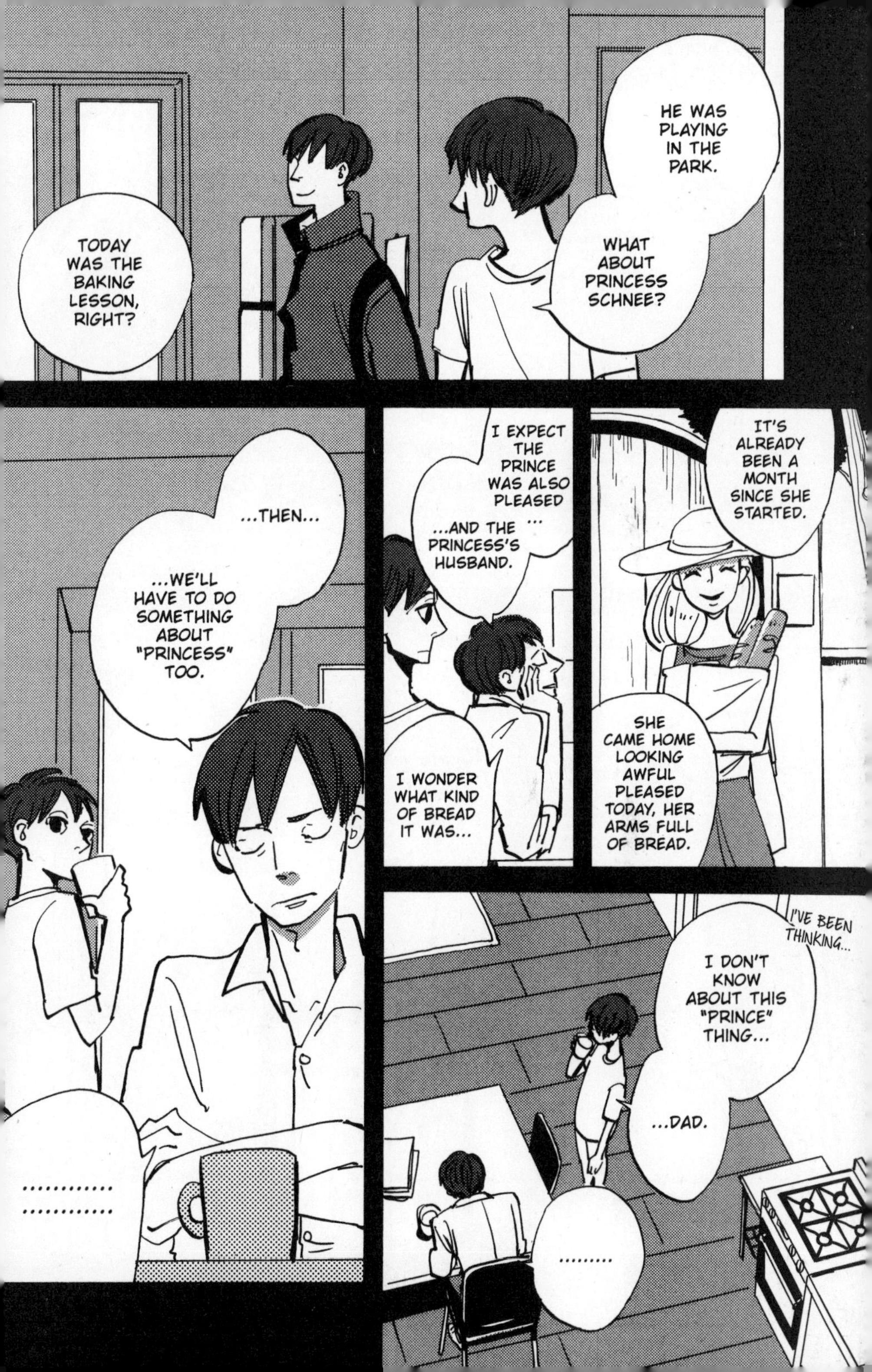
HE WAS PLAYING IN THE PARK.
WHAT ABOUT PRINCESS SCHNEE?
TODAY WAS THE BAKING LESSON, RIGHT?
IT'S ALREADY BEEN A MONTH SINCE SHE STARTED.
SHE CAME HOME LOOKING AWFUL PLEASED TODAY, HER ARMS FULL OF BREAD.
I EXPECT THE PRINCE WAS ALSO PLEASED...
...AND THE PRINCESS'S HUSBAND.
I WONDER WHAT KIND OF BREAD IT WAS...
I'VE BEEN THINKING...
I DON'T KNOW ABOUT THIS "PRINCE" THING...
...DAD.
....
...THEN...
...WE'LL HAVE TO DO SOMETHING ABOUT "PRINCESS" TOO.
....

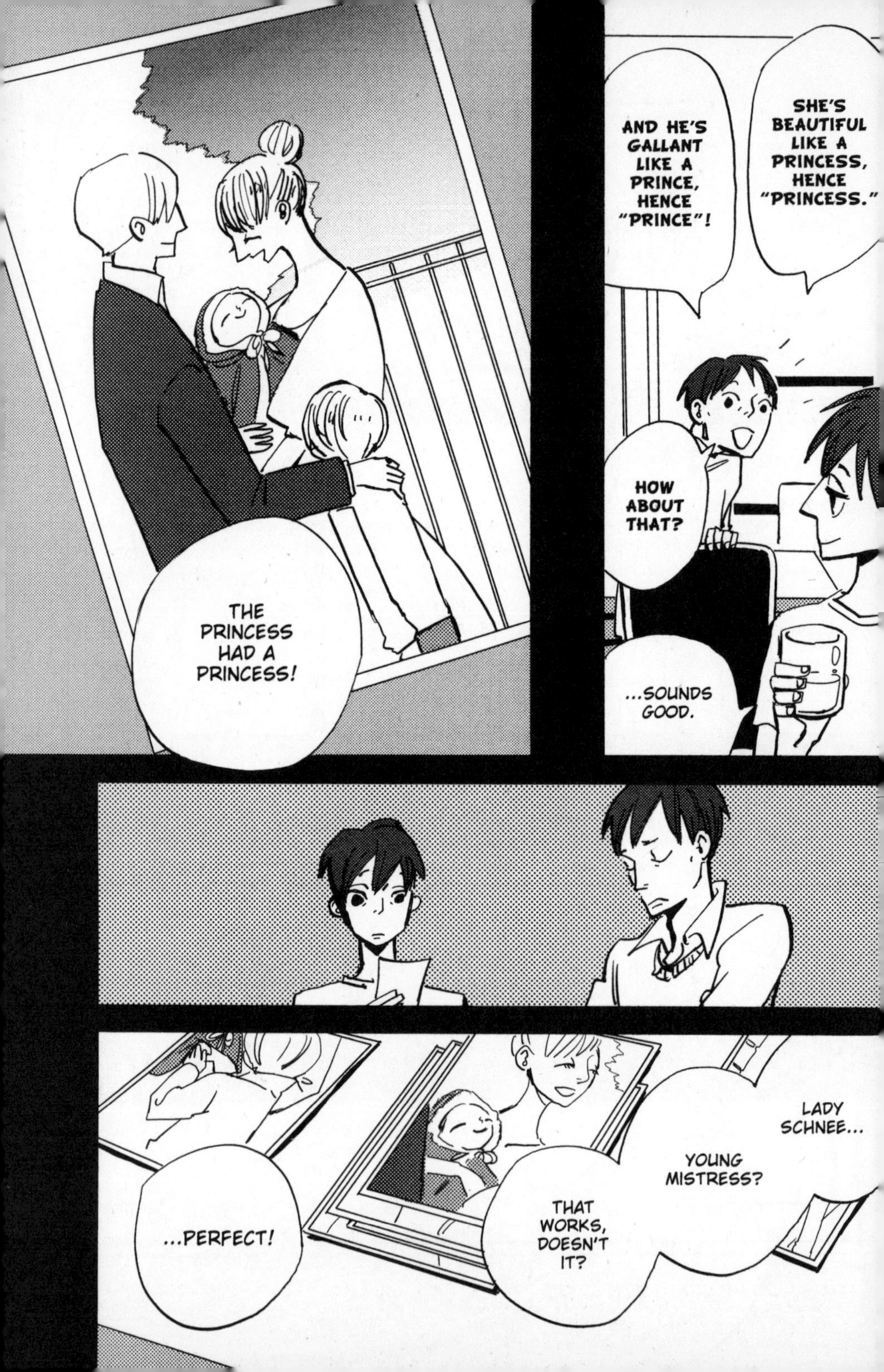
SHE'S BEAUTIFUL LIKE A PRINCESS, HENCE "PRINCESS."
AND HE'S GALLANT LIKE A PRINCE, HENCE "PRINCE"!
HOW ABOUT THAT?
...SOUNDS GOOD.
THE PRINCESS HAD A PRINCESS!
LADY SCHNEE...
YOUNG MISTRESS?
THAT WORKS, DOESN'T IT?
...PERFECT!

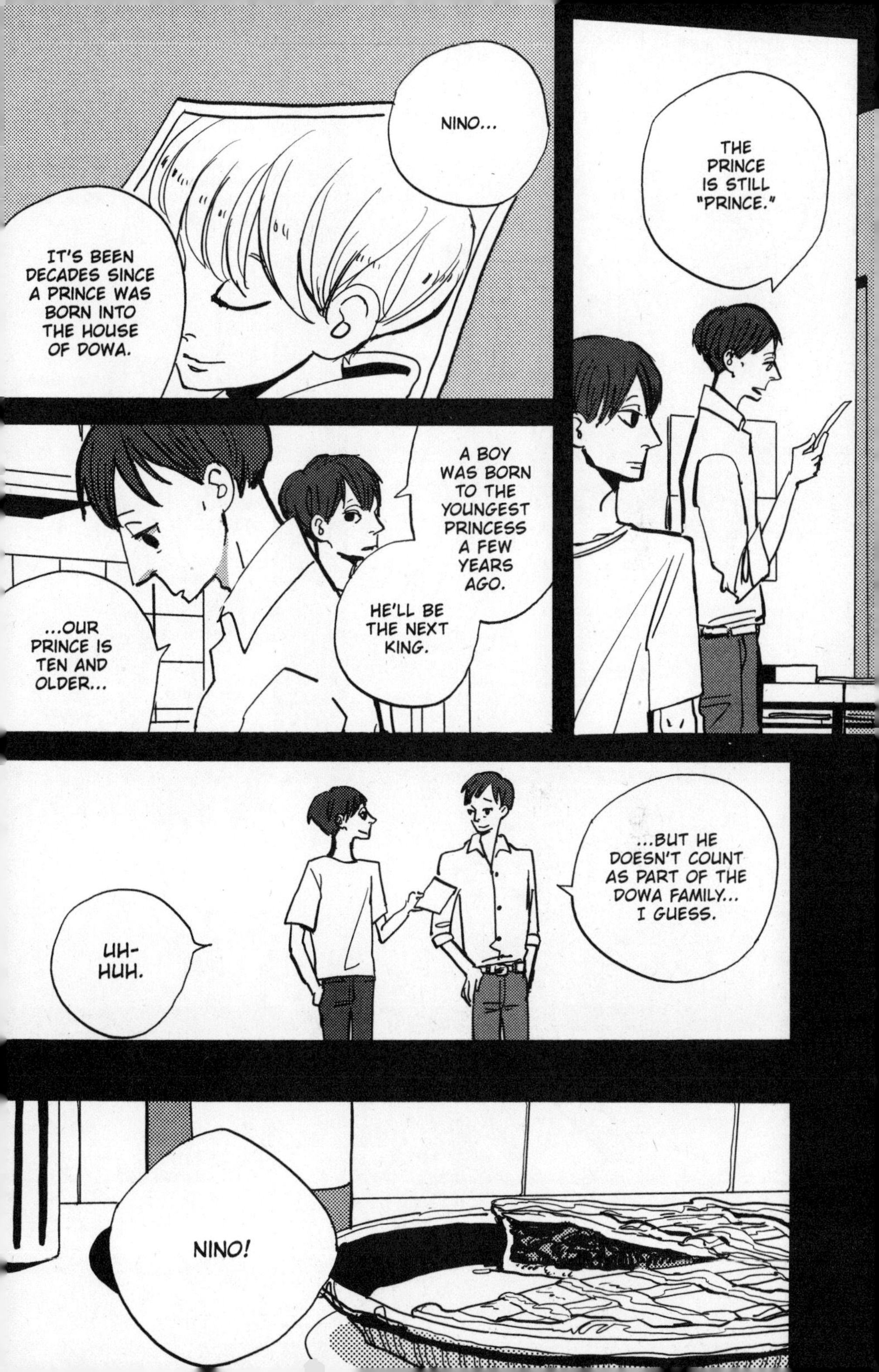
THE PRINCE IS STILL "PRINCE."
NINO...
IT'S BEEN DECADES SINCE A PRINCE WAS BORN INTO THE HOUSE OF DOWA.
A BOY WAS BORN TO THE YOUNGEST PRINCESS A FEW YEARS AGO.
HE'LL BE THE NEXT KING.
...OUR PRINCE IS TEN AND OLDER...
...BUT HE DOESN'T COUNT AS PART OF THE DOWA FAMILY... I GUESS.
UH-HUH.
NINO!

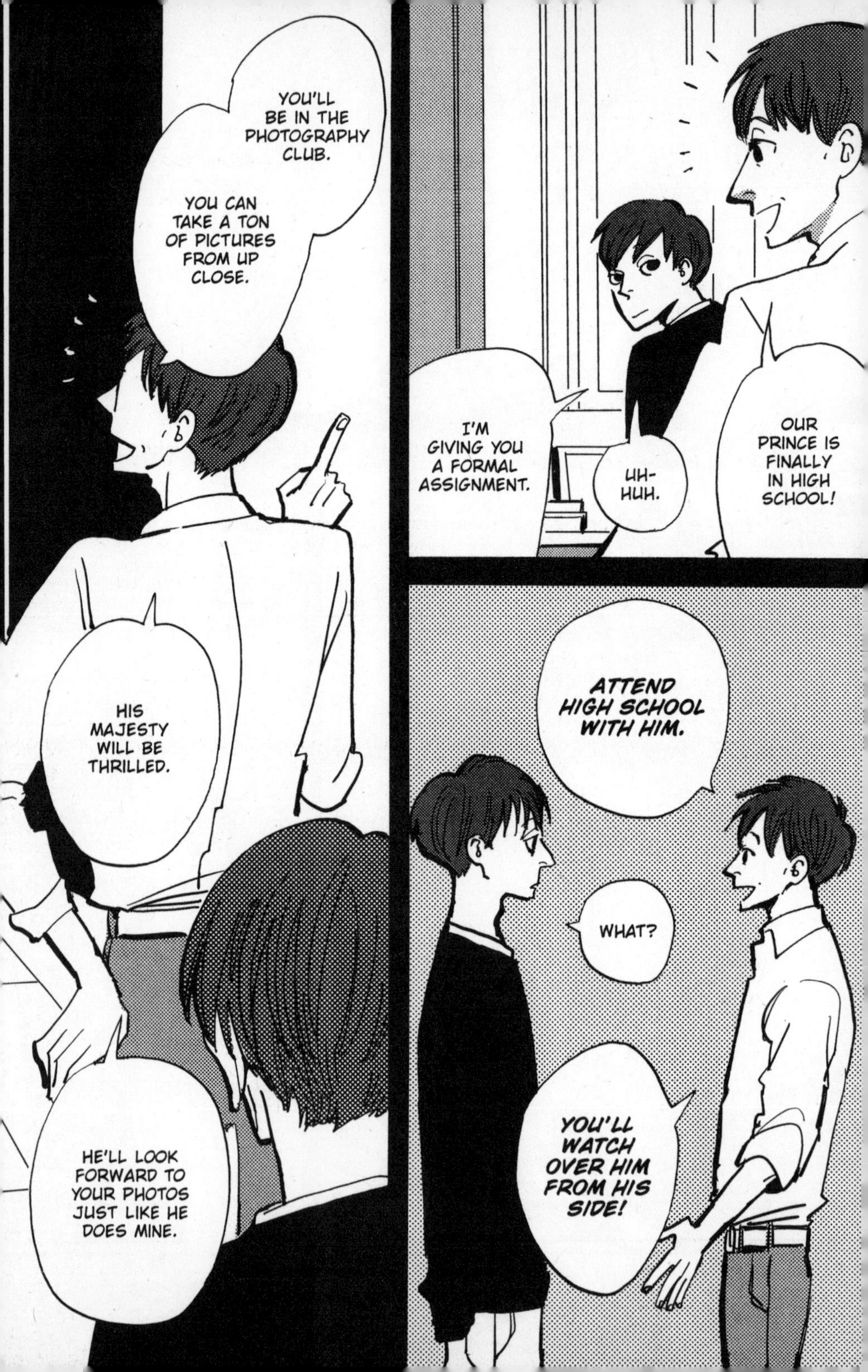
OUR PRINCE IS FINALLY IN HIGH SCHOOL!
UH-HUH.
I'M GIVING YOU A FORMAL ASSIGNMENT.
ATTEND HIGH SCHOOL WITH HIM.
WHAT?
YOU'LL WATCH OVER HIM FROM HIS SIDE!
YOU'LL BE IN THE PHOTOGRAPHY CLUB.
YOU CAN TAKE A TON OF PICTURES FROM UP CLOSE.
HIS MAJESTY WILL BE THRILLED.
HE'LL LOOK FORWARD TO YOUR PHOTOS JUST LIKE HE DOES MINE.

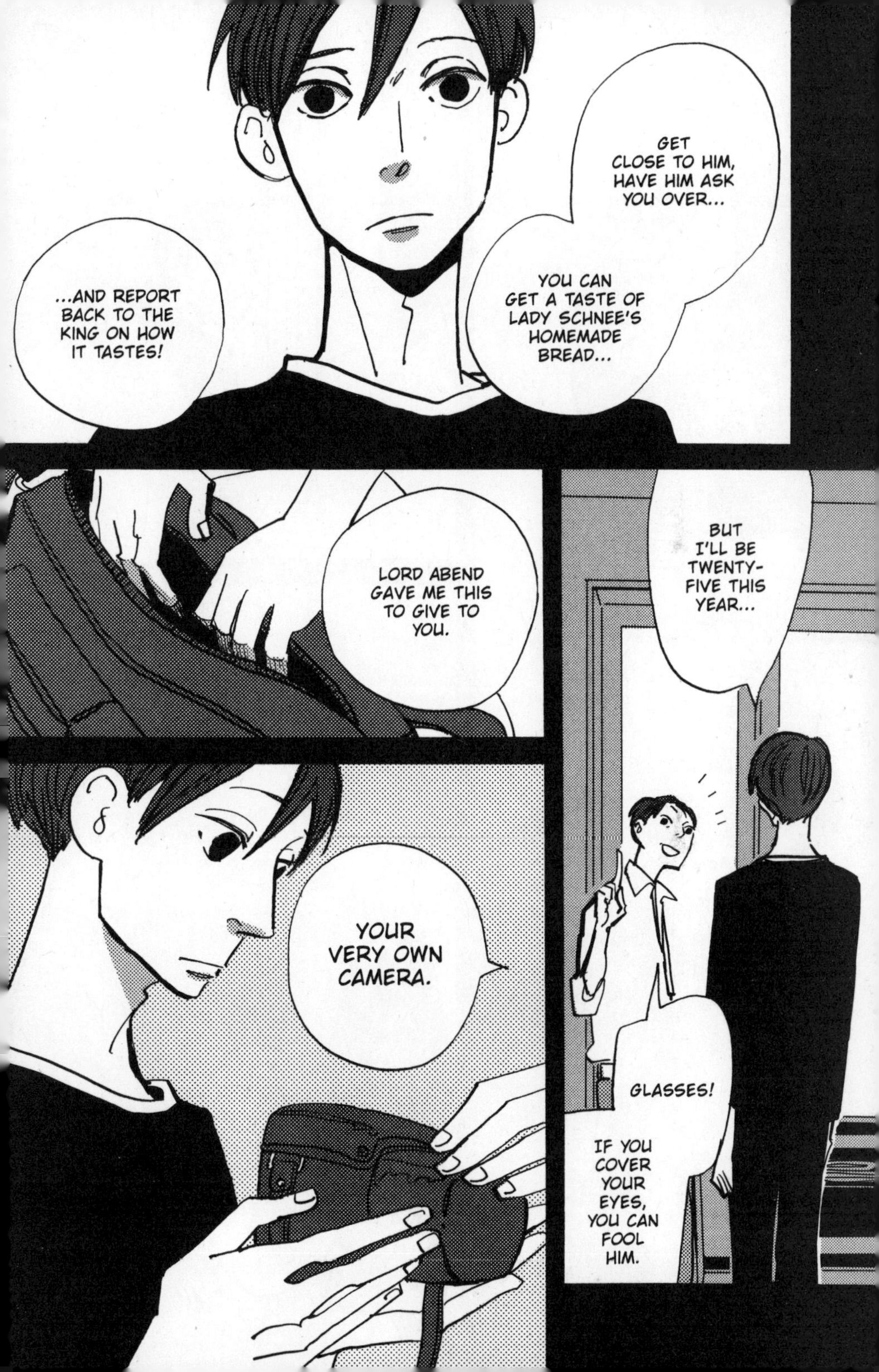
GET CLOSE TO HIM, HAVE HIM ASK YOU OVER...
YOU CAN GET A TASTE OF LADY SCHNEE'S HOMEMADE BREAD...
...AND REPORT BACK TO THE KING ON HOW IT TASTES!
BUT I'LL BE TWENTY-FIVE THIS YEAR...
GLASSES!
IF YOU COVER YOUR EYES, YOU CAN FOOL HIM.
LORD ABEND GAVE ME THIS TO GIVE TO YOU.
YOUR VERY OWN CAMERA.

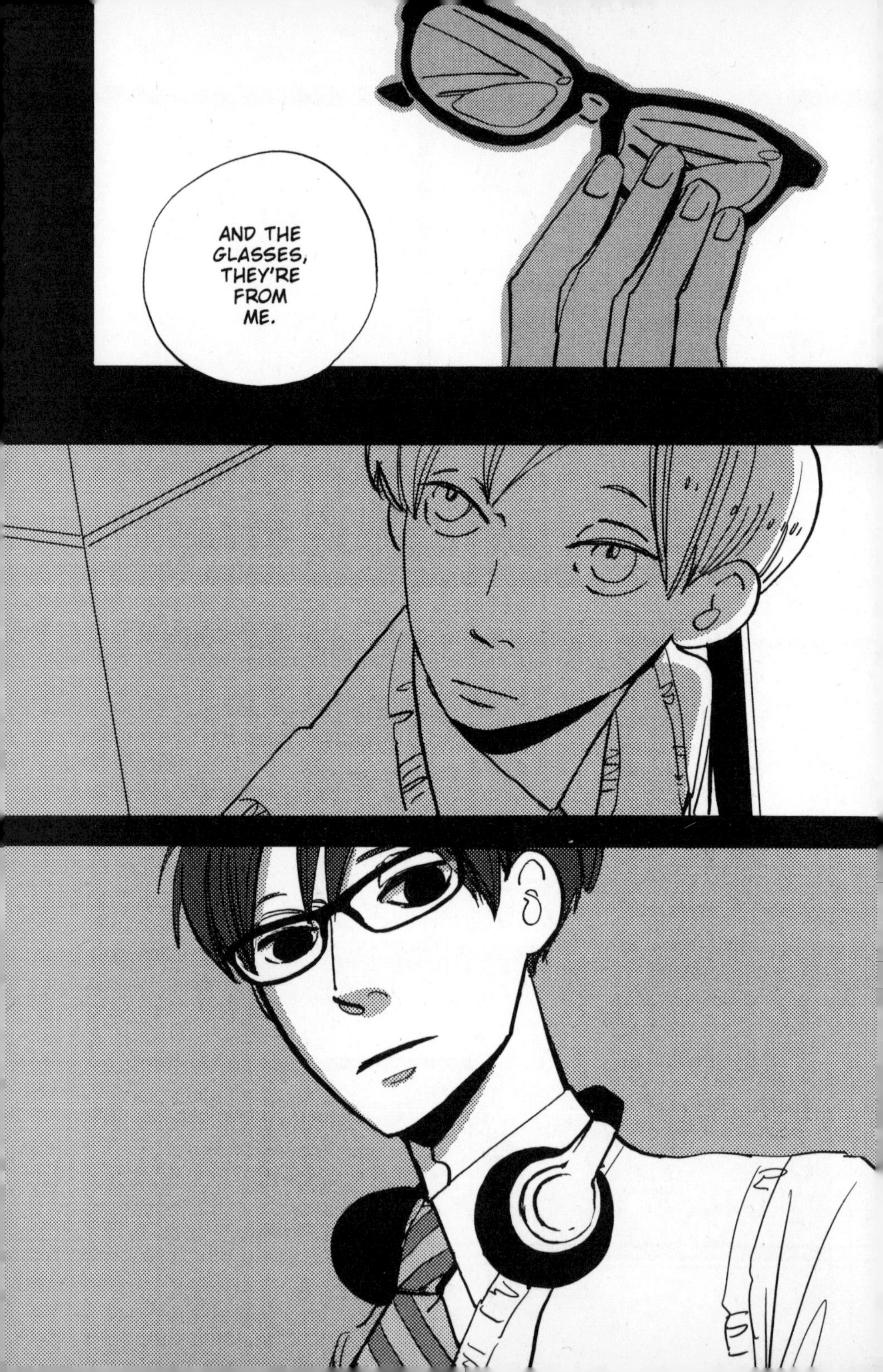
AND THE GLASSES, THEY'RE FROM ME.

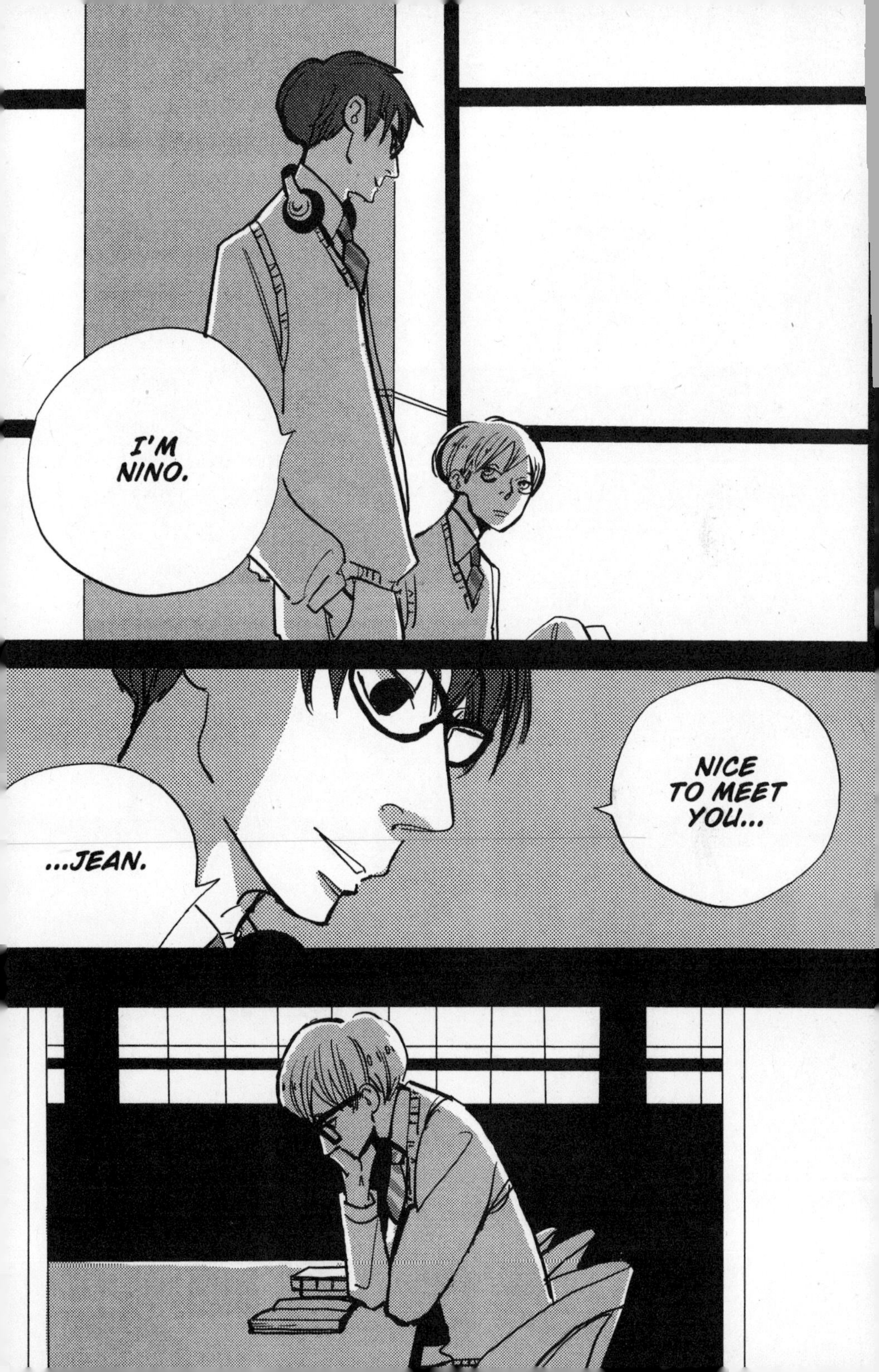
I'M NINO.
NICE TO MEET YOU...
...JEAN.

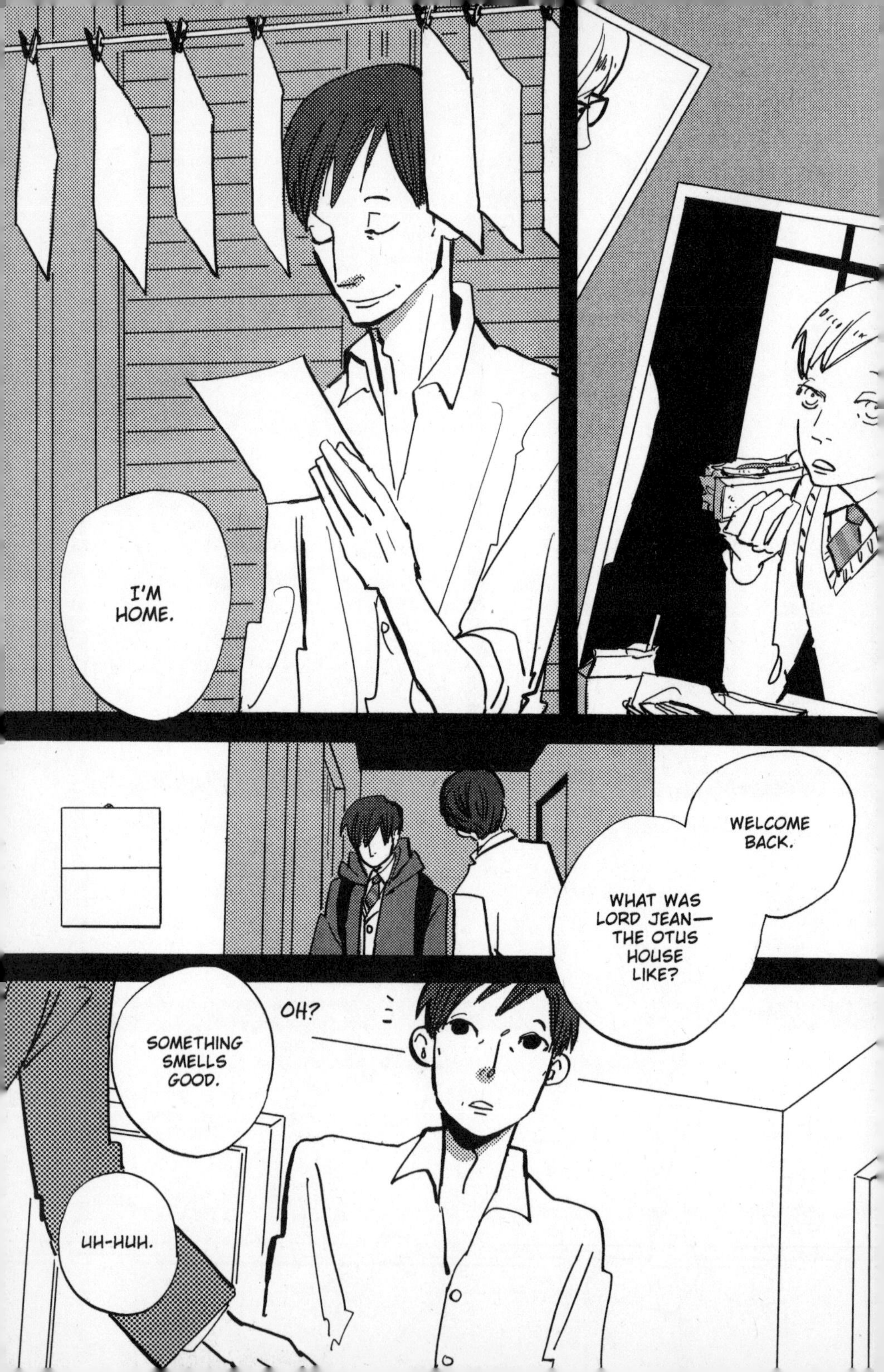
I'M HOME.
WELCOME BACK.
WHAT WAS LORD JEAN—THE OTUS HOUSE LIKE?
OH?
SOMETHING SMELLS GOOD.
UH-HUH.

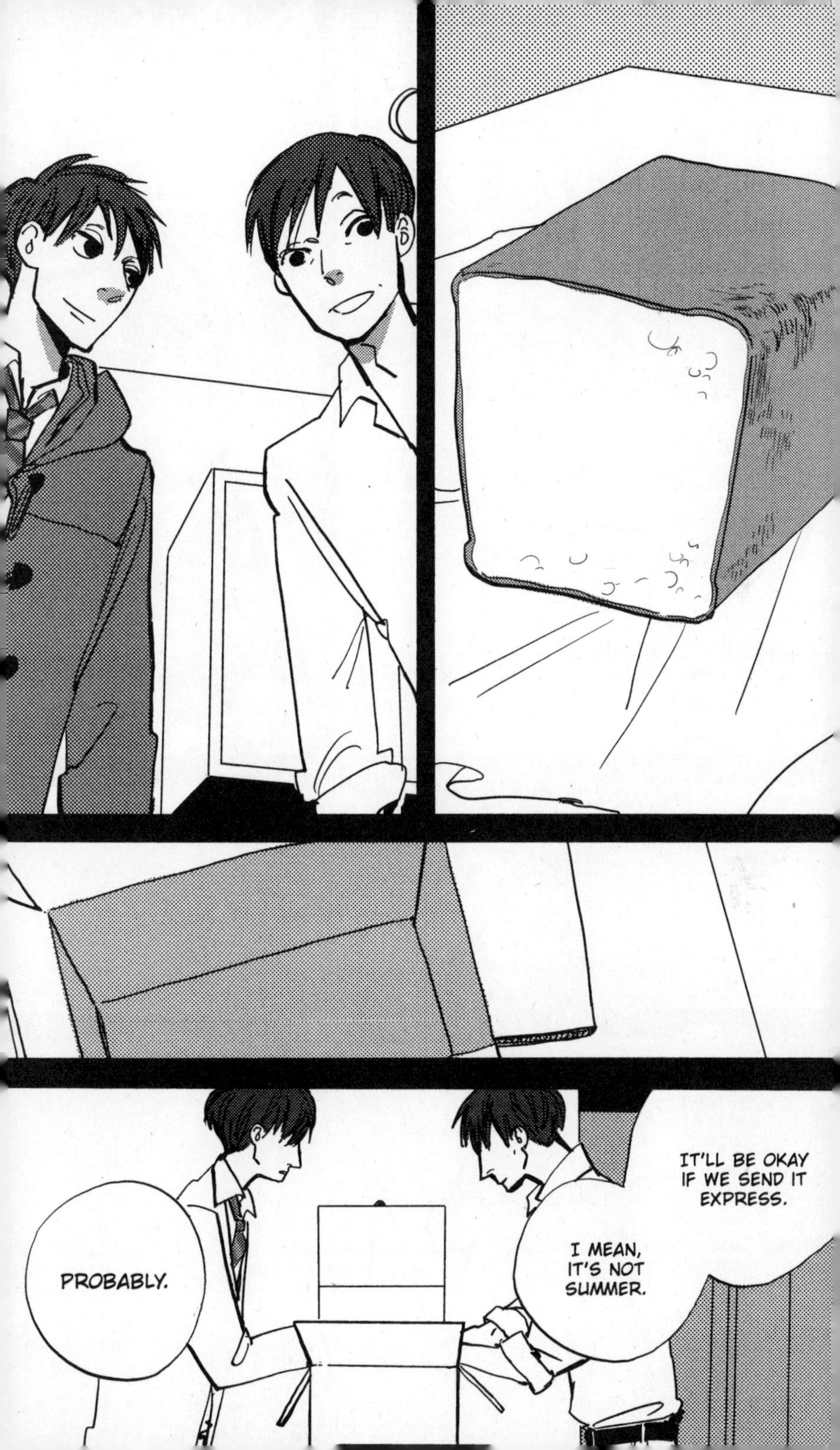
IT'LL BE OKAY IF WE SEND IT EXPRESS.
I MEAN, IT'S NOT SUMMER.
PROBABLY.

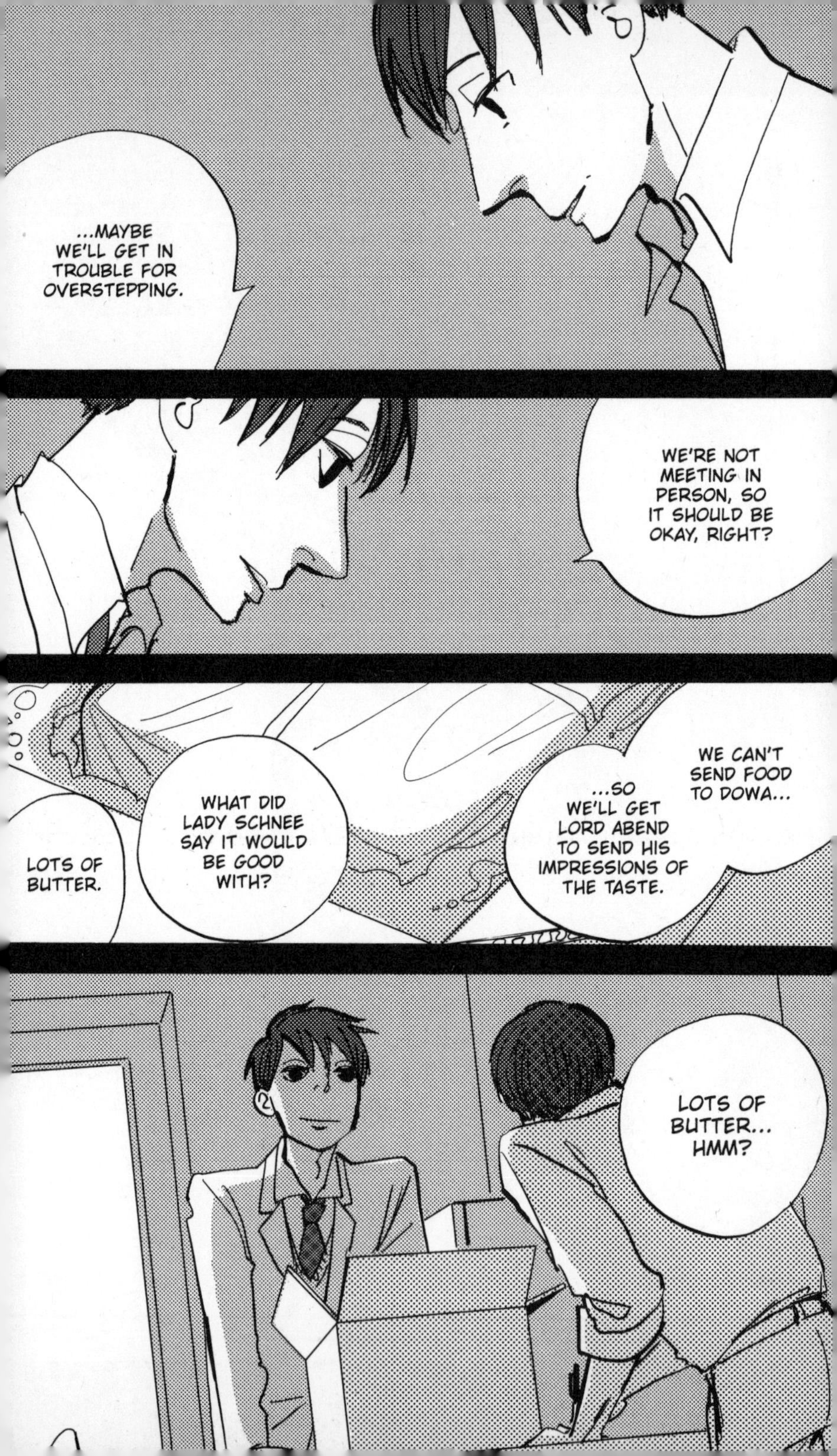
...MAYBE WE'LL GET IN TROUBLE FOR OVERSTEPPING.
WE'RE NOT MEETING IN PERSON, SO IT SHOULD BE OKAY, RIGHT?
WE CAN'T SEND FOOD TO DOWA...
...SO WE'LL GET LORD ABEND TO SEND HIS IMPRESSIONS OF THE TASTE.
WHAT DID LADY SCHNEE SAY IT WOULD BE GOOD WITH?
LOTS OF BUTTER.
LOTS OF BUTTER... HMM?

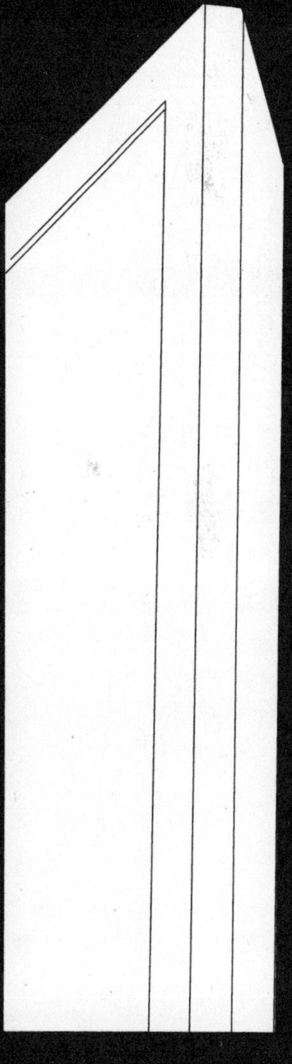

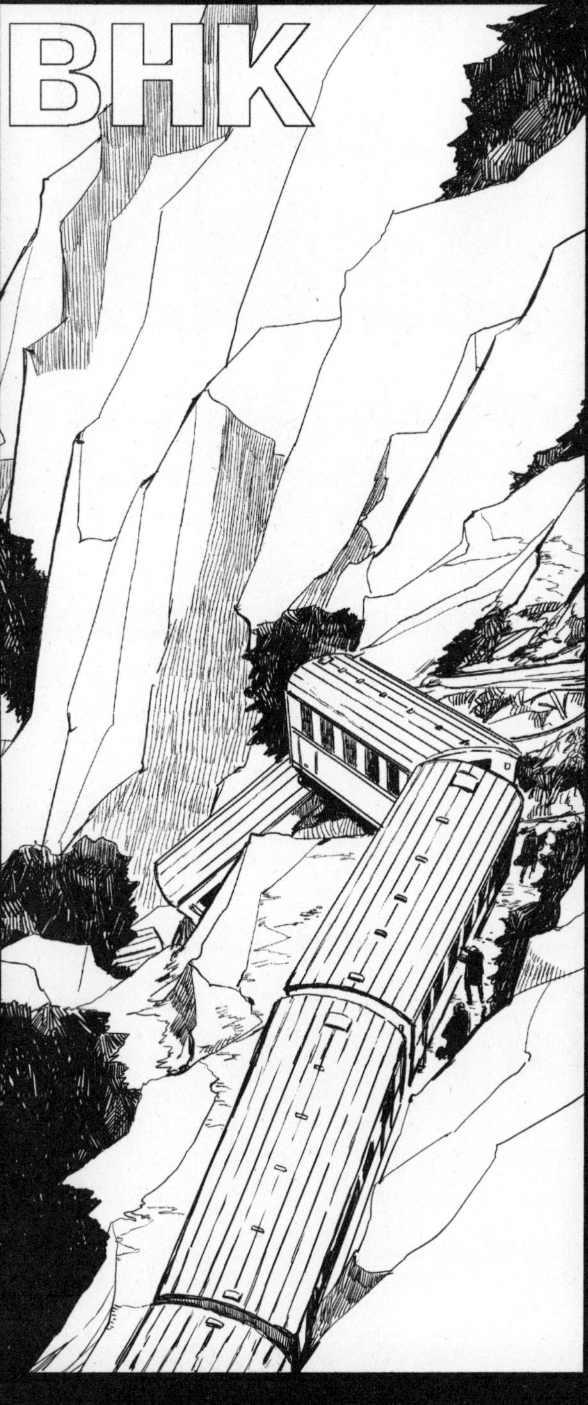
BHK

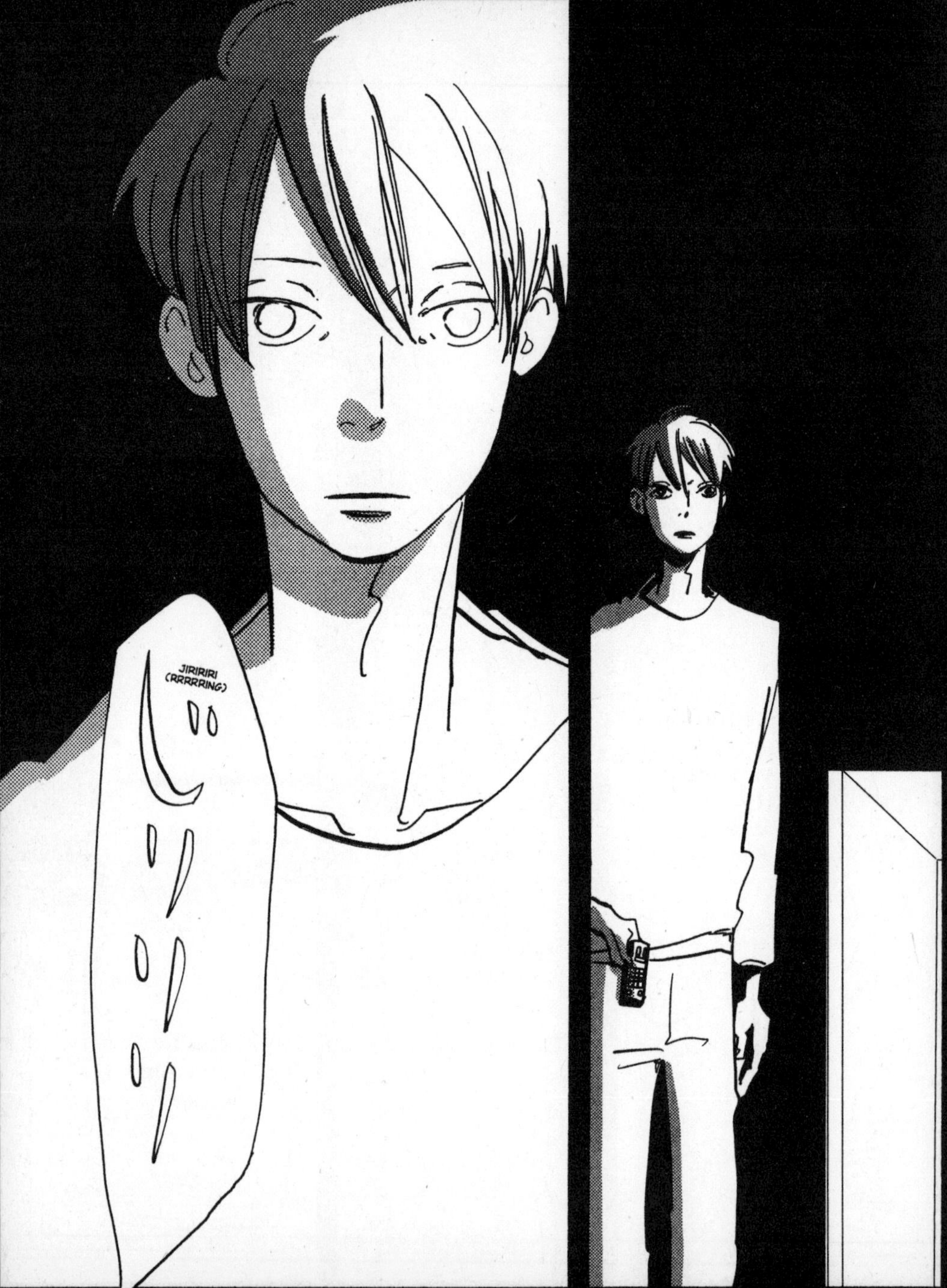
JIRIRIRI
(RRRRRING)

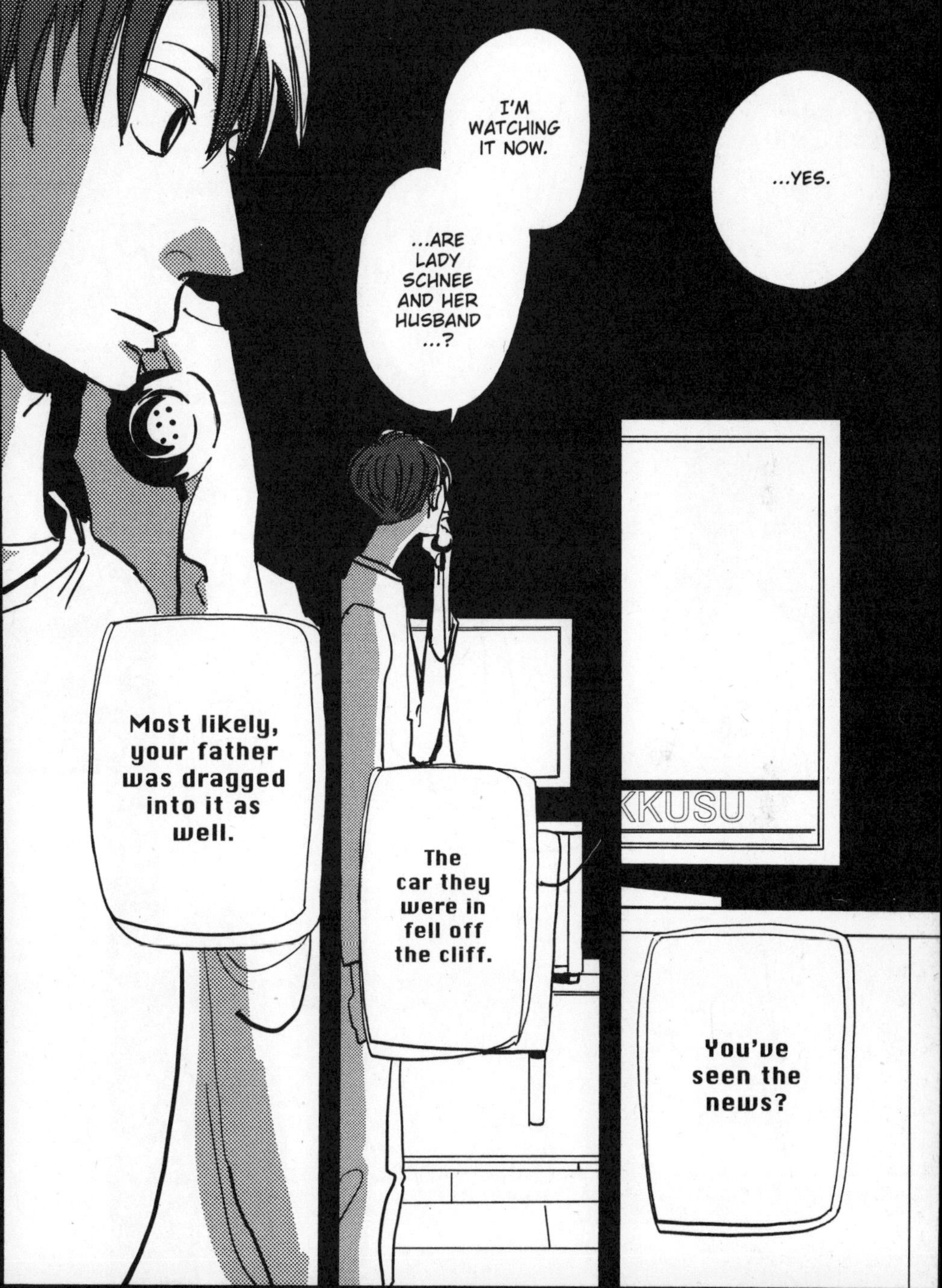
You've seen the news?
...YES.
I'M WATCHING IT NOW.
The car they were in fell off the cliff.
...ARE LADY SCHNEE AND HER HUSBAND ...?
Most likely, your father was dragged into it as well.
KKUSU

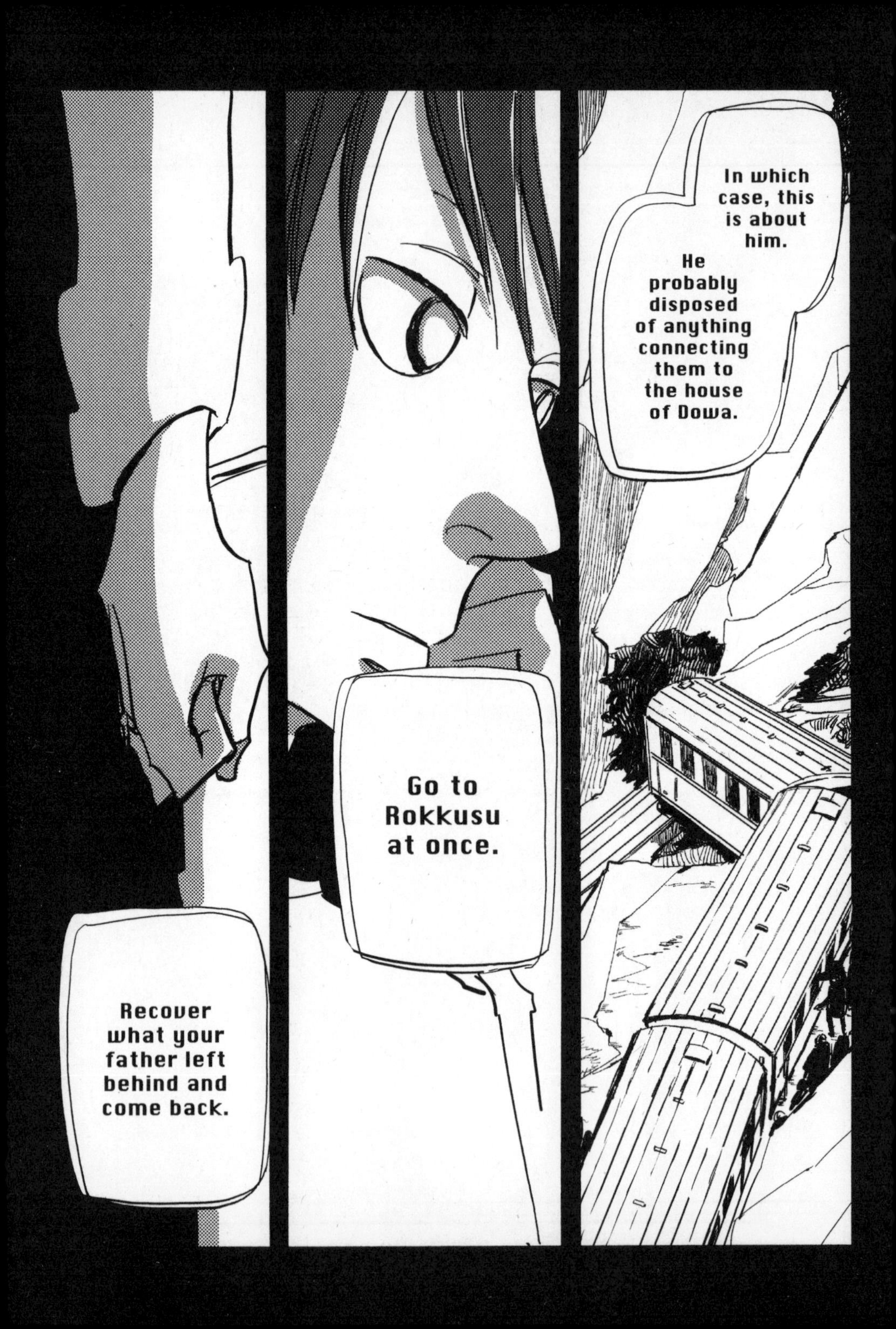
In which case, this is about him.
He probably disposed of anything connecting them to the house of Dowa.
Go to Rokkusu at once.
Recover what your father left behind and come back.

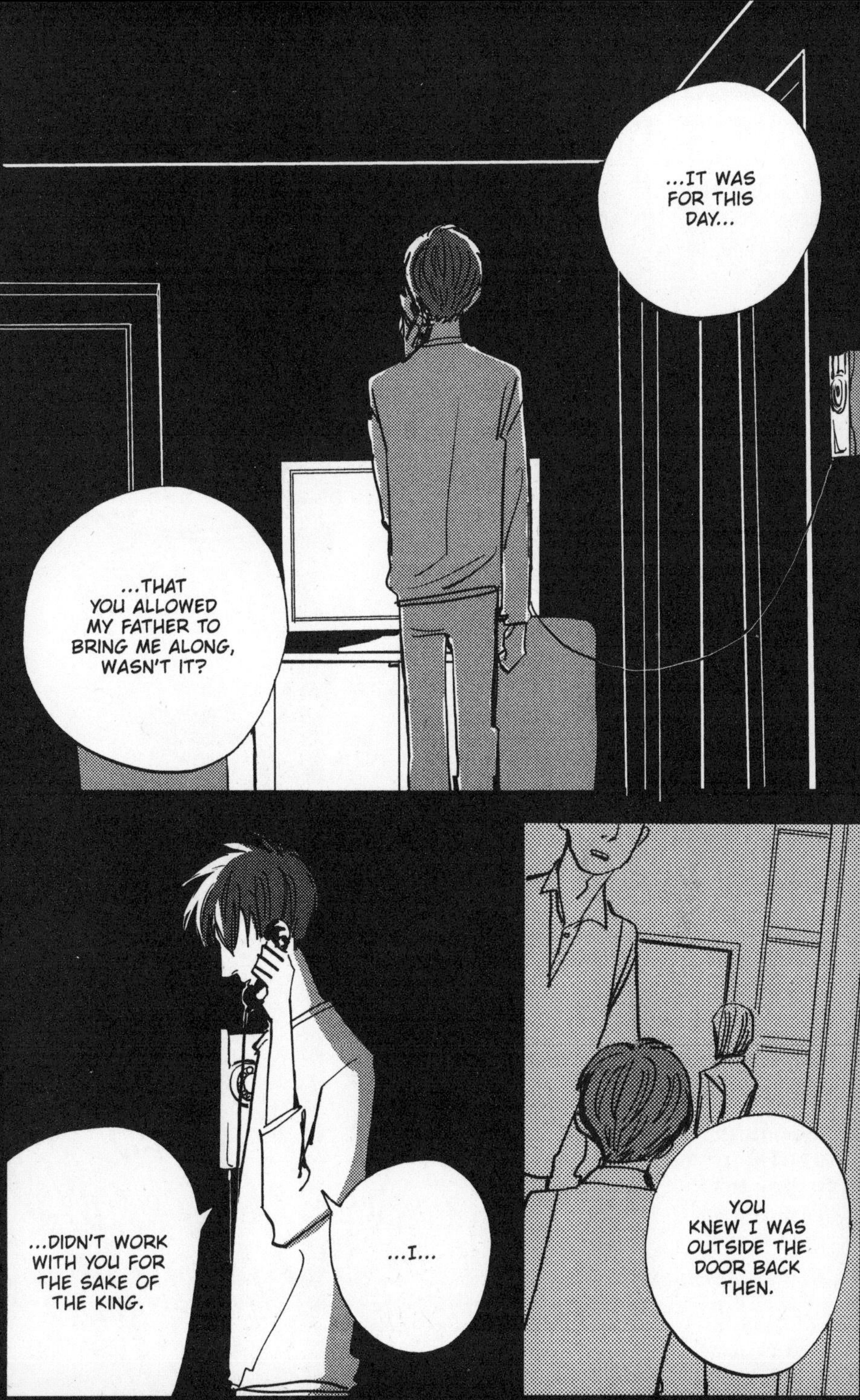
...IT WAS FOR THIS DAY...
...THAT YOU ALLOWED MY FATHER TO BRING ME ALONG, WASN'T IT?
YOU KNEW I WAS OUTSIDE THE DOOR BACK THEN.
...I...
...DIDN'T WORK WITH YOU FOR THE SAKE OF THE KING.

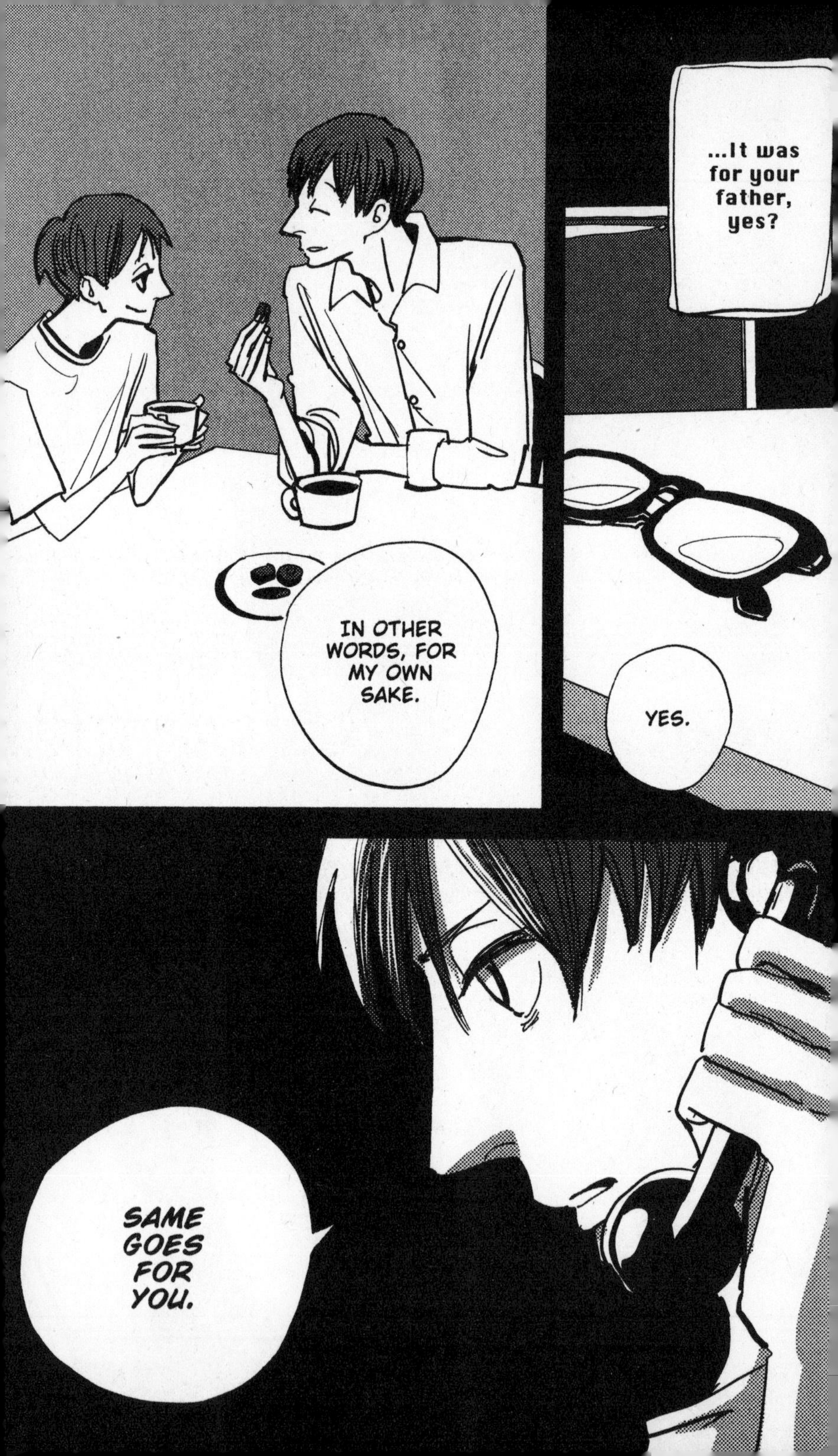
...It was for your father, yes?
YES.
IN OTHER WORDS, FOR MY OWN SAKE.
SAME GOES FOR YOU.

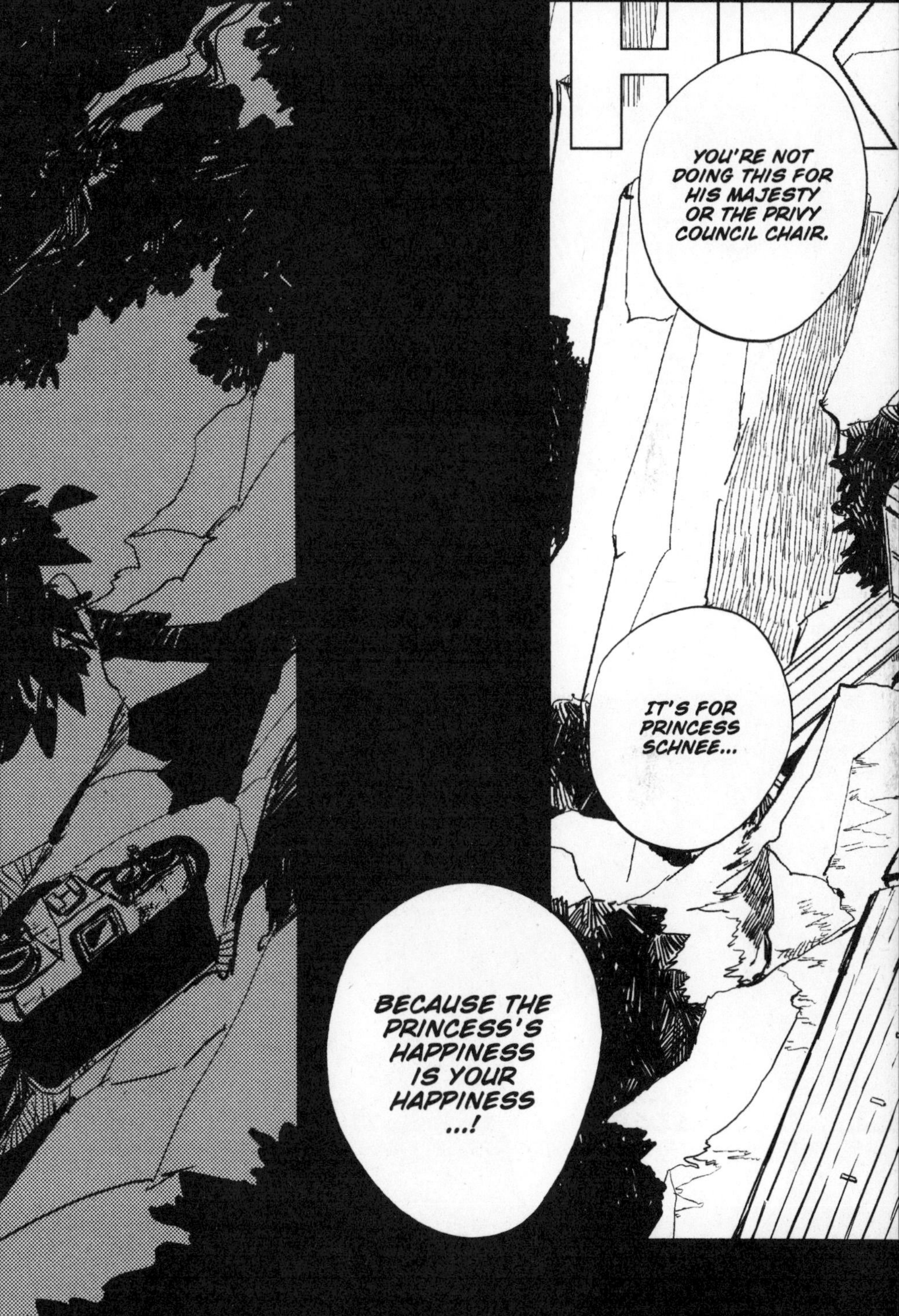
YOU'RE NOT DOING THIS FOR HIS MAJESTY OR THE PRIVY COUNCIL CHAIR.
IT'S FOR PRINCESS SCHNEE...
BECAUSE THE PRINCESS'S HAPPINESS IS YOUR HAPPINESS ...!

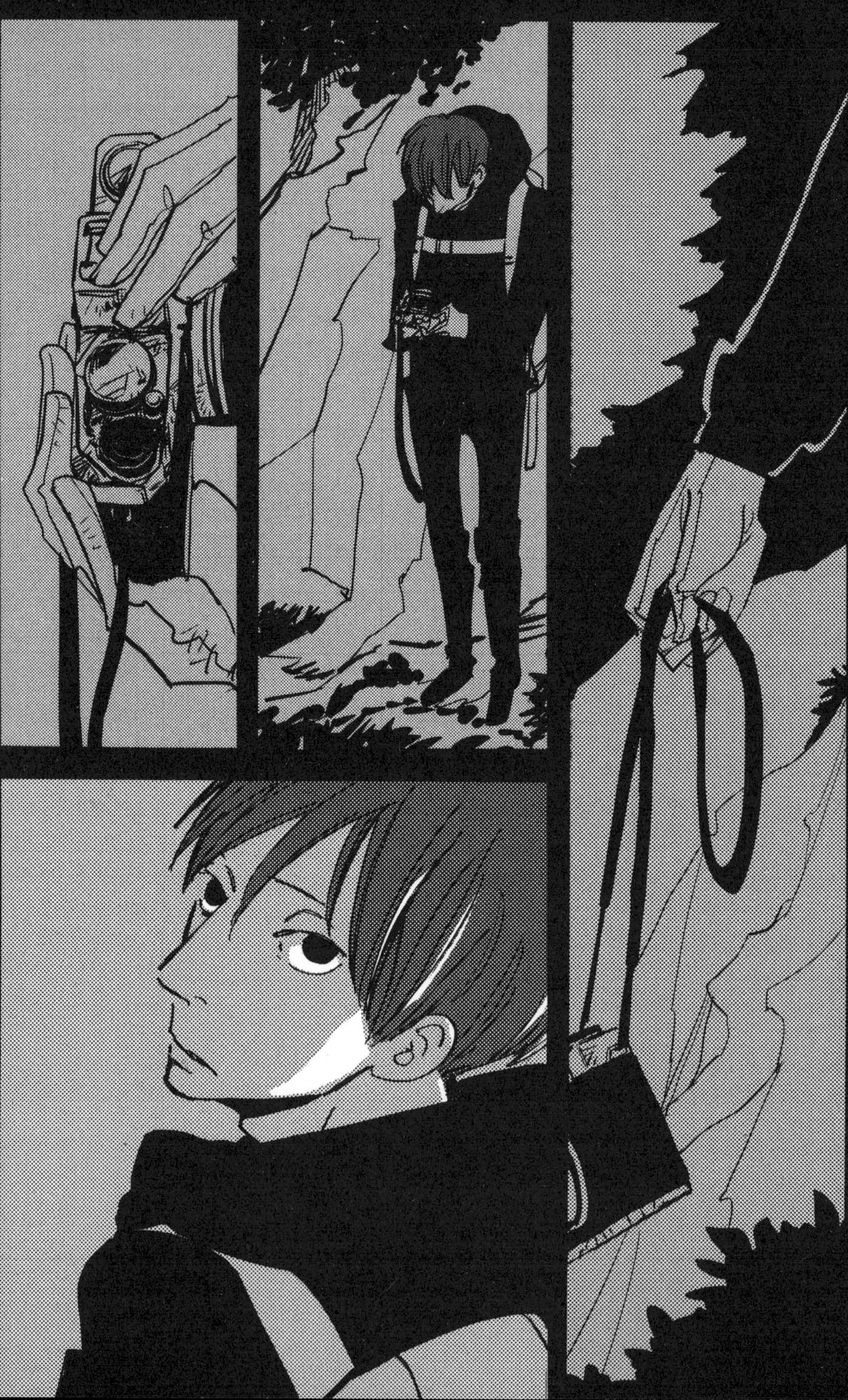

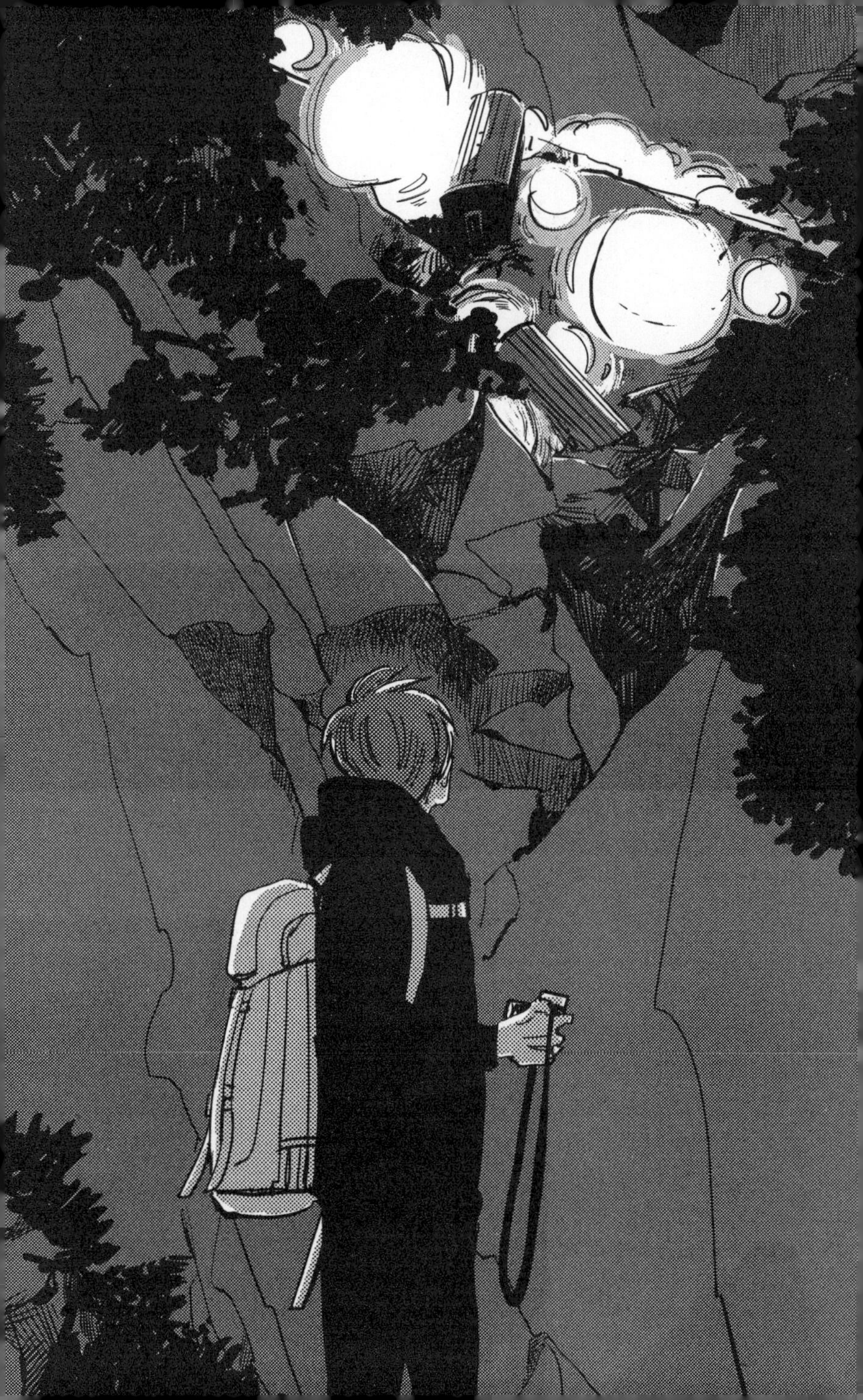

ACCA Branch Uniforms | 8

Many stylish and talented women work in the district of Korore. The ACCA uniforms are tailored to fit the lines of each individual body.

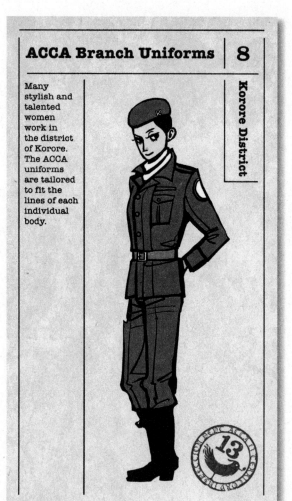

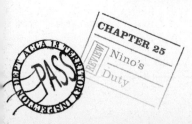

CHAPTER 25

REVIEW

Nino's

Duty

ACCA Branch Uniforms | 9

Noted for
its many
decorative
details, the
traditional
clothing of
the people
is reflected
in the
uniform.

Rokkusu District

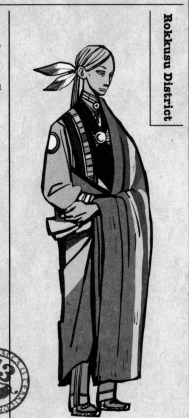

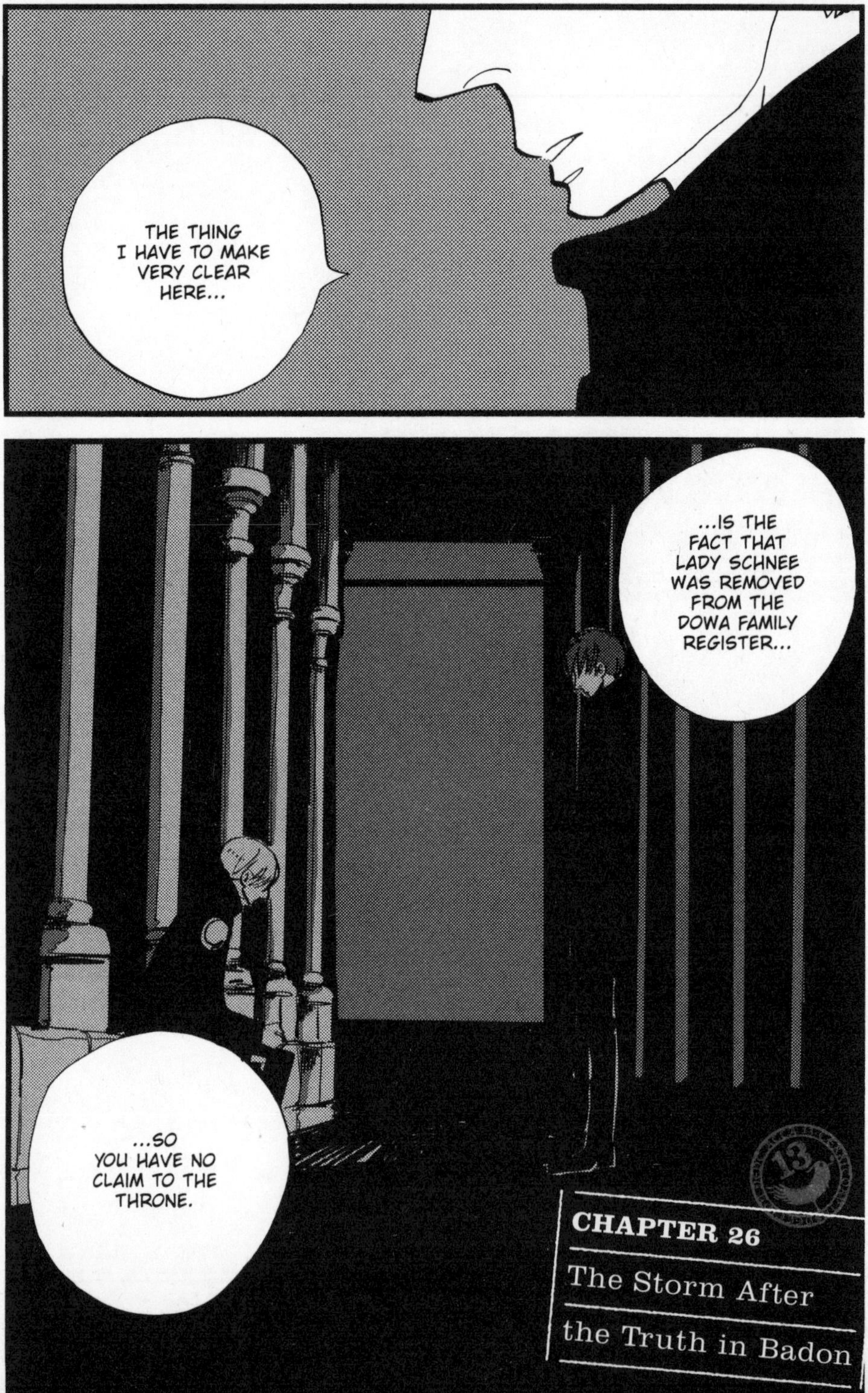
THE THING I HAVE TO MAKE VERY CLEAR HERE...
...IS THE FACT THAT LADY SCHNEE WAS REMOVED FROM THE DOWA FAMILY REGISTER...
...SO YOU HAVE NO CLAIM TO THE THRONE.
CHAPTER 26
The Storm After the Truth in Badon

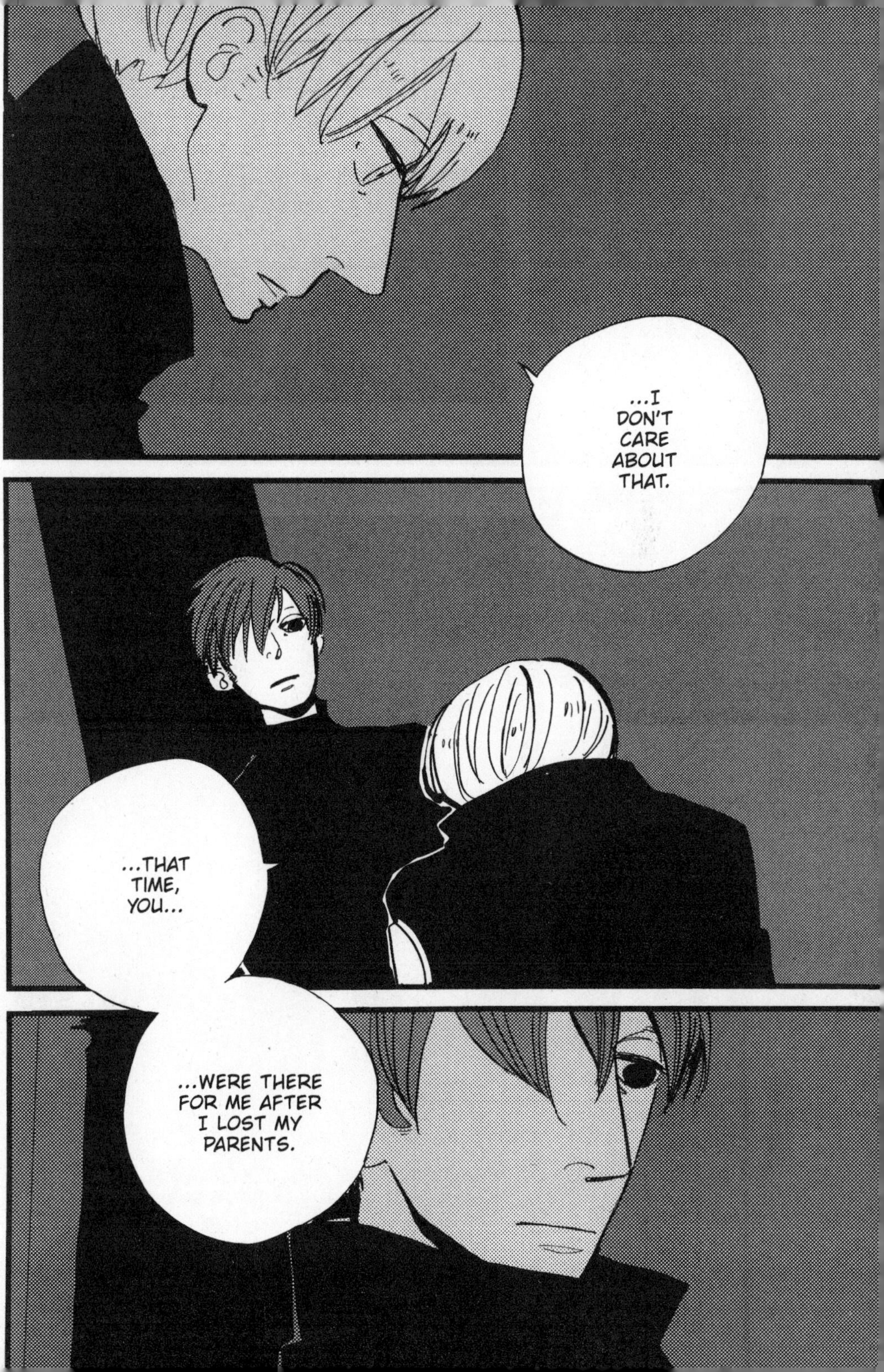
...I DON'T CARE ABOUT THAT.
...THAT TIME, YOU...
...WERE THERE FOR ME AFTER I LOST MY PARENTS.

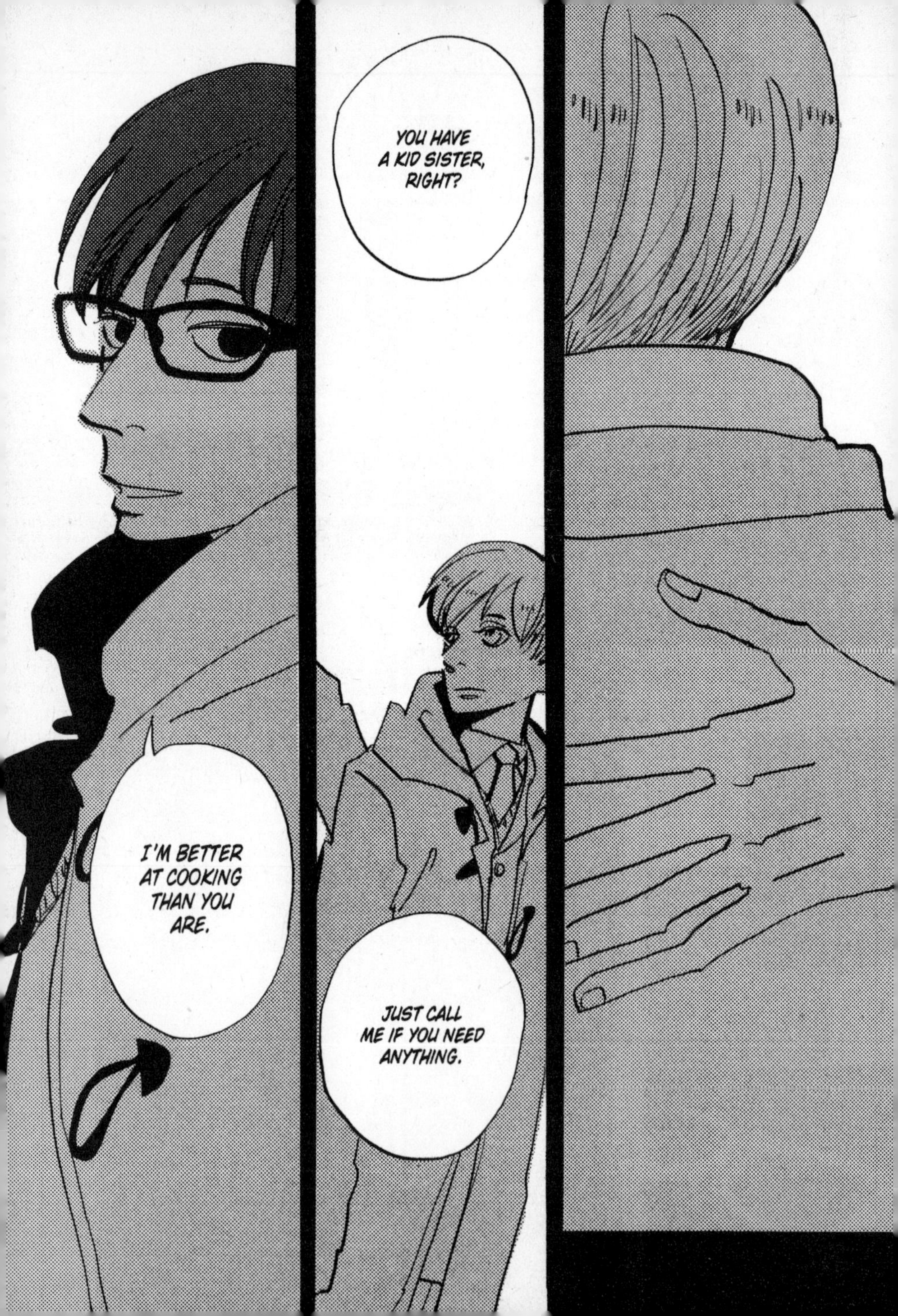
YOU HAVE A KID SISTER, RIGHT?
JUST CALL ME IF YOU NEED ANYTHING.
I'M BETTER AT COOKING THAN YOU ARE.

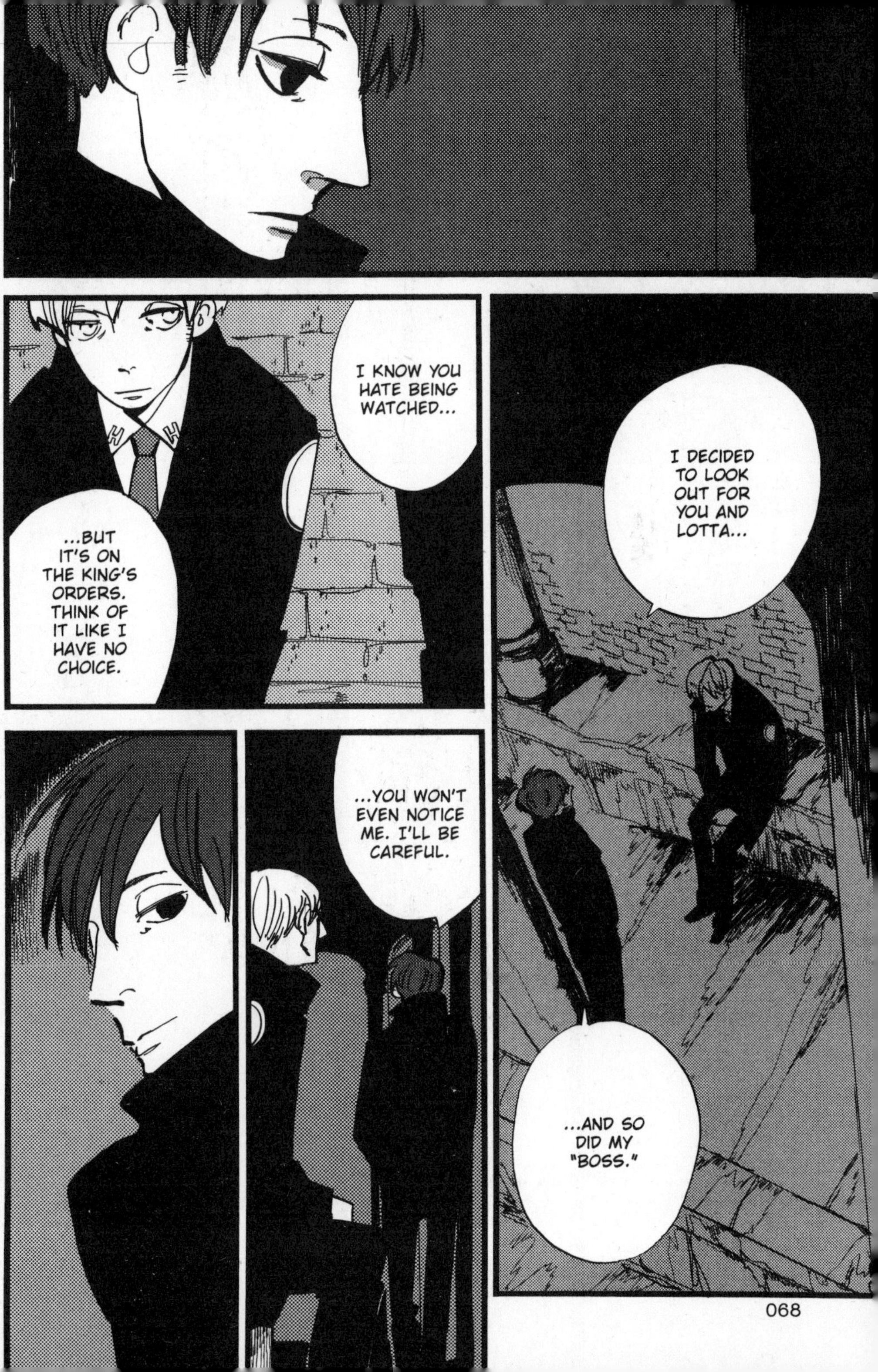
I DECIDED TO LOOK OUT FOR YOU AND LOTTA...
...AND SO DID MY "BOSS."
I KNOW YOU HATE BEING WATCHED...
...BUT IT'S ON THE KING'S ORDERS. THINK OF IT LIKE I HAVE NO CHOICE.
...YOU WON'T EVEN NOTICE ME. I'LL BE CAREFUL.

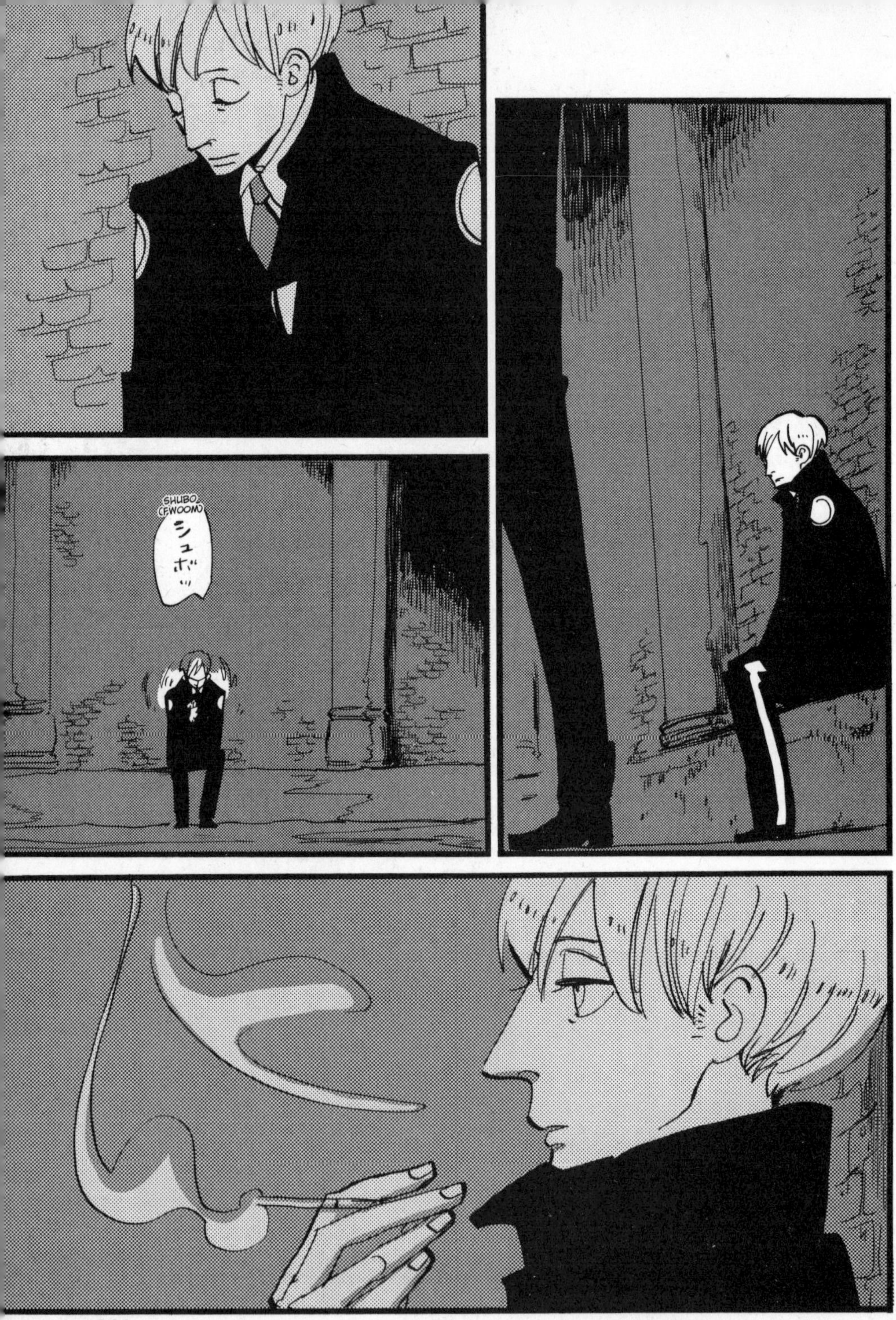
SHUBO (FWOOM)
シュボッ

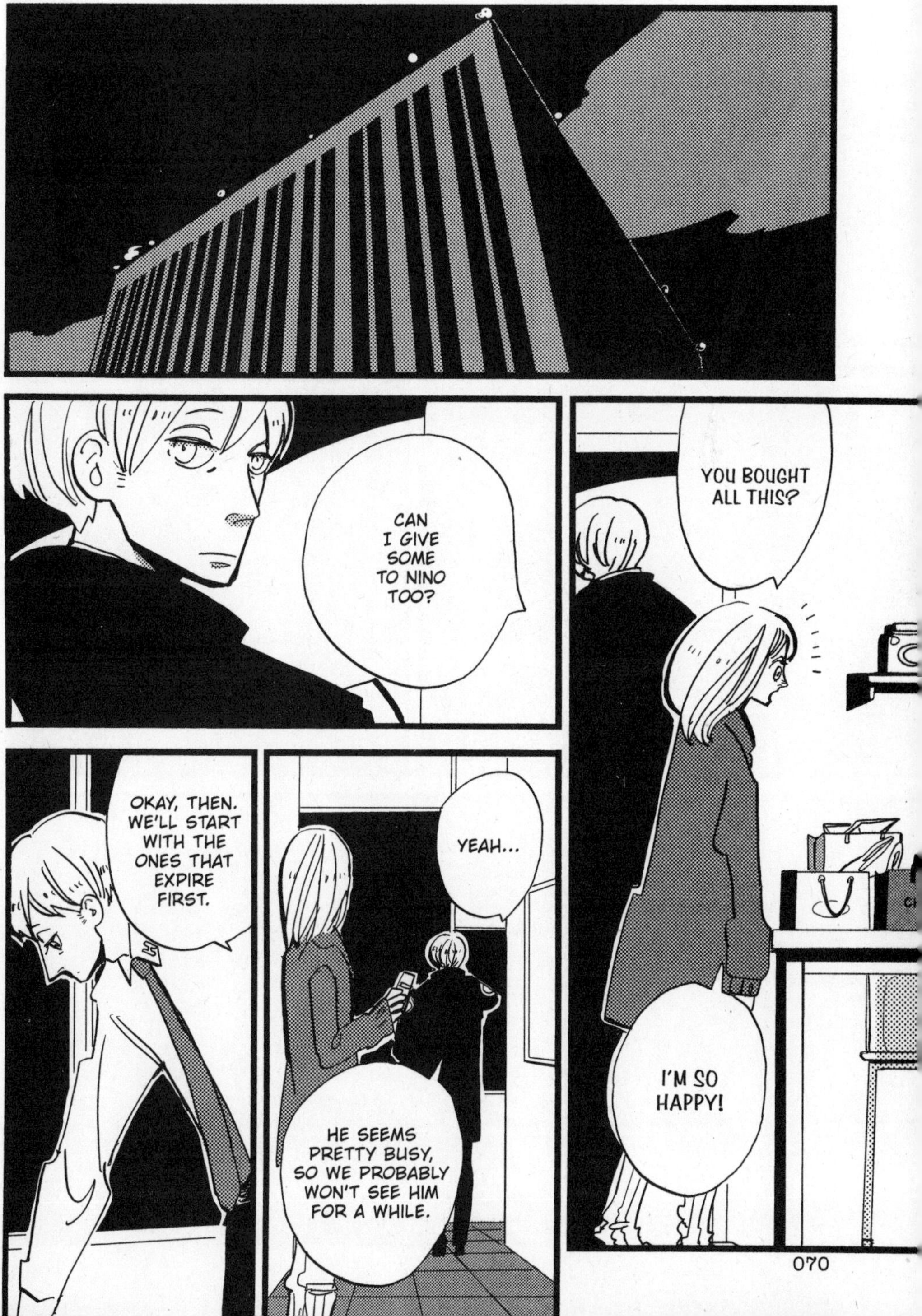
YOU BOUGHT ALL THIS?
I'M SO HAPPY!
CAN I GIVE SOME TO NINO TOO?
YEAH...
HE SEEMS PRETTY BUSY, SO WE PROBABLY WON'T SEE HIM FOR A WHILE.
OKAY, THEN. WE'LL START WITH THE ONES THAT EXPIRE FIRST.

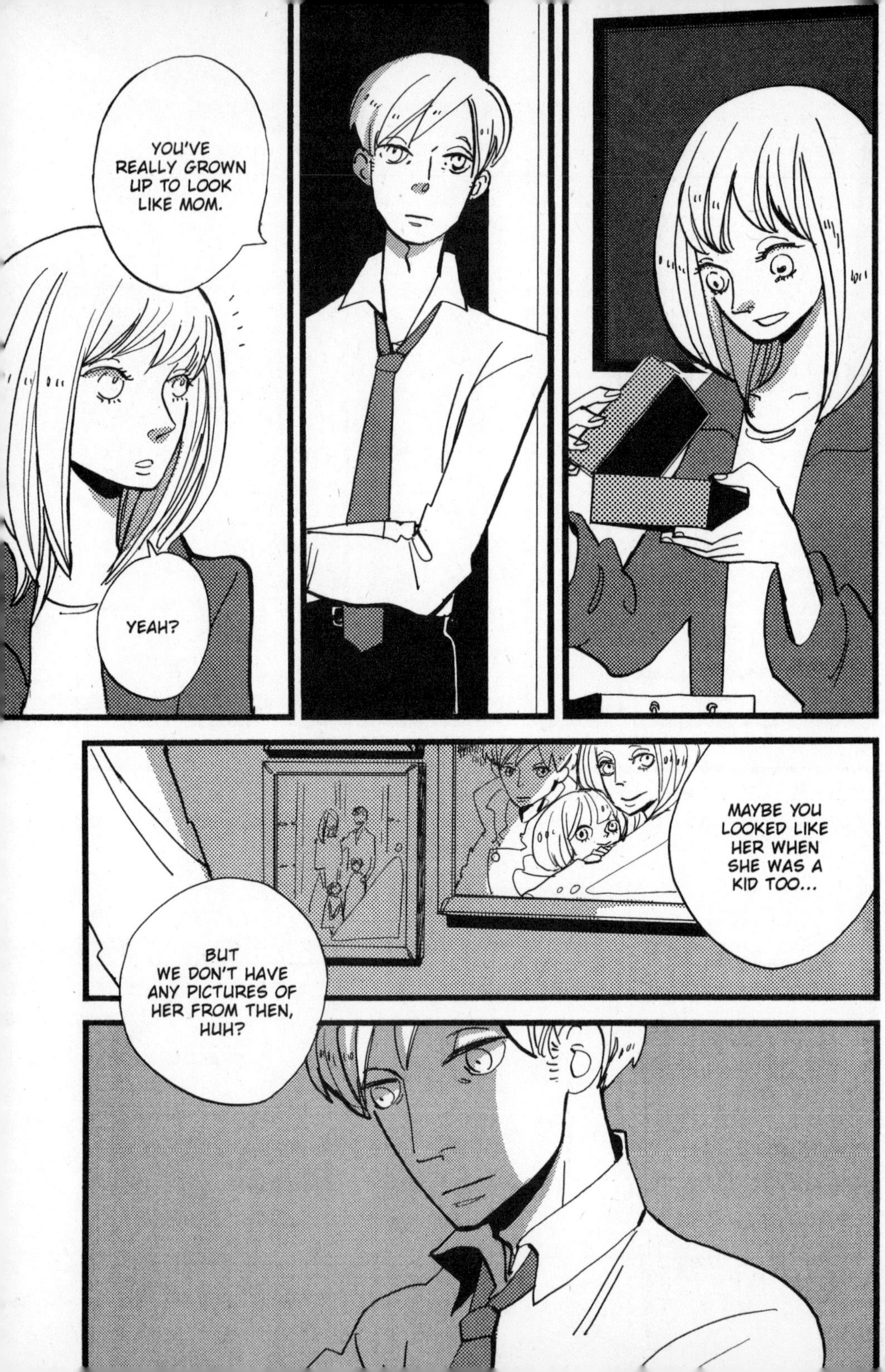
YOU'VE REALLY GROWN UP TO LOOK LIKE MOM.
YEAH?
MAYBE YOU LOOKED LIKE HER WHEN SHE WAS A KID TOO...
BUT WE DON'T HAVE ANY PICTURES OF HER FROM THEN, HUH?

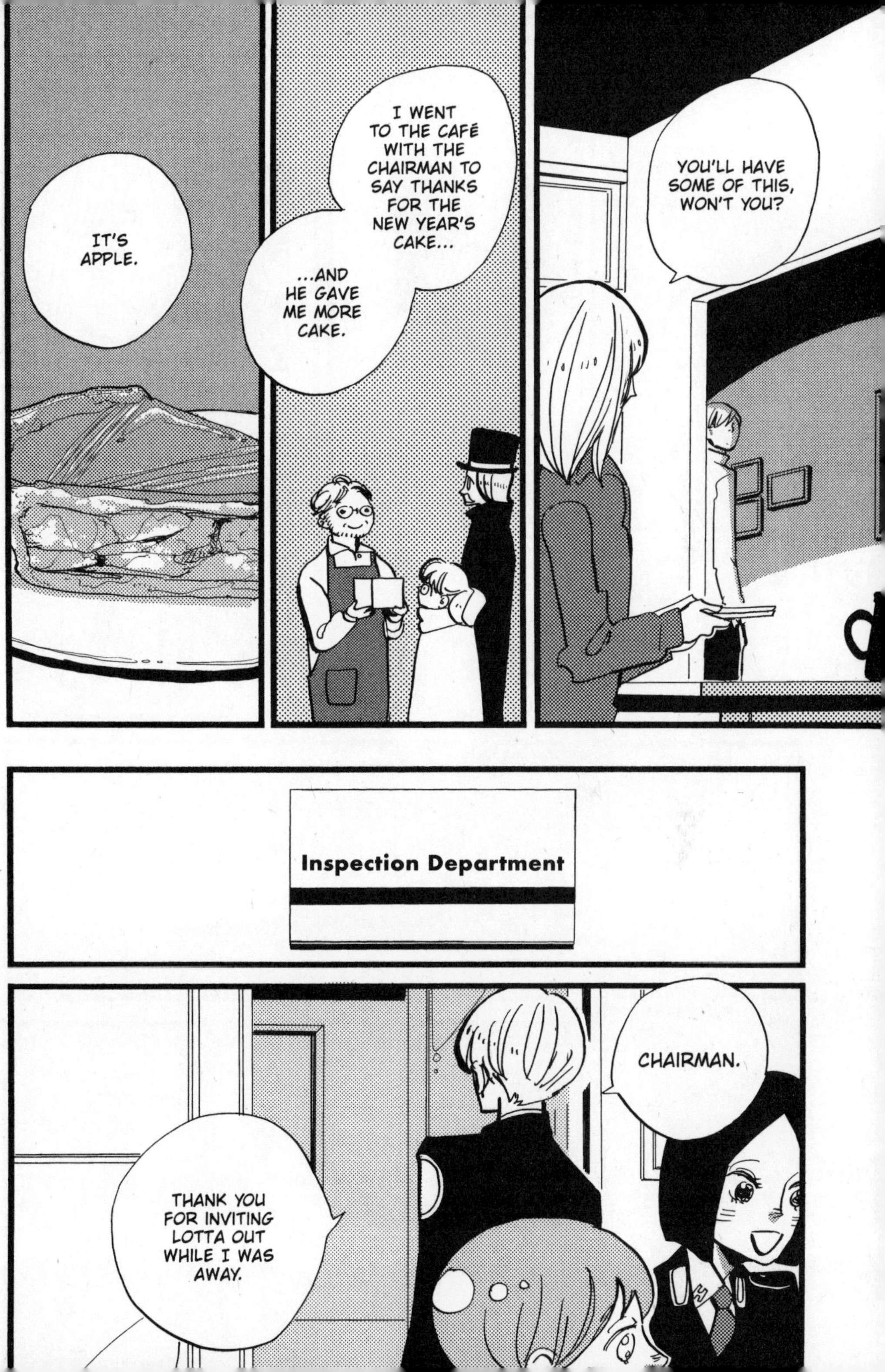
YOU'LL HAVE SOME OF THIS, WON'T YOU?
I WENT TO THE CAFÉ WITH THE CHAIRMAN TO SAY THANKS FOR THE NEW YEAR'S CAKE...
...AND HE GAVE ME MORE CAKE.
IT'S APPLE.
Inspection Department
CHAIRMAN.
THANK YOU FOR INVITING LOTTA OUT WHILE I WAS AWAY.

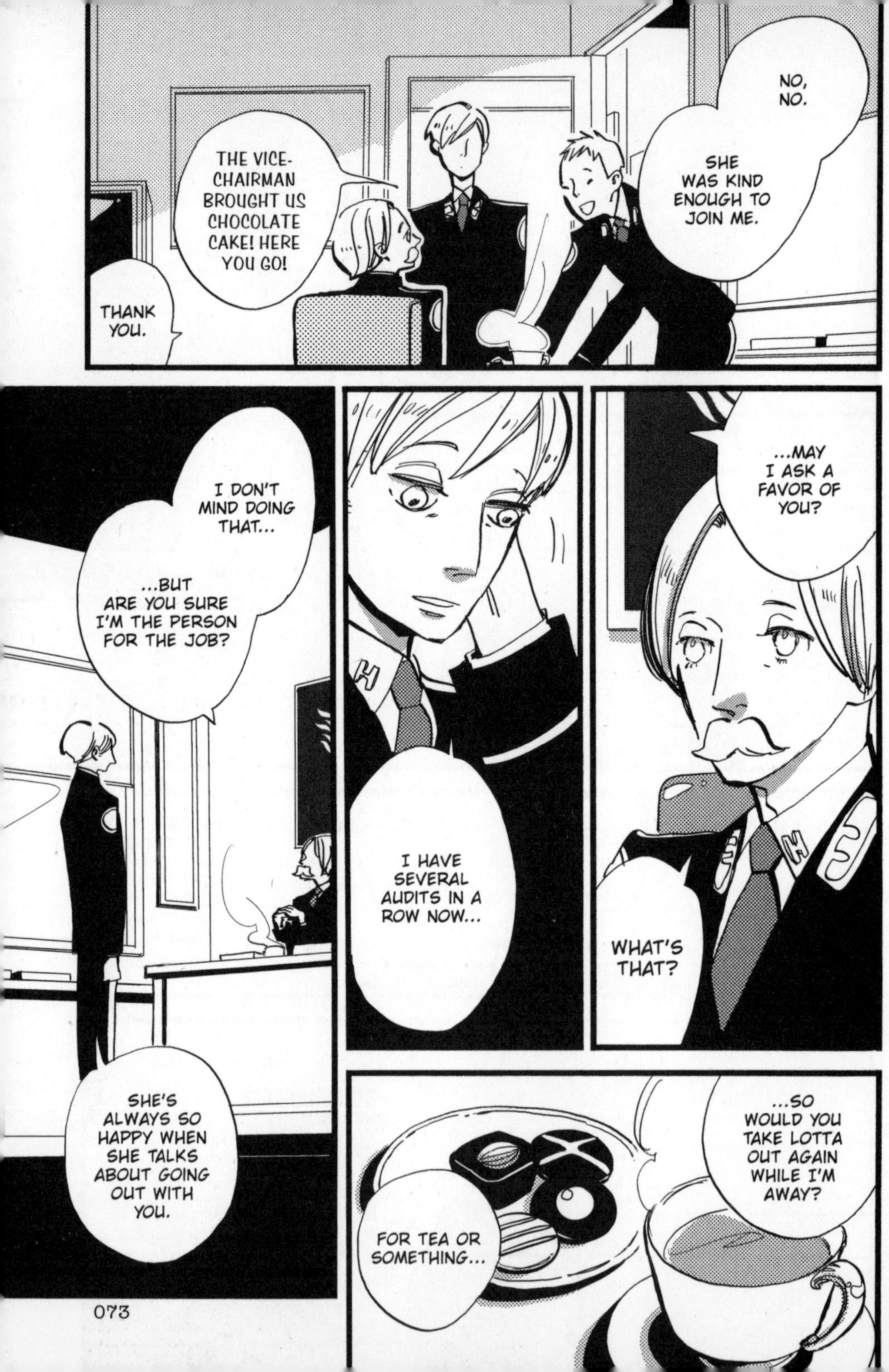
NO, NO.
SHE WAS KIND ENOUGH TO JOIN ME.
THE VICE-CHAIRMAN BROUGHT US CHOCOLATE CAKE! HERE YOU GO!
THANK YOU.
...MAY I ASK A FAVOR OF YOU?
WHAT'S THAT?
I HAVE SEVERAL AUDITS IN A ROW NOW...
...SO WOULD YOU TAKE LOTTA OUT AGAIN WHILE I'M AWAY?
FOR TEA OR SOMETHING...
I DON'T MIND DOING THAT...
...BUT ARE YOU SURE I'M THE PERSON FOR THE JOB?
SHE'S ALWAYS SO HAPPY WHEN SHE TALKS ABOUT GOING OUT WITH YOU.

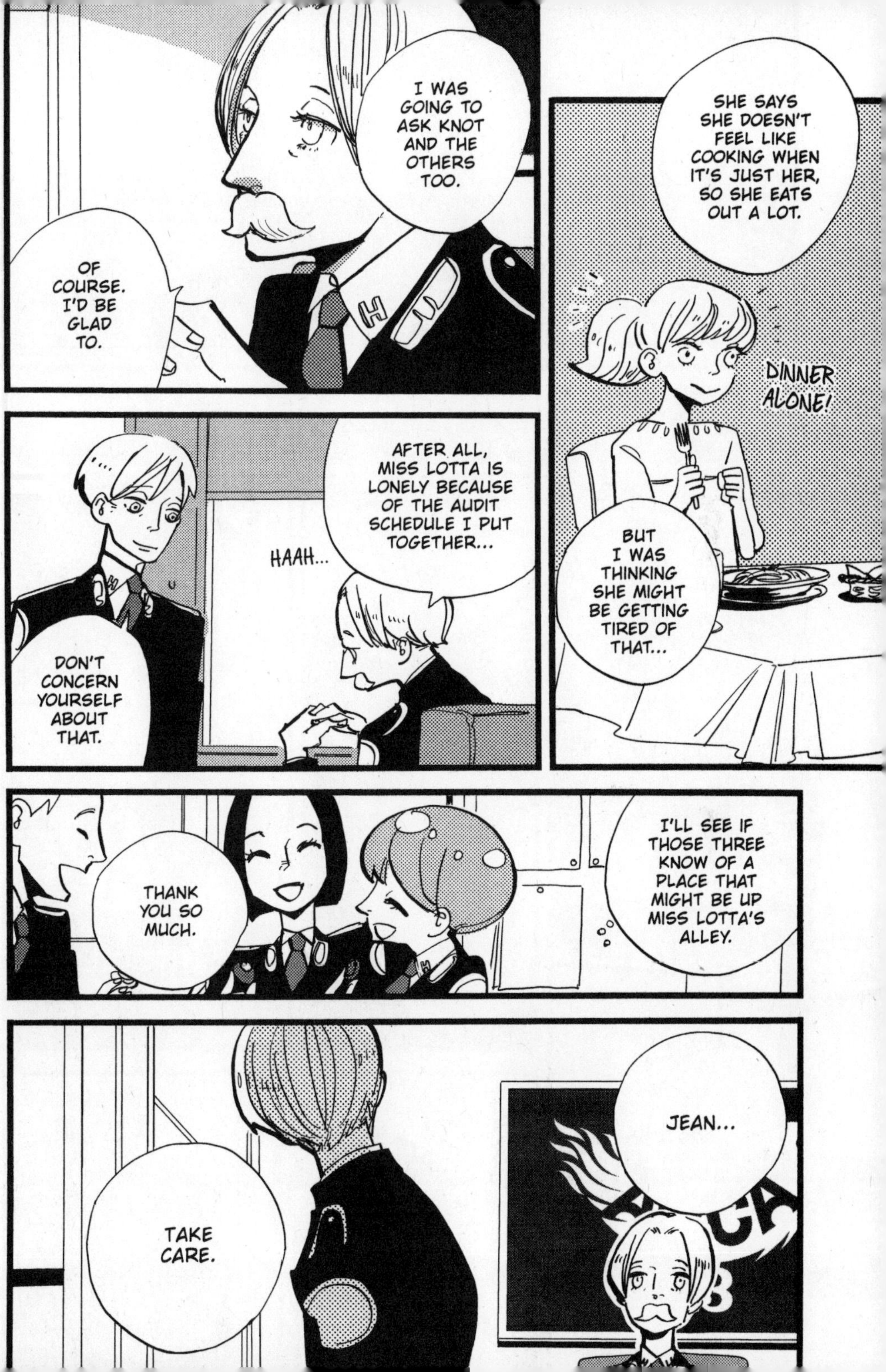
SHE SAYS SHE DOESN'T FEEL LIKE COOKING WHEN IT'S JUST HER, SO SHE EATS OUT A LOT.
DINNER ALONE!
BUT I WAS THINKING SHE MIGHT BE GETTING TIRED OF THAT...
I WAS GOING TO ASK KNOT AND THE OTHERS TOO.
OF COURSE. I'D BE GLAD TO.
AFTER ALL, MISS LOTTA IS LONELY BECAUSE OF THE AUDIT SCHEDULE I PUT TOGETHER...
HAAH...
DON'T CONCERN YOURSELF ABOUT THAT.
I'LL SEE IF THOSE THREE KNOW OF A PLACE THAT MIGHT BE UP MISS LOTTA'S ALLEY.
THANK YOU SO MUCH.
JEAN...
TAKE CARE.

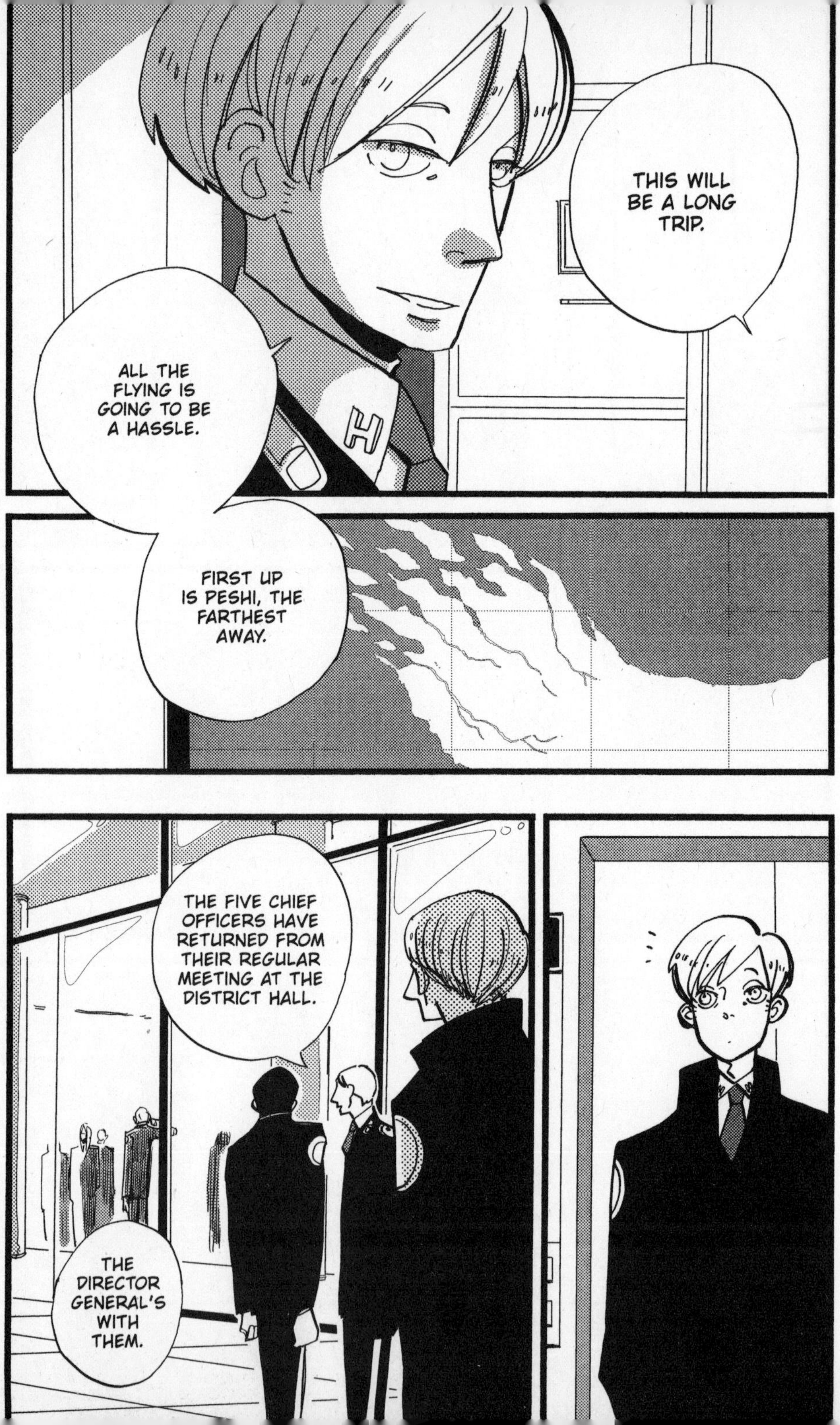
THIS WILL BE A LONG TRIP.
ALL THE FLYING IS GOING TO BE A HASSLE.
FIRST UP IS PESHI, THE FARTHEST AWAY.
THE FIVE CHIEF OFFICERS HAVE RETURNED FROM THEIR REGULAR MEETING AT THE DISTRICT HALL.
THE DIRECTOR GENERAL'S WITH THEM.

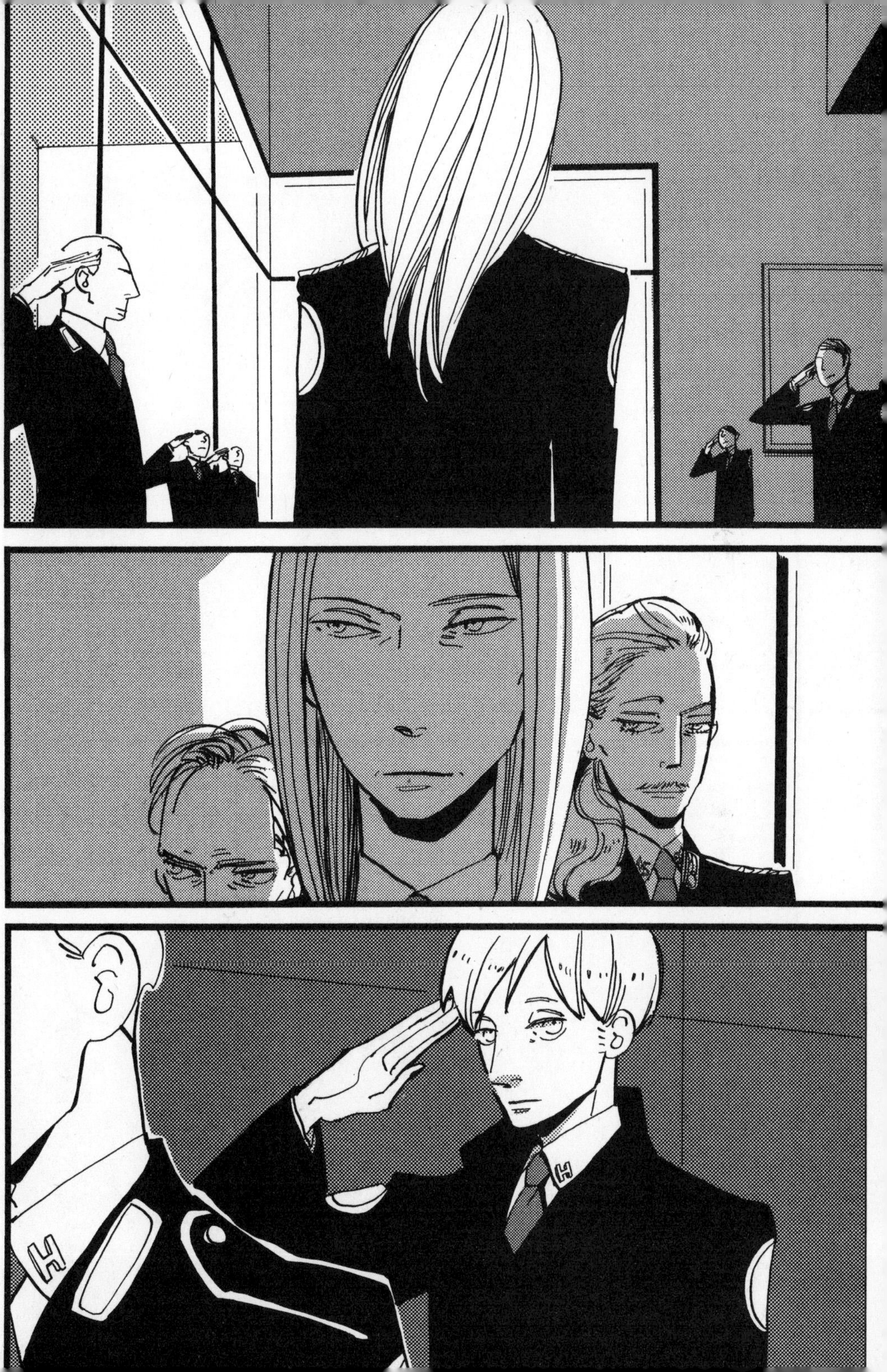

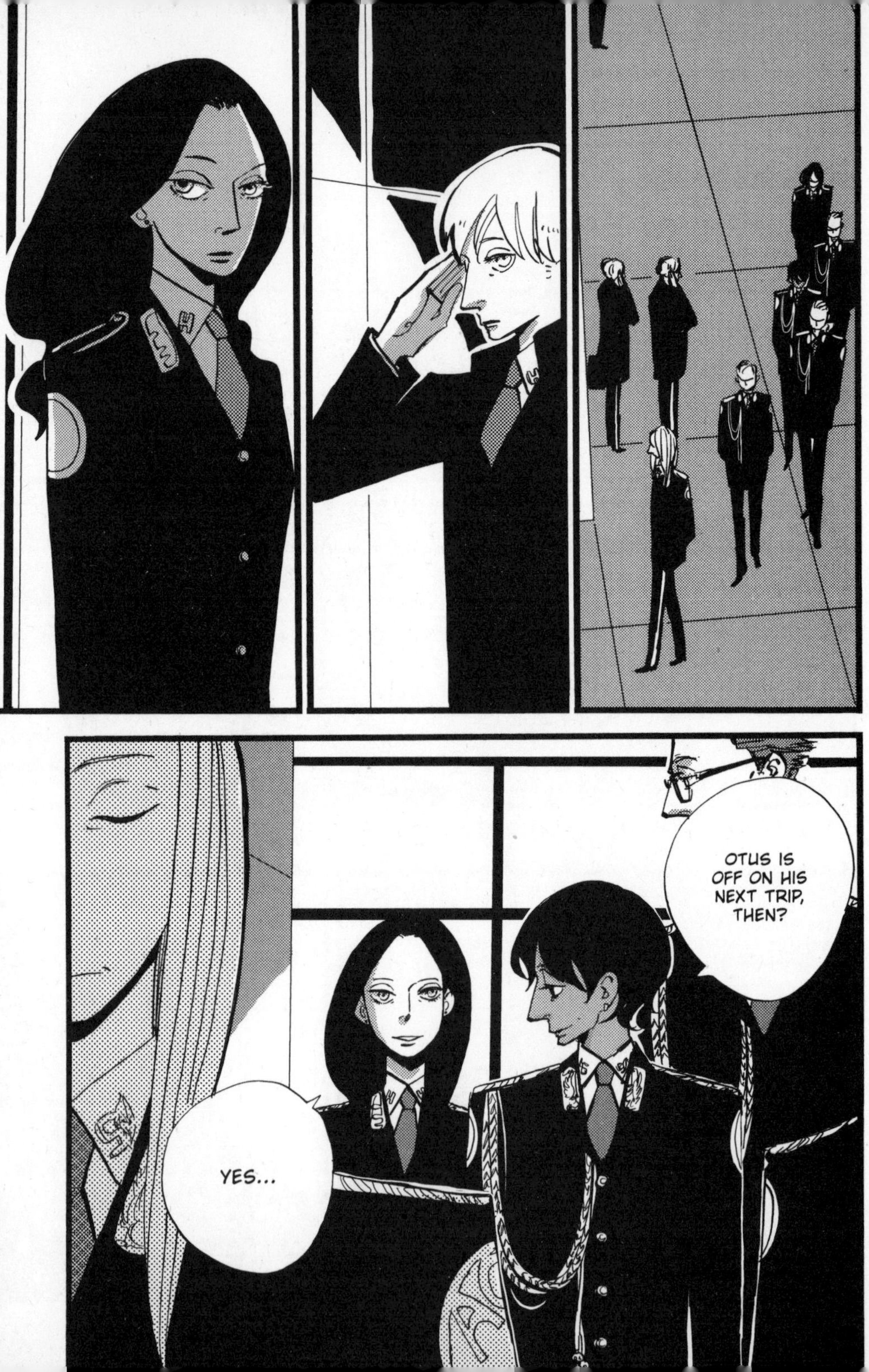
OTUS IS OFF ON HIS NEXT TRIP, THEN?
YES...

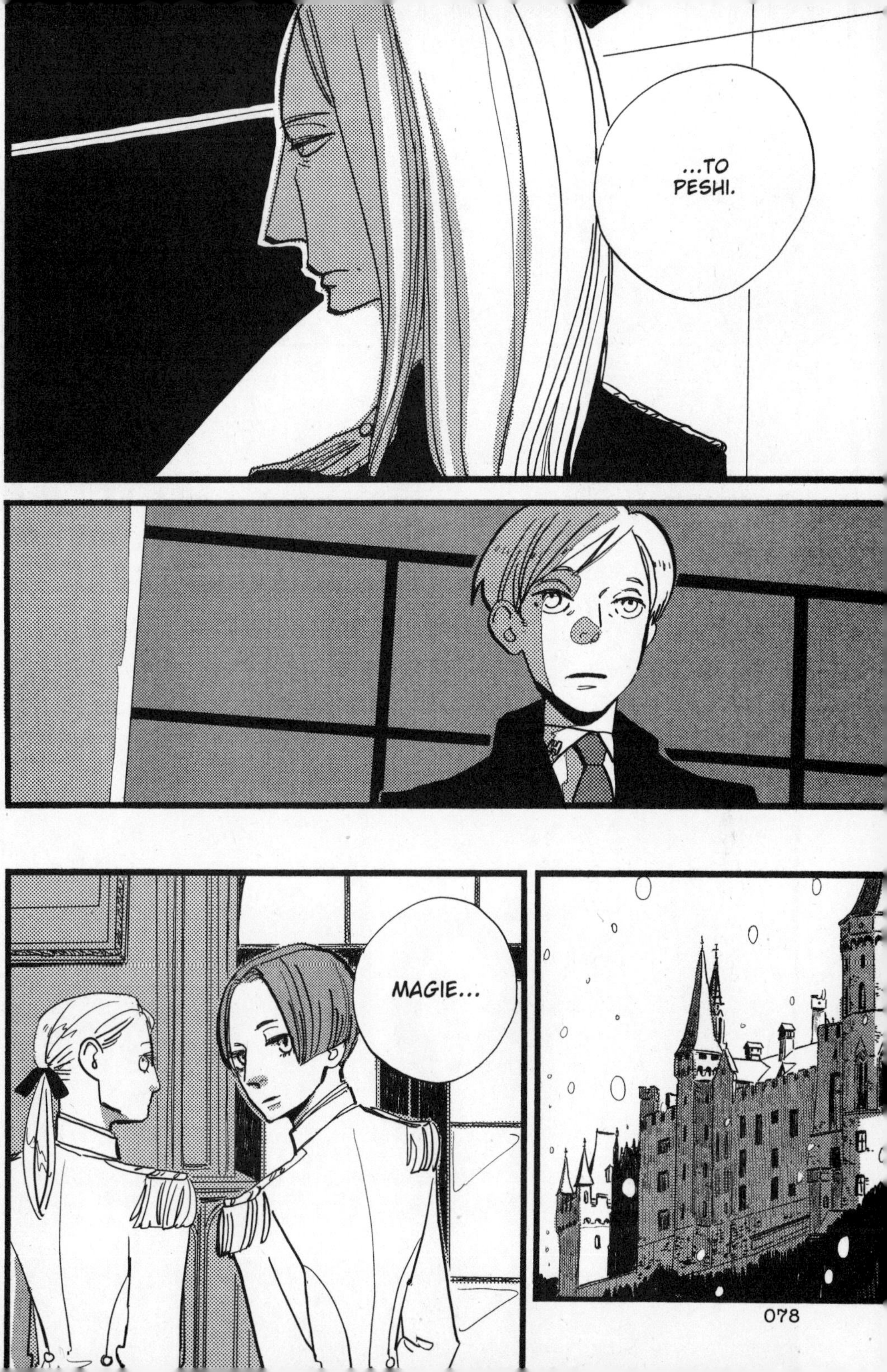
...TO PESHI.
MAGIE...

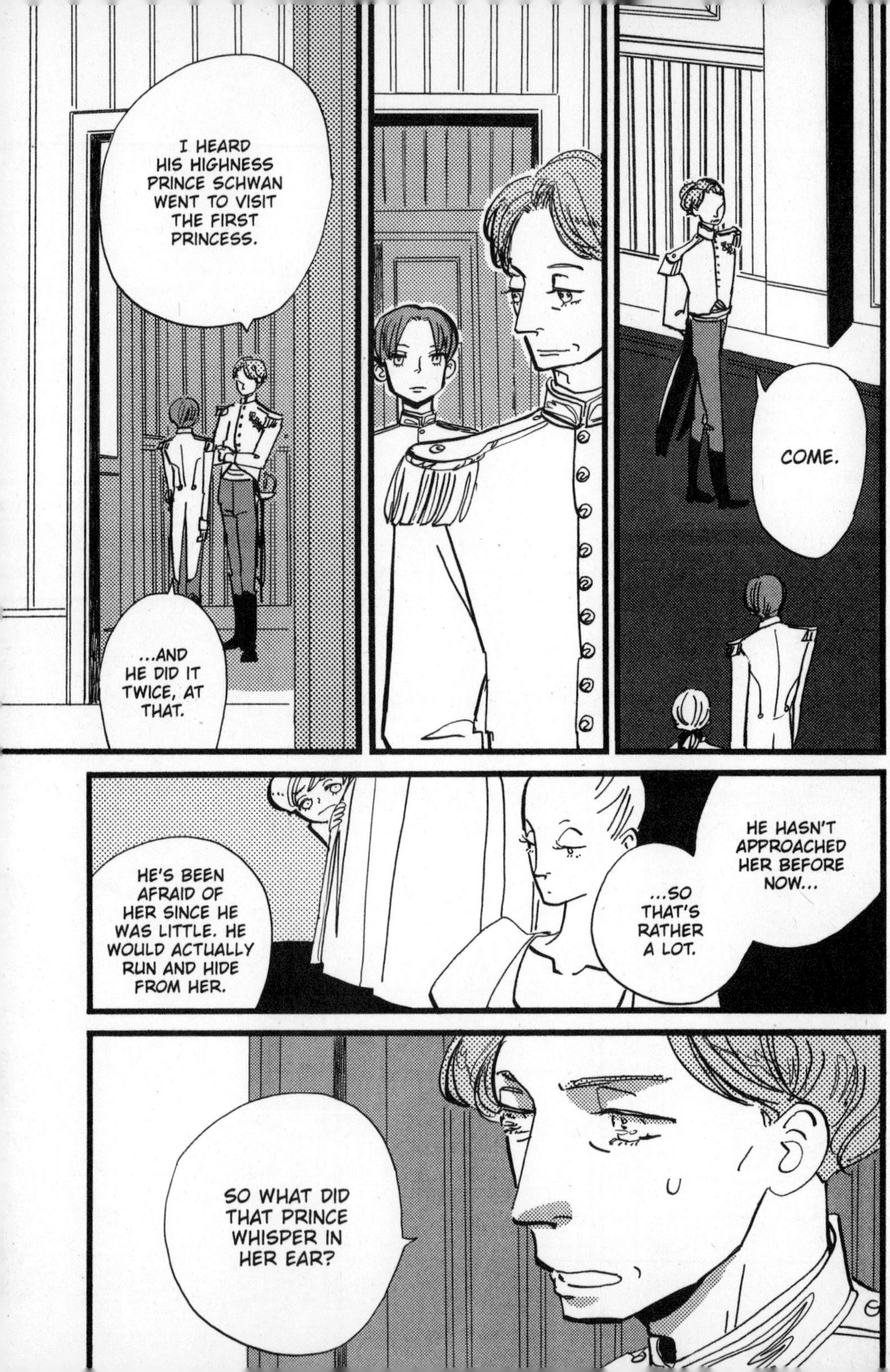
COME.
I HEARD HIS HIGHNESS PRINCE SCHWAN WENT TO VISIT THE FIRST PRINCESS.
...AND HE DID IT TWICE, AT THAT.
HE HASN'T APPROACHED HER BEFORE NOW...
...SO THAT'S RATHER A LOT.
HE'S BEEN AFRAID OF HER SINCE HE WAS LITTLE. HE WOULD ACTUALLY RUN AND HIDE FROM HER.
SO WHAT DID THAT PRINCE WHISPER IN HER EAR?

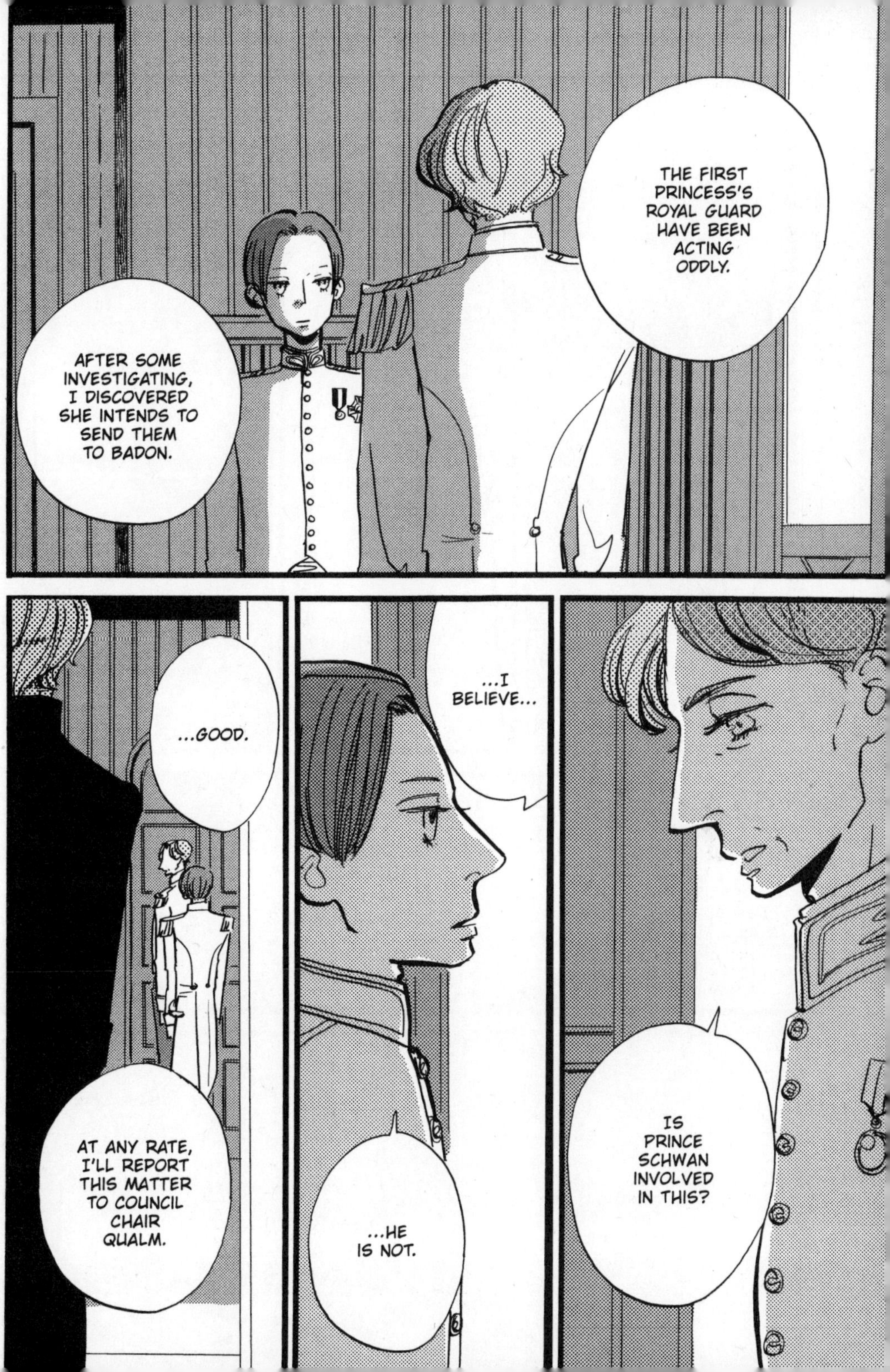
THE FIRST PRINCESS'S ROYAL GUARD HAVE BEEN ACTING ODDLY.
AFTER SOME INVESTIGATING, I DISCOVERED SHE INTENDS TO SEND THEM TO BADON.
IS PRINCE SCHWAN INVOLVED IN THIS?
...I BELIEVE...
...HE IS NOT.
...GOOD.
AT ANY RATE, I'LL REPORT THIS MATTER TO COUNCIL CHAIR QUALM.

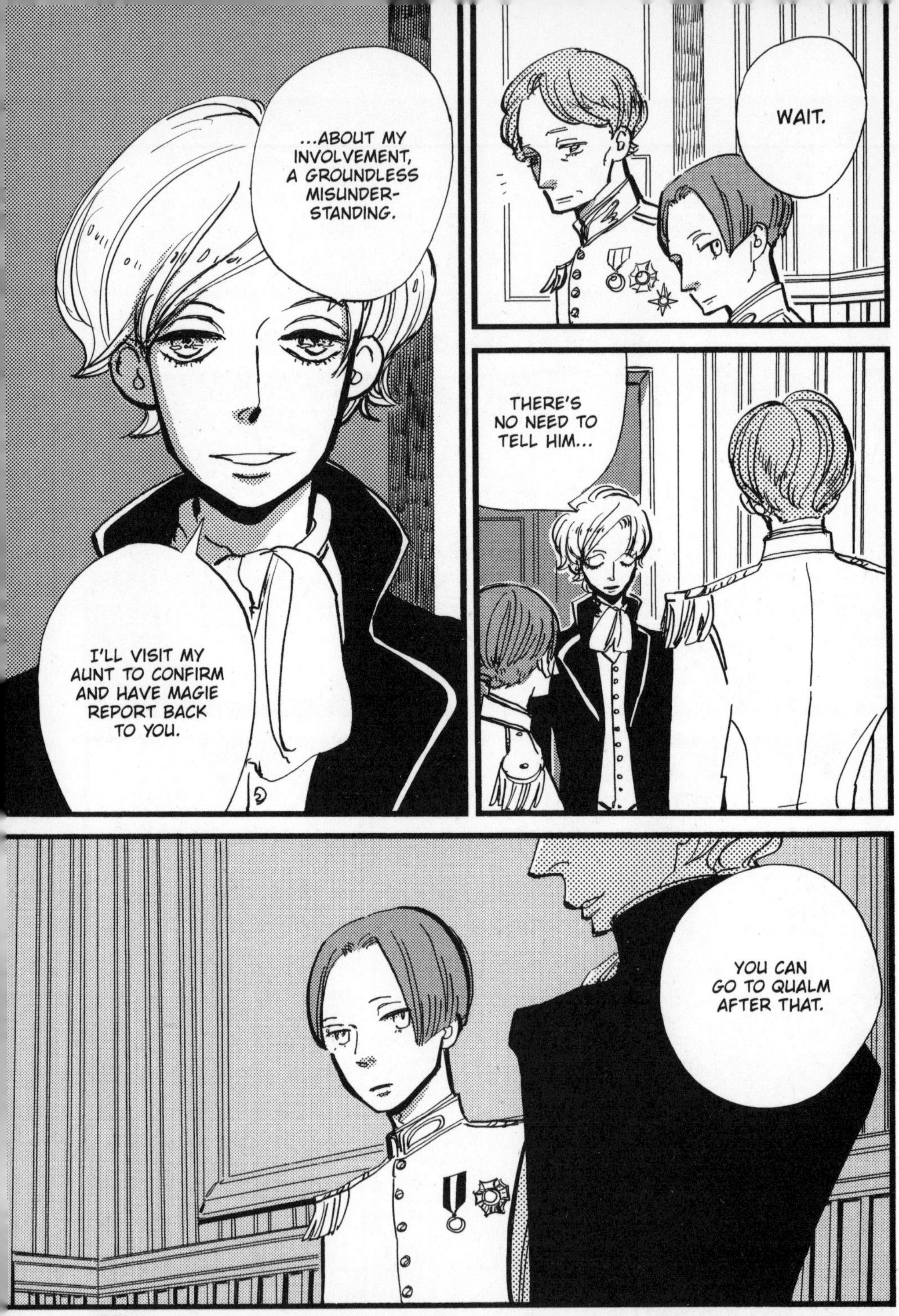
WAIT.
THERE'S NO NEED TO TELL HIM...
...ABOUT MY INVOLVEMENT, A GROUNDLESS MISUNDER-STANDING.
I'LL VISIT MY AUNT TO CONFIRM AND HAVE MAGIE REPORT BACK TO YOU.
YOU CAN GO TO QUALM AFTER THAT.

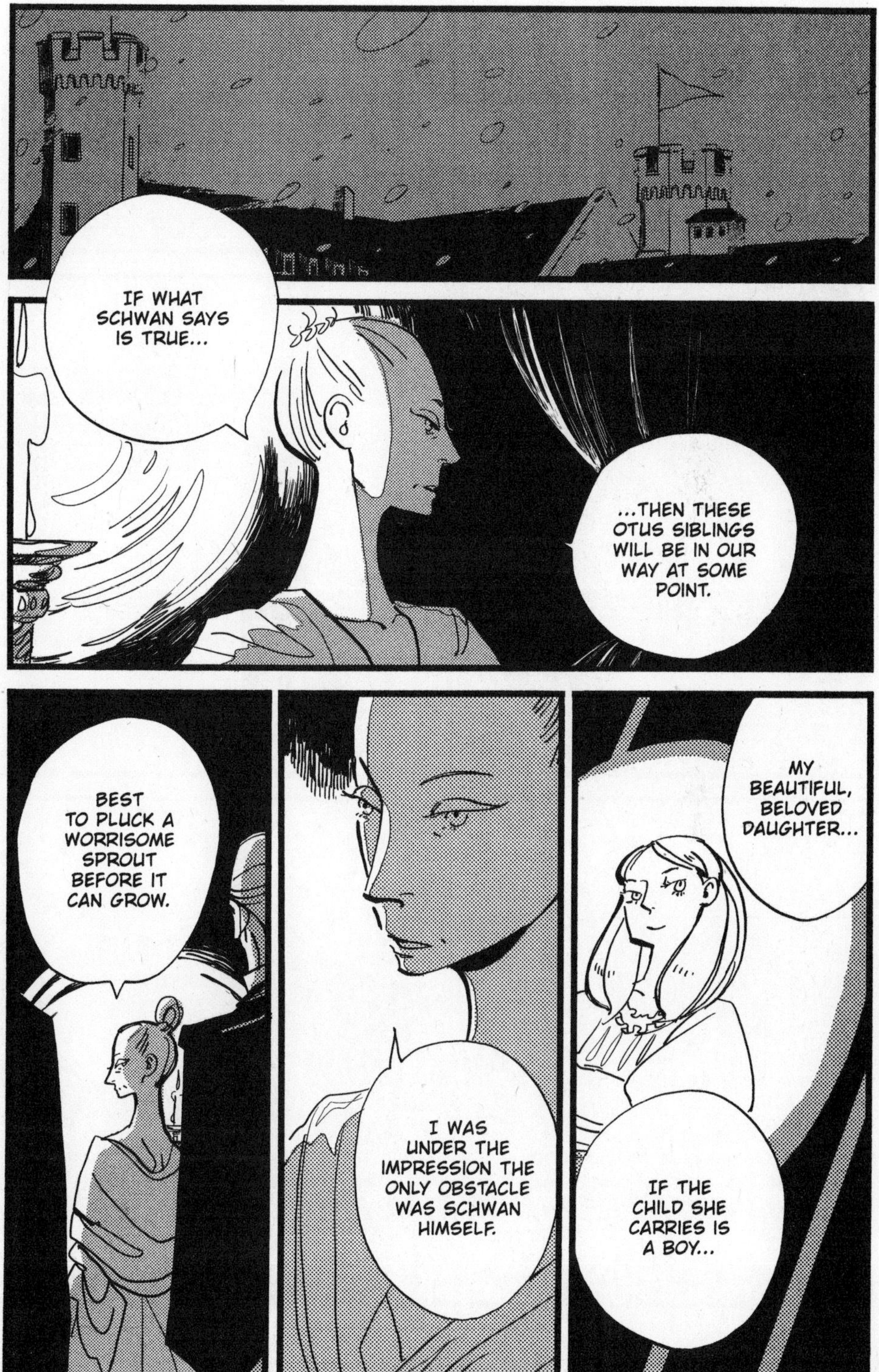
IF WHAT SCHWAN SAYS IS TRUE...
...THEN THESE OTUS SIBLINGS WILL BE IN OUR WAY AT SOME POINT.
MY BEAUTIFUL, BELOVED DAUGHTER...
IF THE CHILD SHE CARRIES IS A BOY...
I WAS UNDER THE IMPRESSION THE ONLY OBSTACLE WAS SCHWAN HIMSELF.
BEST TO PLUCK A WORRISOME SPROUT BEFORE IT CAN GROW.

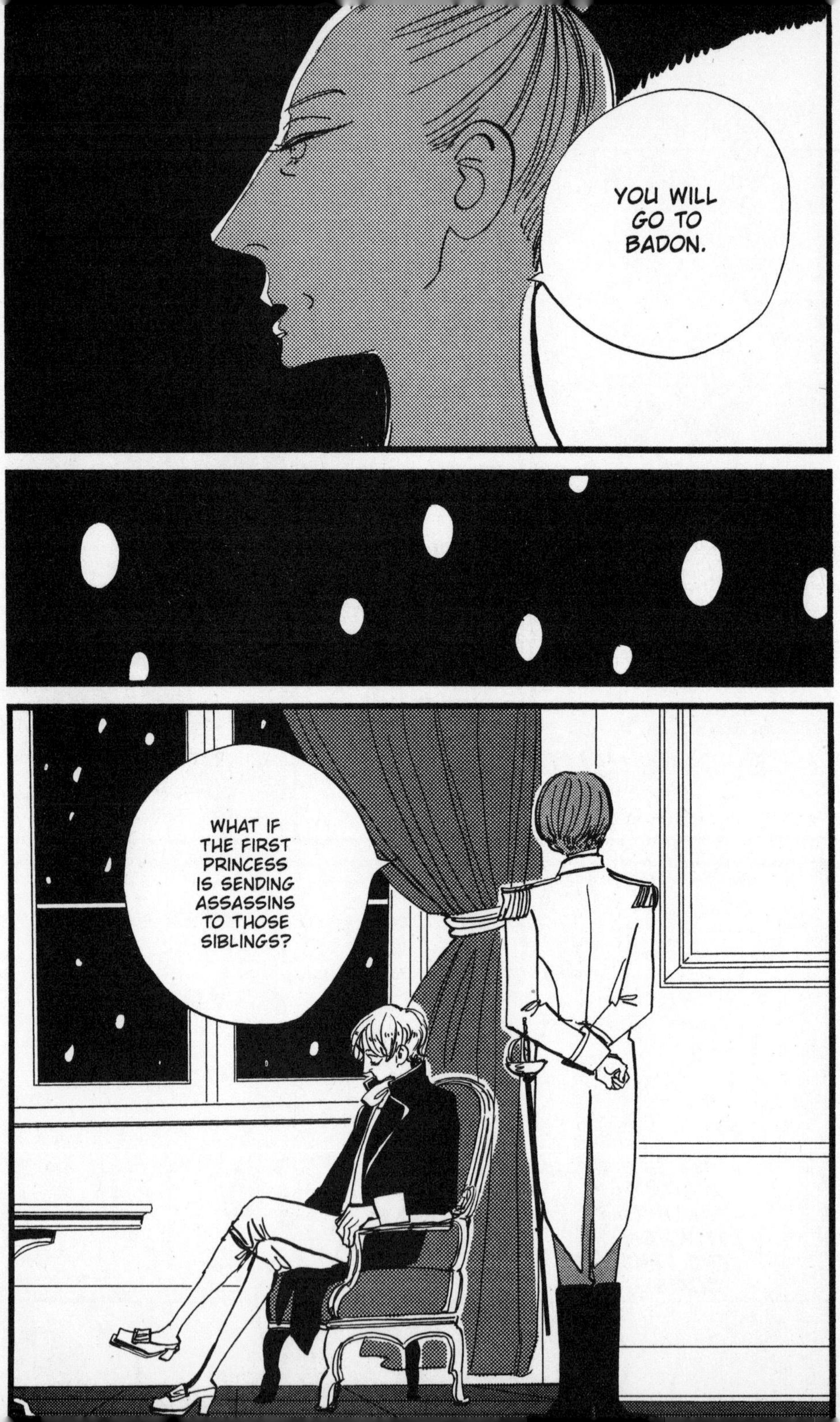
YOU WILL GO TO BADON.
WHAT IF THE FIRST PRINCESS IS SENDING ASSASSINS TO THOSE SIBLINGS?

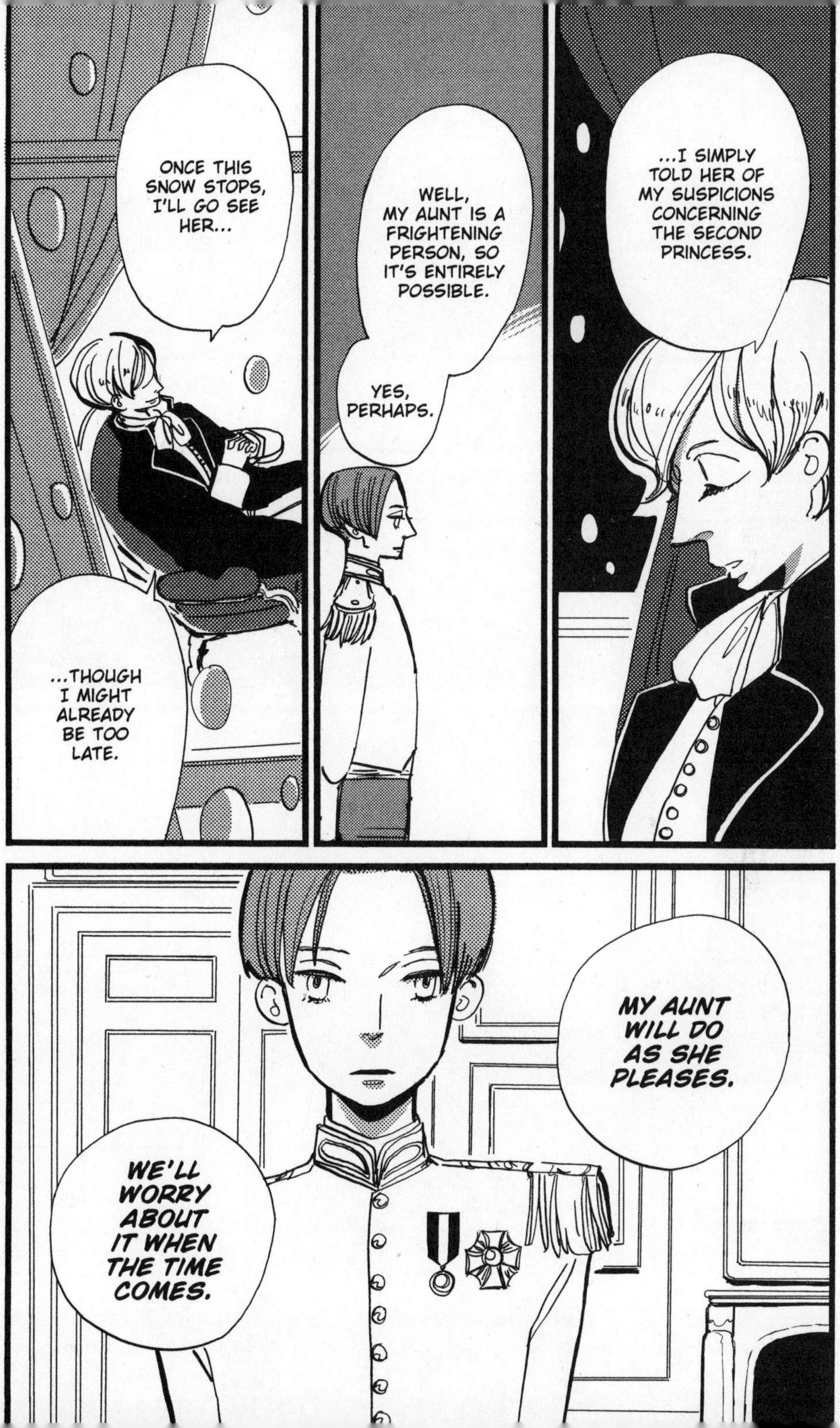
...I SIMPLY TOLD HER OF MY SUSPICIONS CONCERNING THE SECOND PRINCESS.
WELL, MY AUNT IS A FRIGHTENING PERSON, SO IT'S ENTIRELY POSSIBLE.
YES, PERHAPS.
ONCE THIS SNOW STOPS, I'LL GO SEE HER...
...THOUGH I MIGHT ALREADY BE TOO LATE.
MY AUNT WILL DO AS SHE PLEASES.
WE'LL WORRY ABOUT IT WHEN THE TIME COMES.

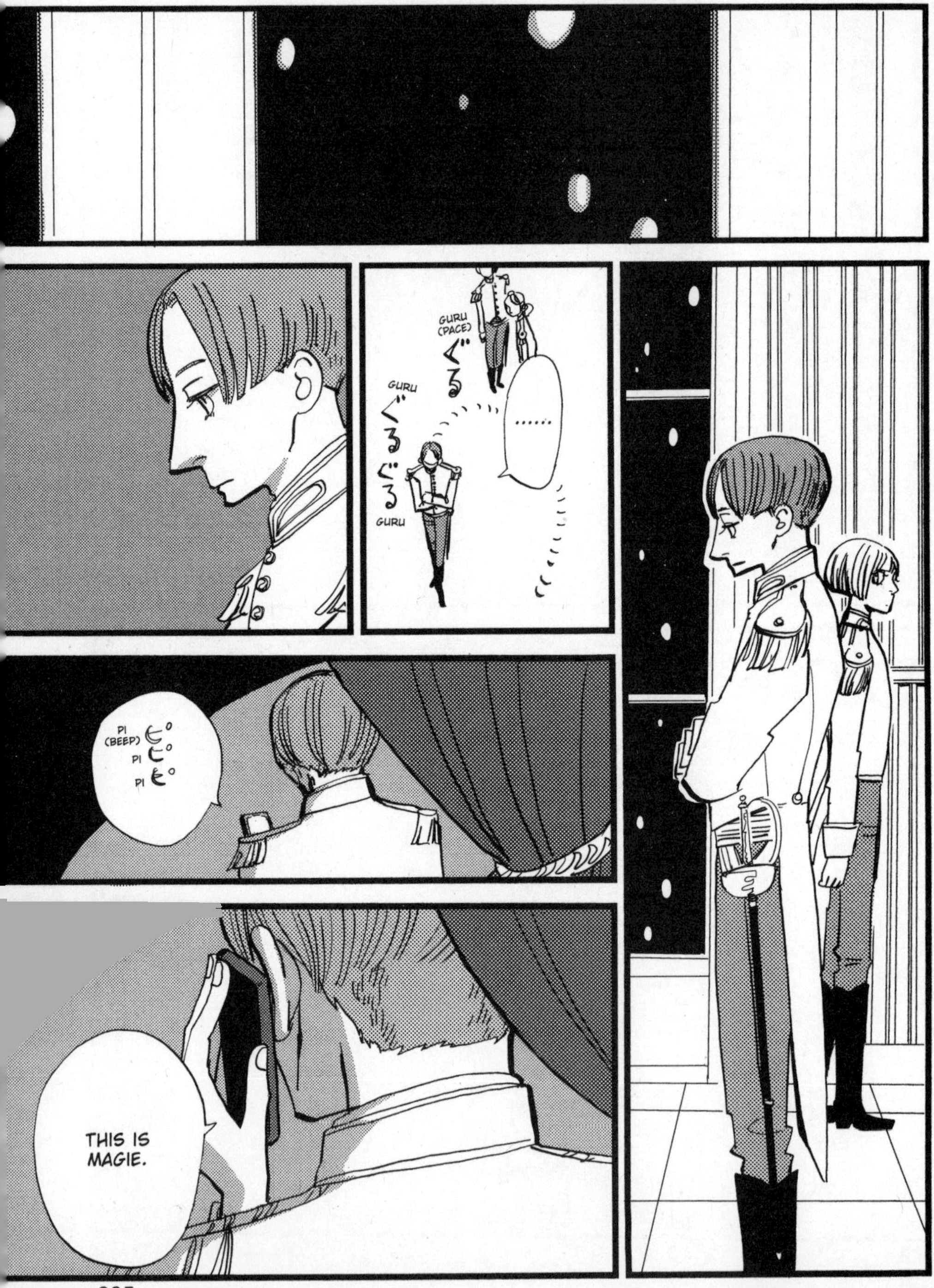
GURU (PACE) ぐる
GURU ぐるぐる GURU
……
PI (BEEP) ピ PI ピ PI ピ
THIS IS MAGIE.

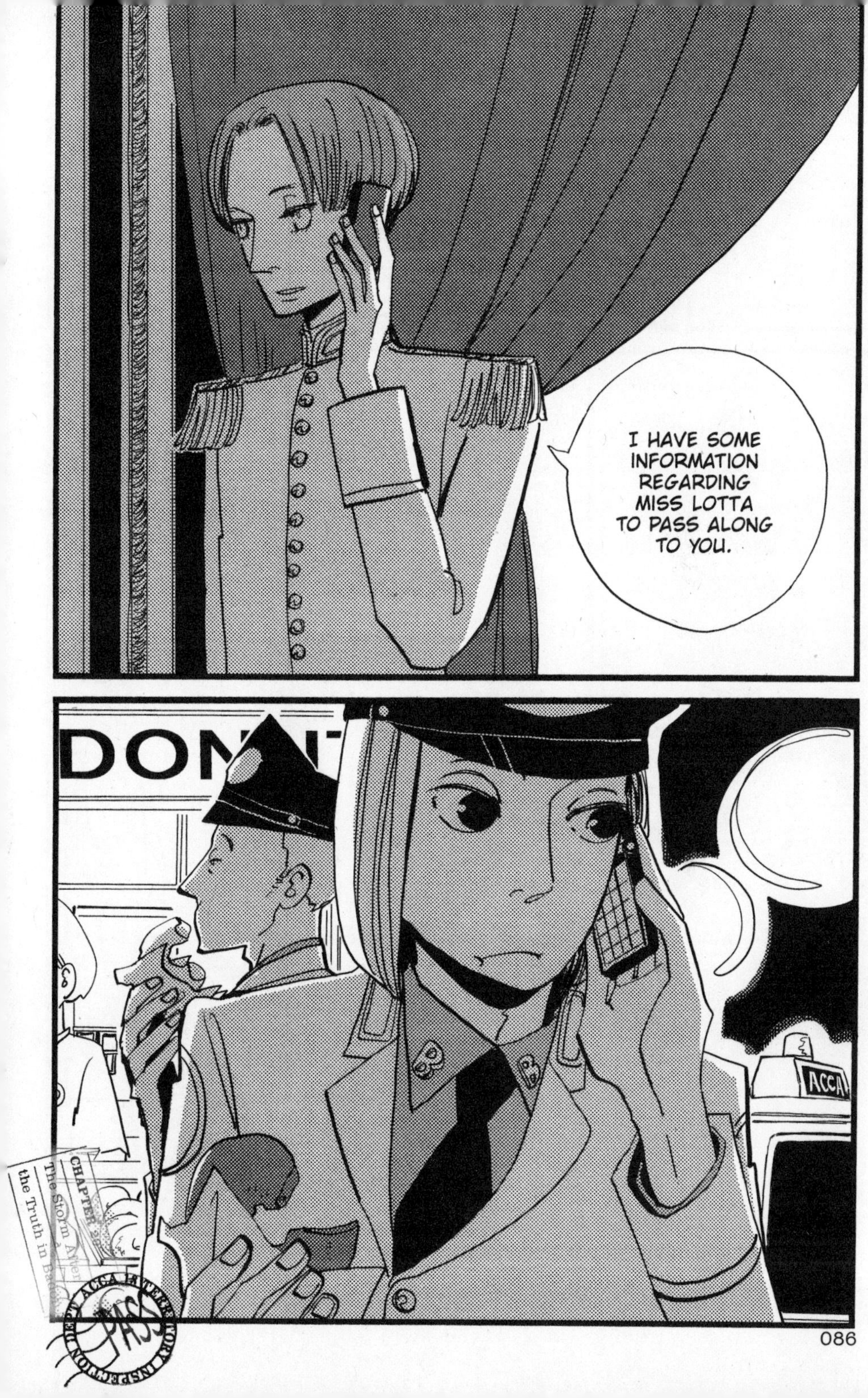
I HAVE SOME INFORMATION REGARDING MISS LOTTA TO PASS ALONG TO YOU.
ACCA

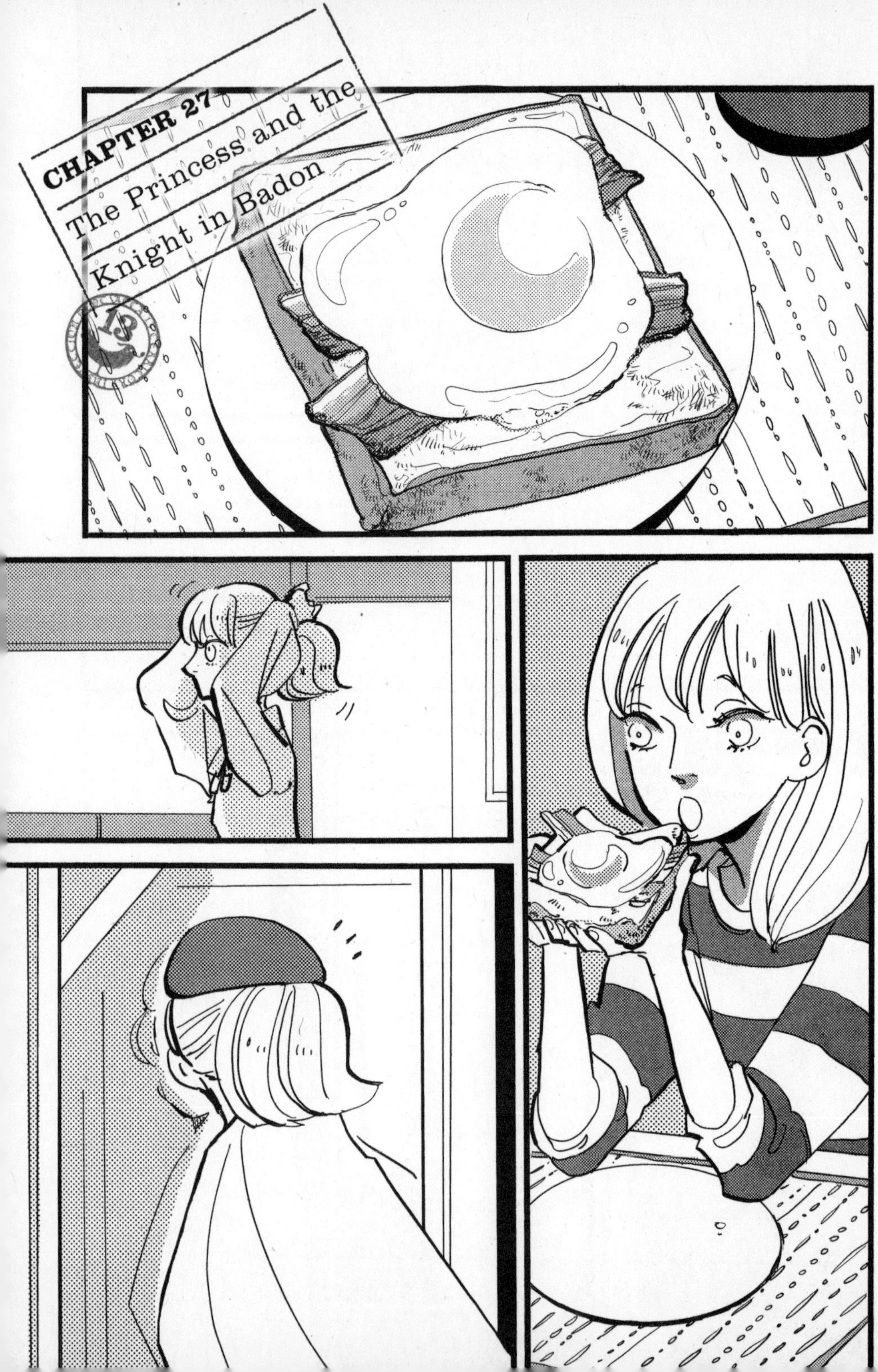
CHAPTER 27
The Princess and the Knight in Badon

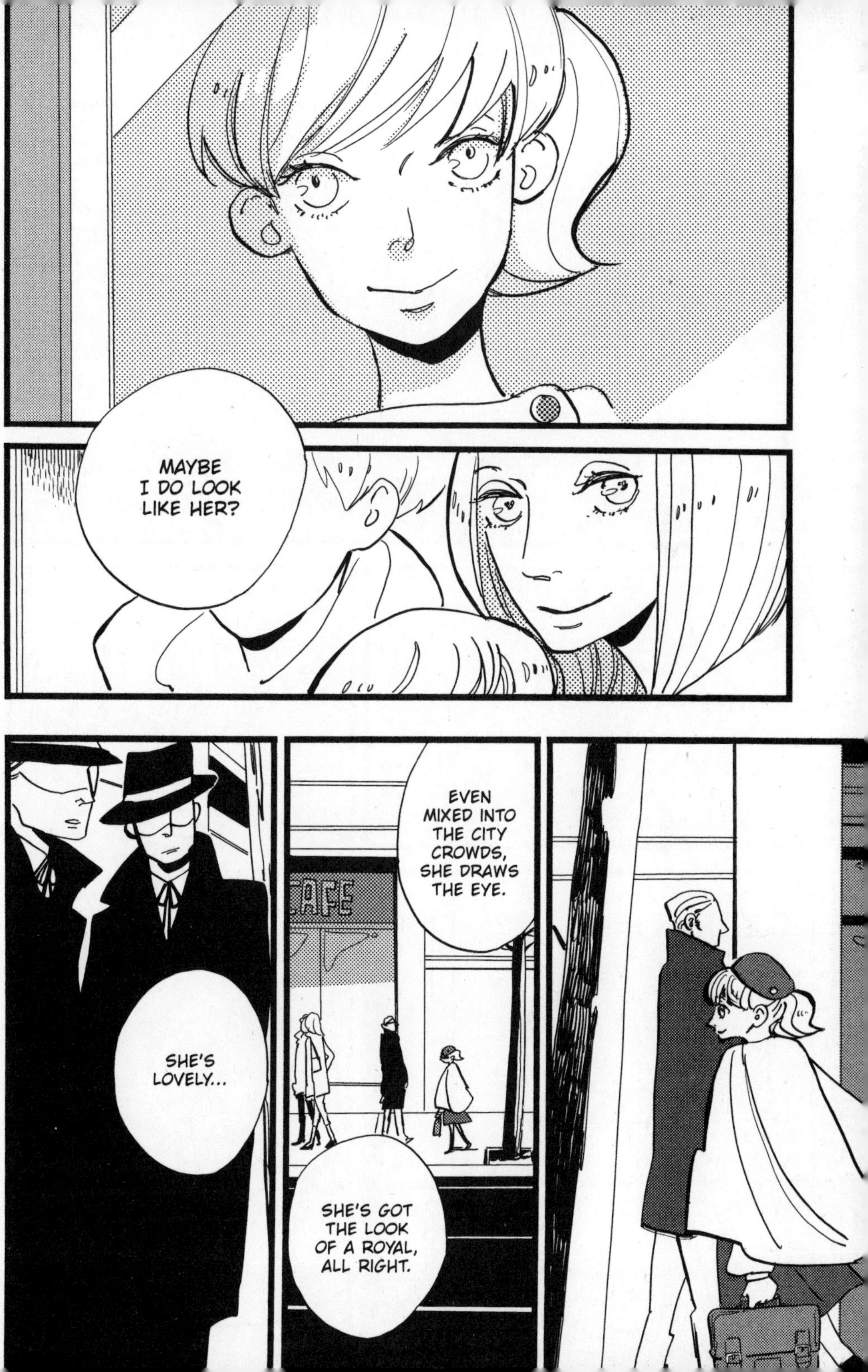
MAYBE I DO LOOK LIKE HER?
EVEN MIXED INTO THE CITY CROWDS, SHE DRAWS THE EYE.
SHE'S LOVELY...
SHE'S GOT THE LOOK OF A ROYAL, ALL RIGHT.

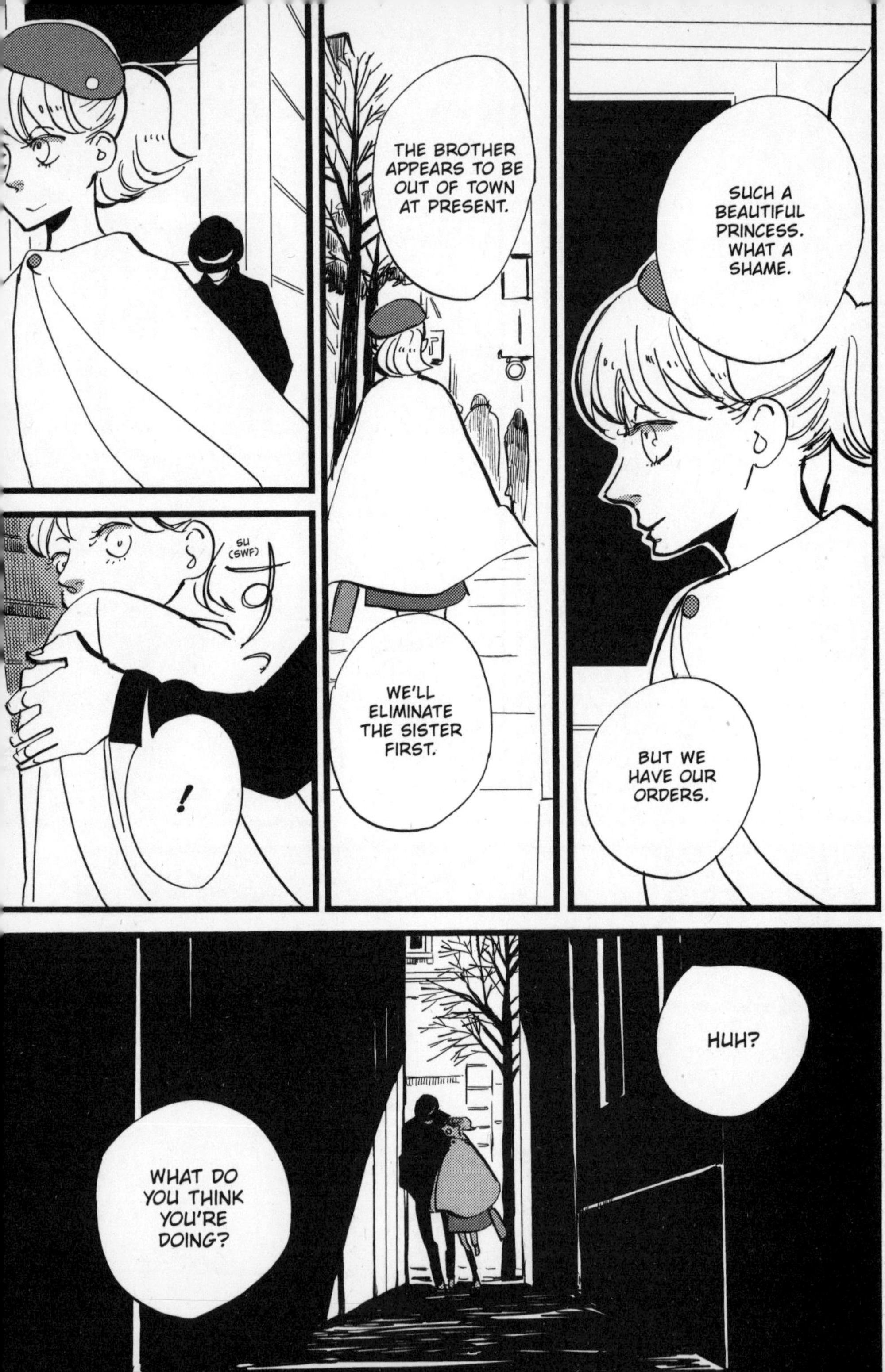
SUCH A BEAUTIFUL PRINCESS. WHAT A SHAME.
BUT WE HAVE OUR ORDERS.
THE BROTHER APPEARS TO BE OUT OF TOWN AT PRESENT.
WE'LL ELIMINATE THE SISTER FIRST.
SU (SWF)
!
HUH?
WHAT DO YOU THINK YOU'RE DOING?

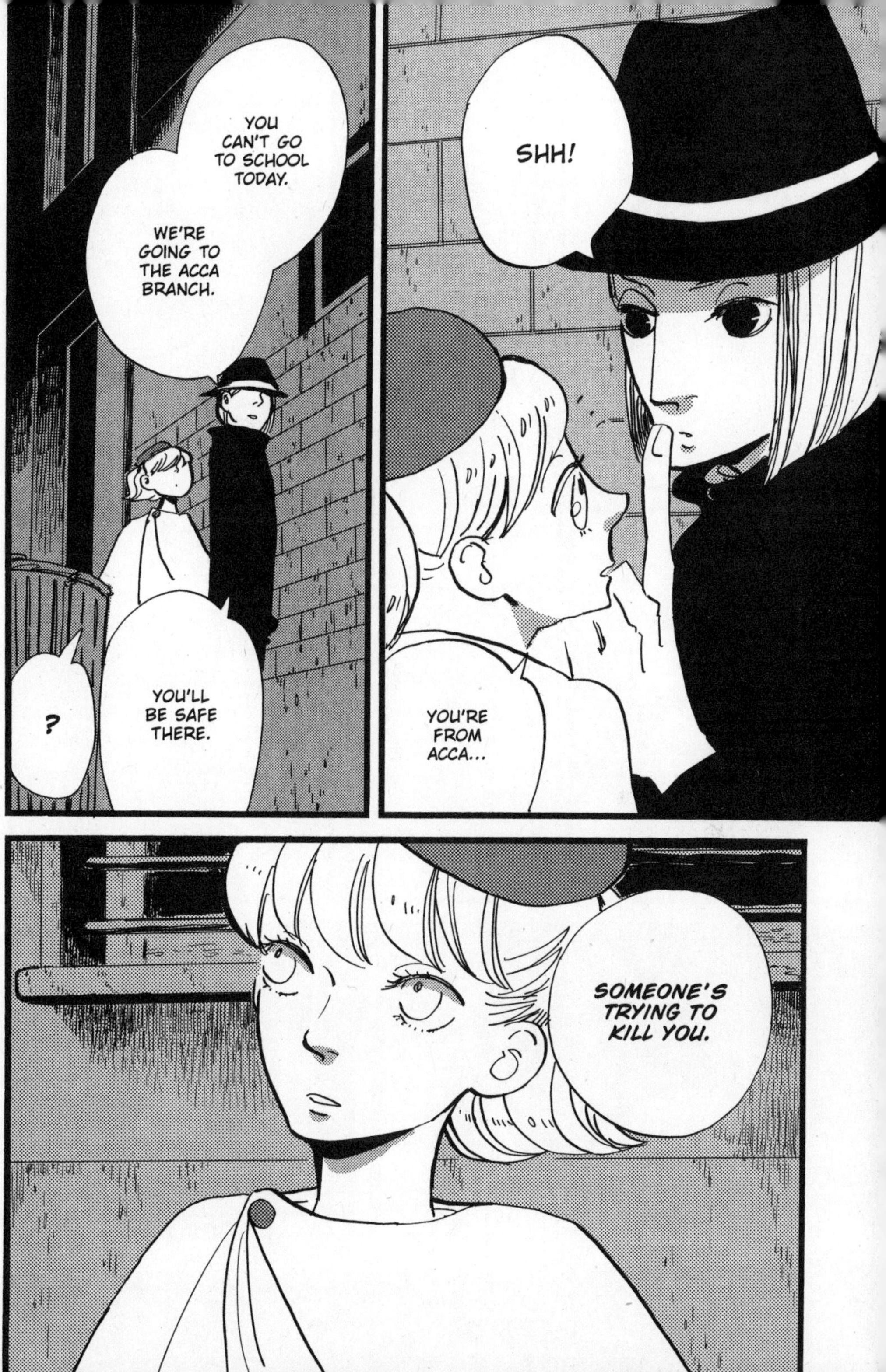
SHH!
YOU'RE FROM ACCA...
YOU CAN'T GO TO SCHOOL TODAY.
WE'RE GOING TO THE ACCA BRANCH.
YOU'LL BE SAFE THERE.
?
SOMEONE'S TRYING TO KILL YOU.

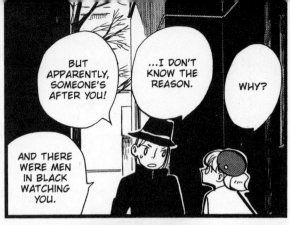

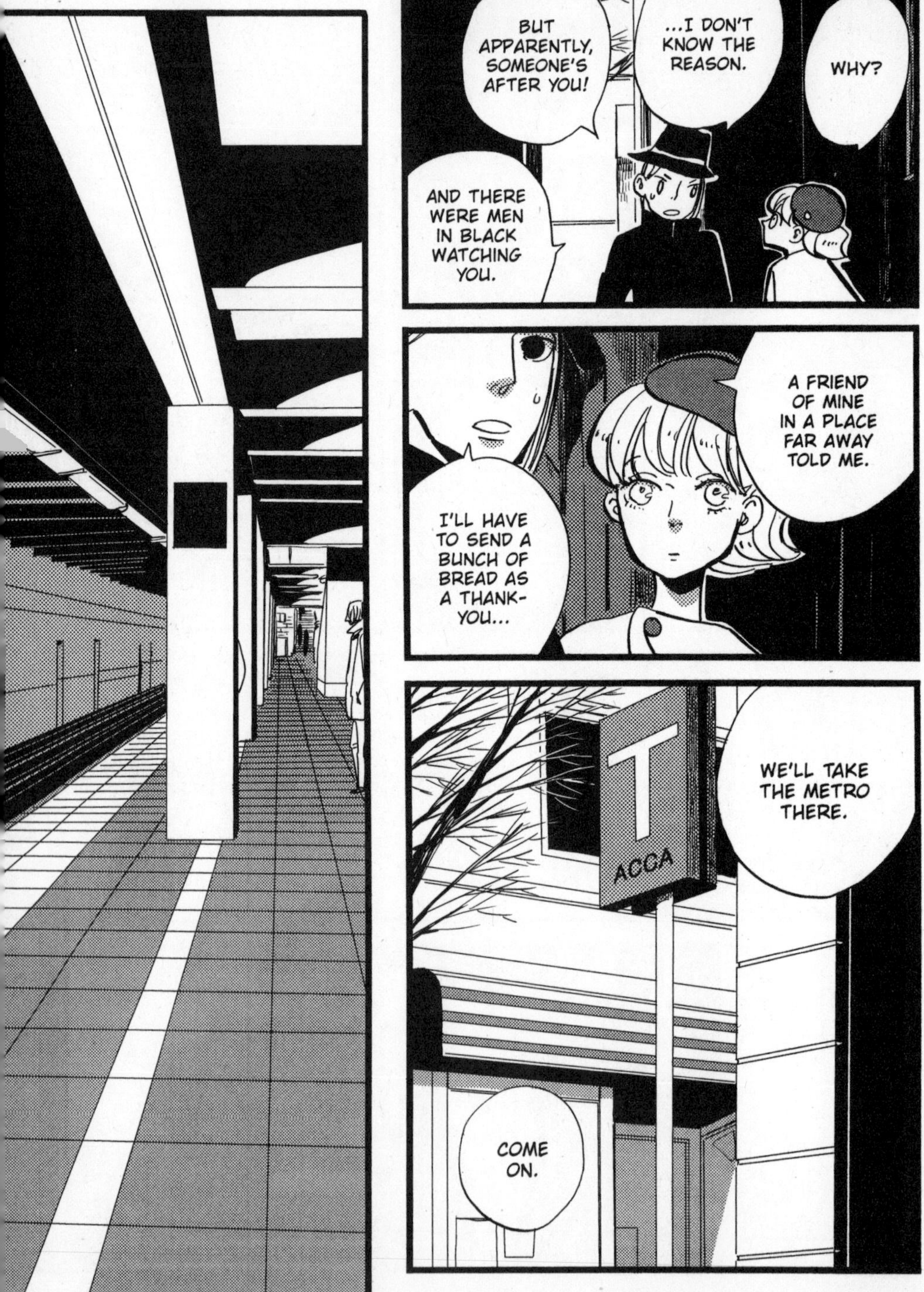
WHY?
...I DON'T KNOW THE REASON.
BUT APPARENTLY, SOMEONE'S AFTER YOU!
AND THERE WERE MEN IN BLACK WATCHING YOU.
A FRIEND OF MINE IN A PLACE FAR AWAY TOLD ME.
I'LL HAVE TO SEND A BUNCH OF BREAD AS A THANK-YOU...
WE'LL TAKE THE METRO THERE.
T
ACCA
COME ON.

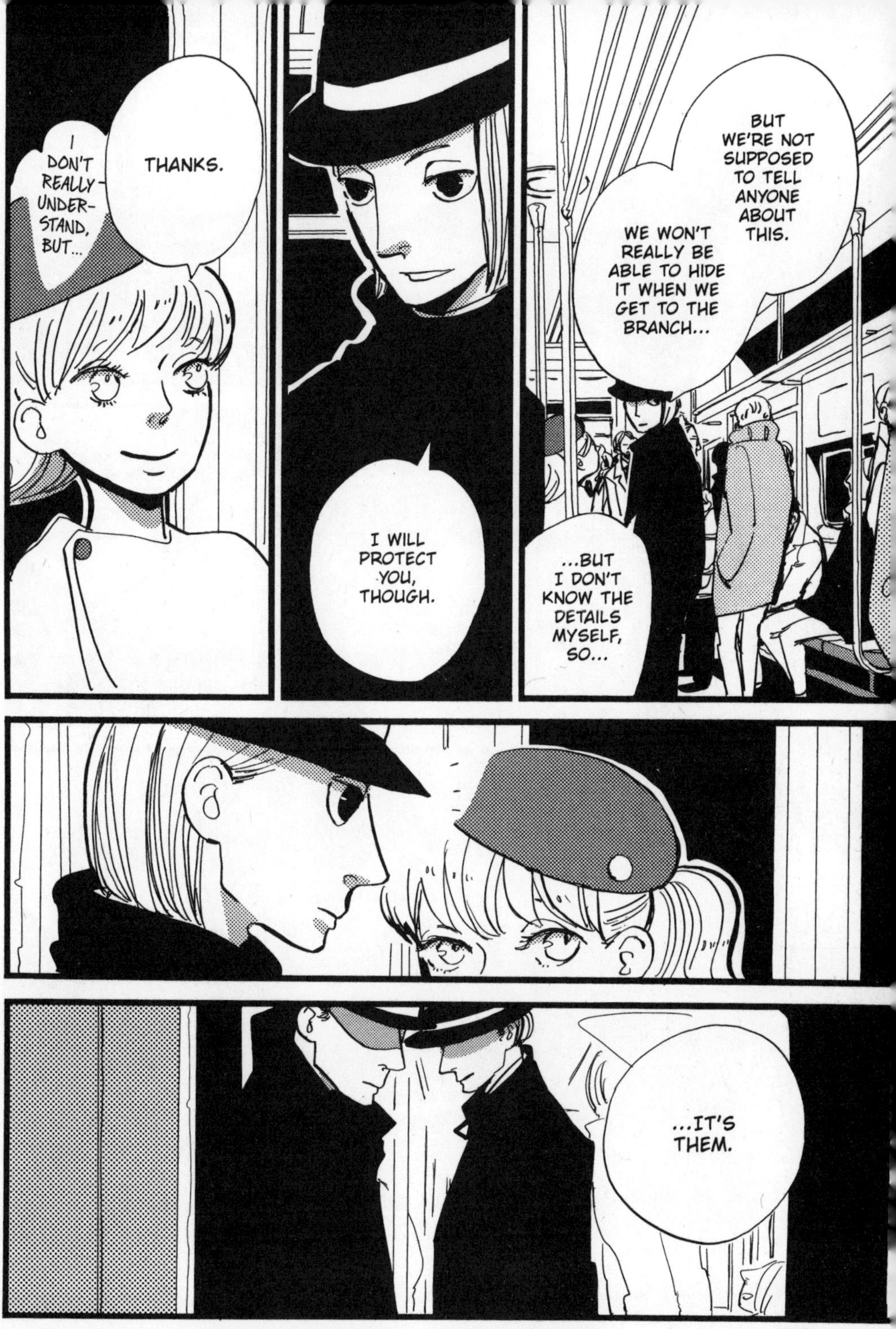
BUT WE'RE NOT SUPPOSED TO TELL ANYONE ABOUT THIS.
WE WON'T REALLY BE ABLE TO HIDE IT WHEN WE GET TO THE BRANCH...
...BUT I DON'T KNOW THE DETAILS MYSELF, SO...
I WILL PROTECT YOU, THOUGH.
THANKS.
I DON'T REALLY UNDER-STAND, BUT...
...IT'S THEM.

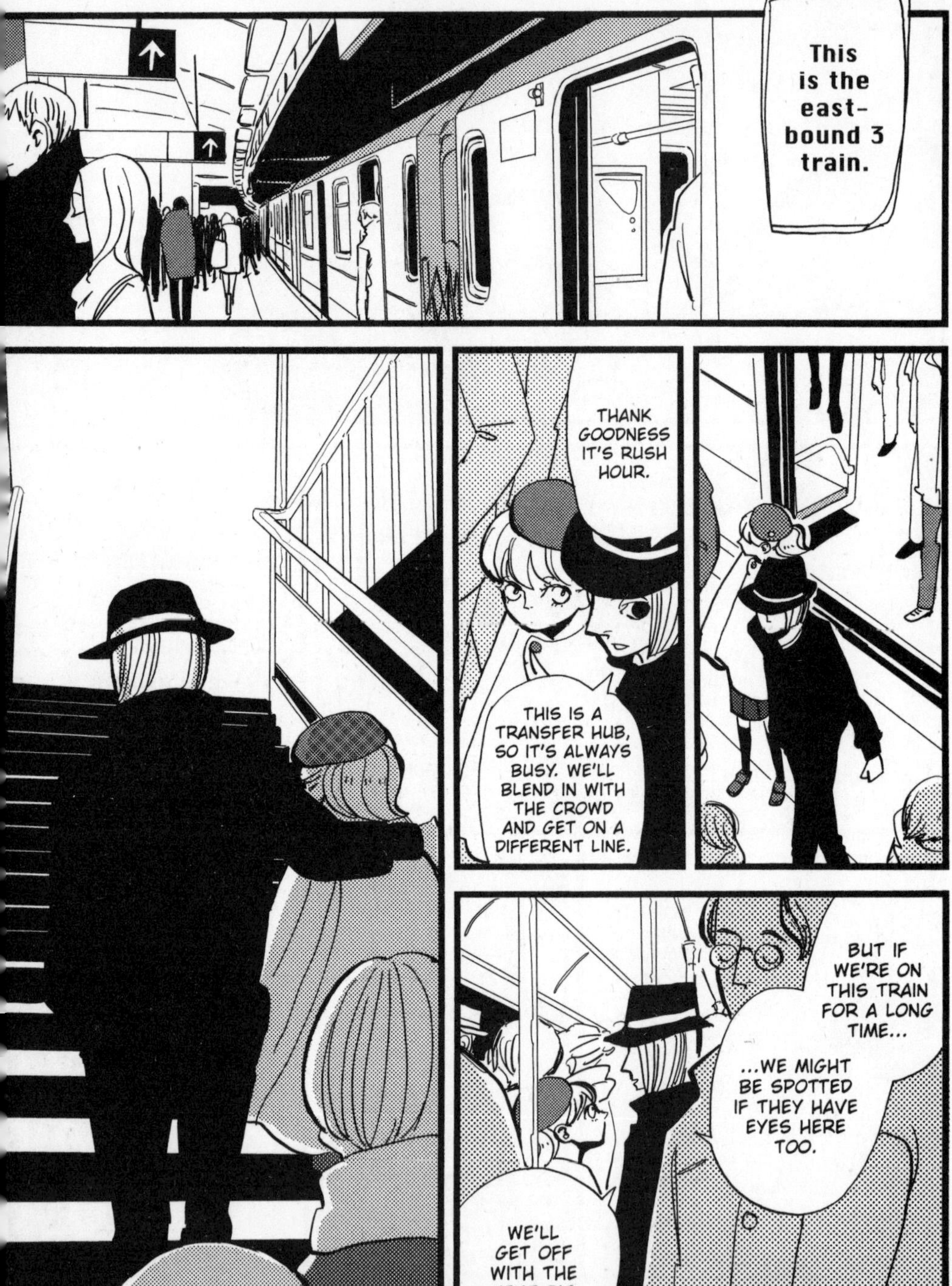
This is the east-bound 3 train.
THANK GOODNESS IT'S RUSH HOUR.
THIS IS A TRANSFER HUB, SO IT'S ALWAYS BUSY. WE'LL BLEND IN WITH THE CROWD AND GET ON A DIFFERENT LINE.
BUT IF WE'RE ON THIS TRAIN FOR A LONG TIME...
...WE MIGHT BE SPOTTED IF THEY HAVE EYES HERE TOO.
WE'LL GET OFF WITH THE NEXT BIG GROUP.

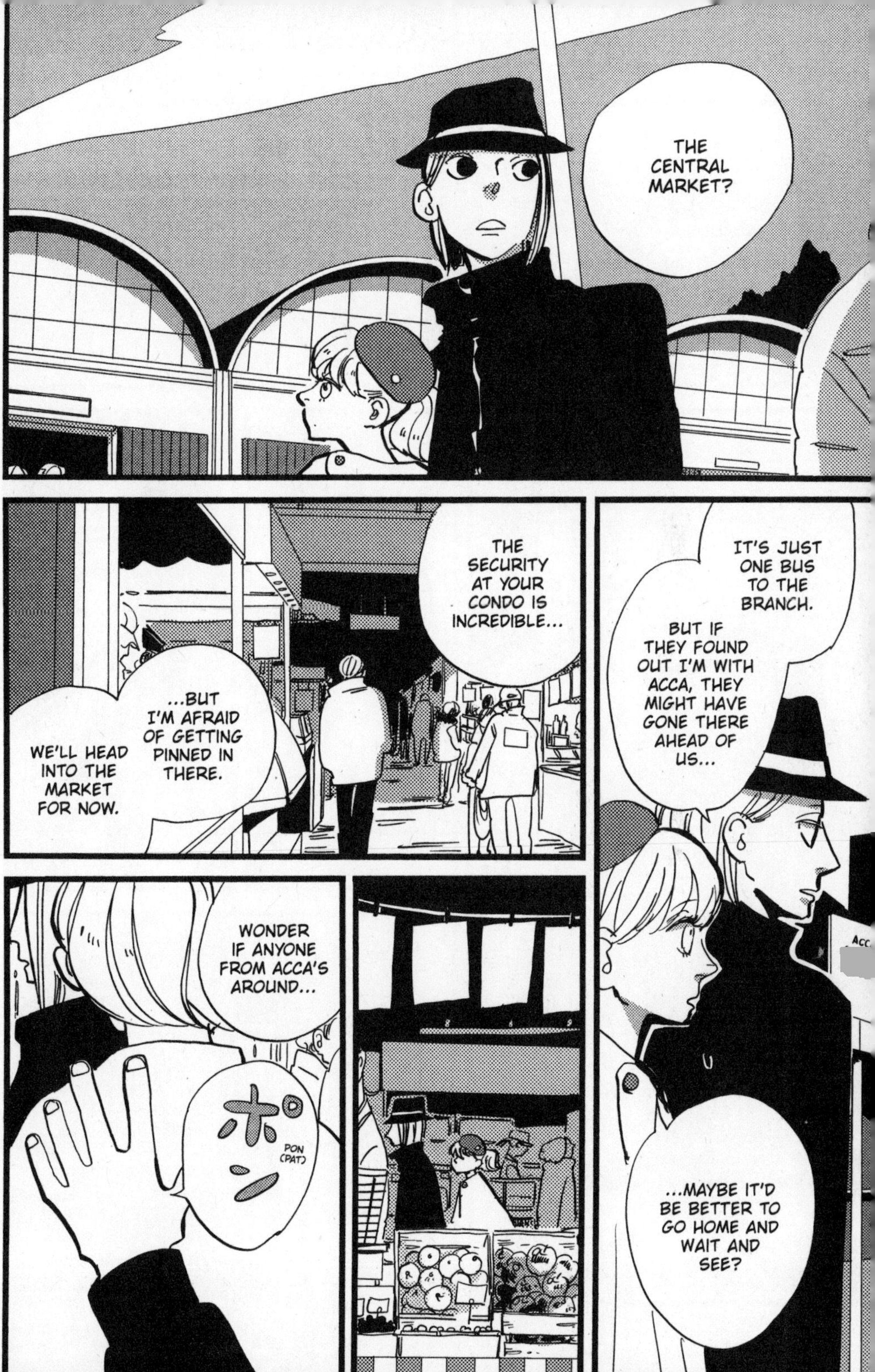
THE CENTRAL MARKET?
IT'S JUST ONE BUS TO THE BRANCH.
BUT IF THEY FOUND OUT I'M WITH ACCA, THEY MIGHT HAVE GONE THERE AHEAD OF US...
...MAYBE IT'D BE BETTER TO GO HOME AND WAIT AND SEE?
THE SECURITY AT YOUR CONDO IS INCREDIBLE...
...BUT I'M AFRAID OF GETTING PINNED IN THERE.
WE'LL HEAD INTO THE MARKET FOR NOW.
WONDER IF ANYONE FROM ACCA'S AROUND...
ポン
PON (PAT)

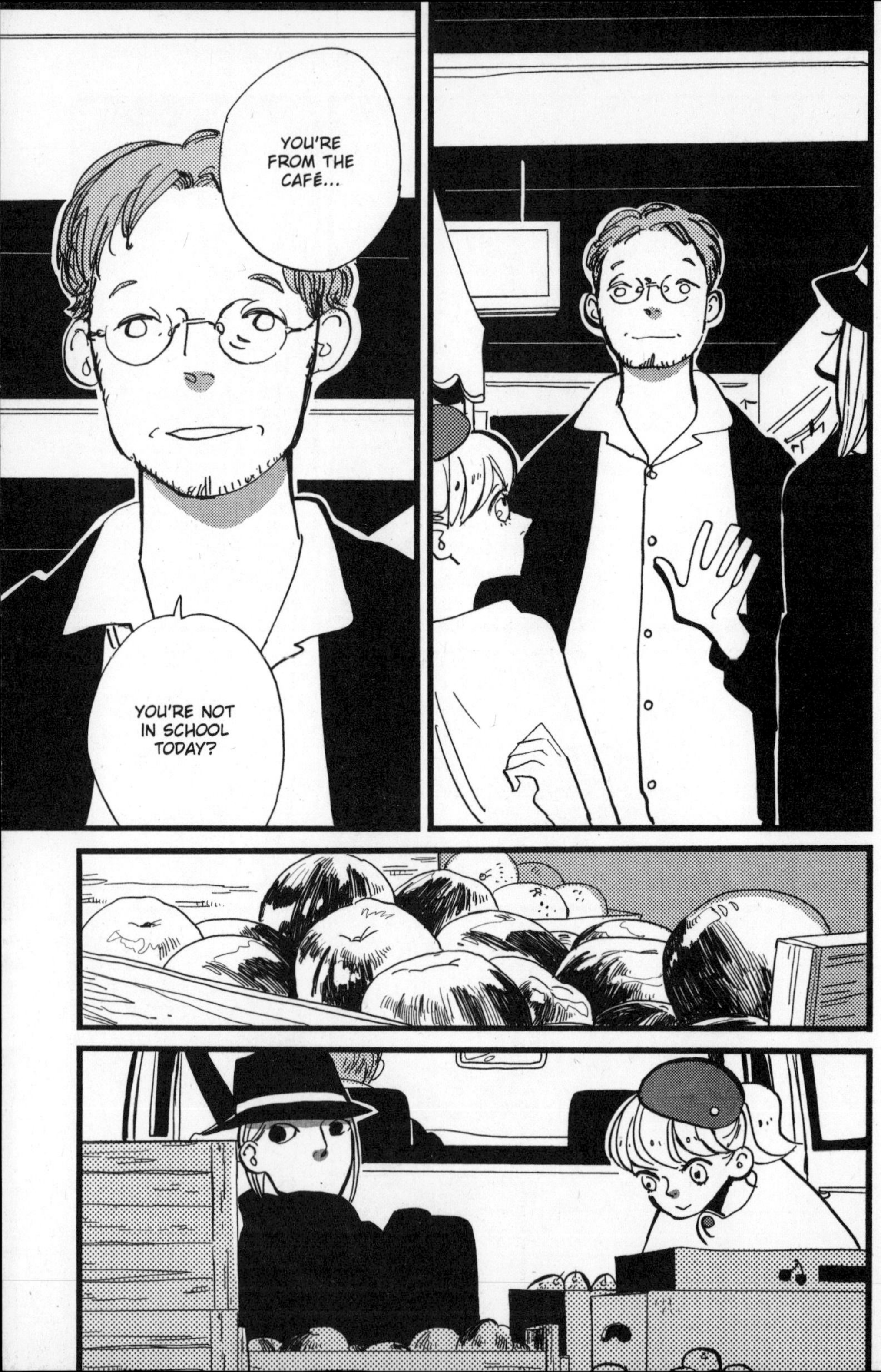
YOU'RE FROM THE CAFÉ...
YOU'RE NOT IN SCHOOL TODAY?

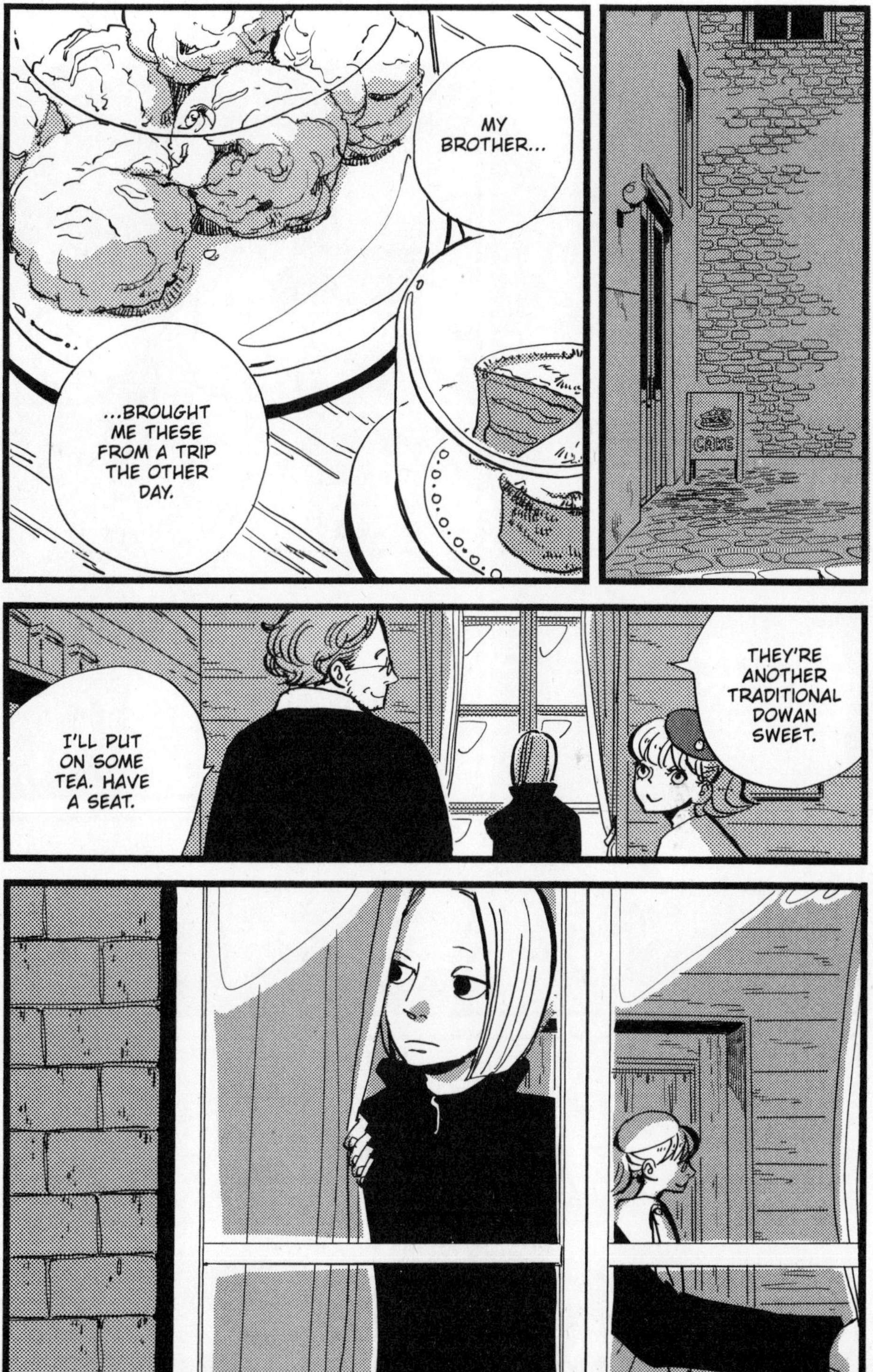
MY BROTHER...
...BROUGHT ME THESE FROM A TRIP THE OTHER DAY.
THEY'RE ANOTHER TRADITIONAL DOWAN SWEET.
I'LL PUT ON SOME TEA. HAVE A SEAT.

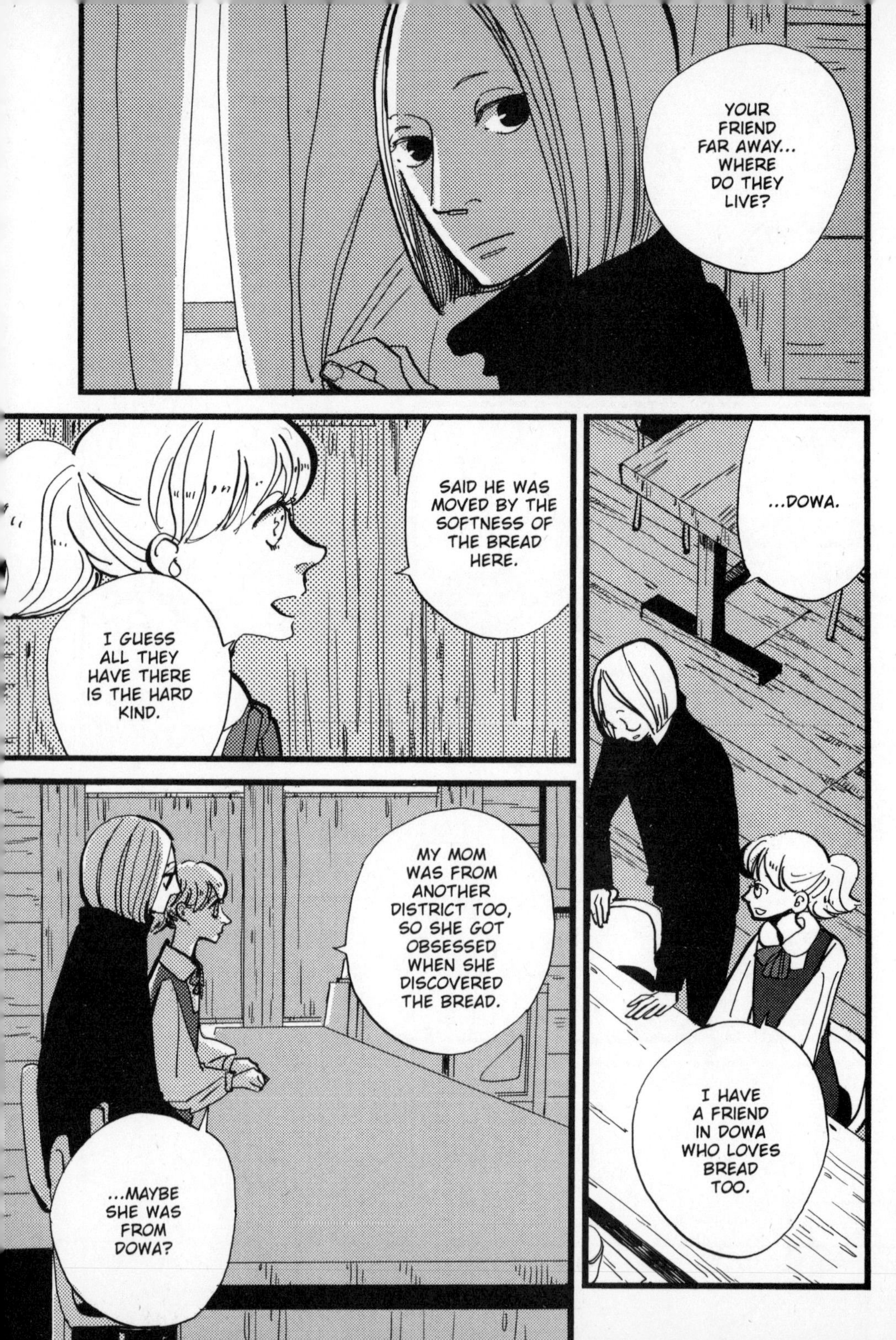
YOUR FRIEND FAR AWAY... WHERE DO THEY LIVE?
...DOWA.
I HAVE A FRIEND IN DOWA WHO LOVES BREAD TOO.
SAID HE WAS MOVED BY THE SOFTNESS OF THE BREAD HERE.
I GUESS ALL THEY HAVE THERE IS THE HARD KIND.
MY MOM WAS FROM ANOTHER DISTRICT TOO, SO SHE GOT OBSESSED WHEN SHE DISCOVERED THE BREAD.
...MAYBE SHE WAS FROM DOWA?

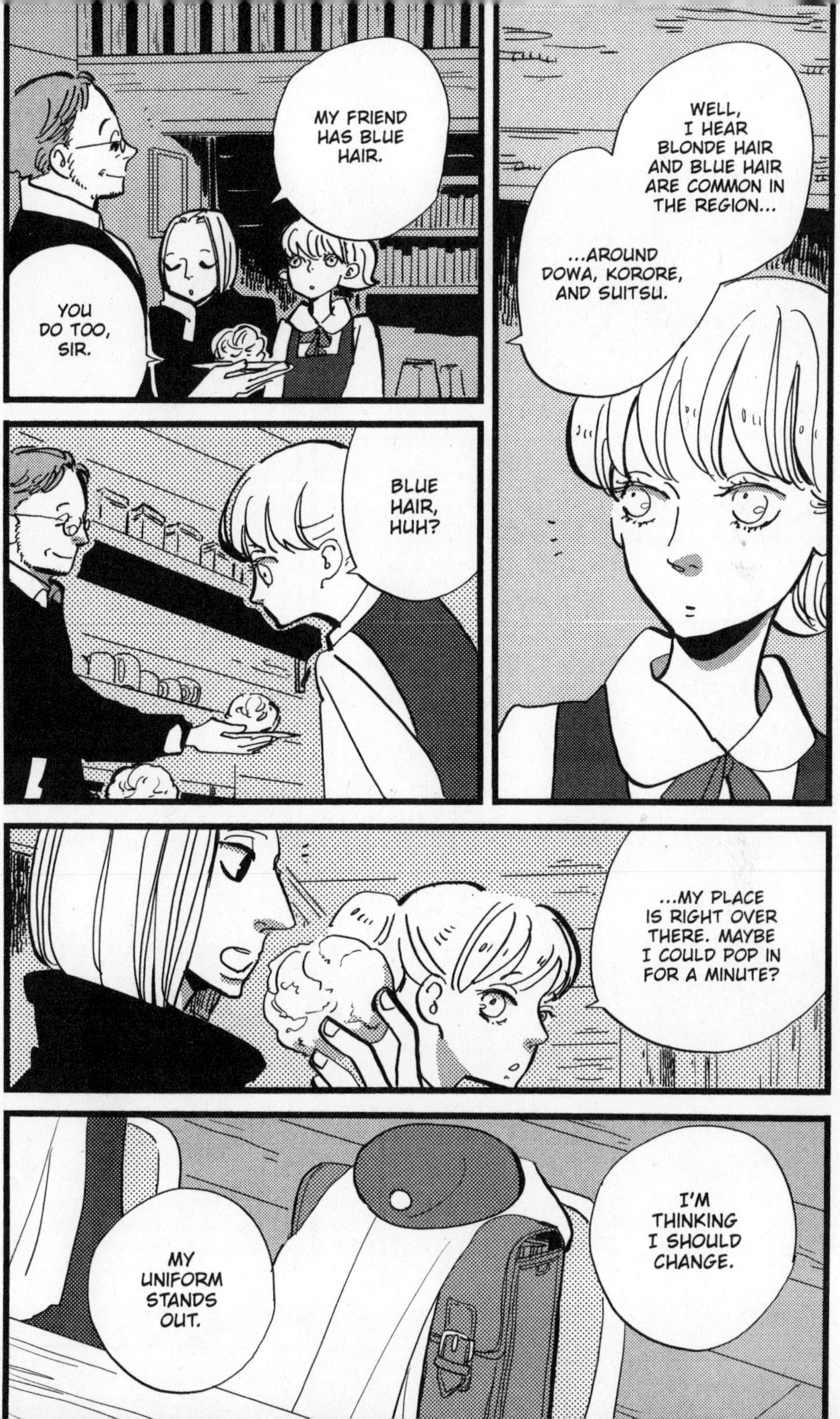
WELL, I HEAR BLONDE HAIR AND BLUE HAIR ARE COMMON IN THE REGION...
...AROUND DOWA, KORORE, AND SUITSU.
MY FRIEND HAS BLUE HAIR.
YOU DO TOO, SIR.
BLUE HAIR, HUH?
...MY PLACE IS RIGHT OVER THERE. MAYBE I COULD POP IN FOR A MINUTE?
I'M THINKING I SHOULD CHANGE.
MY UNIFORM STANDS OUT.

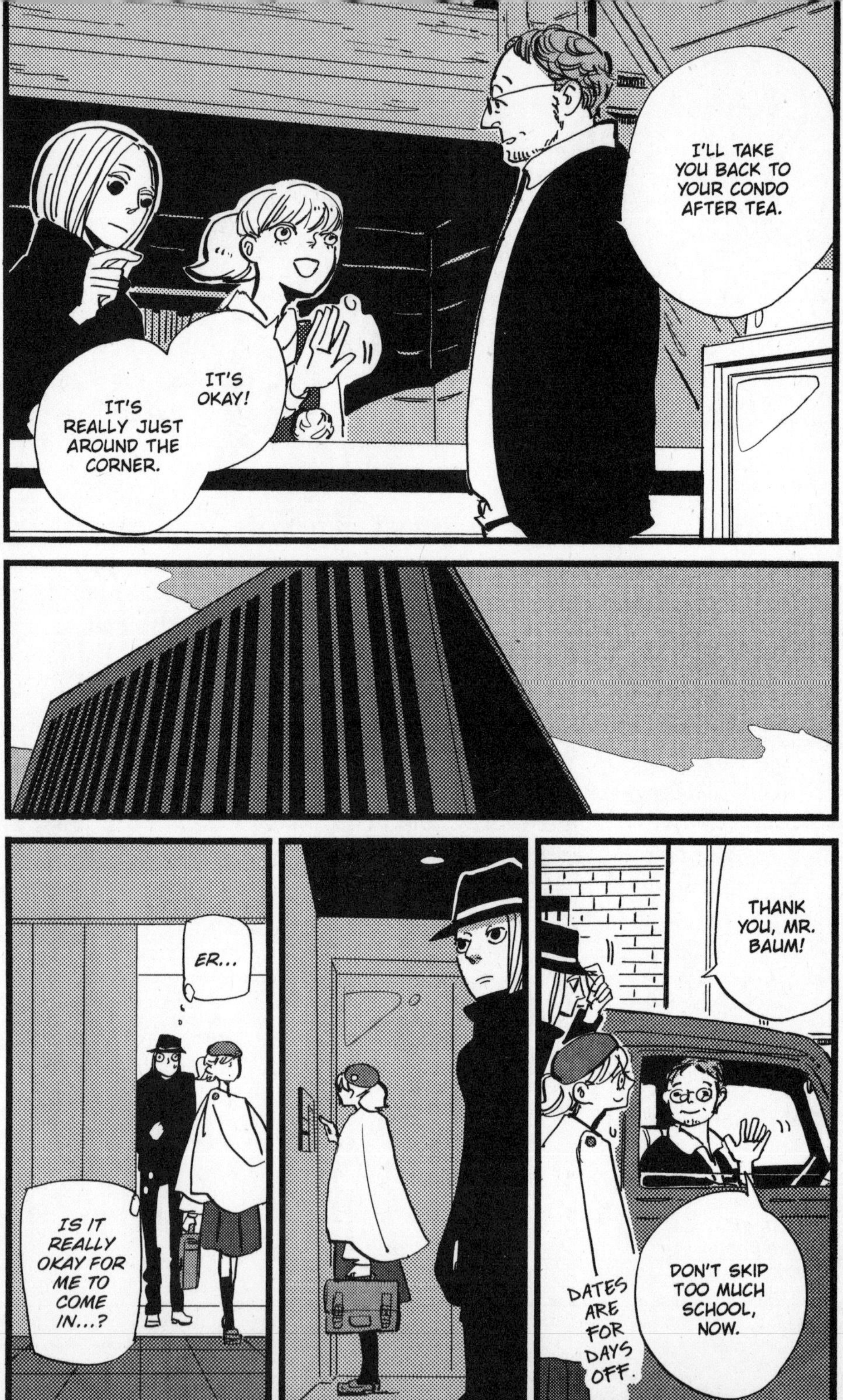
I'LL TAKE YOU BACK TO YOUR CONDO AFTER TEA.
IT'S OKAY!
IT'S REALLY JUST AROUND THE CORNER.
THANK YOU, MR. BAUM!
DON'T SKIP TOO MUCH SCHOOL, NOW.
DATES ARE FOR DAYS OFF.
ER...
IS IT REALLY OKAY FOR ME TO COME IN...?

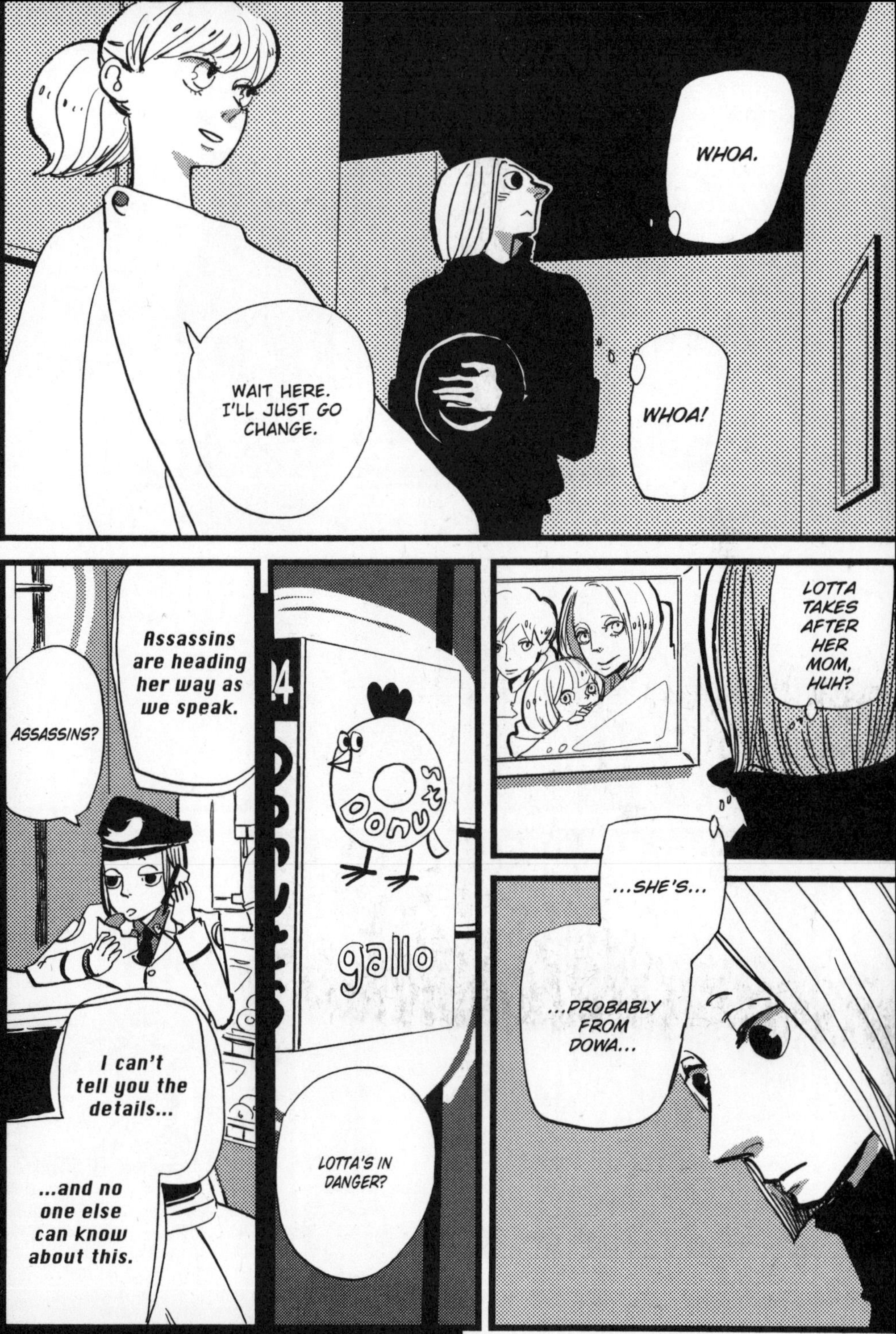
WHOA.
WHOA!
WAIT HERE. I'LL JUST GO CHANGE.
LOTTA TAKES AFTER HER MOM, HUH?
...SHE'S...
...PROBABLY FROM DOWA...
Donuts
gallo
LOTTA'S IN DANGER?
Assassins are heading her way as we speak.
ASSASSINS?
I can't tell you the details...
...and no one else can know about this.

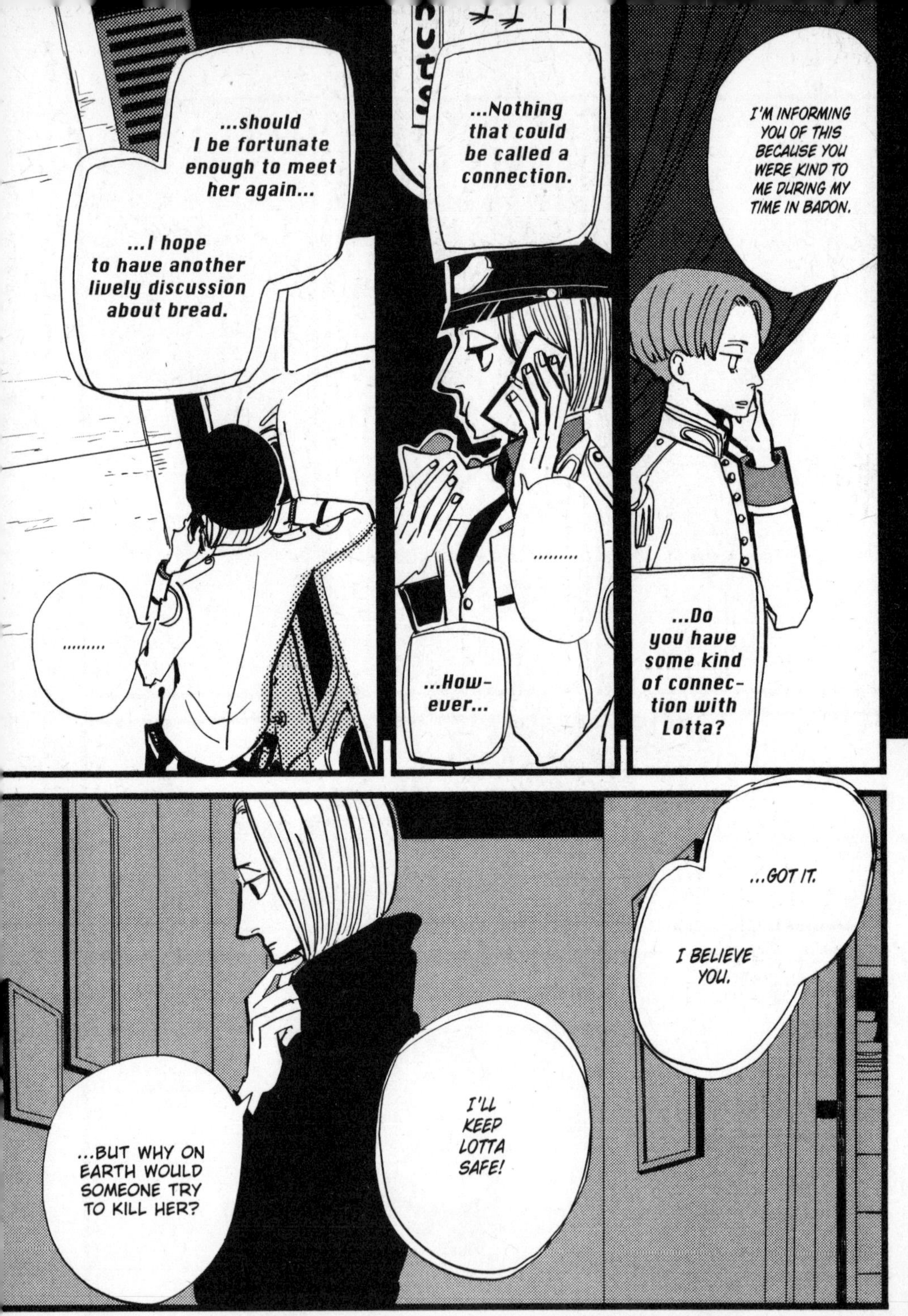

I'M INFORMING YOU OF THIS BECAUSE YOU WERE KIND TO ME DURING MY TIME IN BADON.
...Do you have some kind of connection with Lotta?
...Nothing that could be called a connection.
....
...However...
...should I be fortunate enough to meet her again...
...I hope to have another lively discussion about bread.
....
...GOT IT.
I BELIEVE YOU.
I'LL KEEP LOTTA SAFE!
...BUT WHY ON EARTH WOULD SOMEONE TRY TO KILL HER?

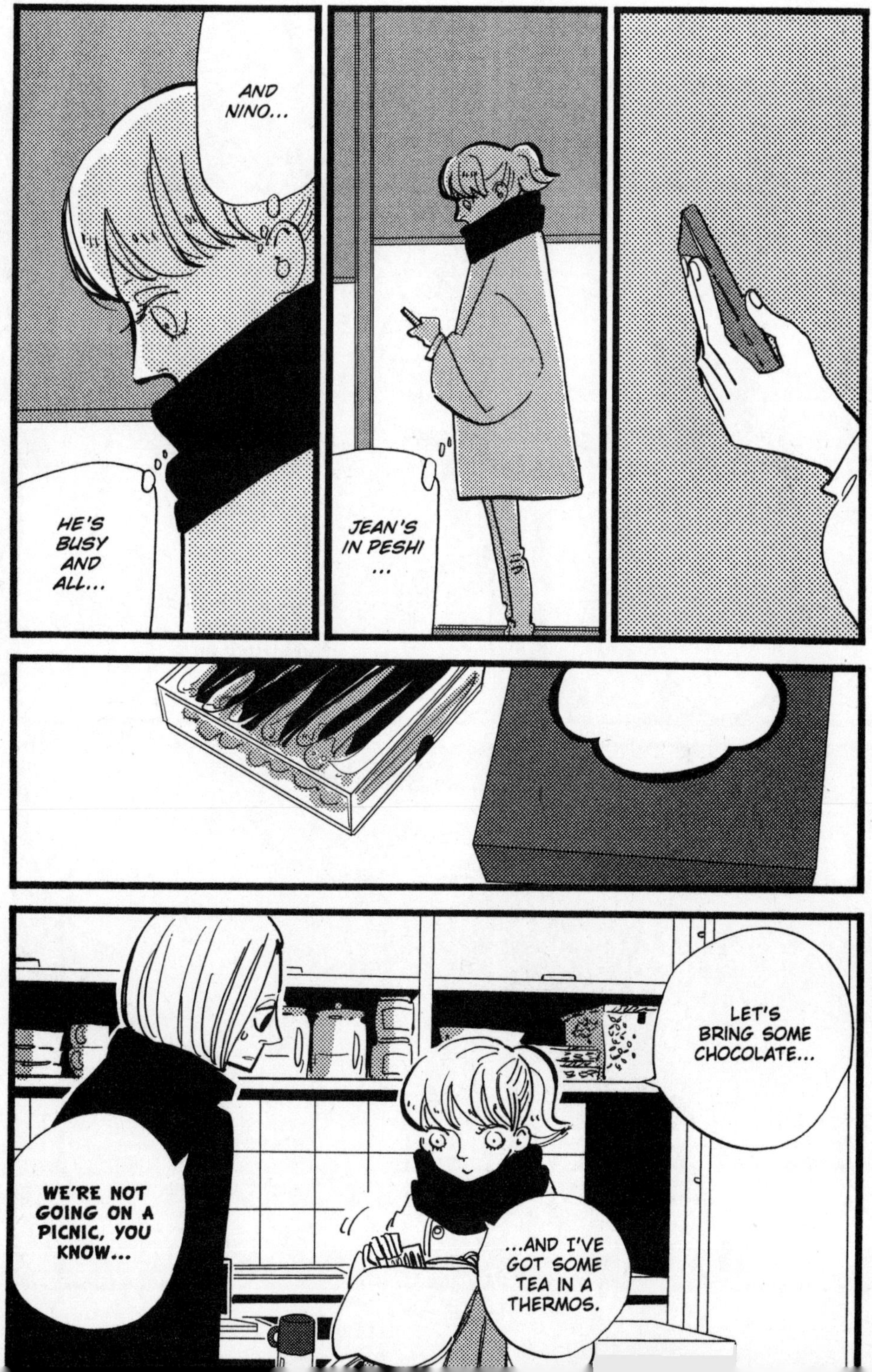
JEAN'S IN PESHI ...
AND NINO...
HE'S BUSY AND ALL...
LET'S BRING SOME CHOCOLATE...
...AND I'VE GOT SOME TEA IN A THERMOS.
WE'RE NOT GOING ON A PICNIC, YOU KNOW...

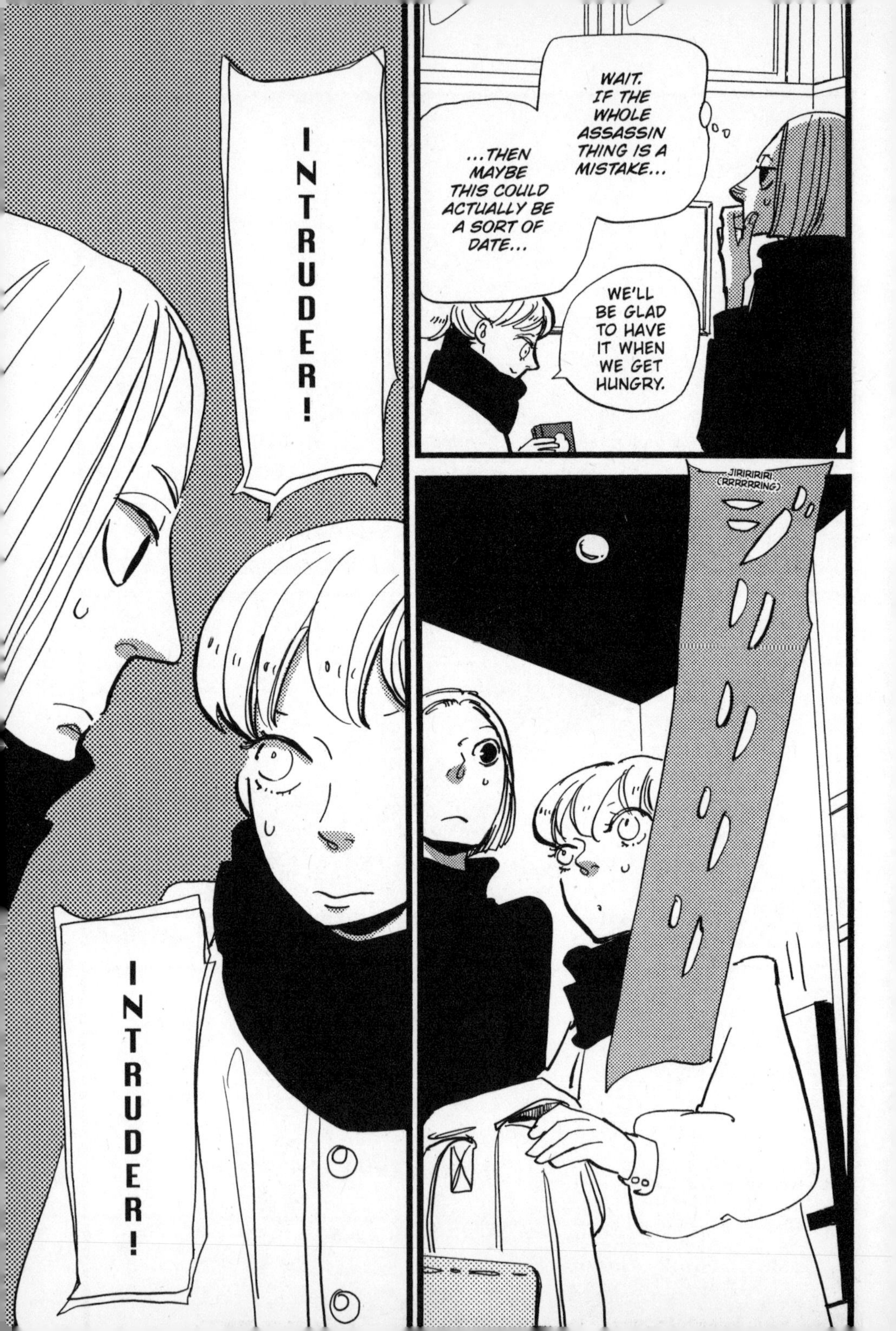
WAIT. IF THE WHOLE ASSASSIN THING IS A MISTAKE...
...THEN MAYBE THIS COULD ACTUALLY BE A SORT OF DATE...
WE'LL BE GLAD TO HAVE IT WHEN WE GET HUNGRY.
JIRIRIRIRI (RRRRRRING)
INTRUDER!
INTRUDER!

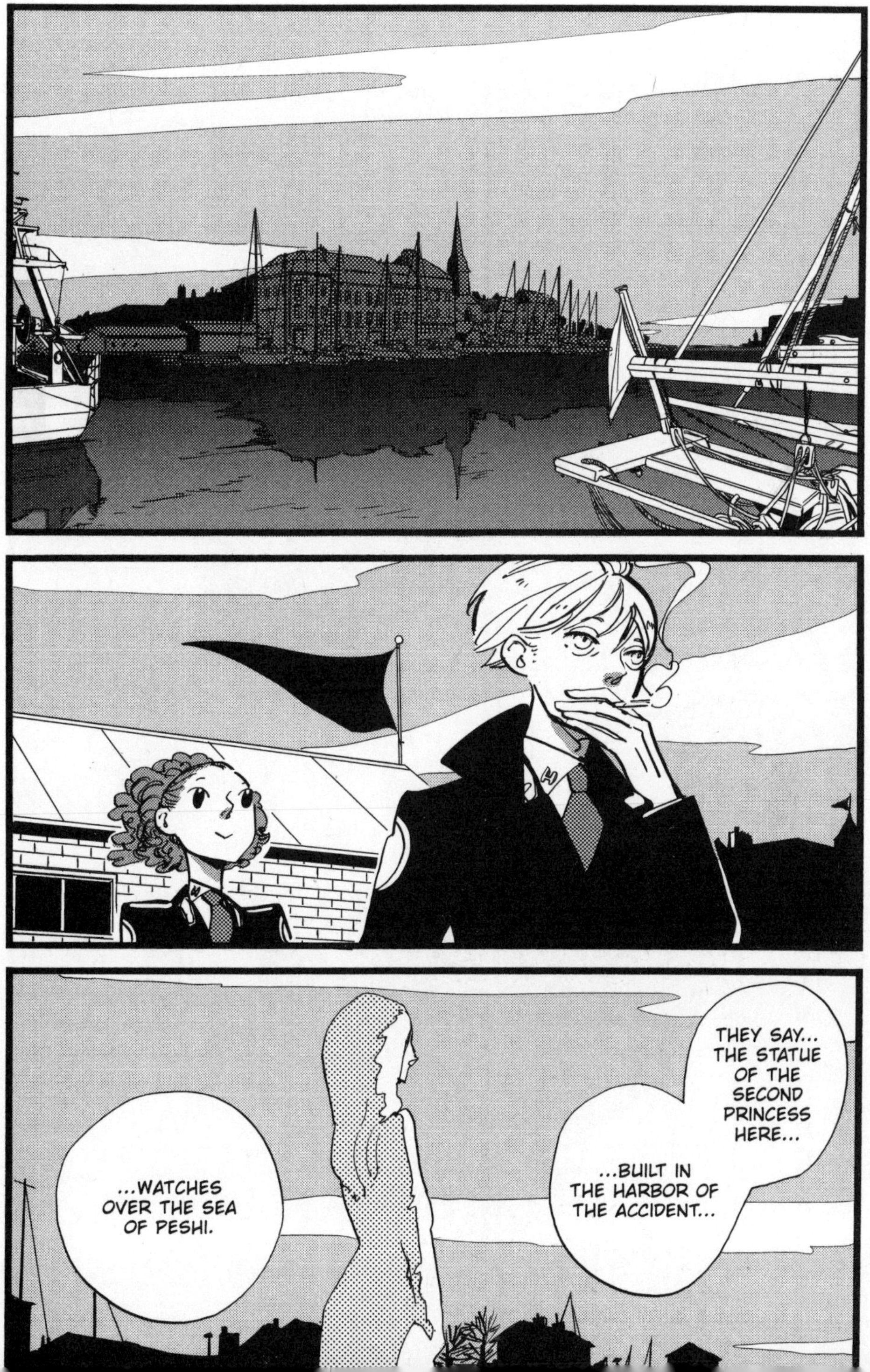
THEY SAY... THE STATUE OF THE SECOND PRINCESS HERE...
...BUILT IN THE HARBOR OF THE ACCIDENT...
...WATCHES OVER THE SEA OF PESHI.

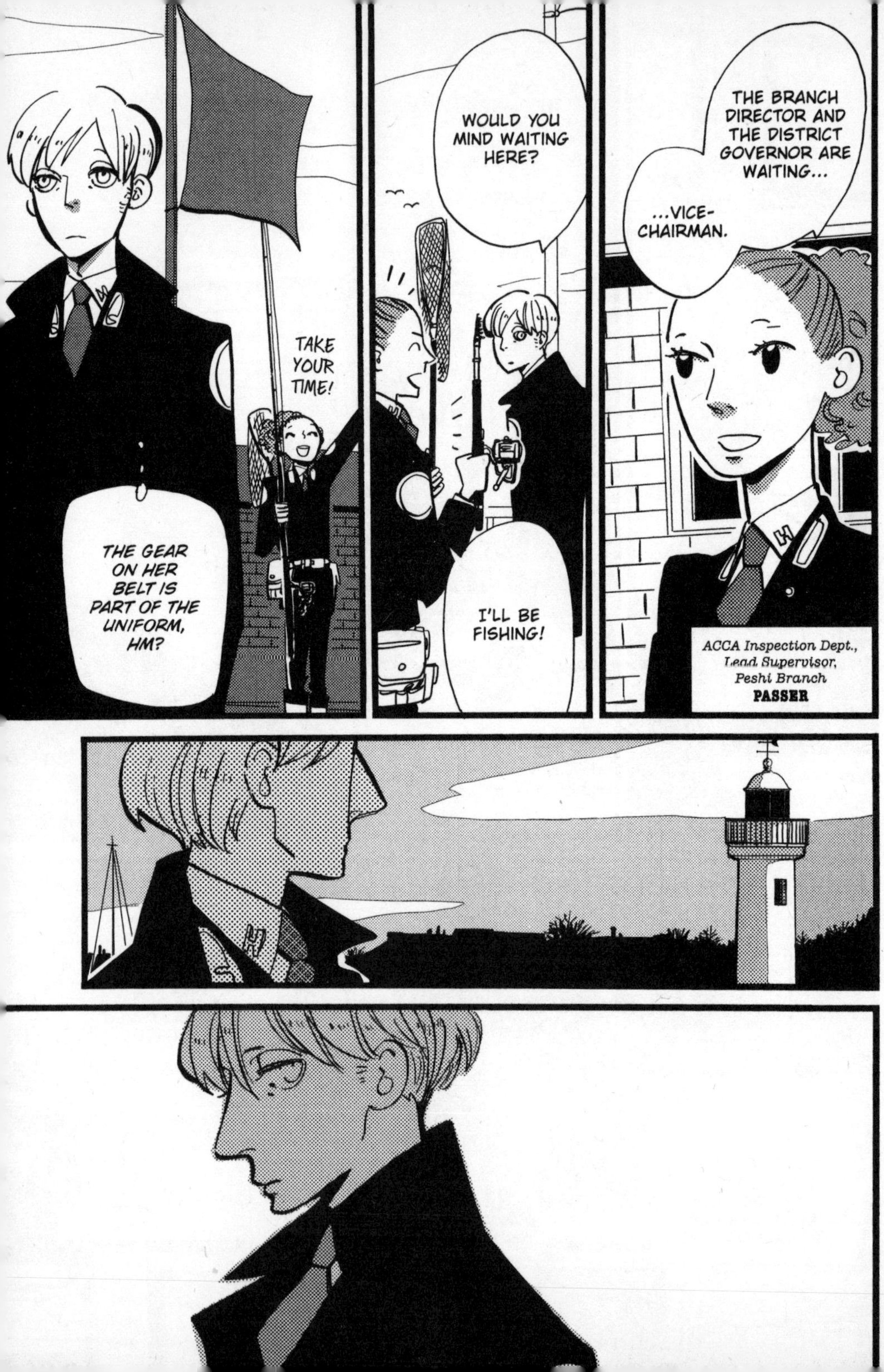
THE BRANCH DIRECTOR AND THE DISTRICT GOVERNOR ARE WAITING...
...VICE-CHAIRMAN.
ACCA Inspection Dept., Lead Supervisor, Peshi Branch PASSER
WOULD YOU MIND WAITING HERE?
I'LL BE FISHING!
TAKE YOUR TIME!
THE GEAR ON HER BELT IS PART OF THE UNIFORM, HM?

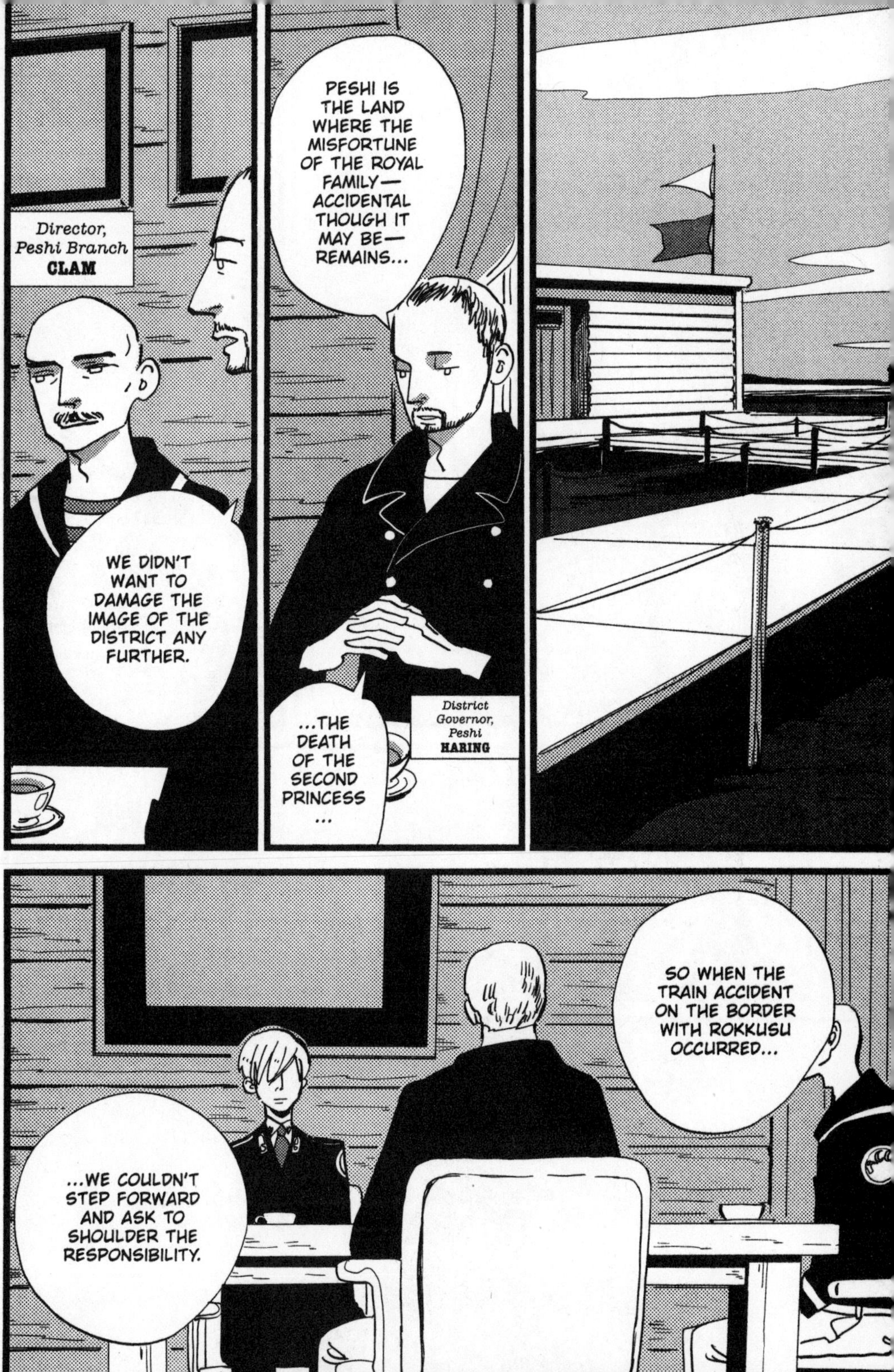
PESHI IS THE LAND WHERE THE MISFORTUNE OF THE ROYAL FAMILY— ACCIDENTAL THOUGH IT MAY BE— REMAINS...
District Governor, Peshi HARING
...THE DEATH OF THE SECOND PRINCESS ...
Director, Peshi Branch CLAM
WE DIDN'T WANT TO DAMAGE THE IMAGE OF THE DISTRICT ANY FURTHER.
SO WHEN THE TRAIN ACCIDENT ON THE BORDER WITH ROKKUSU OCCURRED...
...WE COULDN'T STEP FORWARD AND ASK TO SHOULDER THE RESPONSIBILITY.

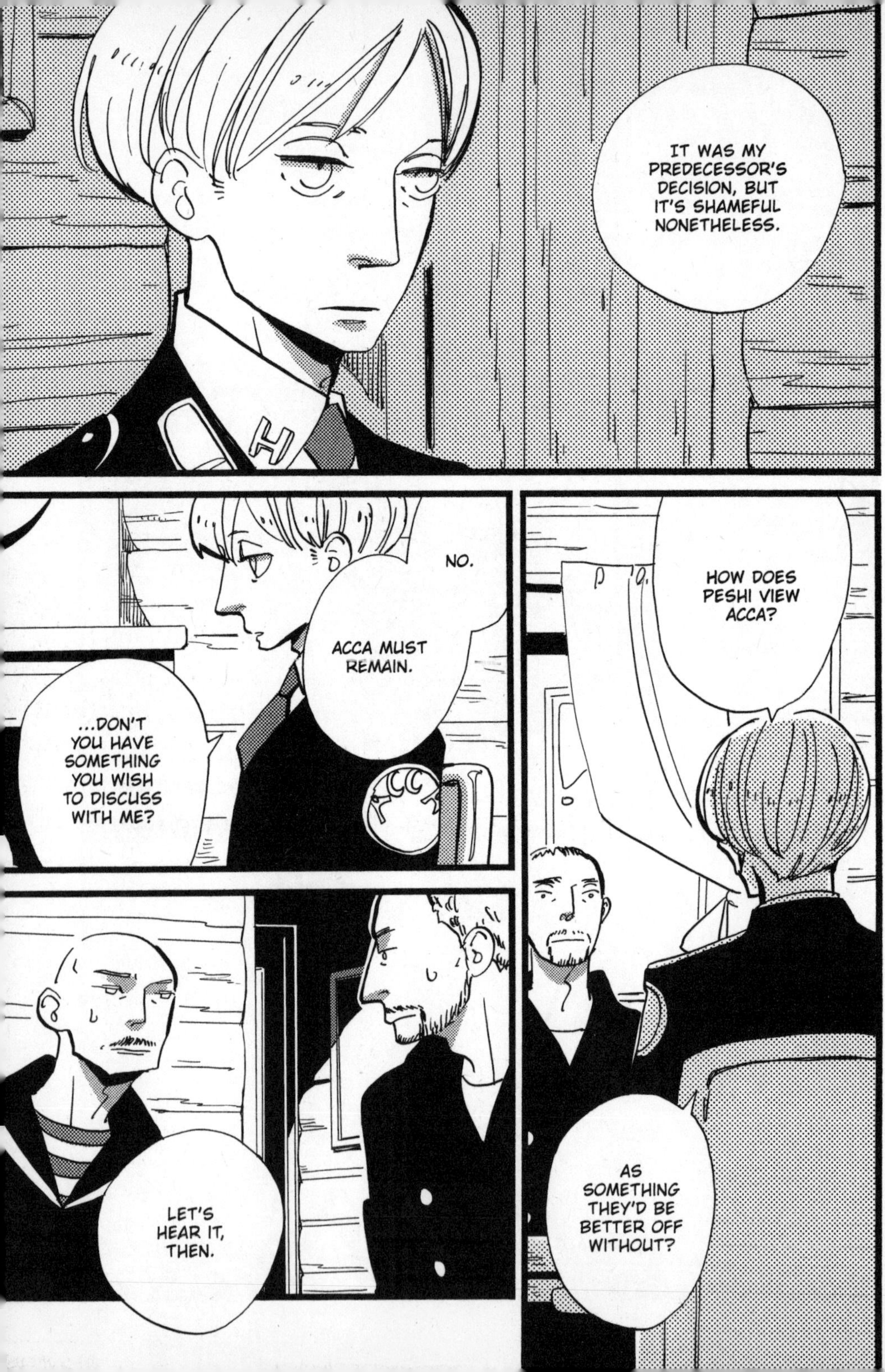
IT WAS MY PREDECESSOR'S DECISION, BUT IT'S SHAMEFUL NONETHELESS.
HOW DOES PESHI VIEW ACCA?
AS SOMETHING THEY'D BE BETTER OFF WITHOUT?
NO.
ACCA MUST REMAIN.
...DON'T YOU HAVE SOMETHING YOU WISH TO DISCUSS WITH ME?
LET'S HEAR IT, THEN.

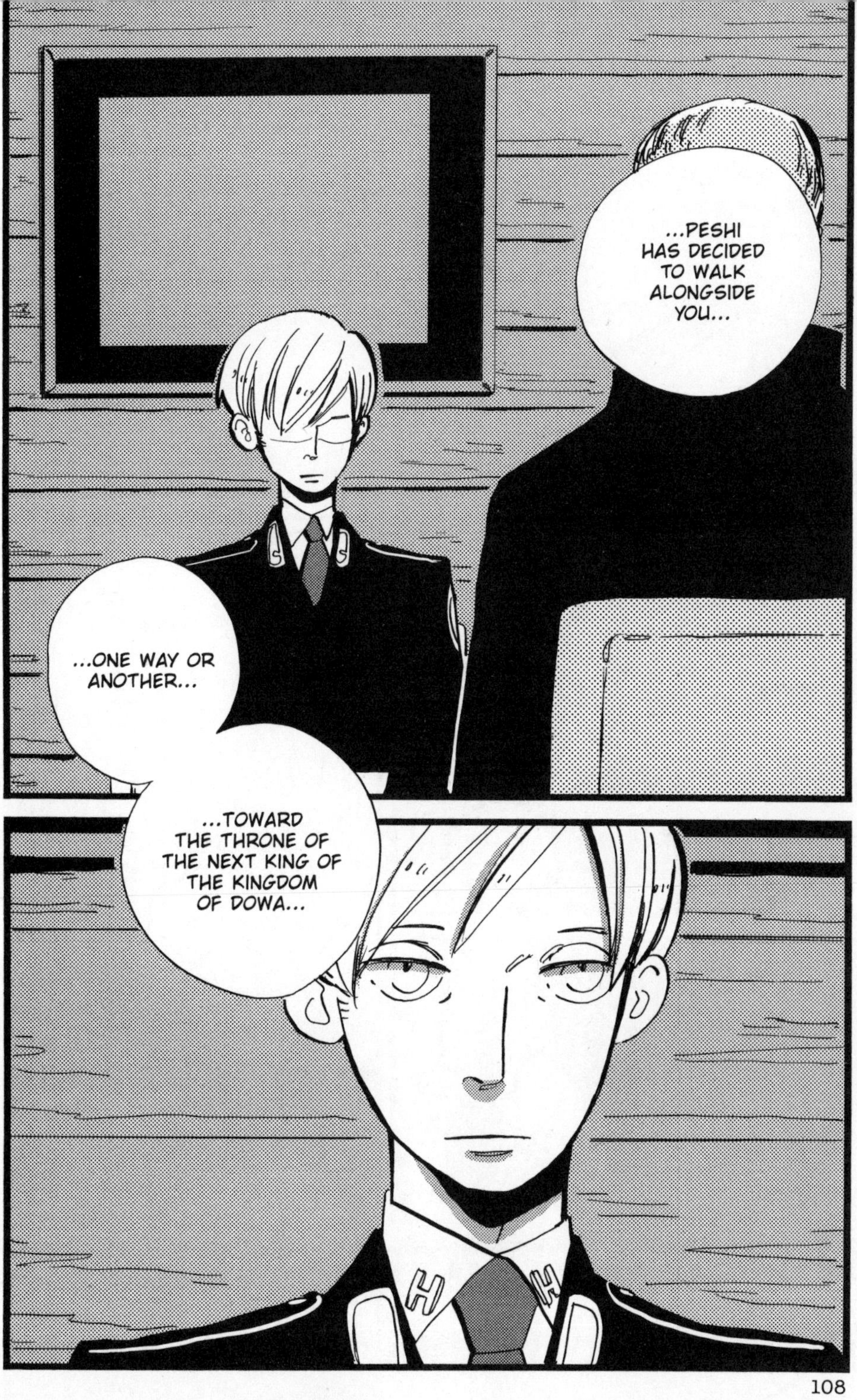
...PESHI HAS DECIDED TO WALK ALONGSIDE YOU...
...ONE WAY OR ANOTHER...
...TOWARD THE THRONE OF THE NEXT KING OF THE KINGDOM OF DOWA...

ACCA Branch Uniforms 10

Peshi District

Given that Peshi is surrounded by the sea, the district uses a sailor-style uniform. To allow easy fishing at the port, the branch agents are often seen carrying fishing equipment. The suntanned, well-built men of the branch office are popular with women.

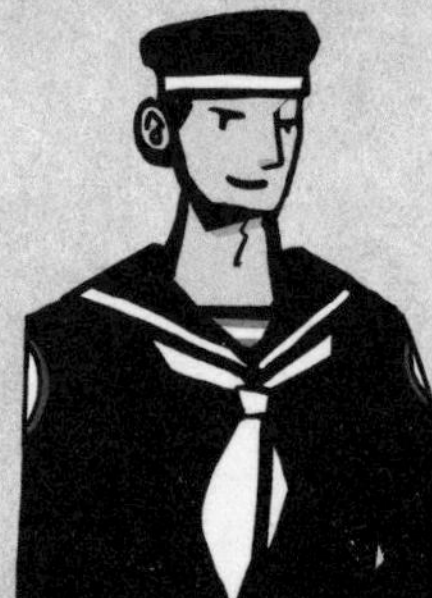

CHAPTER 27

The Princess and the Knight in Badon

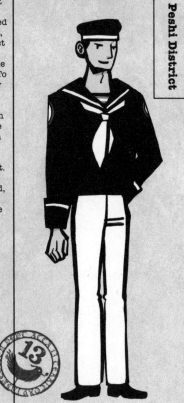

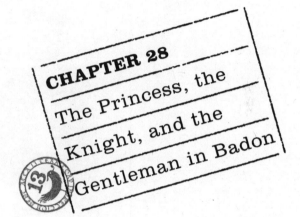

CHAPTER 28

The Princess, the Knight, and the Gentleman in Badon

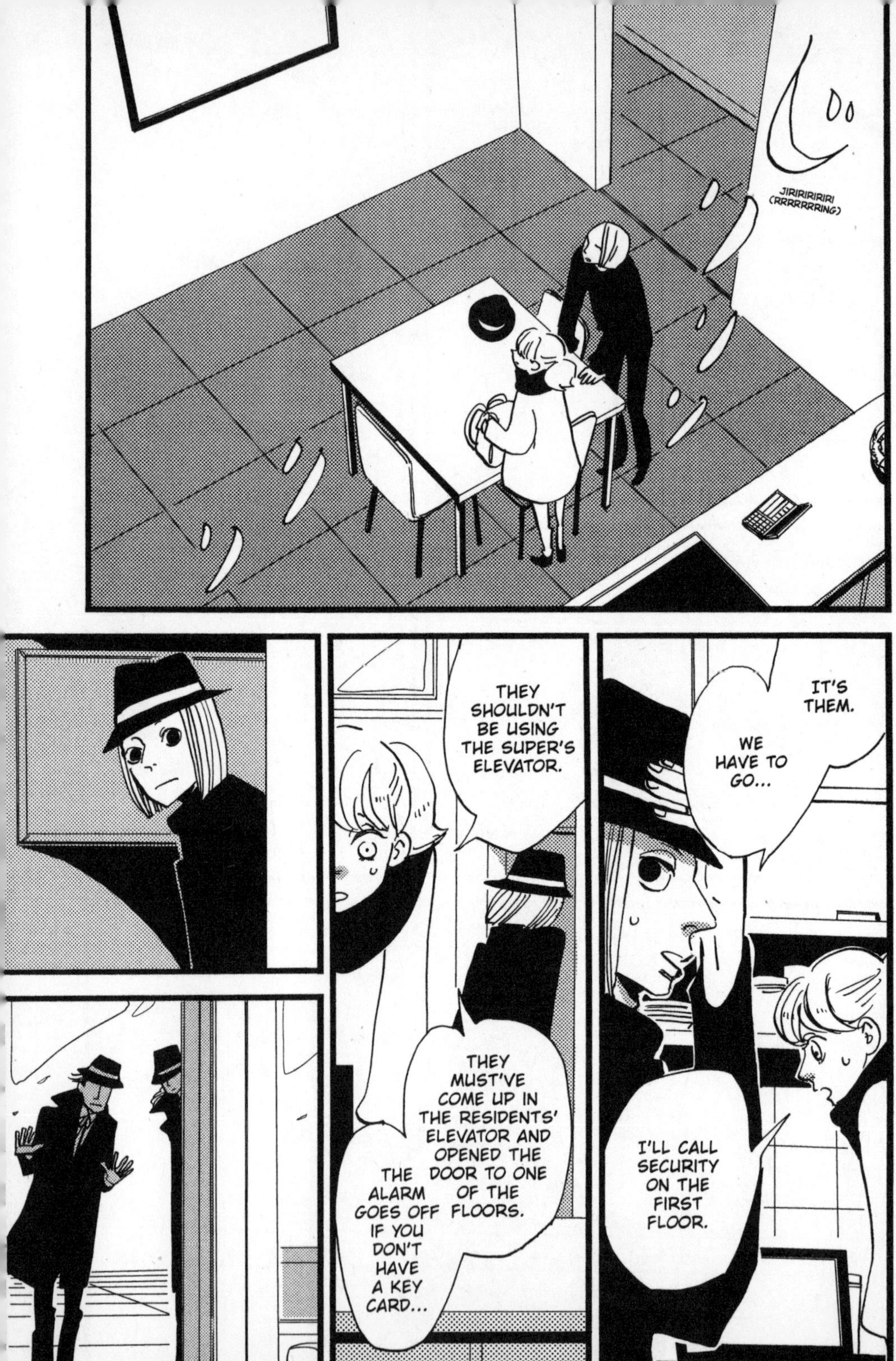
JIRIRIRIRIRI (RRRRRRRING)
IT'S THEM.
WE HAVE TO GO...
I'LL CALL SECURITY ON THE FIRST FLOOR.
THEY SHOULDN'T BE USING THE SUPER'S ELEVATOR.
THEY MUST'VE COME UP IN THE RESIDENTS' ELEVATOR AND OPENED THE DOOR TO ONE OF THE FLOORS.
THE ALARM GOES OFF IF YOU DON'T HAVE A KEY CARD...

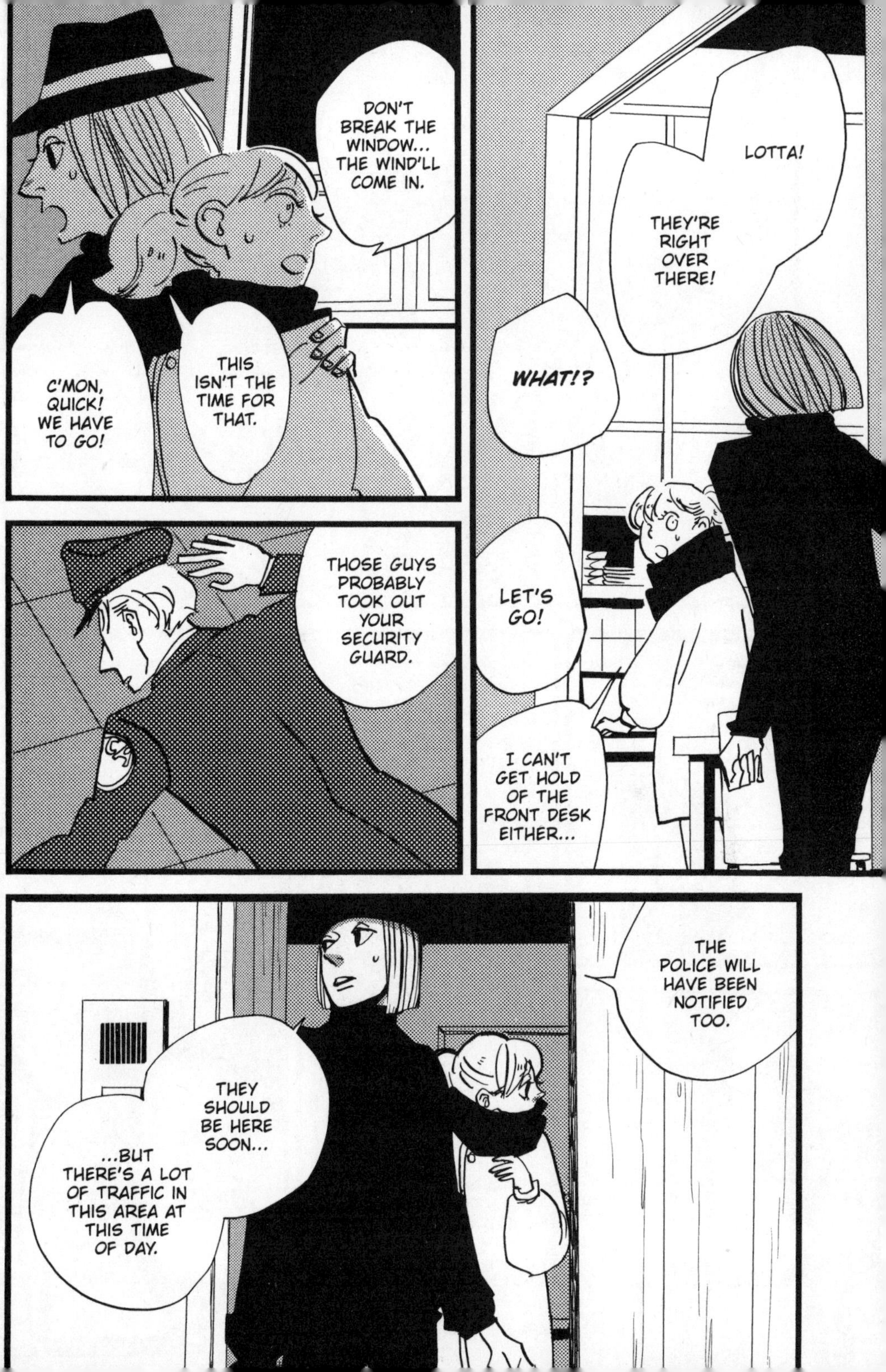
LOTTA!
THEY'RE RIGHT OVER THERE!
WHAT!?
LET'S GO!
I CAN'T GET HOLD OF THE FRONT DESK EITHER...
DON'T BREAK THE WINDOW... THE WIND'LL COME IN.
THIS ISN'T THE TIME FOR THAT.
C'MON, QUICK! WE HAVE TO GO!
THOSE GUYS PROBABLY TOOK OUT YOUR SECURITY GUARD.
THE POLICE WILL HAVE BEEN NOTIFIED TOO.
THEY SHOULD BE HERE SOON...
...BUT THERE'S A LOT OF TRAFFIC IN THIS AREA AT THIS TIME OF DAY.

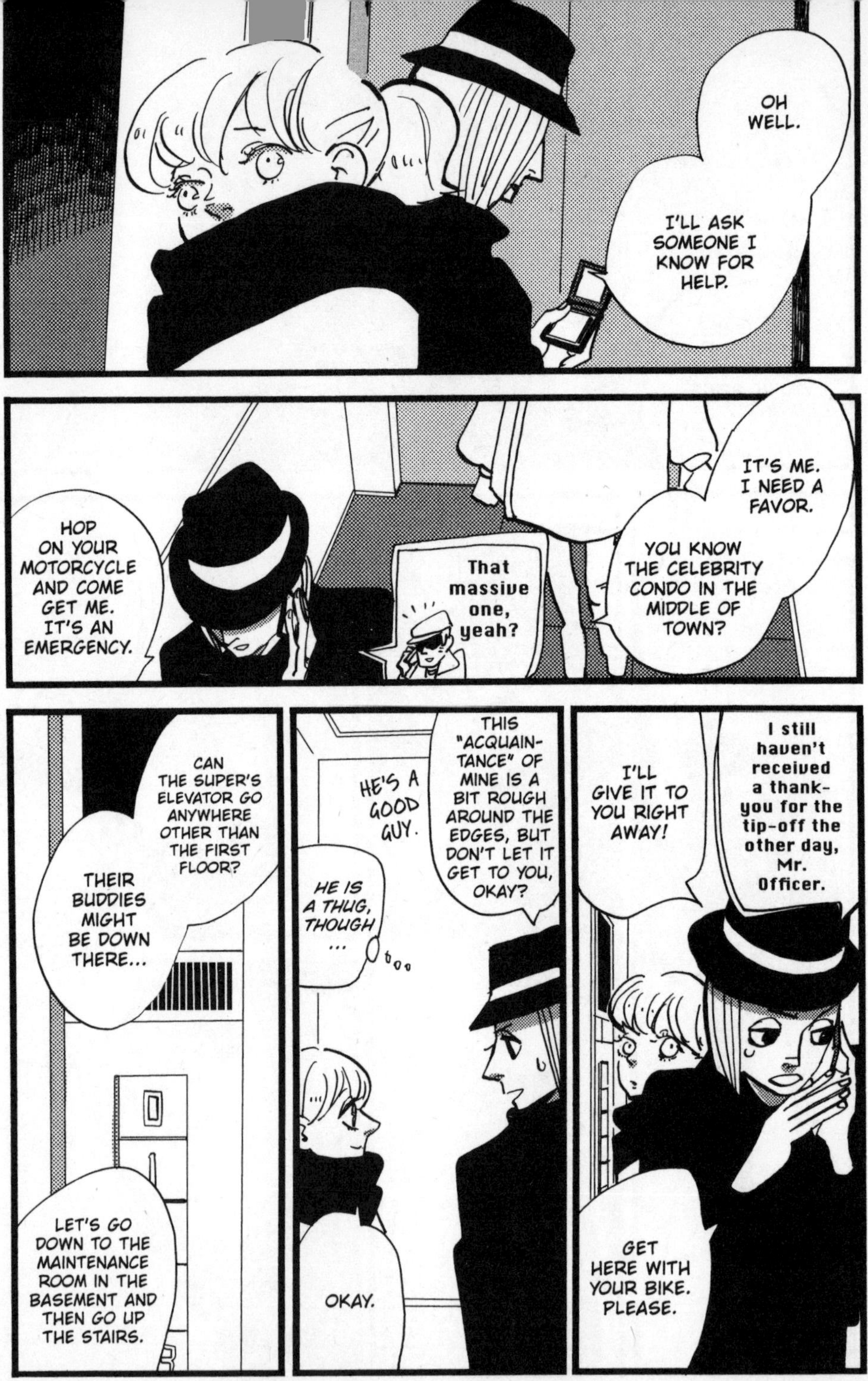
OH WELL.
I'LL ASK SOMEONE I KNOW FOR HELP.
IT'S ME. I NEED A FAVOR.
YOU KNOW THE CELEBRITY CONDO IN THE MIDDLE OF TOWN?
That massive one, yeah?
HOP ON YOUR MOTORCYCLE AND COME GET ME. IT'S AN EMERGENCY.
I still haven't received a thank-you for the tip-off the other day, Mr. Officer.
I'LL GIVE IT TO YOU RIGHT AWAY!
GET HERE WITH YOUR BIKE. PLEASE.
THIS "ACQUAINTANCE" OF MINE IS A BIT ROUGH AROUND THE EDGES, BUT DON'T LET IT GET TO YOU, OKAY?
HE'S A GOOD GUY.
HE IS A THUG, THOUGH ...
OKAY.
CAN THE SUPER'S ELEVATOR GO ANYWHERE OTHER THAN THE FIRST FLOOR?
THEIR BUDDIES MIGHT BE DOWN THERE...
LET'S GO DOWN TO THE MAINTENANCE ROOM IN THE BASEMENT AND THEN GO UP THE STAIRS.

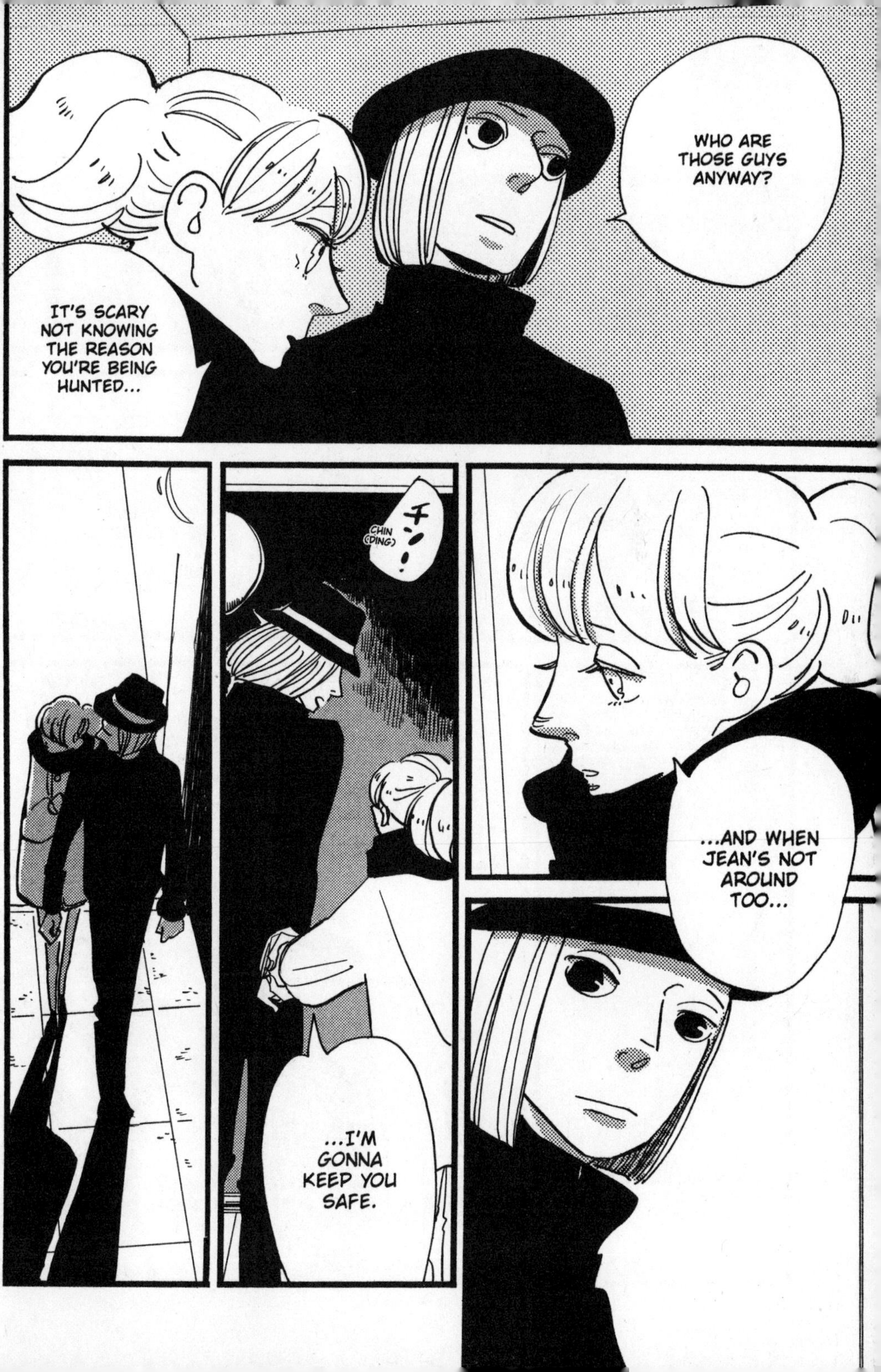
WHO ARE THOSE GUYS ANYWAY?
IT'S SCARY NOT KNOWING THE REASON YOU'RE BEING HUNTED...
...AND WHEN JEAN'S NOT AROUND TOO...
チン…
CHIN (DING)
...I'M GONNA KEEP YOU SAFE.

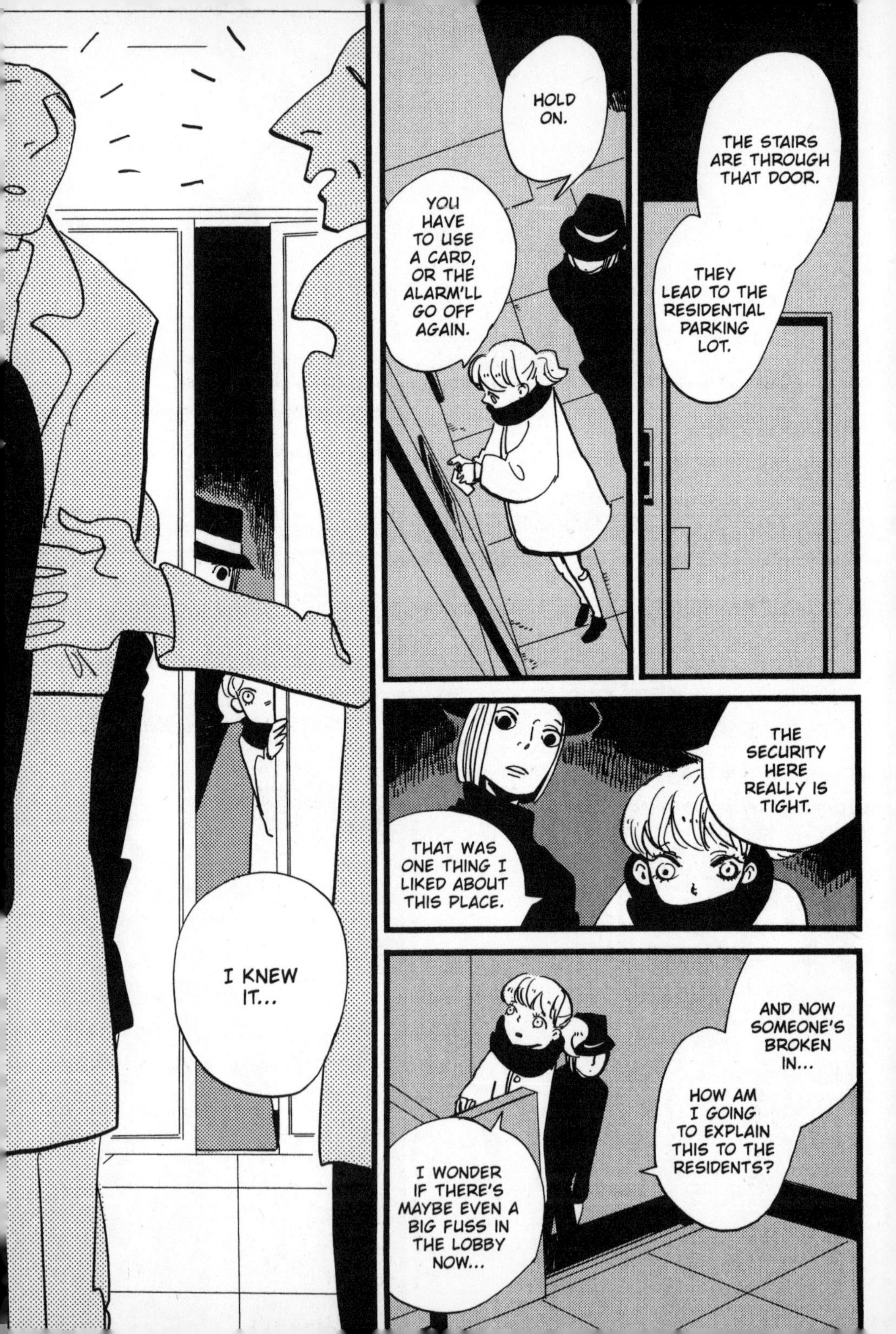
THE STAIRS ARE THROUGH THAT DOOR.
THEY LEAD TO THE RESIDENTIAL PARKING LOT.
HOLD ON.
YOU HAVE TO USE A CARD, OR THE ALARM'LL GO OFF AGAIN.
THE SECURITY HERE REALLY IS TIGHT.
THAT WAS ONE THING I LIKED ABOUT THIS PLACE.
AND NOW SOMEONE'S BROKEN IN...
HOW AM I GOING TO EXPLAIN THIS TO THE RESIDENTS?
I WONDER IF THERE'S MAYBE EVEN A BIG FUSS IN THE LOBBY NOW...
I KNEW IT...

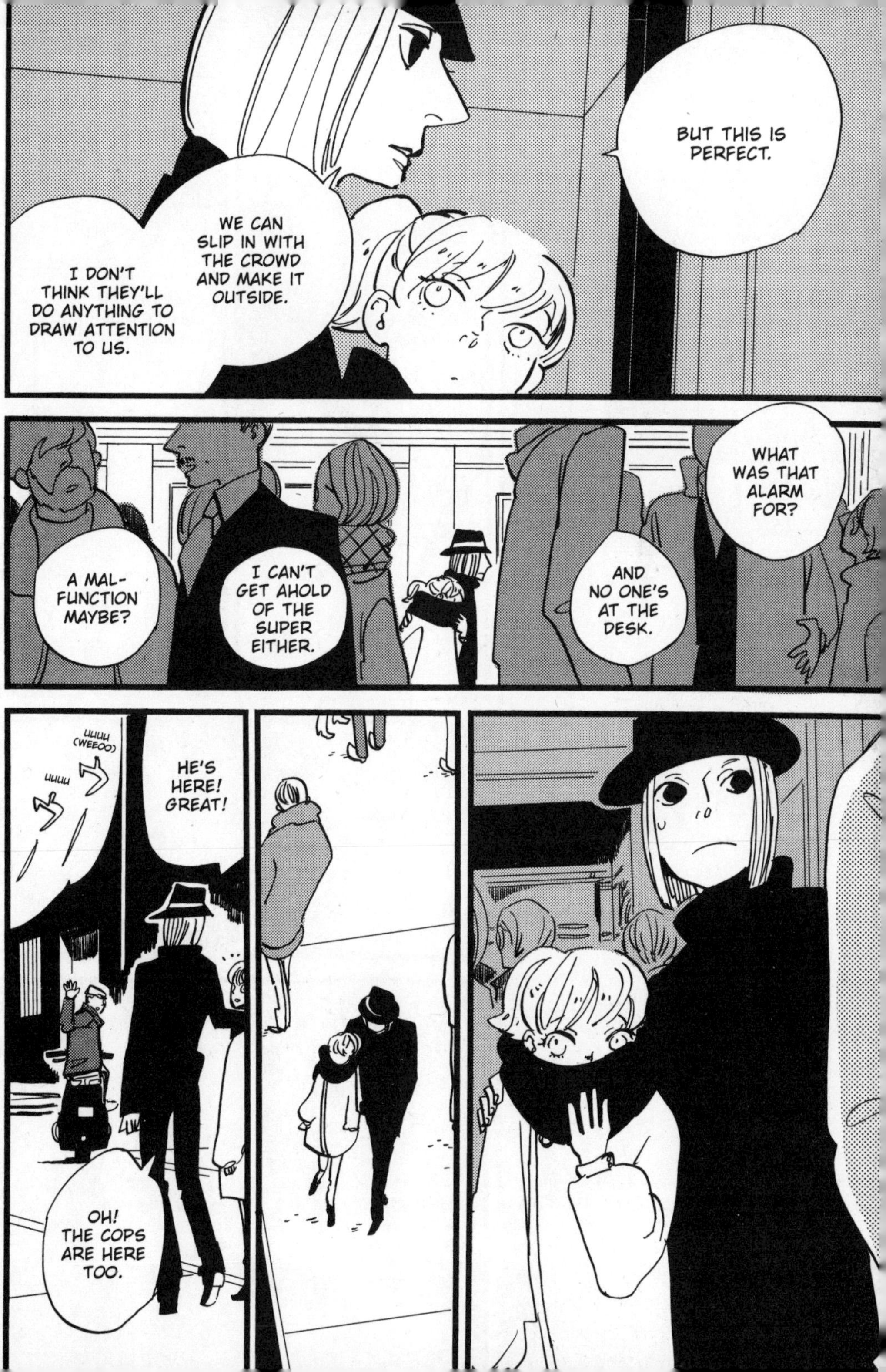
BUT THIS IS PERFECT.
WE CAN SLIP IN WITH THE CROWD AND MAKE IT OUTSIDE.
I DON'T THINK THEY'LL DO ANYTHING TO DRAW ATTENTION TO US.
WHAT WAS THAT ALARM FOR?
AND NO ONE'S AT THE DESK.
I CAN'T GET AHOLD OF THE SUPER EITHER.
A MAL-FUNCTION MAYBE?
uuuu (WEEOO)
uuuu
HE'S HERE! GREAT!
OH! THE COPS ARE HERE TOO.

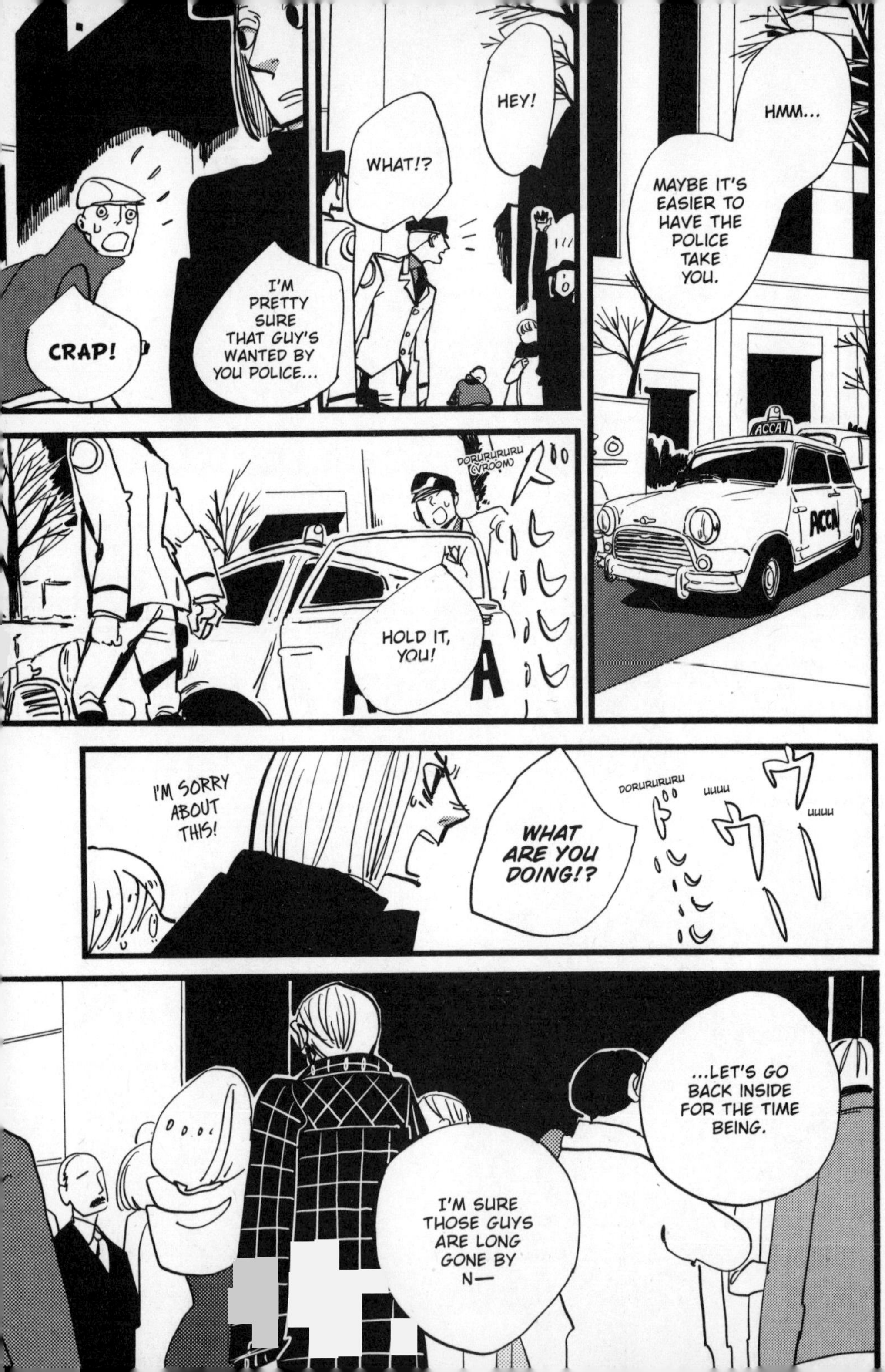
HMM...
MAYBE IT'S EASIER TO HAVE THE POLICE TAKE YOU.
ACCA
ACCA
HEY!
WHAT!?
I'M PRETTY SURE THAT GUY'S WANTED BY YOU POLICE...
CRAP!
DORURURURU (VROOM)
HOLD IT, YOU!
DORURURURU
UUUU
UUUU
WHAT ARE YOU DOING!?
I'M SORRY ABOUT THIS!
...LET'S GO BACK INSIDE FOR THE TIME BEING.
I'M SURE THOSE GUYS ARE LONG GONE BY N—

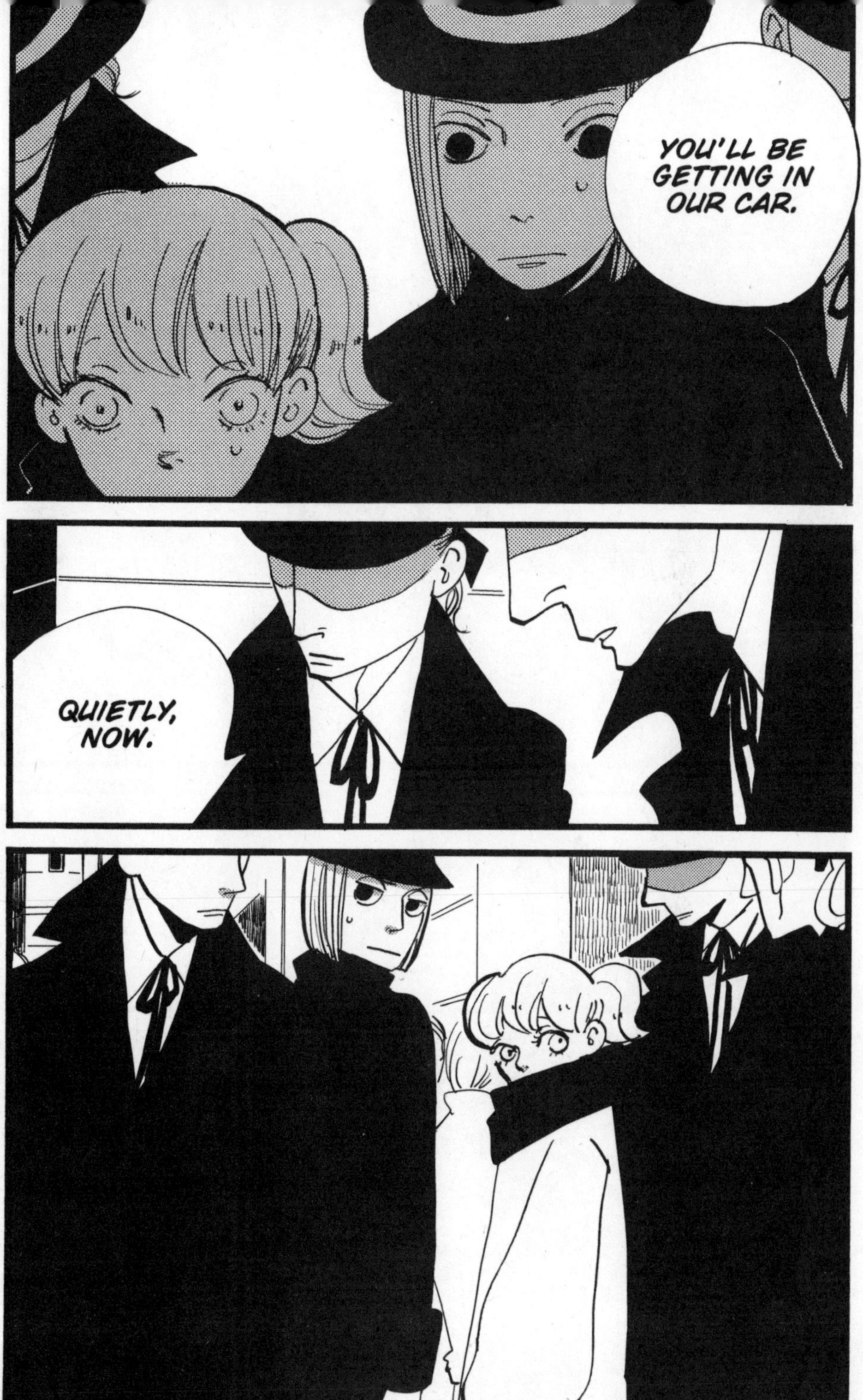
YOU'LL BE GETTING IN OUR CAR.
QUIETLY, NOW.

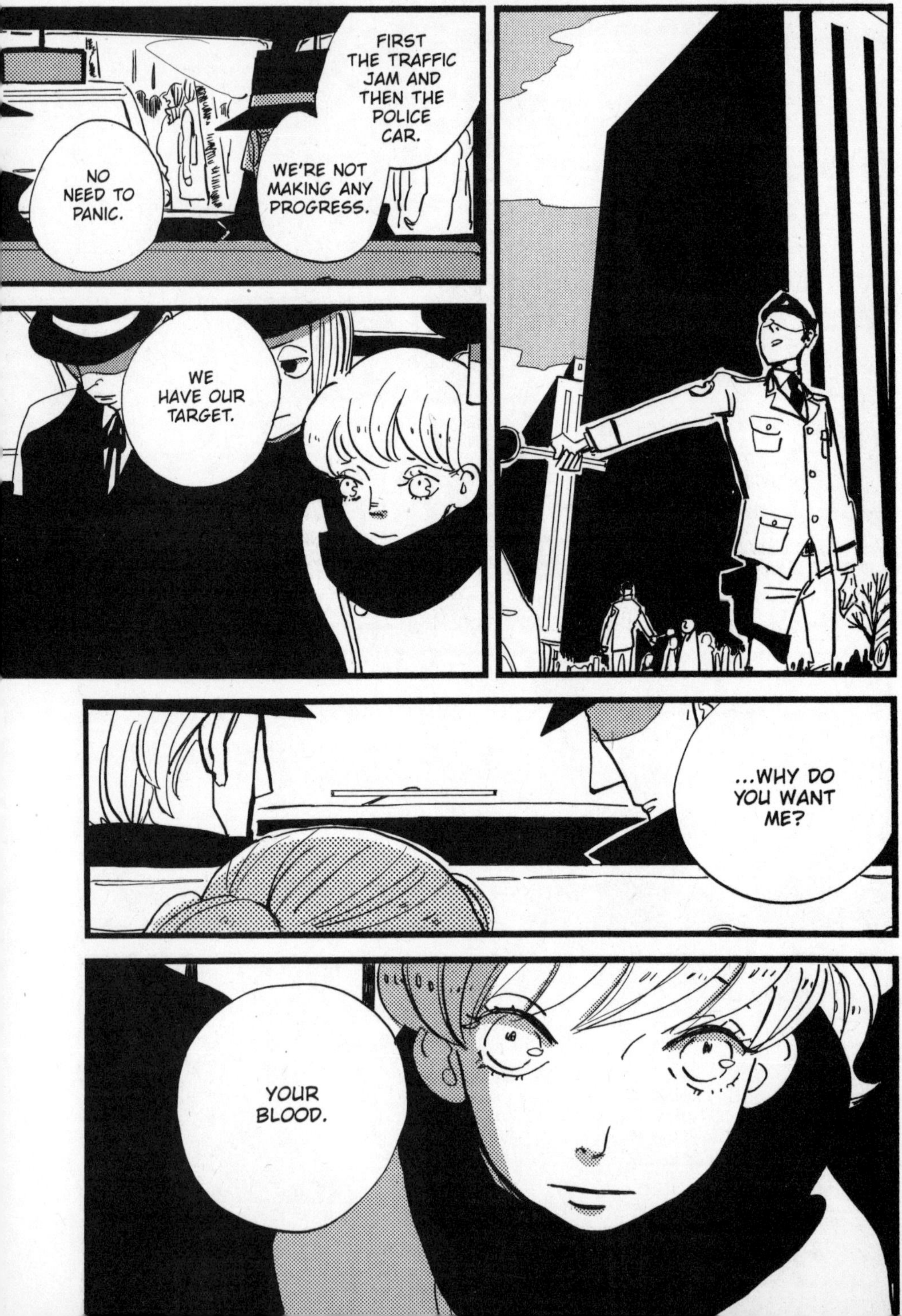
FIRST THE TRAFFIC JAM AND THEN THE POLICE CAR.
WE'RE NOT MAKING ANY PROGRESS.
NO NEED TO PANIC.
WE HAVE OUR TARGET.
...WHY DO YOU WANT ME?
YOUR BLOOD.

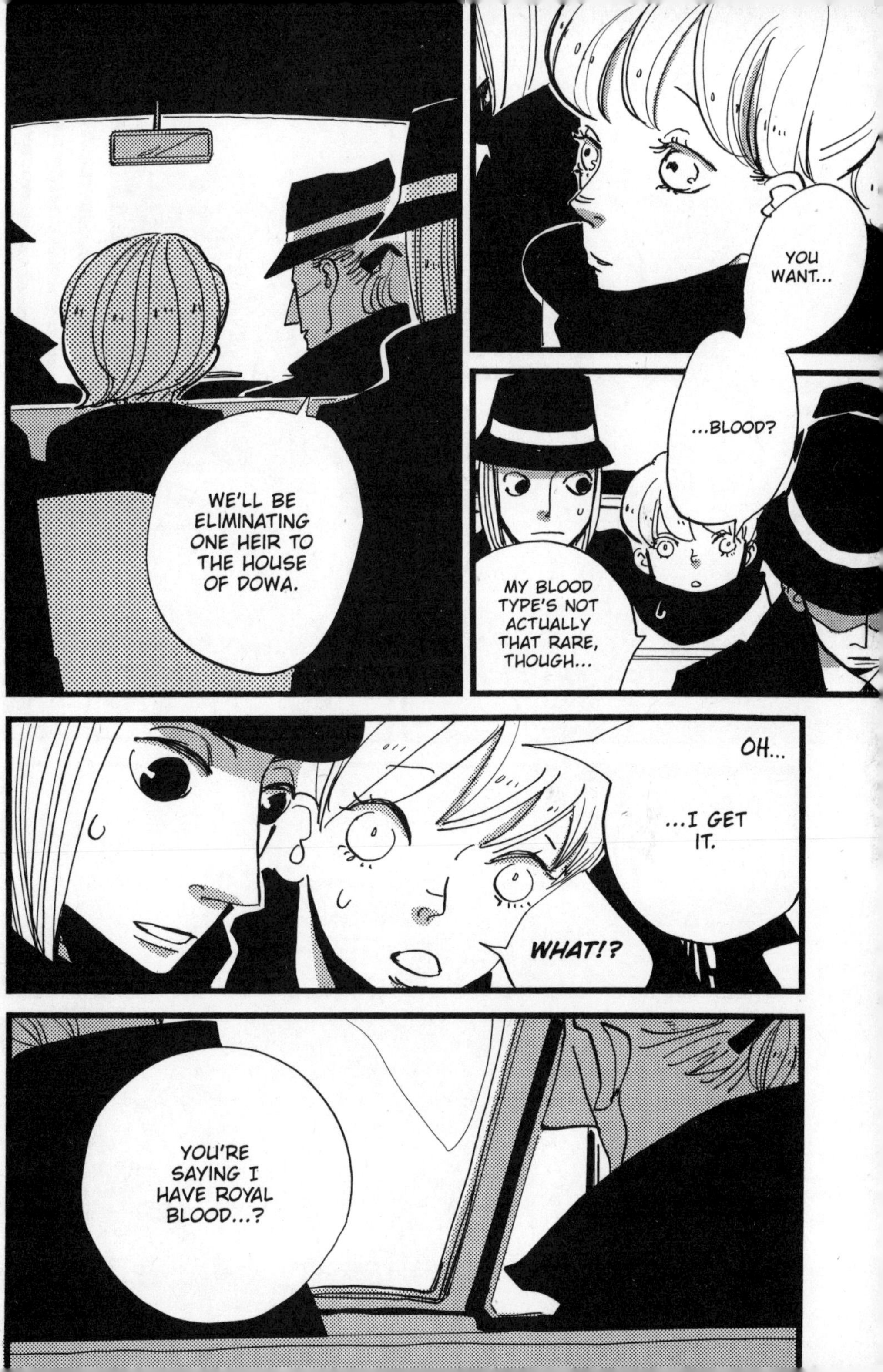
YOU WANT...
...BLOOD?
MY BLOOD TYPE'S NOT ACTUALLY THAT RARE, THOUGH...
WE'LL BE ELIMINATING ONE HEIR TO THE HOUSE OF DOWA.
OH...
...I GET IT.
WHAT!?
YOU'RE SAYING I HAVE ROYAL BLOOD...?

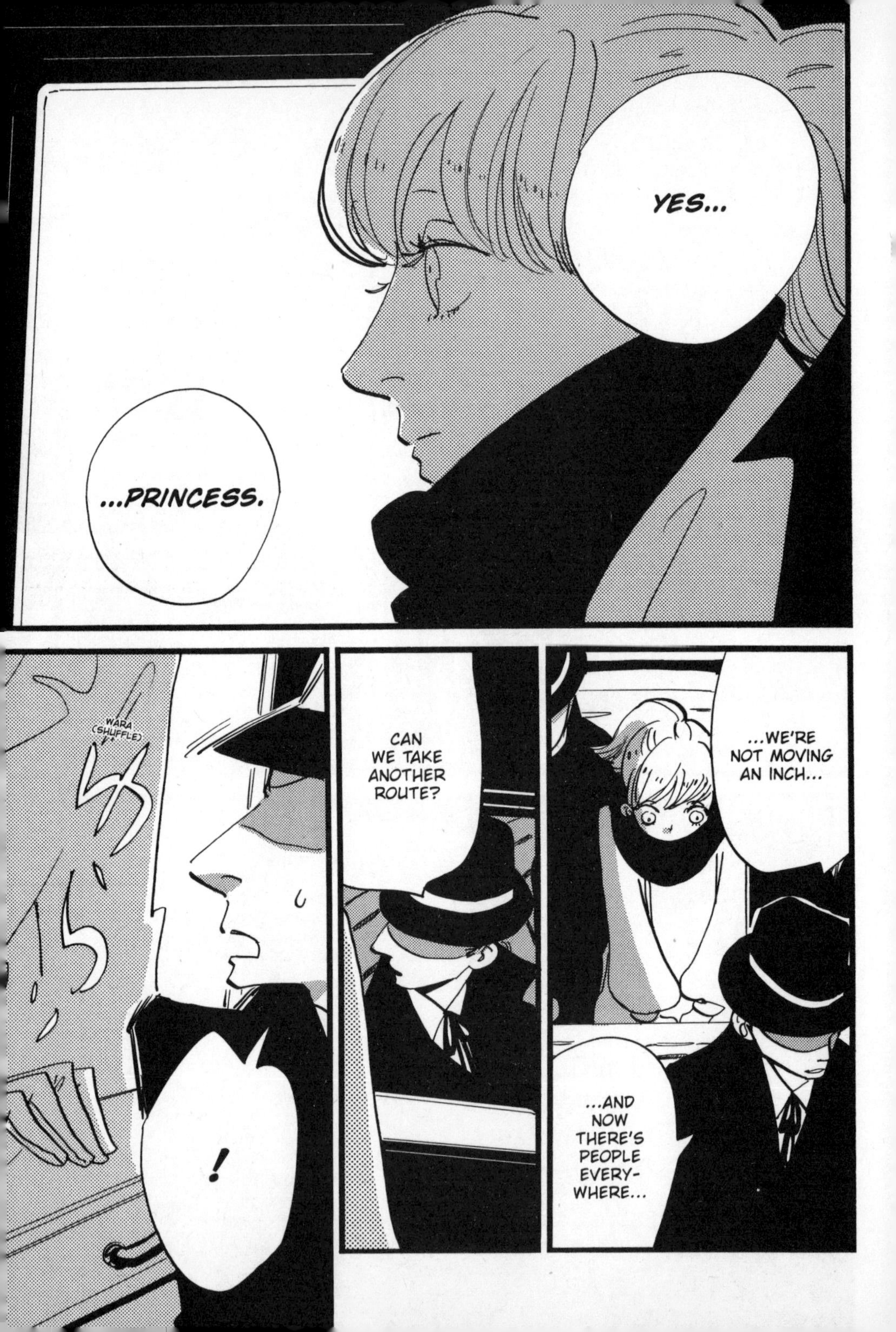
YES...
...PRINCESS.
...WE'RE NOT MOVING AN INCH...
...AND NOW THERE'S PEOPLE EVERY-WHERE...
CAN WE TAKE ANOTHER ROUTE?
WARA (SHUFFLE)
!

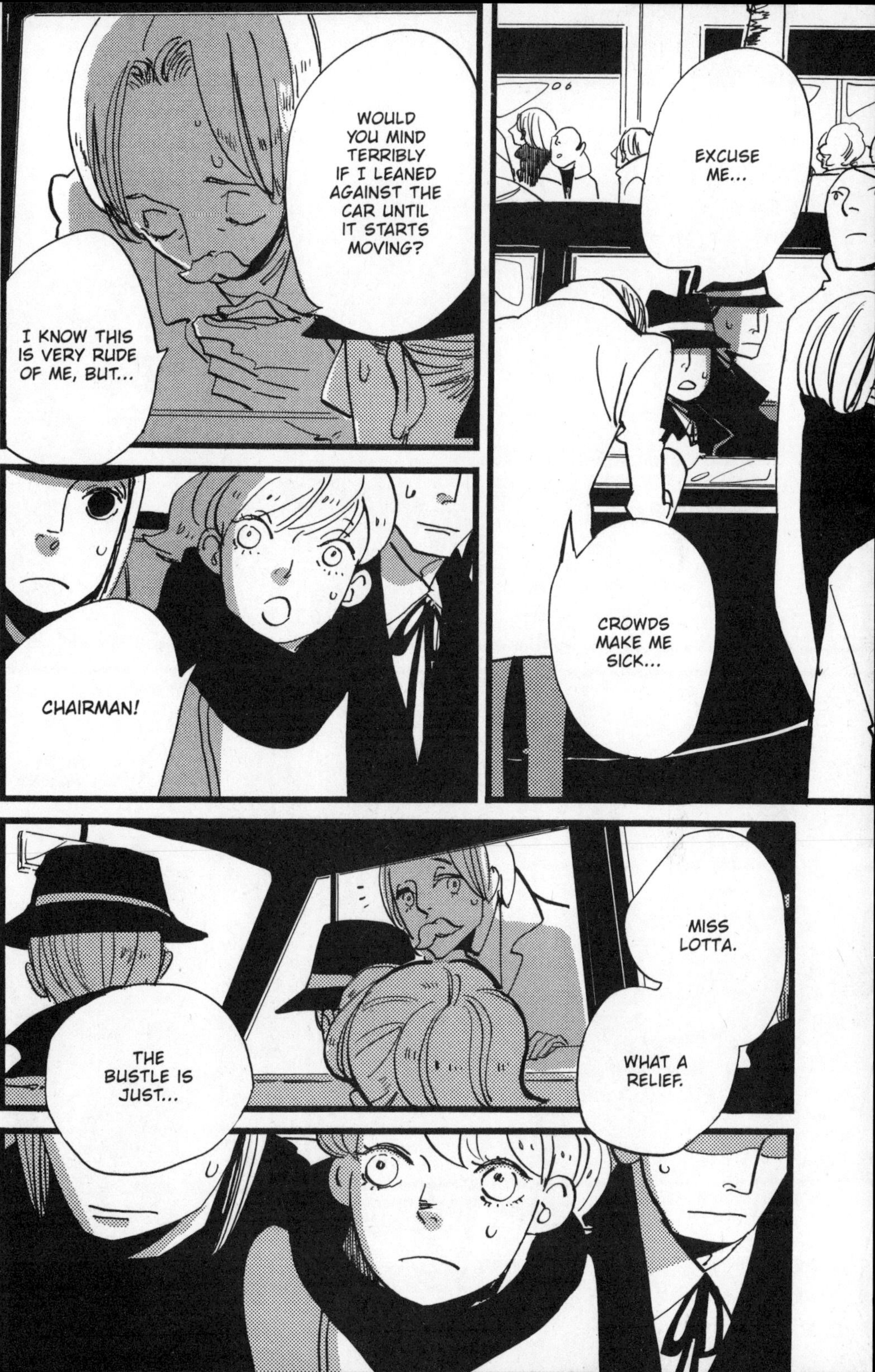
EXCUSE ME...
CROWDS MAKE ME SICK...
WOULD YOU MIND TERRIBLY IF I LEANED AGAINST THE CAR UNTIL IT STARTS MOVING?
I KNOW THIS IS VERY RUDE OF ME, BUT...
CHAIRMAN!
MISS LOTTA.
WHAT A RELIEF.
THE BUSTLE IS JUST...

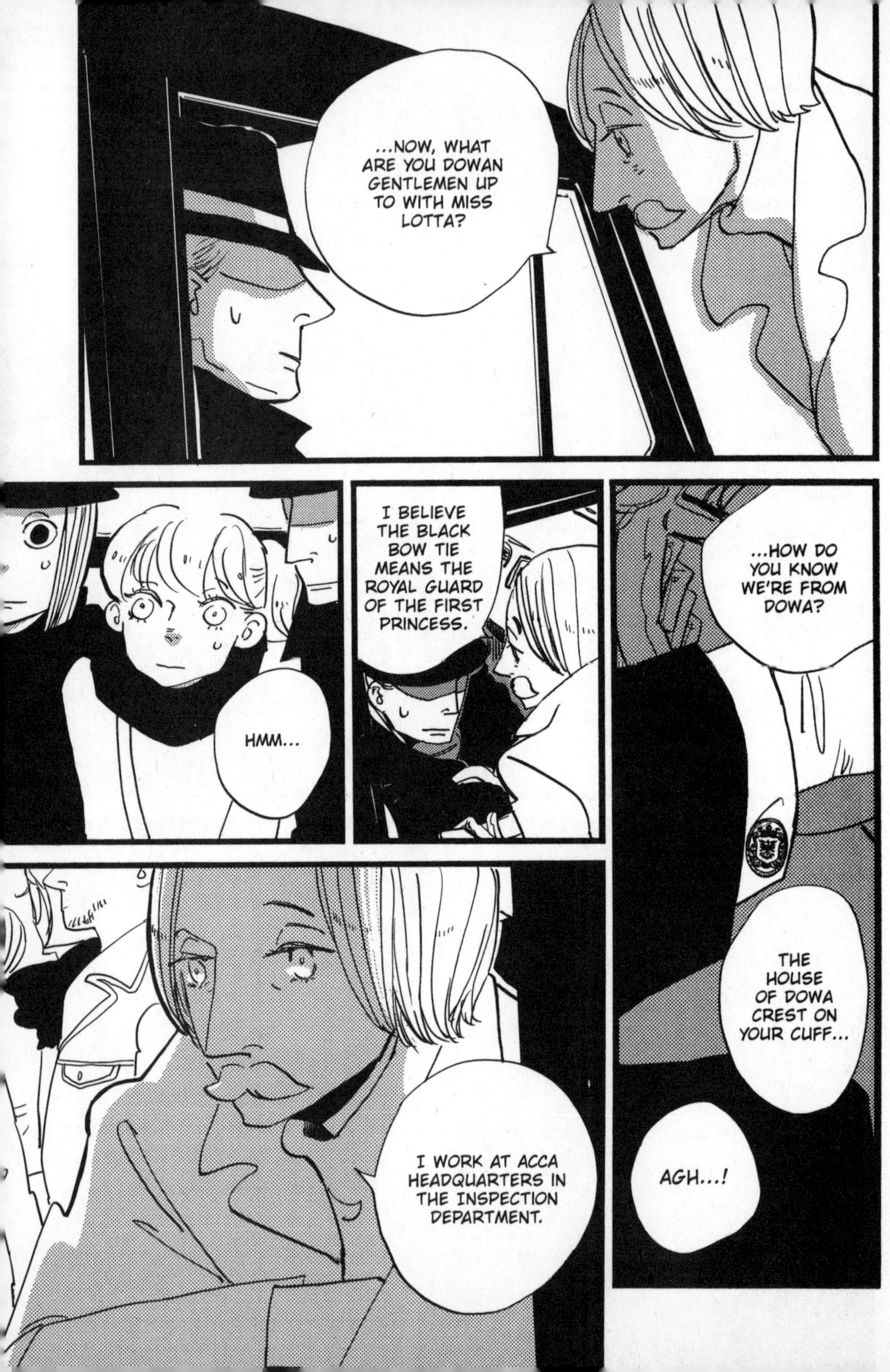
...NOW, WHAT ARE YOU DOWAN GENTLEMEN UP TO WITH MISS LOTTA?
...HOW DO YOU KNOW WE'RE FROM DOWA?
THE HOUSE OF DOWA CREST ON YOUR CUFF...
AGH...!
I BELIEVE THE BLACK BOW TIE MEANS THE ROYAL GUARD OF THE FIRST PRINCESS.
HMM...
I WORK AT ACCA HEADQUARTERS IN THE INSPECTION DEPARTMENT.

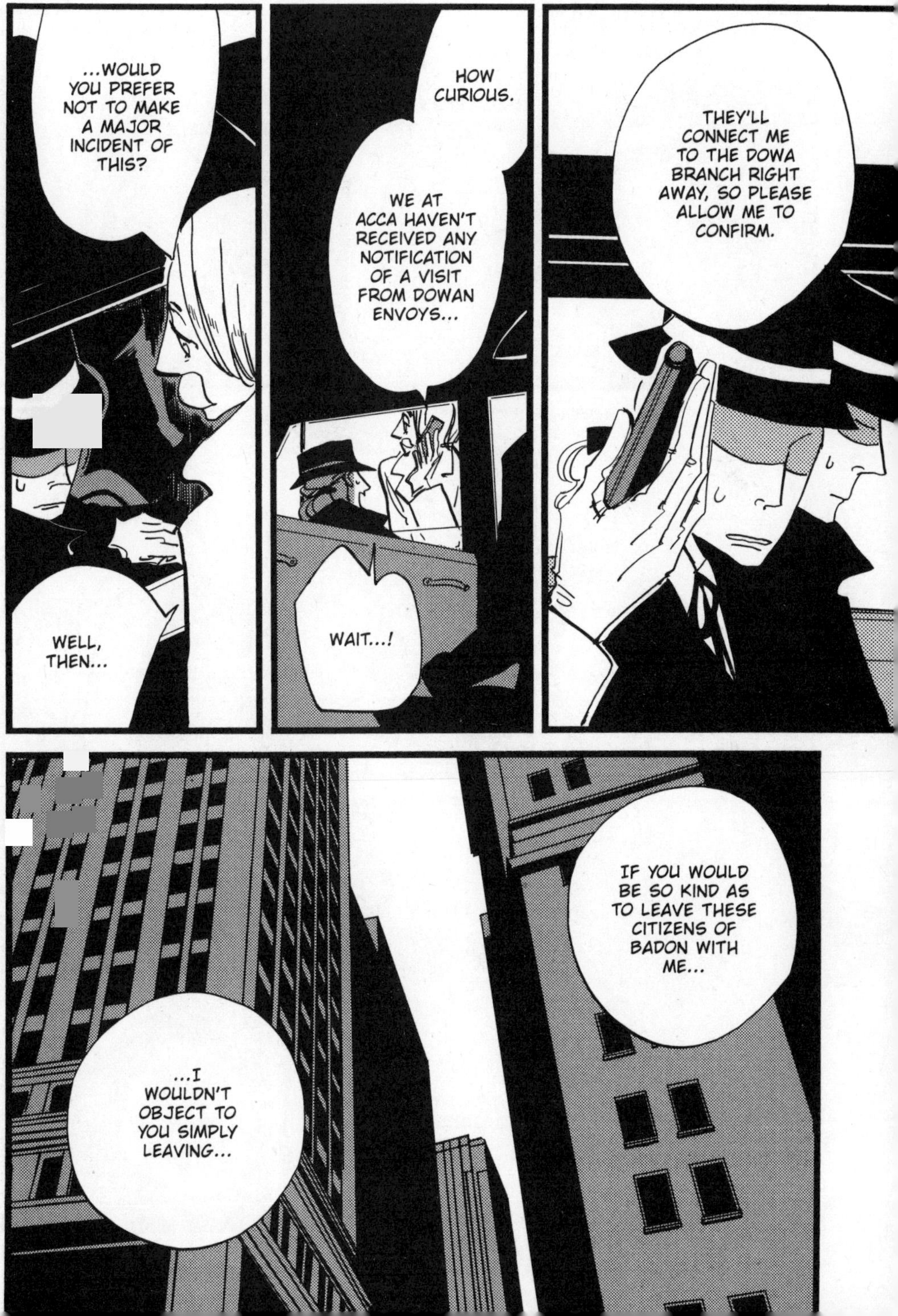
THEY'LL CONNECT ME TO THE DOWA BRANCH RIGHT AWAY, SO PLEASE ALLOW ME TO CONFIRM.
HOW CURIOUS.
WE AT ACCA HAVEN'T RECEIVED ANY NOTIFICATION OF A VISIT FROM DOWAN ENVOYS...
WAIT...!
...WOULD YOU PREFER NOT TO MAKE A MAJOR INCIDENT OF THIS?
WELL, THEN...
IF YOU WOULD BE SO KIND AS TO LEAVE THESE CITIZENS OF BADON WITH ME...
...I WOULDN'T OBJECT TO YOU SIMPLY LEAVING...

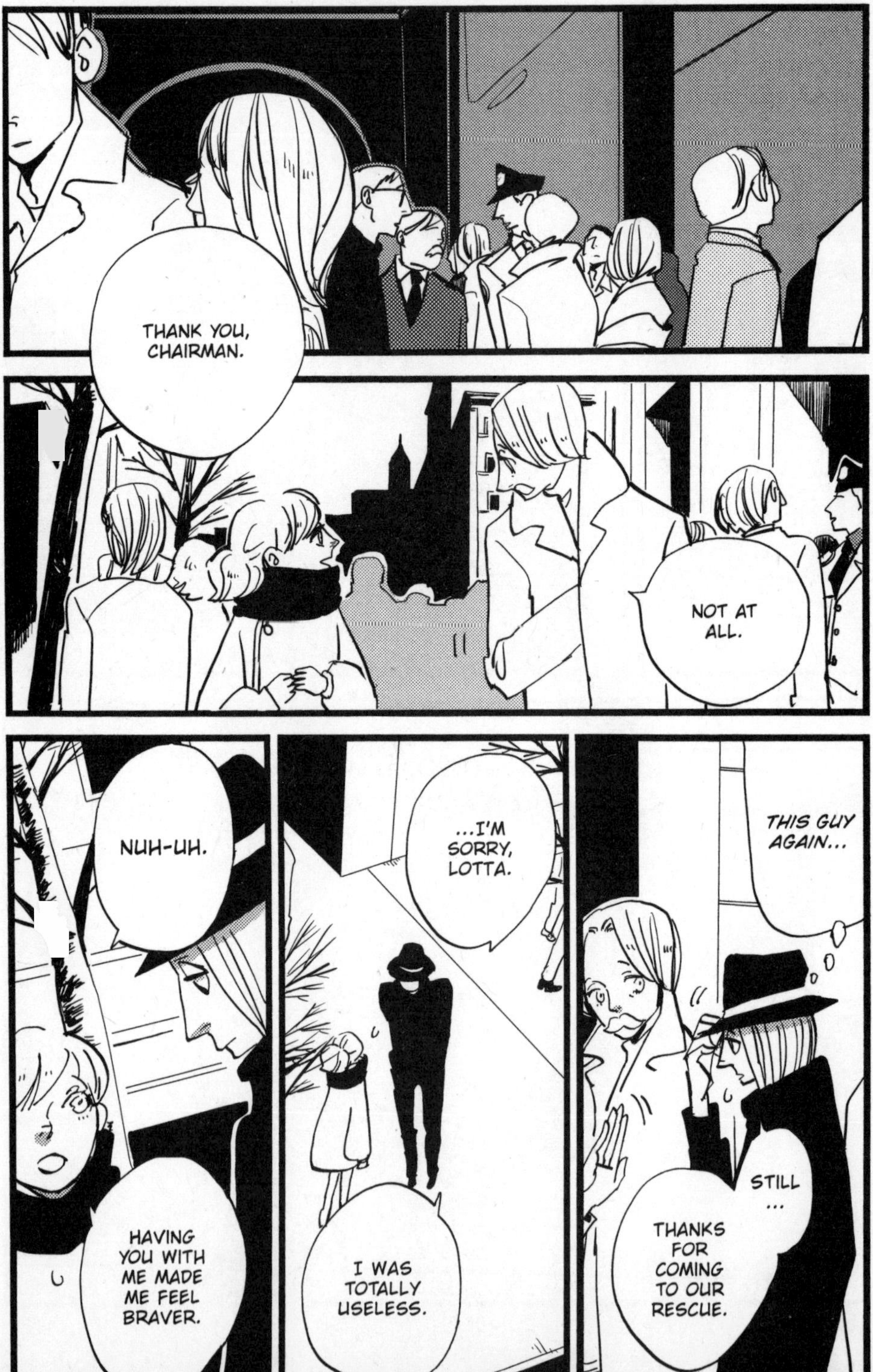
THANK YOU, CHAIRMAN.
NOT AT ALL.
THIS GUY AGAIN...
STILL...
THANKS FOR COMING TO OUR RESCUE.
...I'M SORRY, LOTTA.
I WAS TOTALLY USELESS.
NUH-UH.
HAVING YOU WITH ME MADE ME FEEL BRAVER.

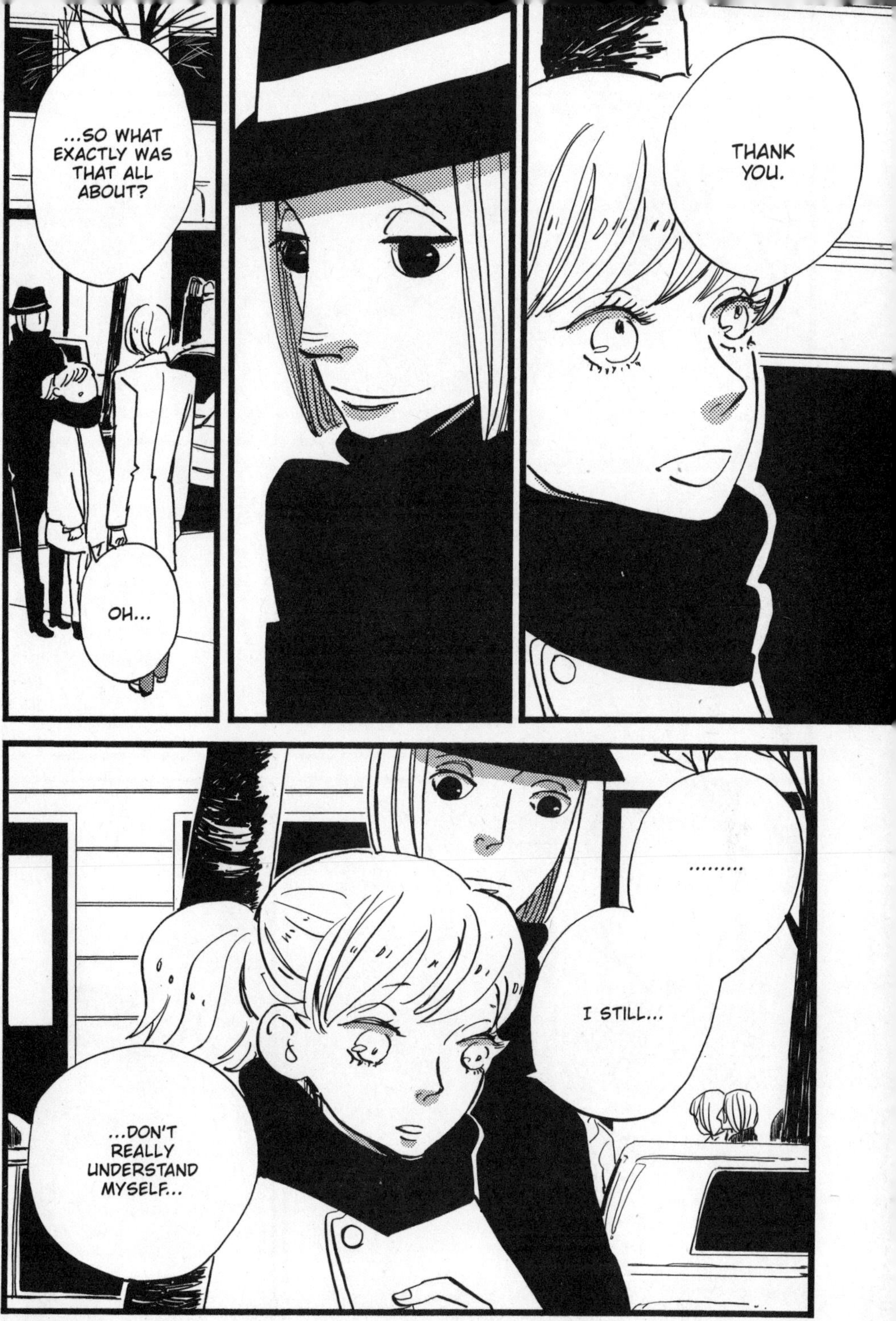
THANK YOU.
...SO WHAT EXACTLY WAS THAT ALL ABOUT?
OH...
....
I STILL...
...DON'T REALLY UNDERSTAND MYSELF...

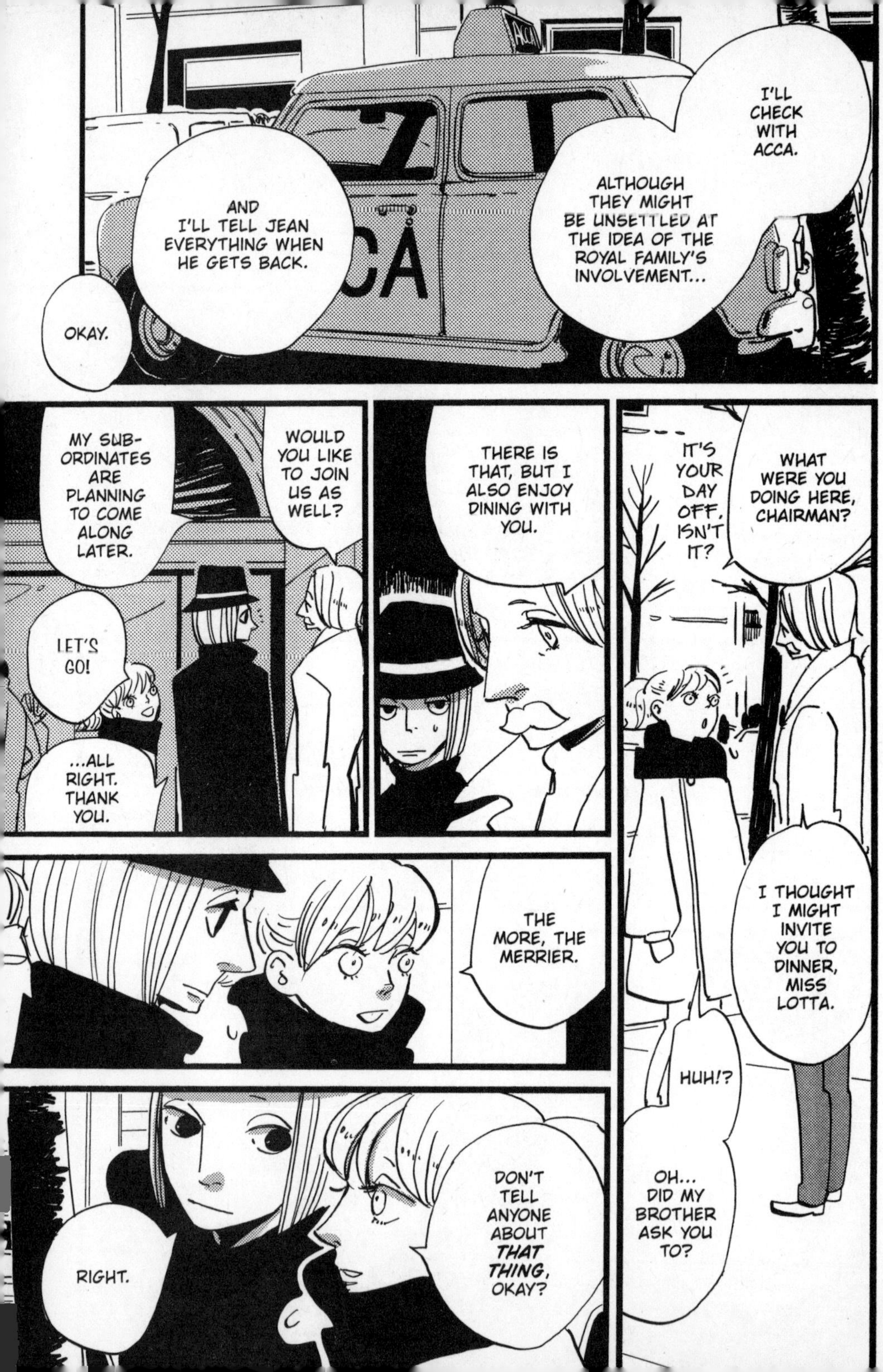
I'LL CHECK WITH ACCA.
ALTHOUGH THEY MIGHT BE UNSETTLED AT THE IDEA OF THE ROYAL FAMILY'S INVOLVEMENT...
AND I'LL TELL JEAN EVERYTHING WHEN HE GETS BACK.
OKAY.
WHAT WERE YOU DOING HERE, CHAIRMAN?
IT'S YOUR DAY OFF, ISN'T IT?
I THOUGHT I MIGHT INVITE YOU TO DINNER, MISS LOTTA.
HUH!?
OH... DID MY BROTHER ASK YOU TO?
THERE IS THAT, BUT I ALSO ENJOY DINING WITH YOU.
WOULD YOU LIKE TO JOIN US AS WELL?
MY SUB-ORDINATES ARE PLANNING TO COME ALONG LATER.
LET'S GO!
...ALL RIGHT. THANK YOU.
THE MORE, THE MERRIER.
DON'T TELL ANYONE ABOUT *THAT THING*, OKAY?
RIGHT.

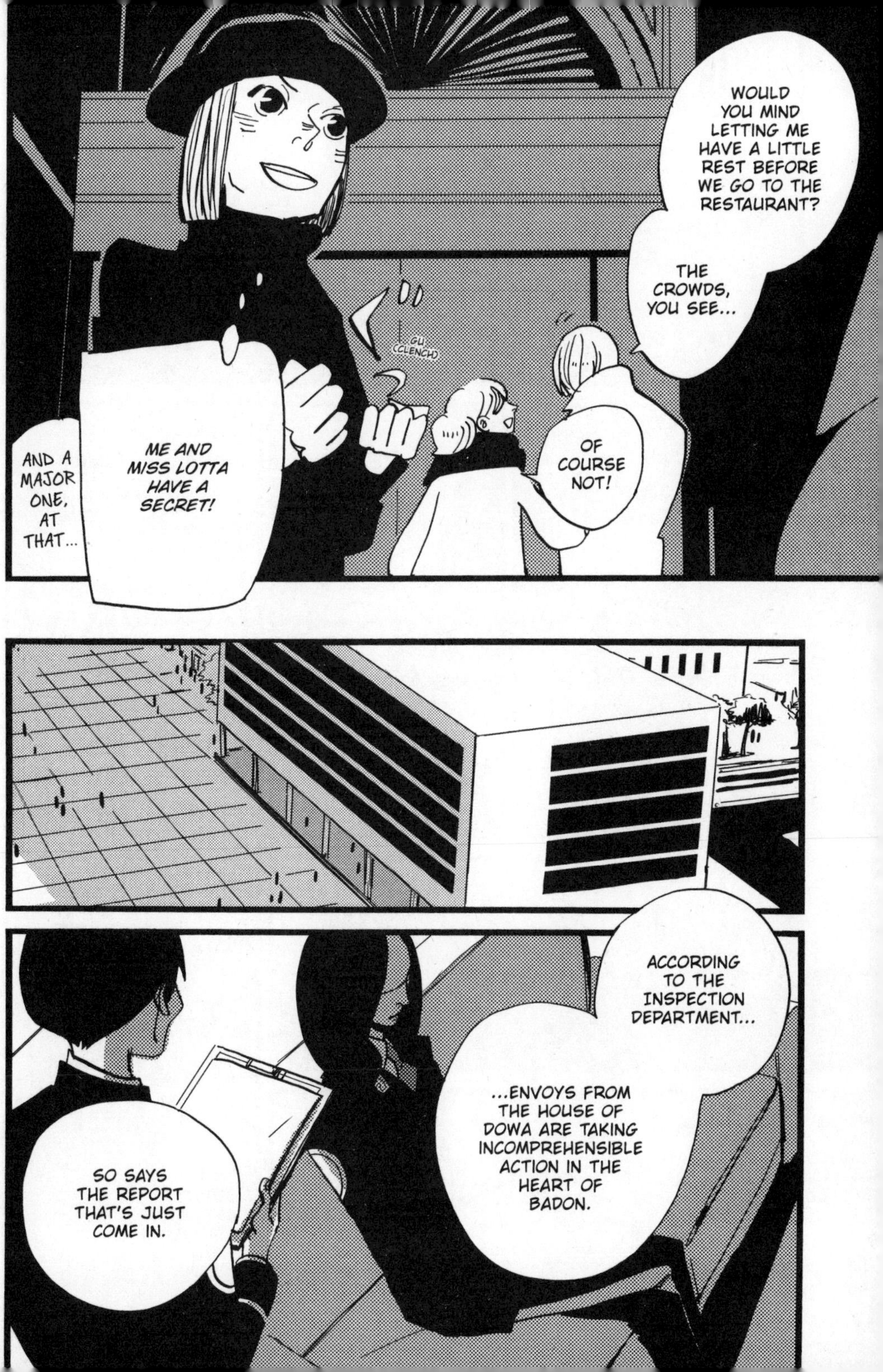
WOULD YOU MIND LETTING ME HAVE A LITTLE REST BEFORE WE GO TO THE RESTAURANT?
THE CROWDS, YOU SEE...
OF COURSE NOT!
GU (CLENCH)
ME AND MISS LOTTA HAVE A SECRET!
AND A MAJOR ONE, AT THAT...
ACCORDING TO THE INSPECTION DEPARTMENT...
...ENVOYS FROM THE HOUSE OF DOWA ARE TAKING INCOMPREHENSIBLE ACTION IN THE HEART OF BADON.
SO SAYS THE REPORT THAT'S JUST COME IN.

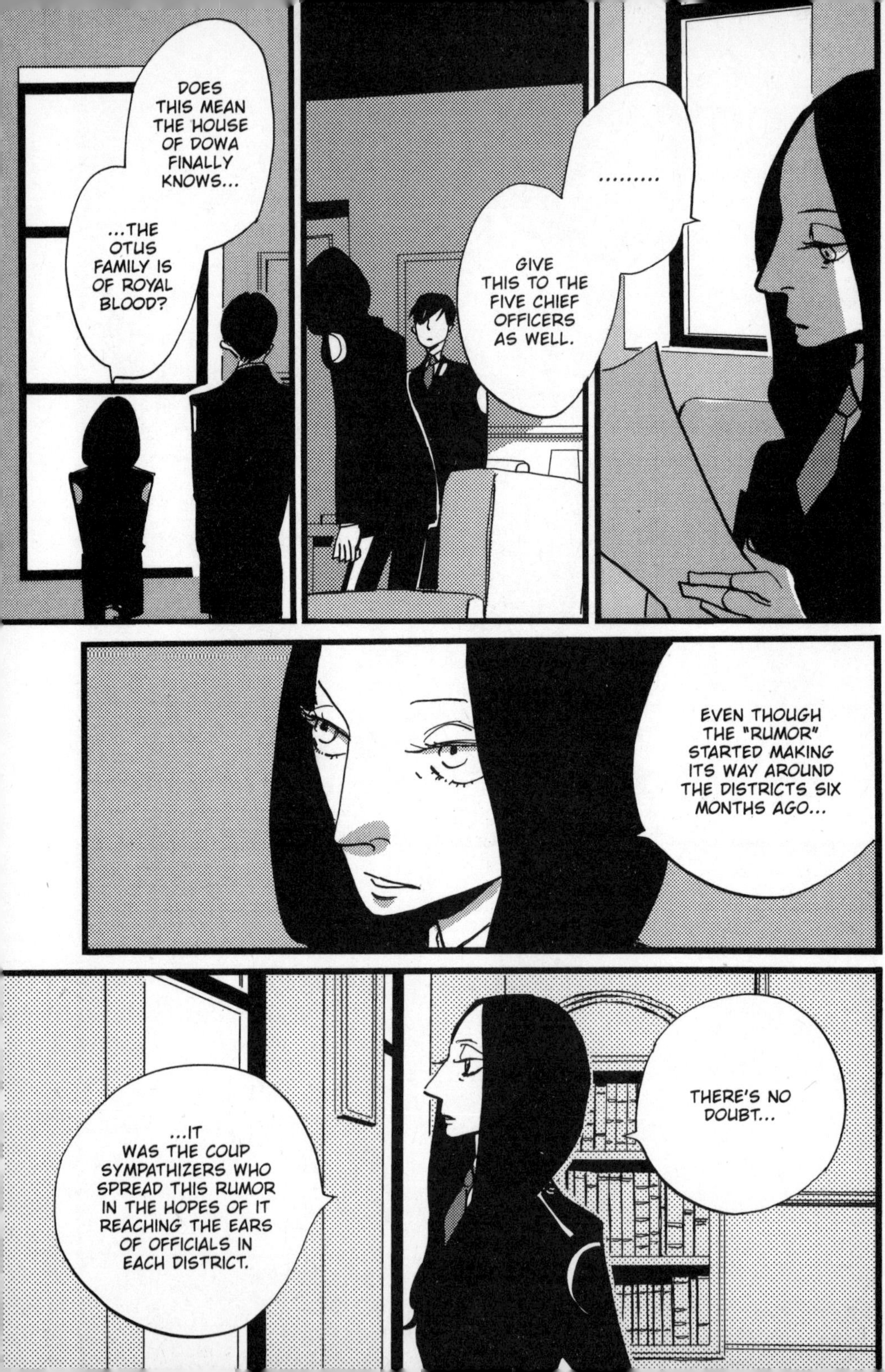
....
GIVE THIS TO THE FIVE CHIEF OFFICERS AS WELL.
DOES THIS MEAN THE HOUSE OF DOWA FINALLY KNOWS...
...THE OTUS FAMILY IS OF ROYAL BLOOD?
EVEN THOUGH THE "RUMOR" STARTED MAKING ITS WAY AROUND THE DISTRICTS SIX MONTHS AGO...
THERE'S NO DOUBT...
...IT WAS THE COUP SYMPATHIZERS WHO SPREAD THIS RUMOR IN THE HOPES OF IT REACHING THE EARS OF OFFICIALS IN EACH DISTRICT.

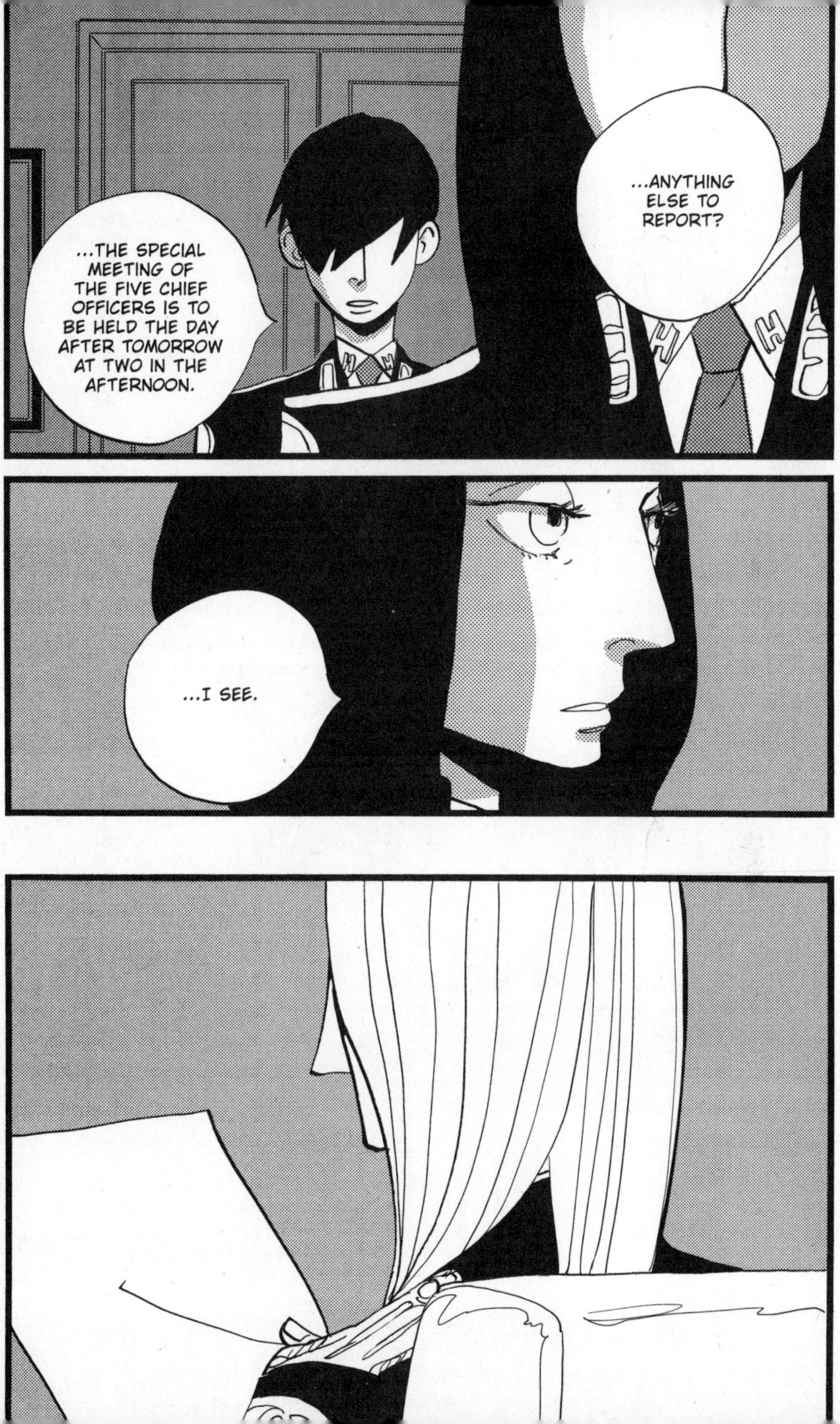
...ANYTHING ELSE TO REPORT?
...THE SPECIAL MEETING OF THE FIVE CHIEF OFFICERS IS TO BE HELD THE DAY AFTER TOMORROW AT TWO IN THE AFTERNOON.
...I SEE.

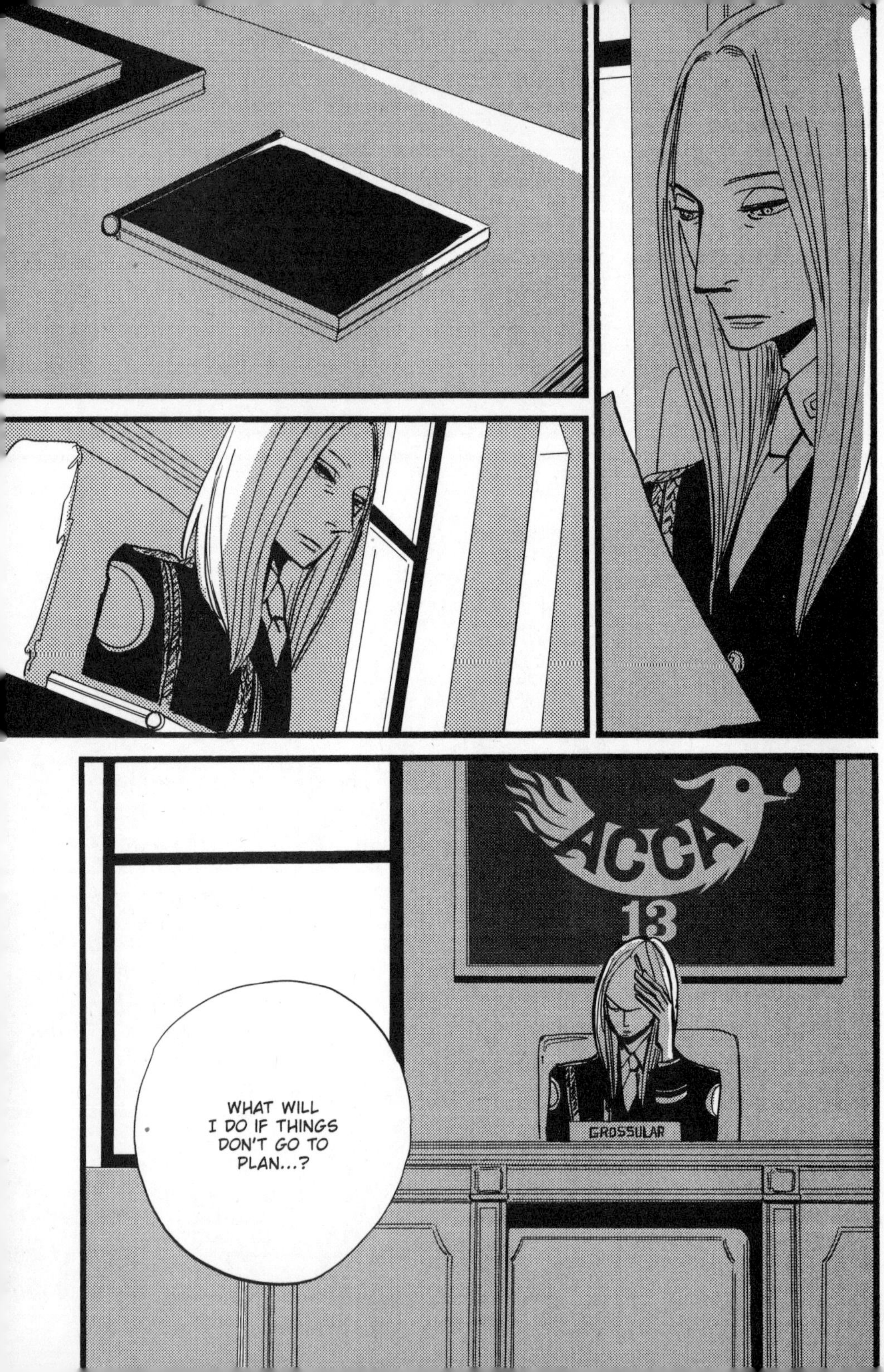
ACCA
13
GROSSULAR
WHAT WILL I DO IF THINGS DON'T GO TO PLAN...?

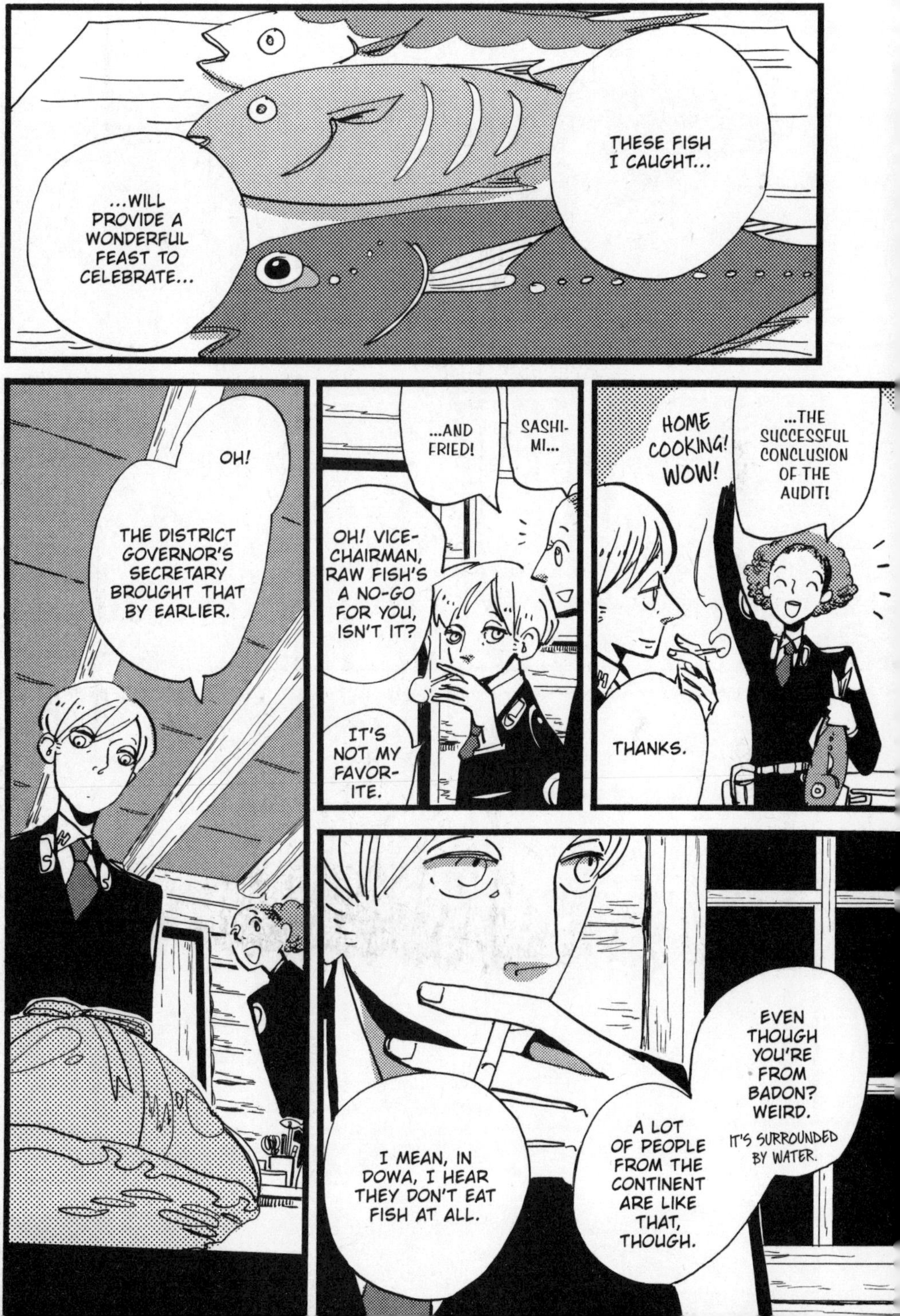
THESE FISH I CAUGHT...
...WILL PROVIDE A WONDERFUL FEAST TO CELEBRATE...
...THE SUCCESSFUL CONCLUSION OF THE AUDIT!
HOME COOKING! WOW!
THANKS.
SASHI-MI...
...AND FRIED!
OH! VICE-CHAIRMAN, RAW FISH'S A NO-GO FOR YOU, ISN'T IT?
IT'S NOT MY FAVOR-ITE.
EVEN THOUGH YOU'RE FROM BADON? WEIRD.
IT'S SURROUNDED BY WATER.
A LOT OF PEOPLE FROM THE CONTINENT ARE LIKE THAT, THOUGH.
I MEAN, IN DOWA, I HEAR THEY DON'T EAT FISH AT ALL.
OH!
THE DISTRICT GOVERNOR'S SECRETARY BROUGHT THAT BY EARLIER.

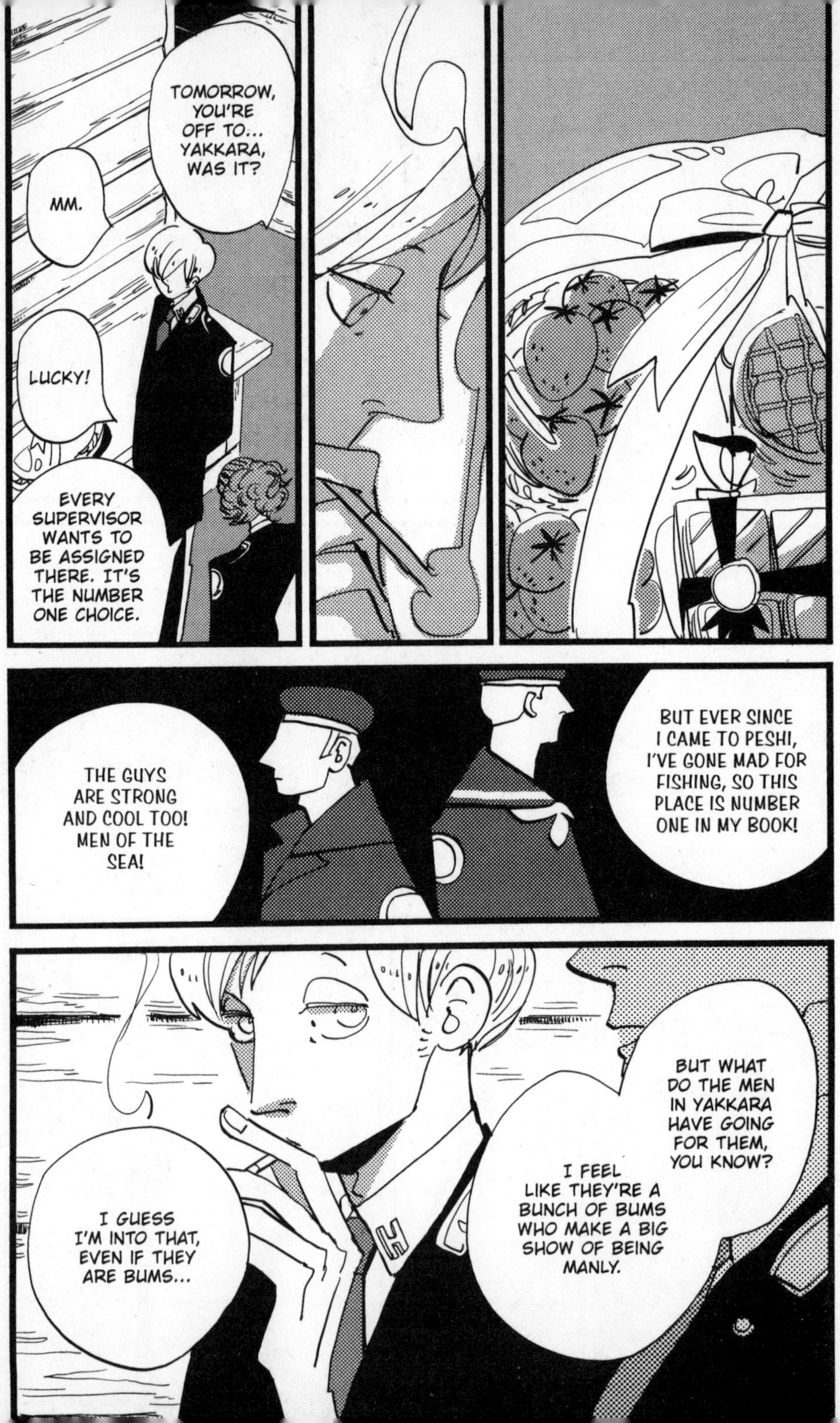
TOMORROW, YOU'RE OFF TO... YAKKARA, WAS IT?
MM.
LUCKY!
EVERY SUPERVISOR WANTS TO BE ASSIGNED THERE. IT'S THE NUMBER ONE CHOICE.
BUT EVER SINCE I CAME TO PESHI, I'VE GONE MAD FOR FISHING, SO THIS PLACE IS NUMBER ONE IN MY BOOK!
THE GUYS ARE STRONG AND COOL TOO! MEN OF THE SEA!
BUT WHAT DO THE MEN IN YAKKARA HAVE GOING FOR THEM, YOU KNOW?
I FEEL LIKE THEY'RE A BUNCH OF BUMS WHO MAKE A BIG SHOW OF BEING MANLY.
I GUESS I'M INTO THAT, EVEN IF THEY ARE BUMS...

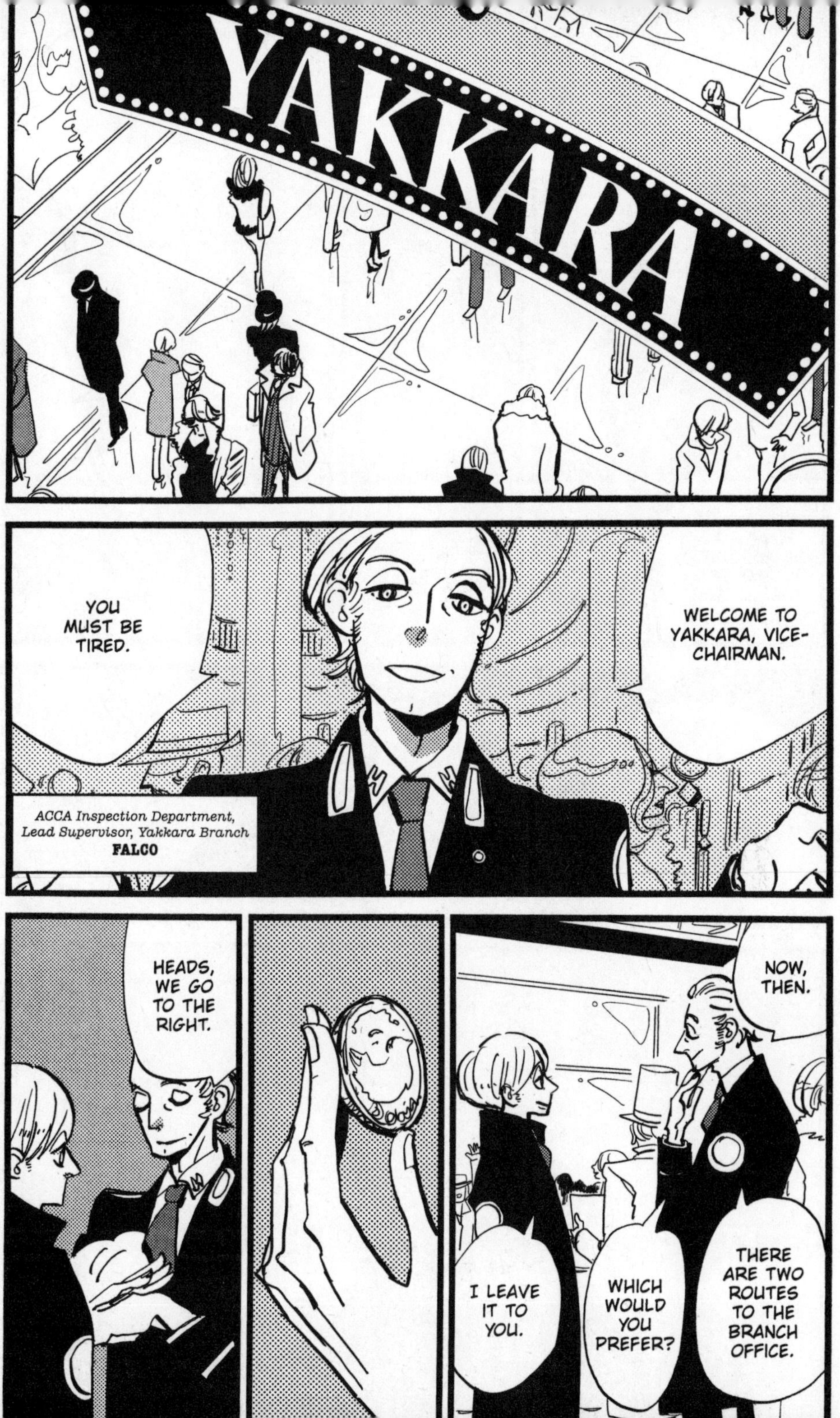
YAKKARA
WELCOME TO YAKKARA, VICE-CHAIRMAN.
YOU MUST BE TIRED.
ACCA Inspection Department, Lead Supervisor, Yakkara Branch FALCO
NOW, THEN.
THERE ARE TWO ROUTES TO THE BRANCH OFFICE.
WHICH WOULD YOU PREFER?
I LEAVE IT TO YOU.
HEADS, WE GO TO THE RIGHT.

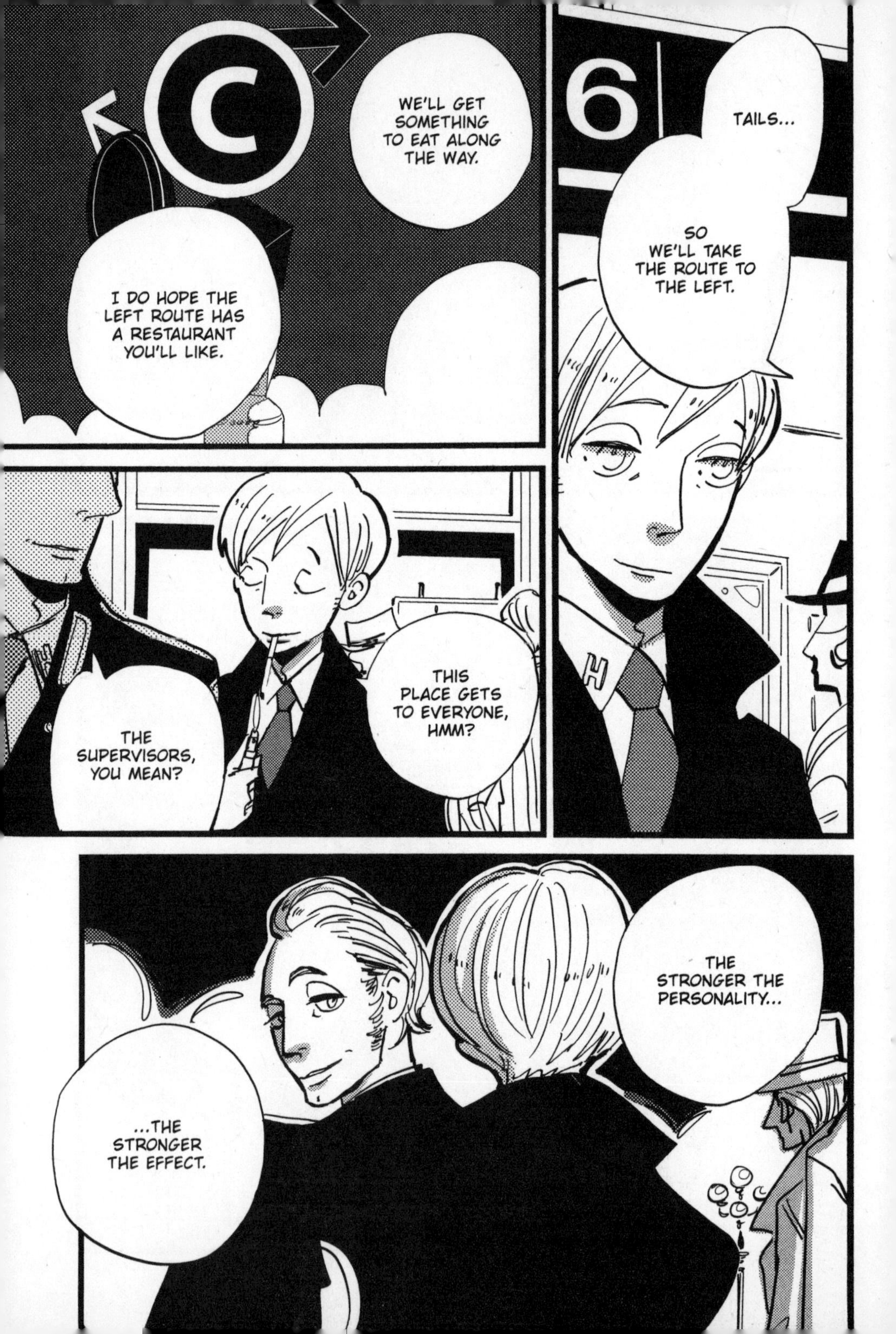
TAILS...
SO WE'LL TAKE THE ROUTE TO THE LEFT.
WE'LL GET SOMETHING TO EAT ALONG THE WAY.
I DO HOPE THE LEFT ROUTE HAS A RESTAURANT YOU'LL LIKE.
THIS PLACE GETS TO EVERYONE, HMM?
THE SUPERVISORS, YOU MEAN?
THE STRONGER THE PERSONALITY...
...THE STRONGER THE EFFECT.

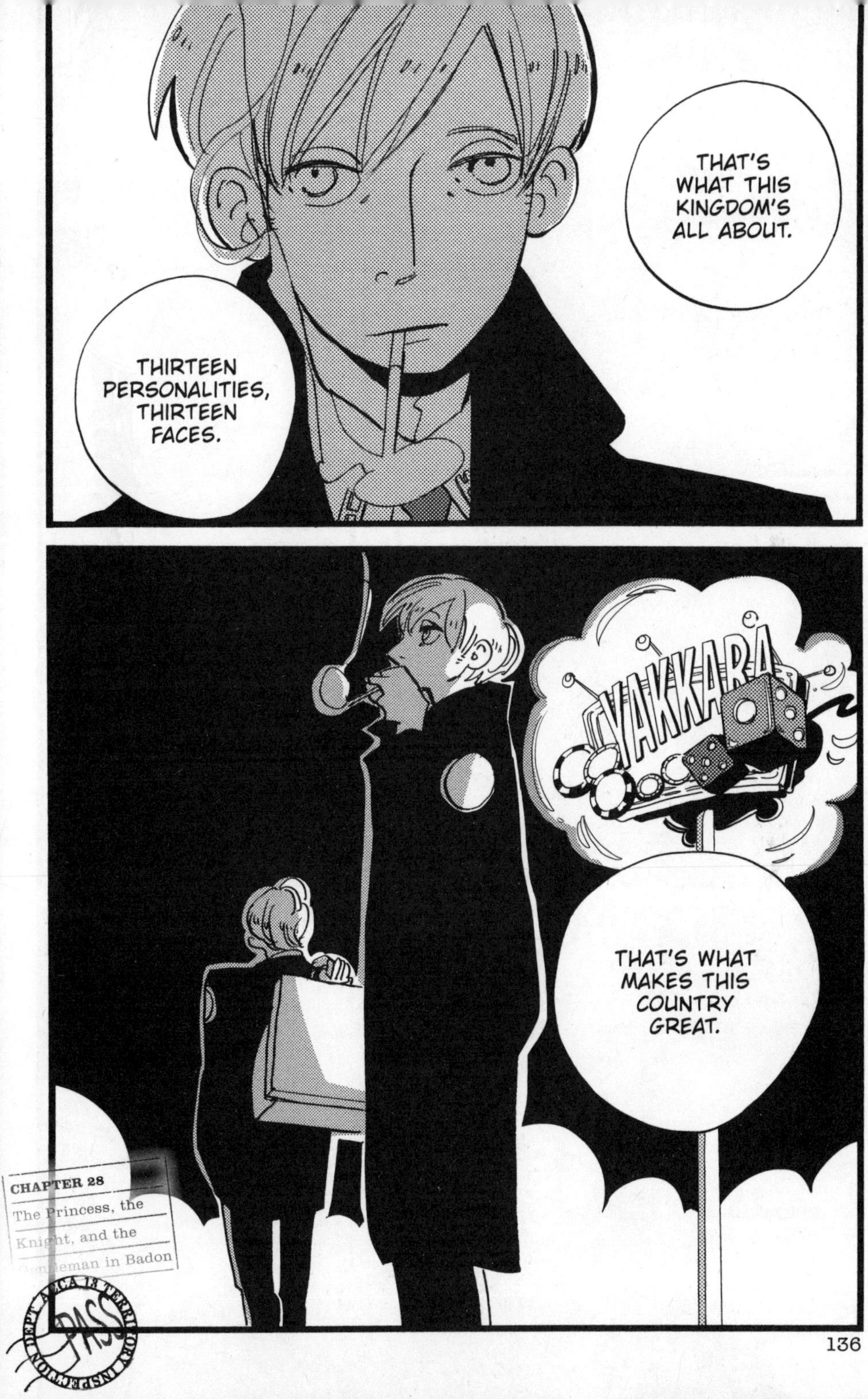
THAT'S WHAT THIS KINGDOM'S ALL ABOUT.
THIRTEEN PERSONALITIES, THIRTEEN FACES.
YAKKARA
THAT'S WHAT MAKES THIS COUNTRY GREAT.
CHAPTER 28
The Princess, the Knight, and the Gentleman in Badon
DEPT. ALCA 13 TERRITORY INSPECTION
PASS

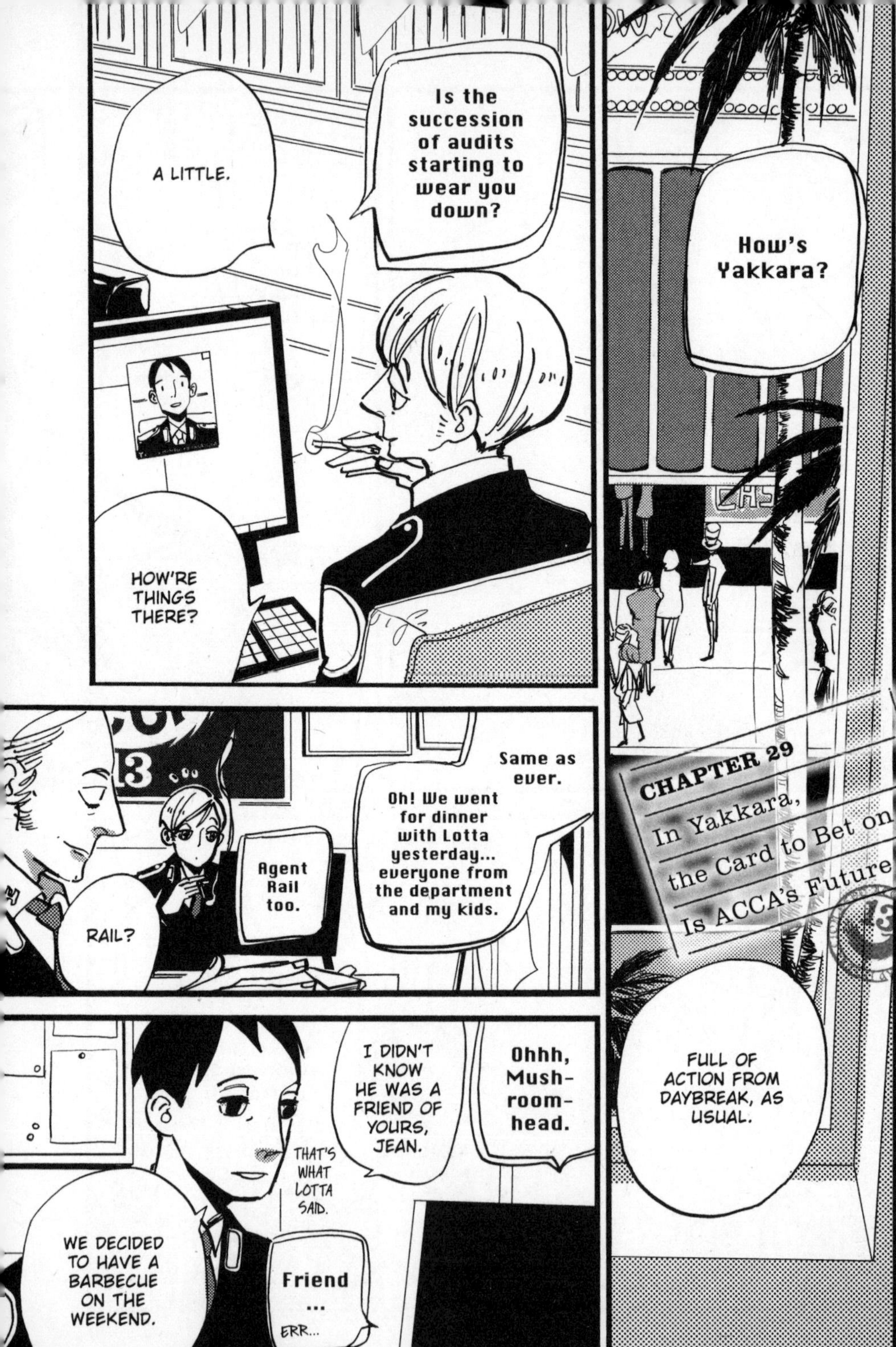

How's Yakkara?
CHAPTER 29
In Yakkara, the Card to Bet on Is ACCA's Future
FULL OF ACTION FROM DAYBREAK, AS USUAL.
Is the succession of audits starting to wear you down?
A LITTLE.
HOW'RE THINGS THERE?
Same as ever.
Oh! We went for dinner with Lotta yesterday... everyone from the department and my kids.
Agent Rail too.
RAIL?
Ohhh, Mush-room-head.
I DIDN'T KNOW HE WAS A FRIEND OF YOURS, JEAN.
THAT'S WHAT LOTTA SAID.
Friend ...
ERR...
WE DECIDED TO HAVE A BARBECUE ON THE WEEKEND.

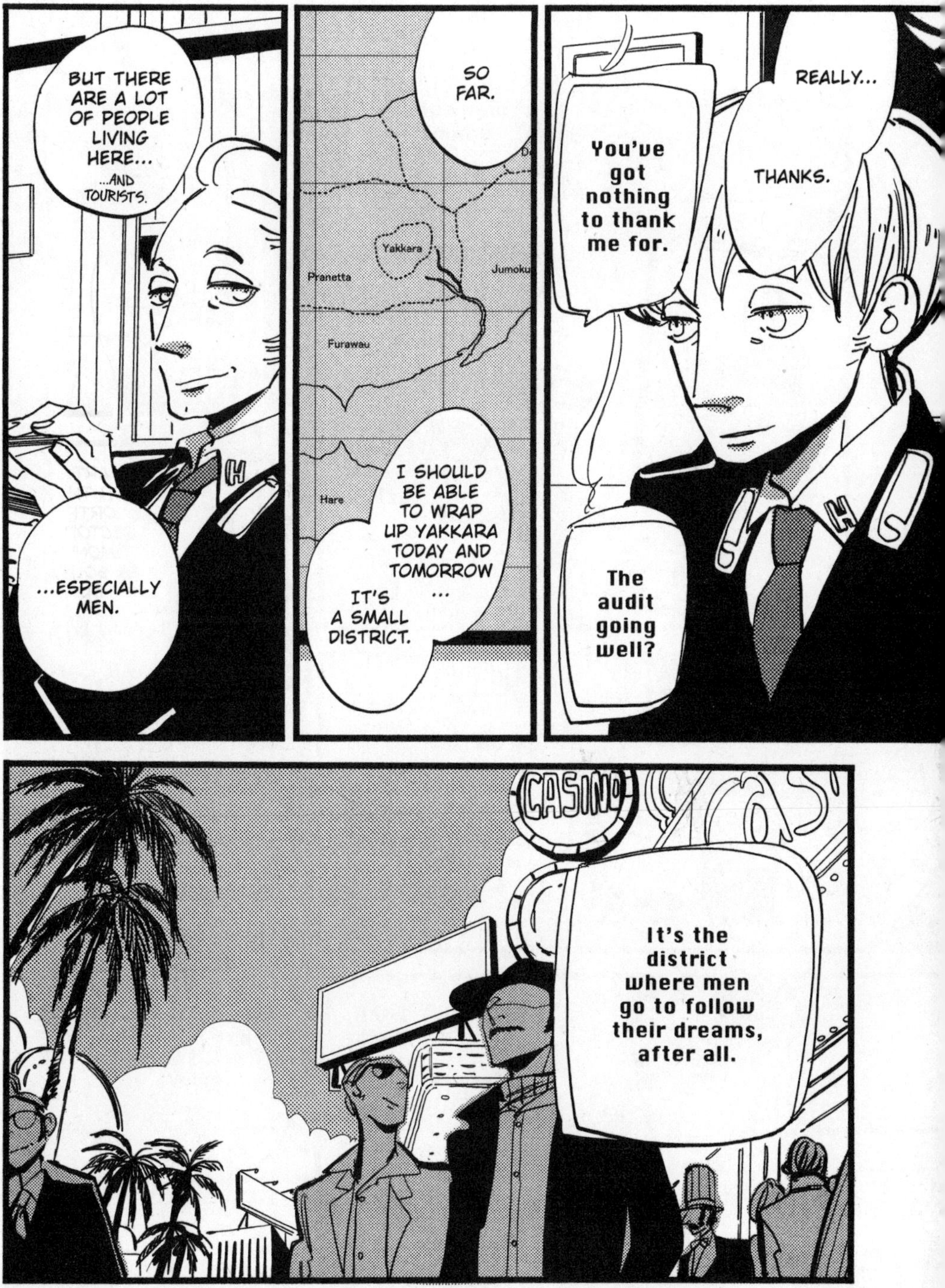
REALLY...
THANKS.
You've got nothing to thank me for.
The audit going well?
SO FAR.
Yakkara
Pranetta
Jumoku
Furawau
Hare
I SHOULD BE ABLE TO WRAP UP YAKKARA TODAY AND TOMORROW ...
IT'S A SMALL DISTRICT.
BUT THERE ARE A LOT OF PEOPLE LIVING HERE...
...AND TOURISTS.
...ESPECIALLY MEN.
CASINO
It's the district where men go to follow their dreams, after all.

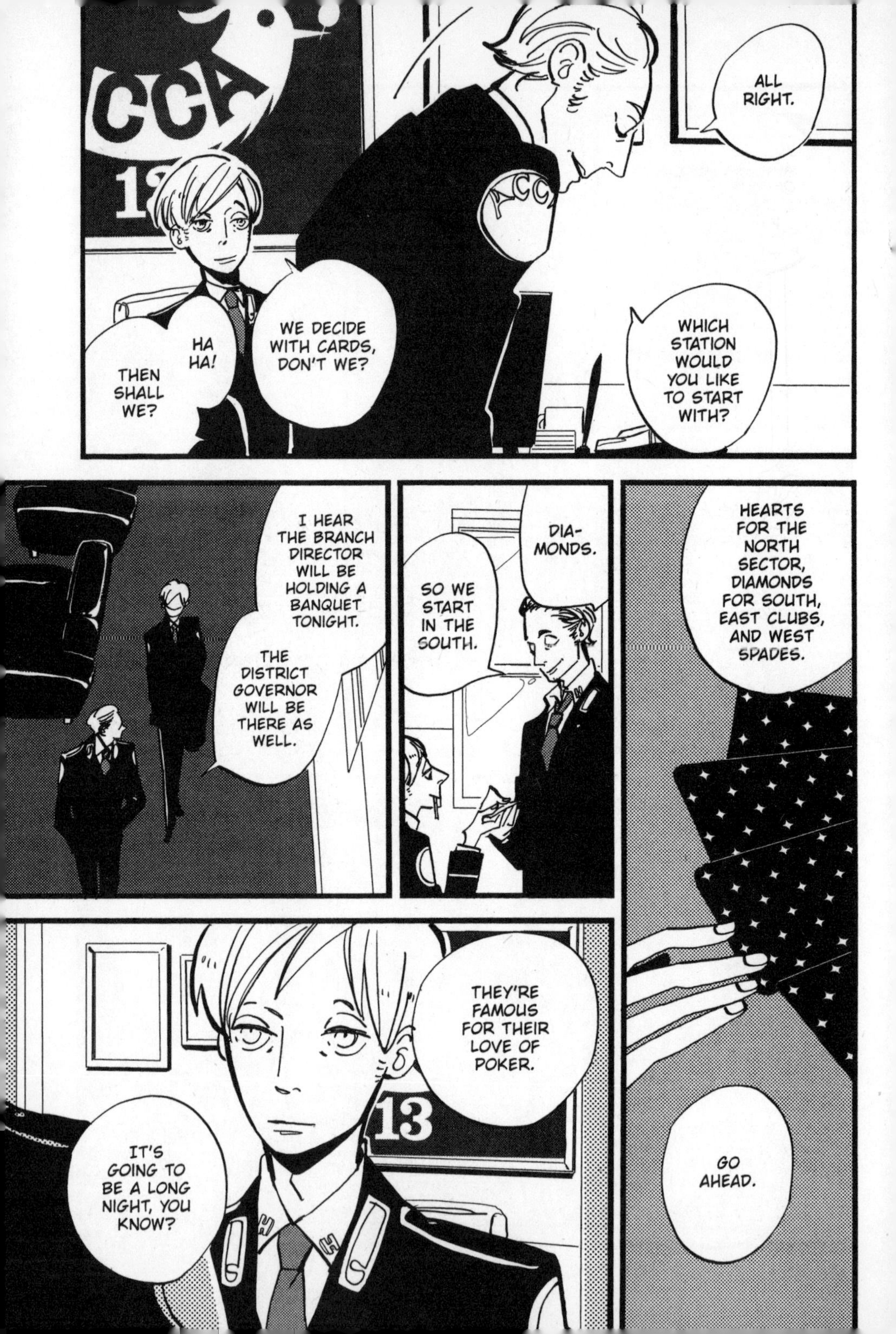

ALL RIGHT.
WHICH STATION WOULD YOU LIKE TO START WITH?
WE DECIDE WITH CARDS, DON'T WE?
HA HA!
THEN SHALL WE?
HEARTS FOR THE NORTH SECTOR, DIAMONDS FOR SOUTH, EAST CLUBS, AND WEST SPADES.
GO AHEAD.
DIA-MONDS.
SO WE START IN THE SOUTH.
I HEAR THE BRANCH DIRECTOR WILL BE HOLDING A BANQUET TONIGHT.
THE DISTRICT GOVERNOR WILL BE THERE AS WELL.
THEY'RE FAMOUS FOR THEIR LOVE OF POKER.
IT'S GOING TO BE A LONG NIGHT, YOU KNOW?

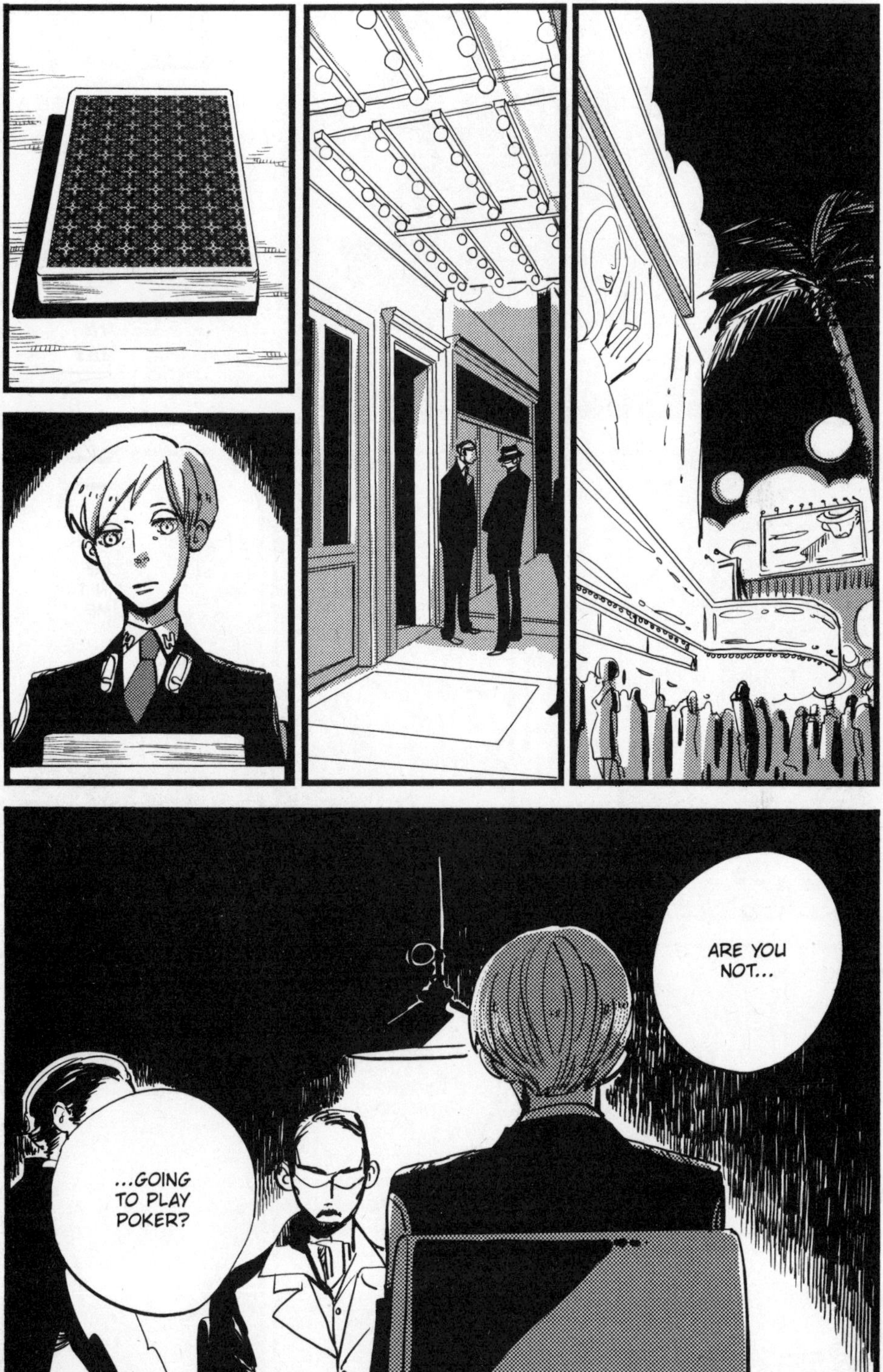
ARE YOU NOT...
...GOING TO PLAY POKER?

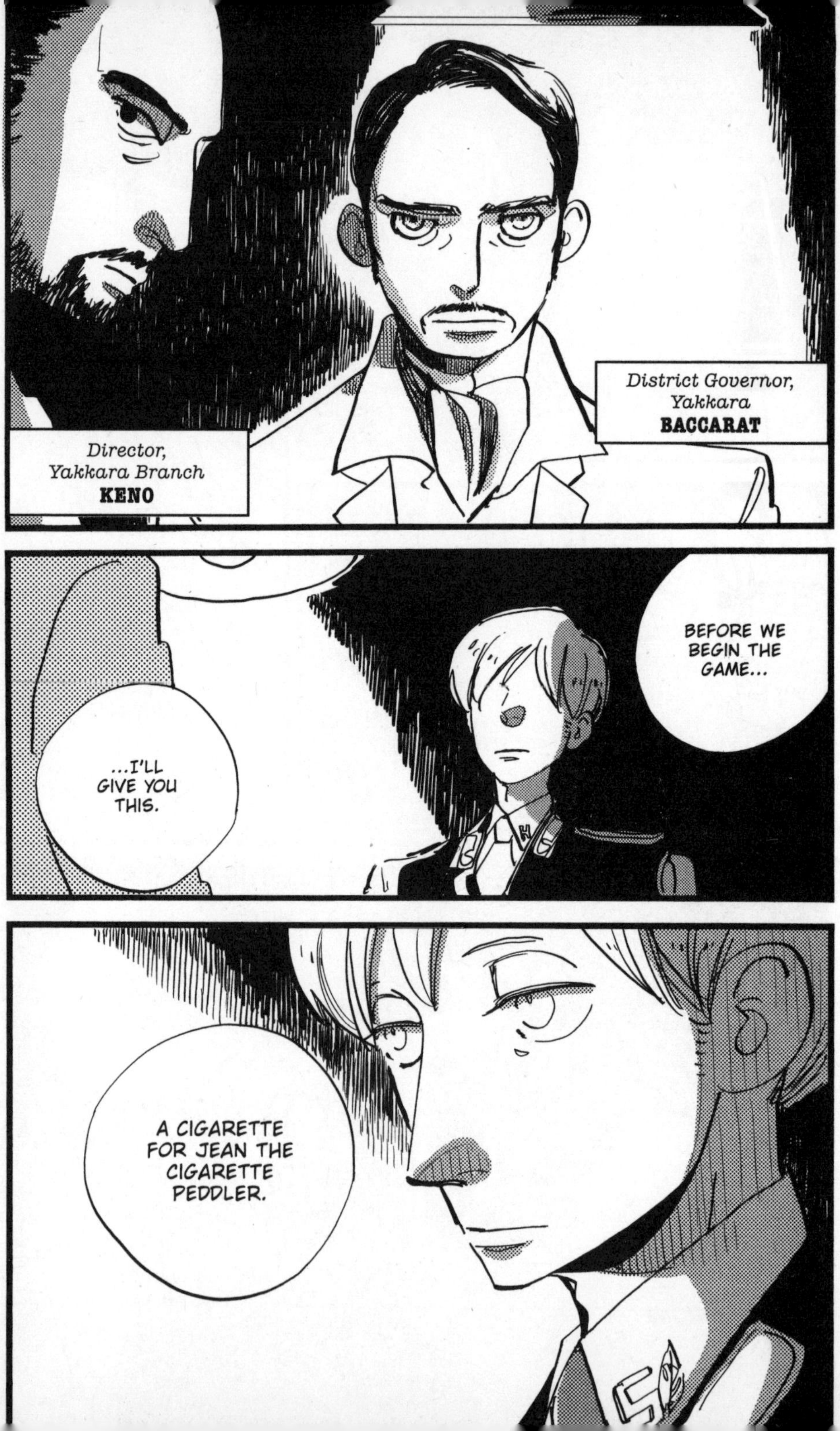
District Governor, Yakkara
BACCARAT
Director, Yakkara Branch
KENO
BEFORE WE BEGIN THE GAME...
...I'LL GIVE YOU THIS.
A CIGARETTE FOR JEAN THE CIGARETTE PEDDLER.

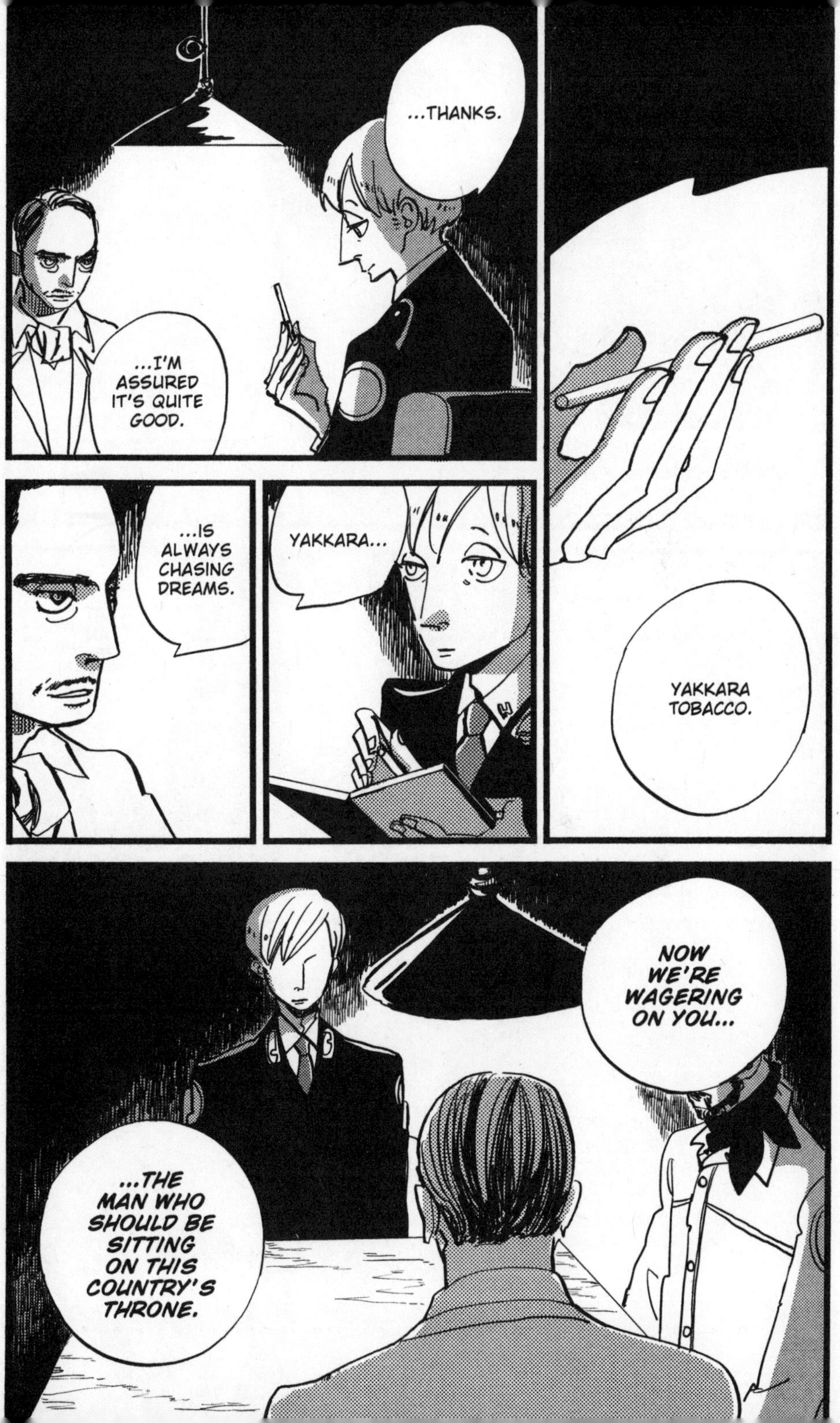
YAKKARA TOBACCO.
...THANKS.
...I'M ASSURED IT'S QUITE GOOD.
YAKKARA...
...IS ALWAYS CHASING DREAMS.
NOW WE'RE WAGERING ON YOU...
...THE MAN WHO SHOULD BE SITTING ON THIS COUNTRY'S THRONE.

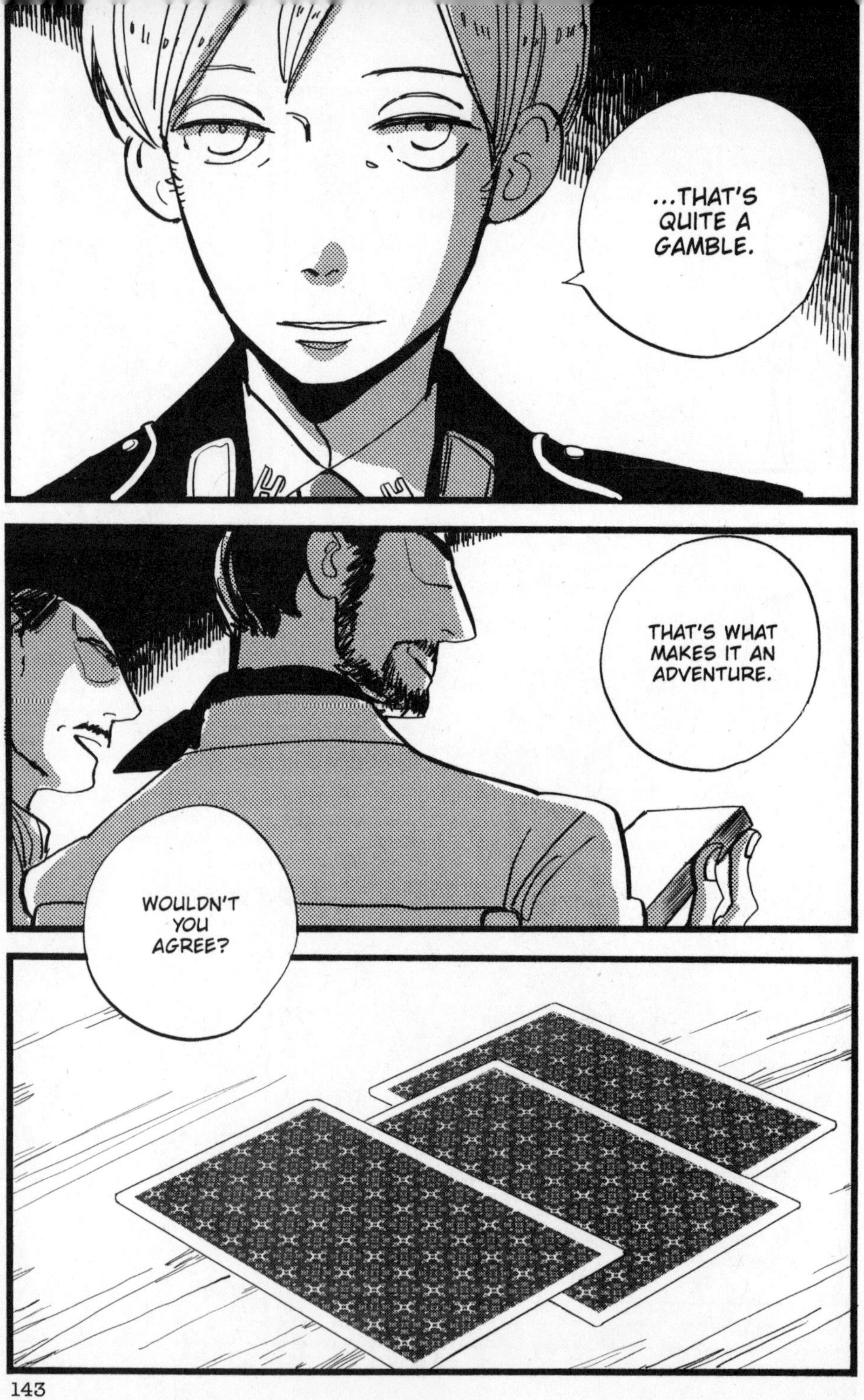
...THAT'S QUITE A GAMBLE.
THAT'S WHAT MAKES IT AN ADVENTURE.
WOULDN'T YOU AGREE?

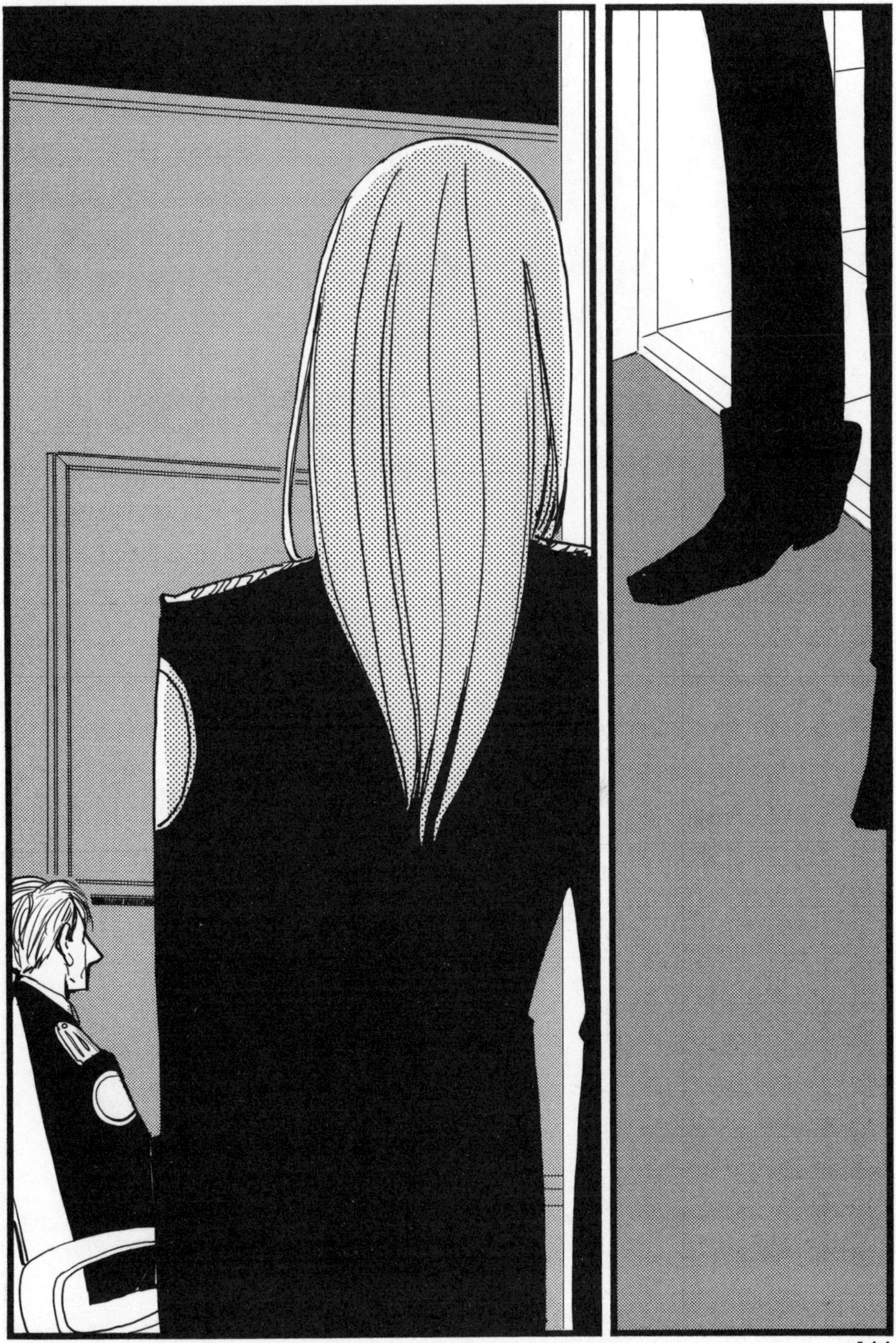

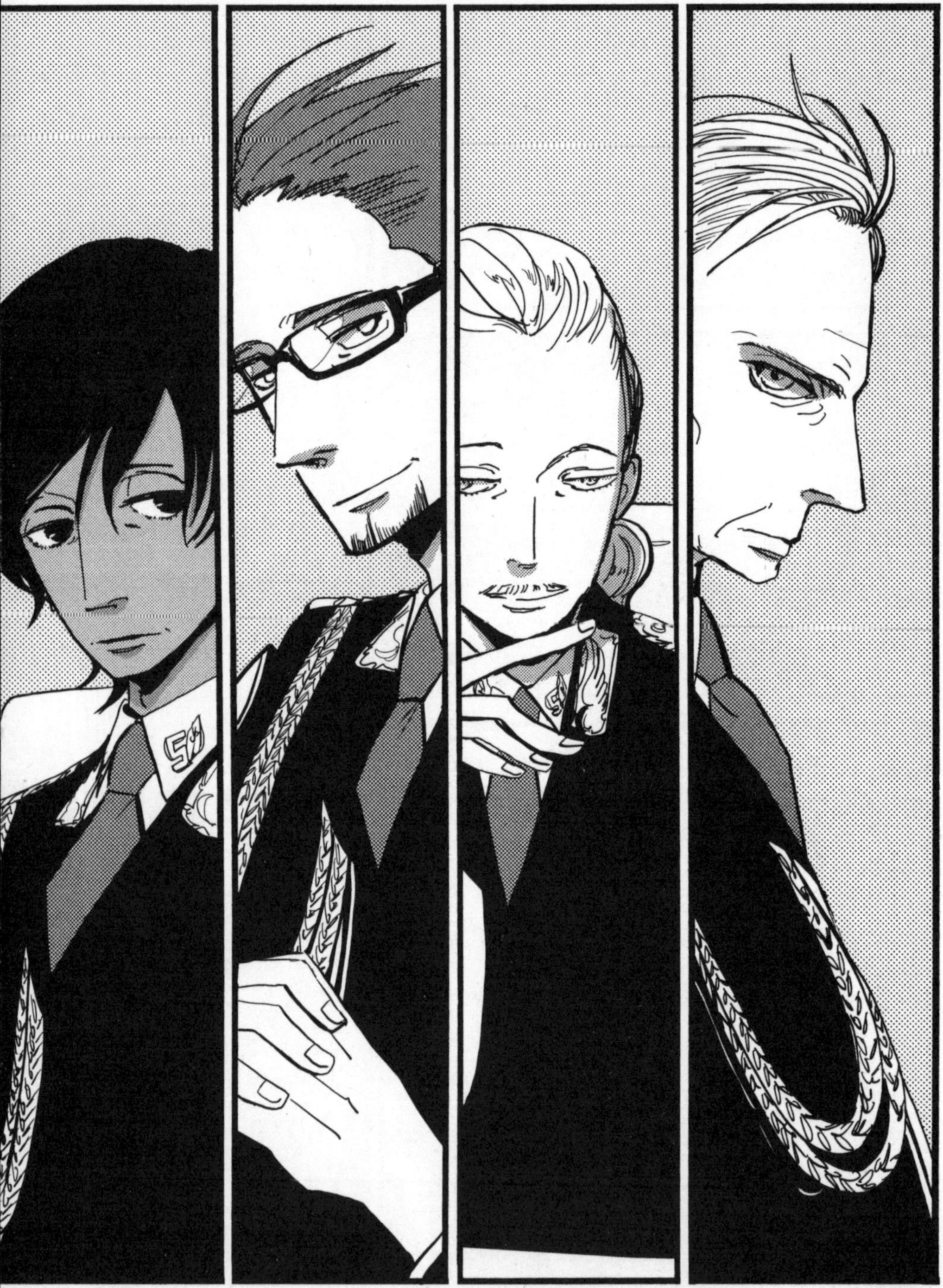

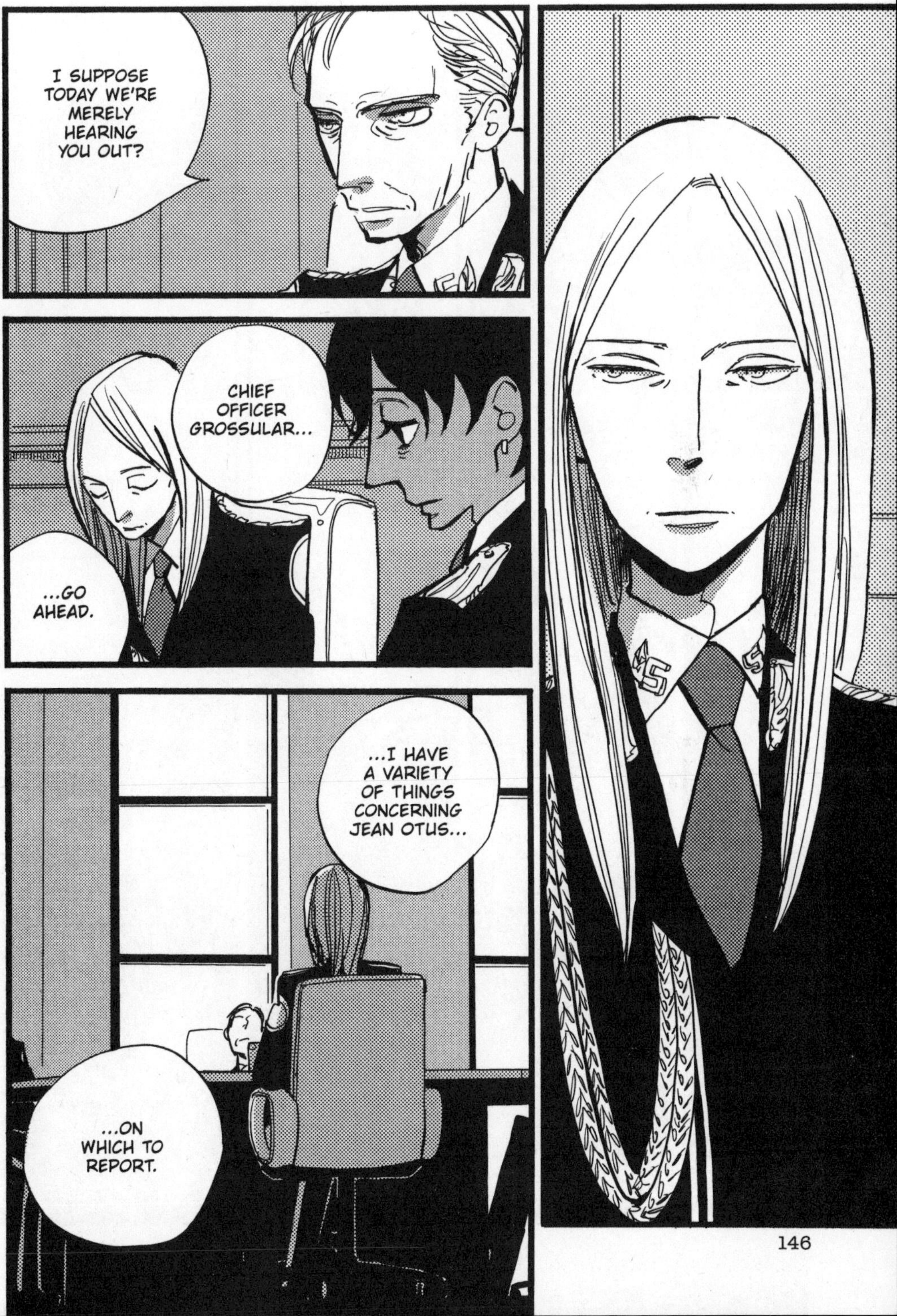
I SUPPOSE TODAY WE'RE MERELY HEARING YOU OUT?
CHIEF OFFICER GROSSULAR...
...GO AHEAD.
...I HAVE A VARIETY OF THINGS CONCERNING JEAN OTUS...
...ON WHICH TO REPORT.

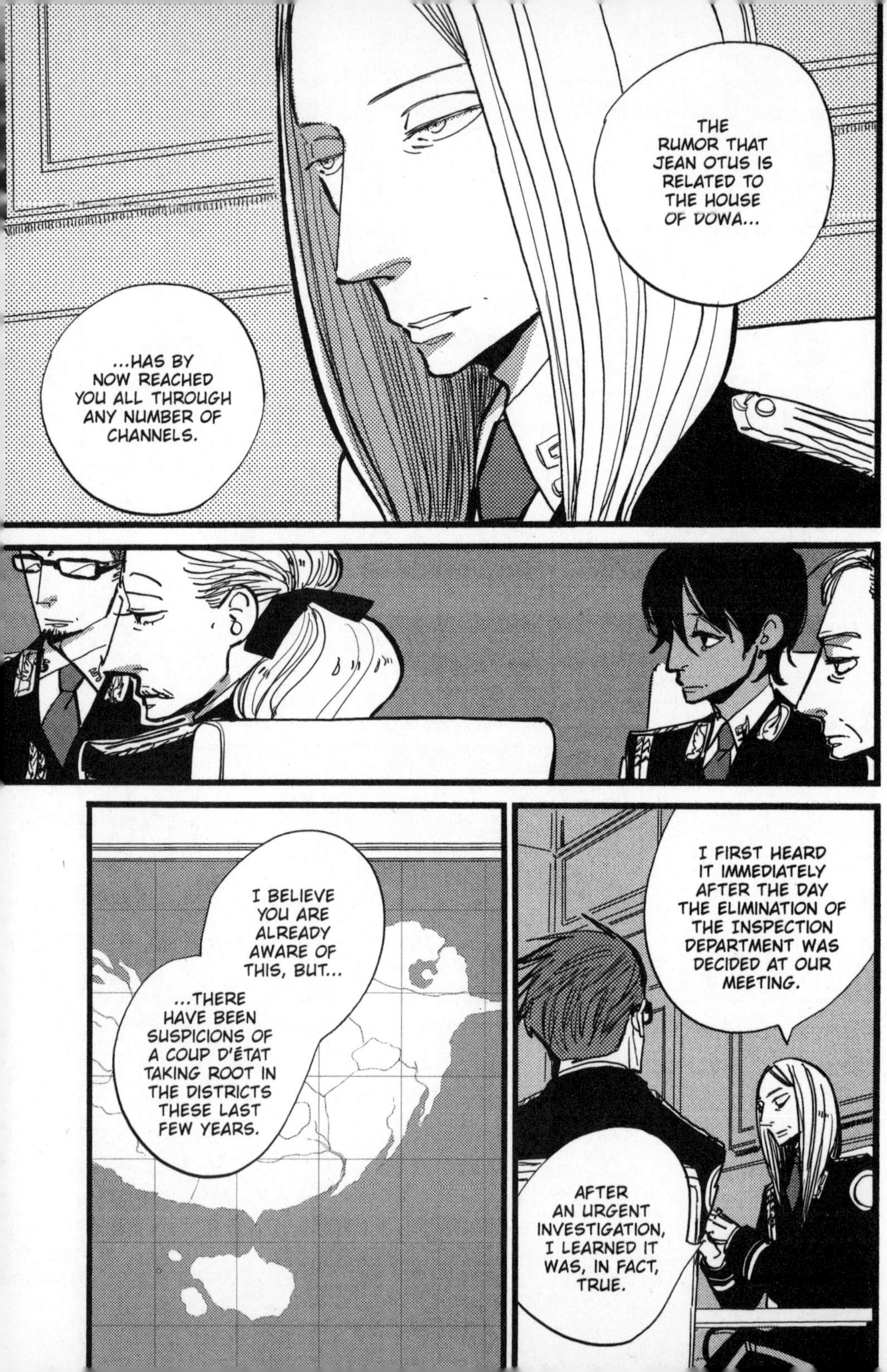
THE RUMOR THAT JEAN OTUS IS RELATED TO THE HOUSE OF DOWA...
...HAS BY NOW REACHED YOU ALL THROUGH ANY NUMBER OF CHANNELS.
I FIRST HEARD IT IMMEDIATELY AFTER THE DAY THE ELIMINATION OF THE INSPECTION DEPARTMENT WAS DECIDED AT OUR MEETING.
AFTER AN URGENT INVESTIGATION, I LEARNED IT WAS, IN FACT, TRUE.
I BELIEVE YOU ARE ALREADY AWARE OF THIS, BUT...
...THERE HAVE BEEN SUSPICIONS OF A COUP D'ÉTAT TAKING ROOT IN THE DISTRICTS THESE LAST FEW YEARS.

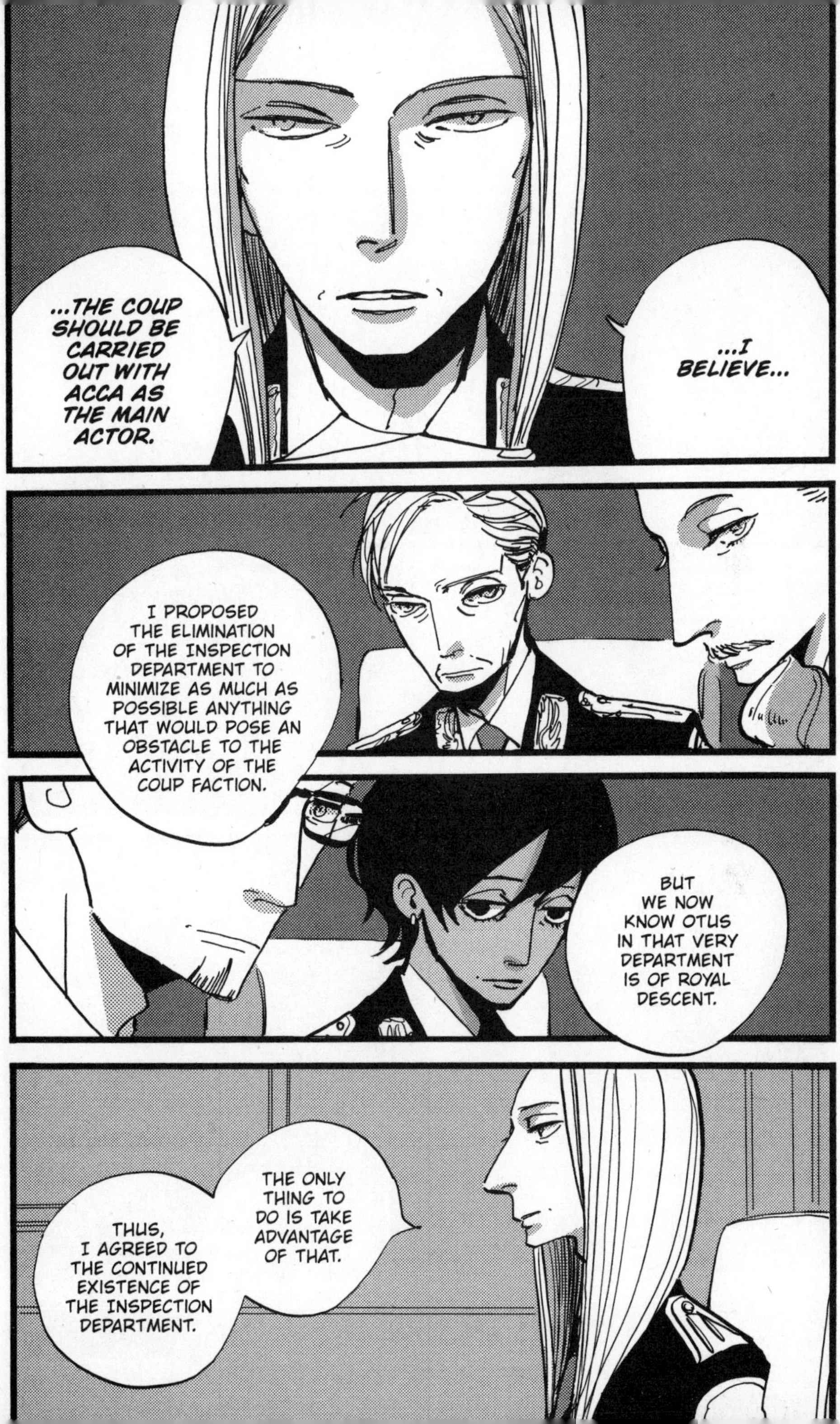
...THE COUP SHOULD BE CARRIED OUT WITH ACCA AS THE MAIN ACTOR.
...I BELIEVE...
I PROPOSED THE ELIMINATION OF THE INSPECTION DEPARTMENT TO MINIMIZE AS MUCH AS POSSIBLE ANYTHING THAT WOULD POSE AN OBSTACLE TO THE ACTIVITY OF THE COUP FACTION.
BUT WE NOW KNOW OTUS IN THAT VERY DEPARTMENT IS OF ROYAL DESCENT.
THE ONLY THING TO DO IS TAKE ADVANTAGE OF THAT.
THUS, I AGREED TO THE CONTINUED EXISTENCE OF THE INSPECTION DEPARTMENT.

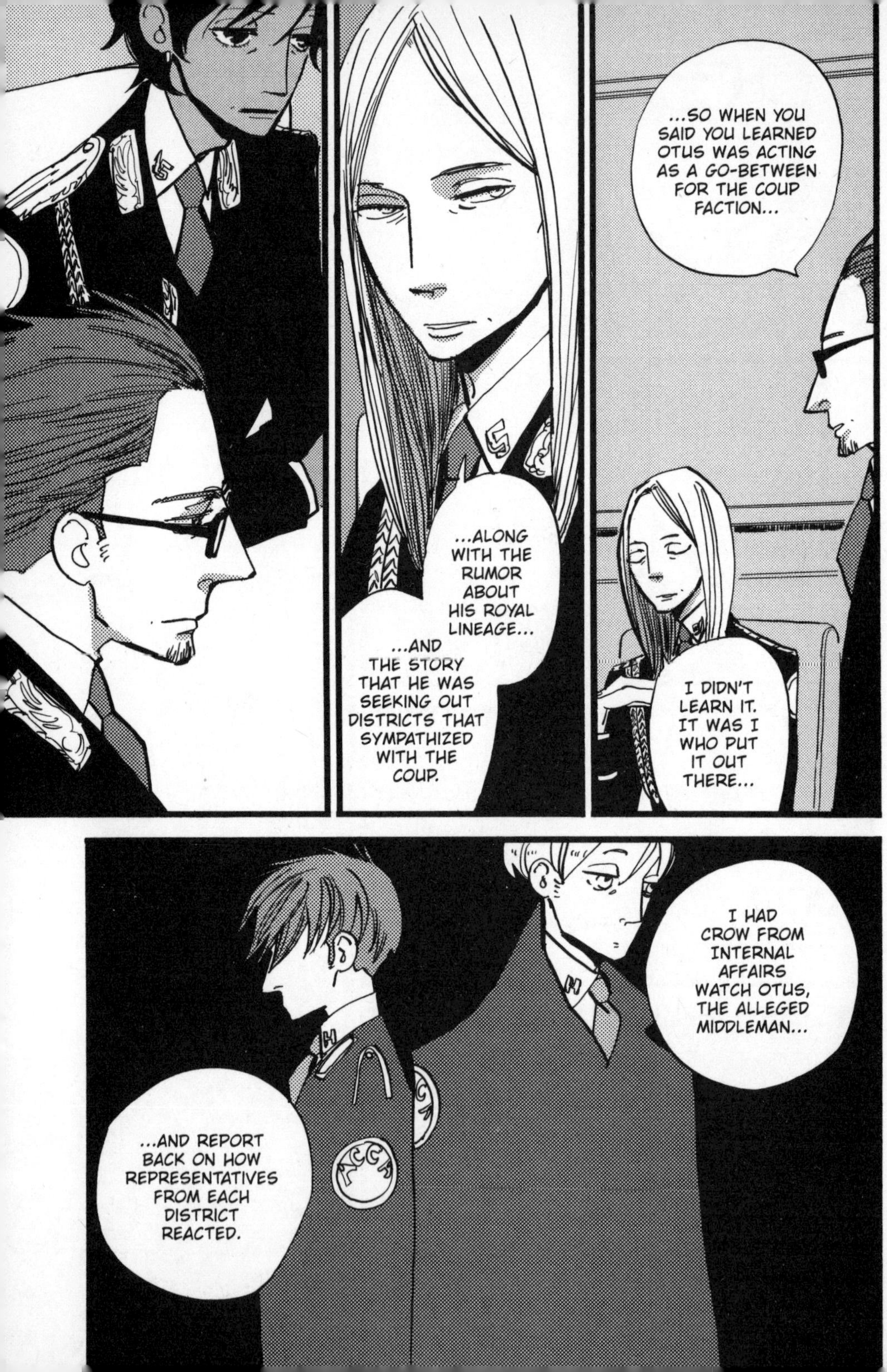
...SO WHEN YOU SAID YOU LEARNED OTUS WAS ACTING AS A GO-BETWEEN FOR THE COUP FACTION...
I DIDN'T LEARN IT. IT WAS I WHO PUT IT OUT THERE...
...ALONG WITH THE RUMOR ABOUT HIS ROYAL LINEAGE...
...AND THE STORY THAT HE WAS SEEKING OUT DISTRICTS THAT SYMPATHIZED WITH THE COUP.
I HAD CROW FROM INTERNAL AFFAIRS WATCH OTUS, THE ALLEGED MIDDLEMAN...
...AND REPORT BACK ON HOW REPRESENTATIVES FROM EACH DISTRICT REACTED.

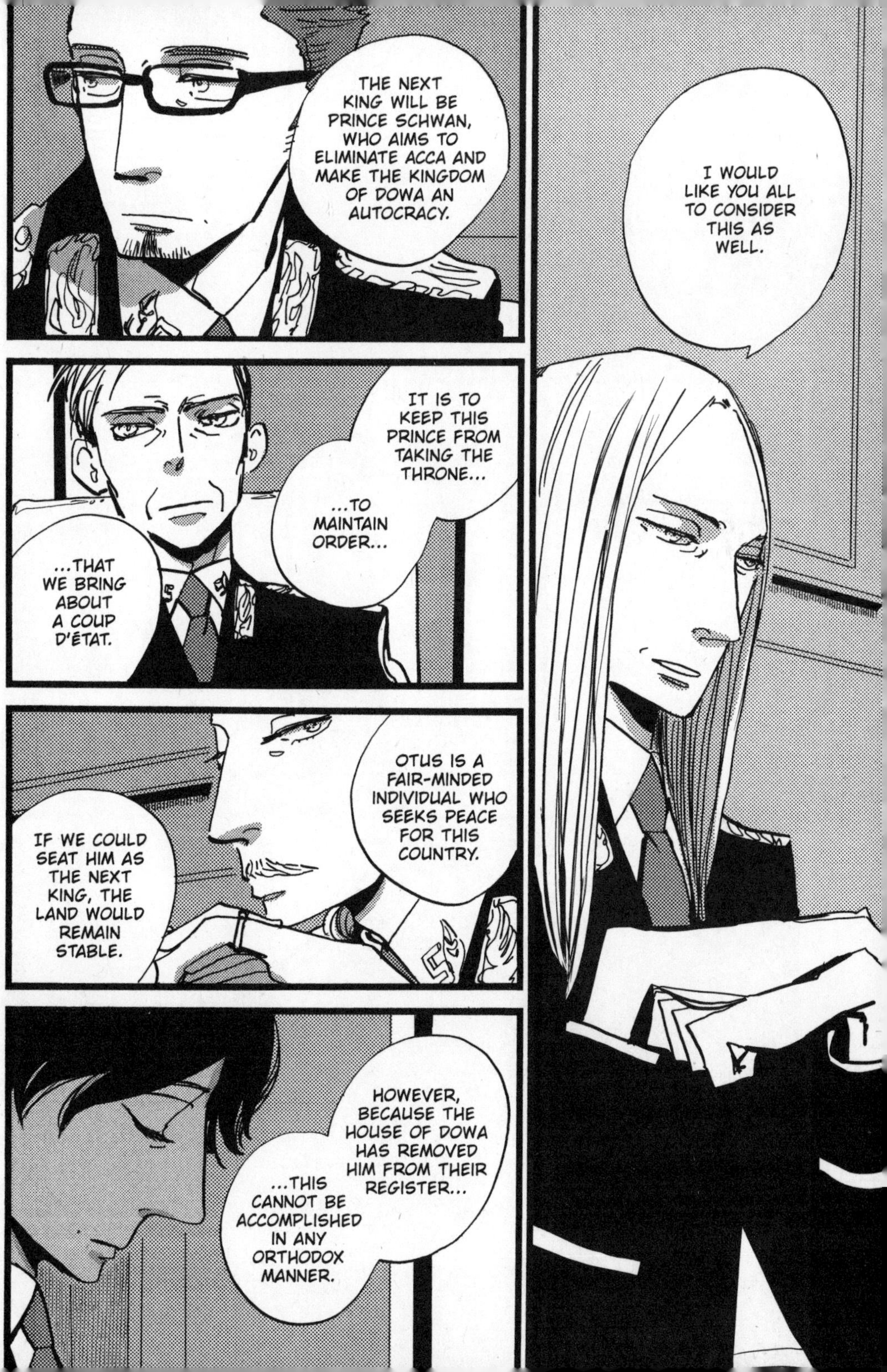
I WOULD LIKE YOU ALL TO CONSIDER THIS AS WELL.
THE NEXT KING WILL BE PRINCE SCHWAN, WHO AIMS TO ELIMINATE ACCA AND MAKE THE KINGDOM OF DOWA AN AUTOCRACY.
IT IS TO KEEP THIS PRINCE FROM TAKING THE THRONE...
...TO MAINTAIN ORDER...
...THAT WE BRING ABOUT A COUP D'ÉTAT.
OTUS IS A FAIR-MINDED INDIVIDUAL WHO SEEKS PEACE FOR THIS COUNTRY.
IF WE COULD SEAT HIM AS THE NEXT KING, THE LAND WOULD REMAIN STABLE.
HOWEVER, BECAUSE THE HOUSE OF DOWA HAS REMOVED HIM FROM THEIR REGISTER...
...THIS CANNOT BE ACCOMPLISHED IN ANY ORTHODOX MANNER.

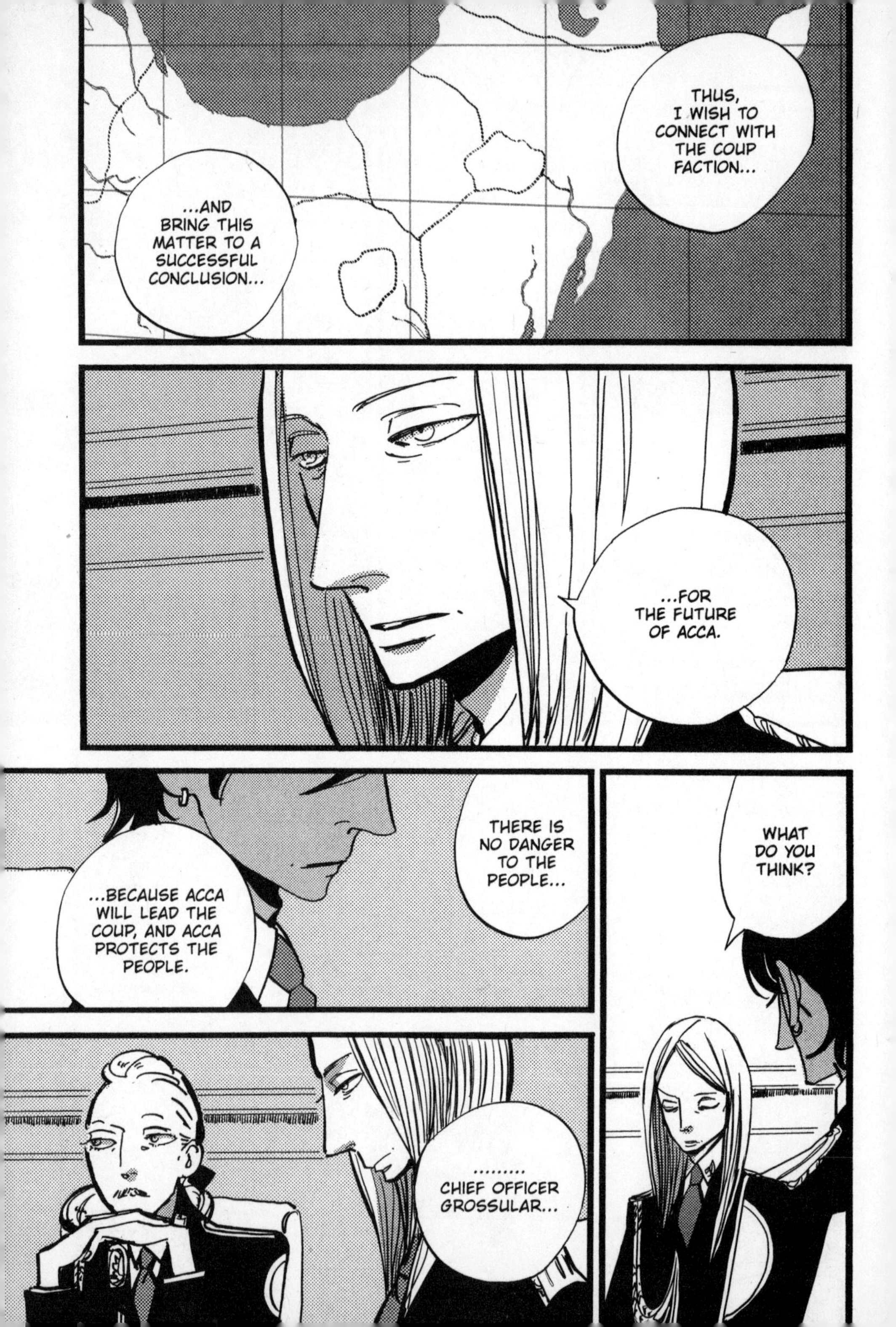
THUS, I WISH TO CONNECT WITH THE COUP FACTION...
...AND BRING THIS MATTER TO A SUCCESSFUL CONCLUSION...
...FOR THE FUTURE OF ACCA.
WHAT DO YOU THINK?
THERE IS NO DANGER TO THE PEOPLE...
...BECAUSE ACCA WILL LEAD THE COUP, AND ACCA PROTECTS THE PEOPLE.
....
CHIEF OFFICER GROSSULAR...

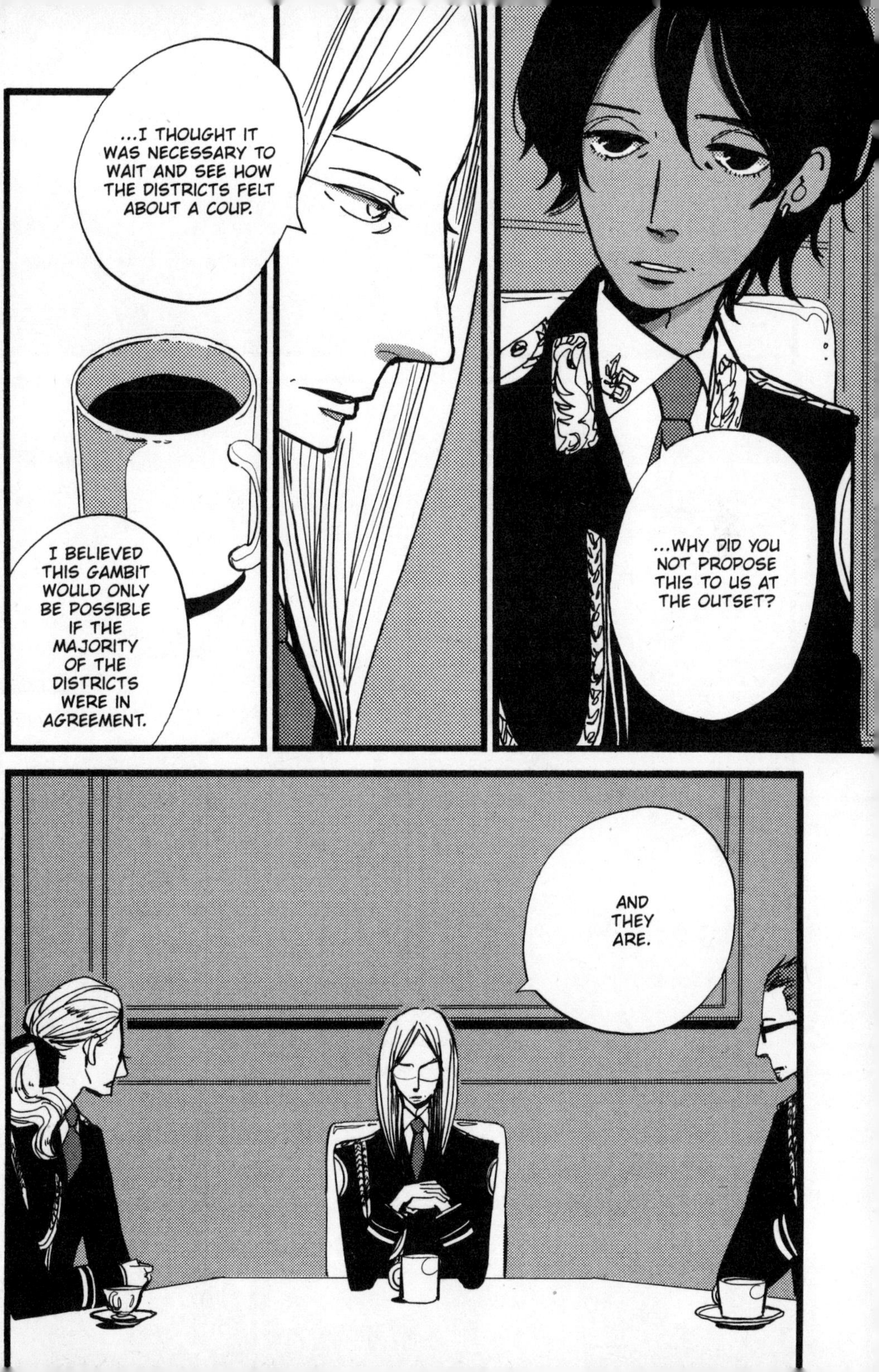
...WHY DID YOU NOT PROPOSE THIS TO US AT THE OUTSET?
...I THOUGHT IT WAS NECESSARY TO WAIT AND SEE HOW THE DISTRICTS FELT ABOUT A COUP.
I BELIEVED THIS GAMBIT WOULD ONLY BE POSSIBLE IF THE MAJORITY OF THE DISTRICTS WERE IN AGREEMENT.
AND THEY ARE.

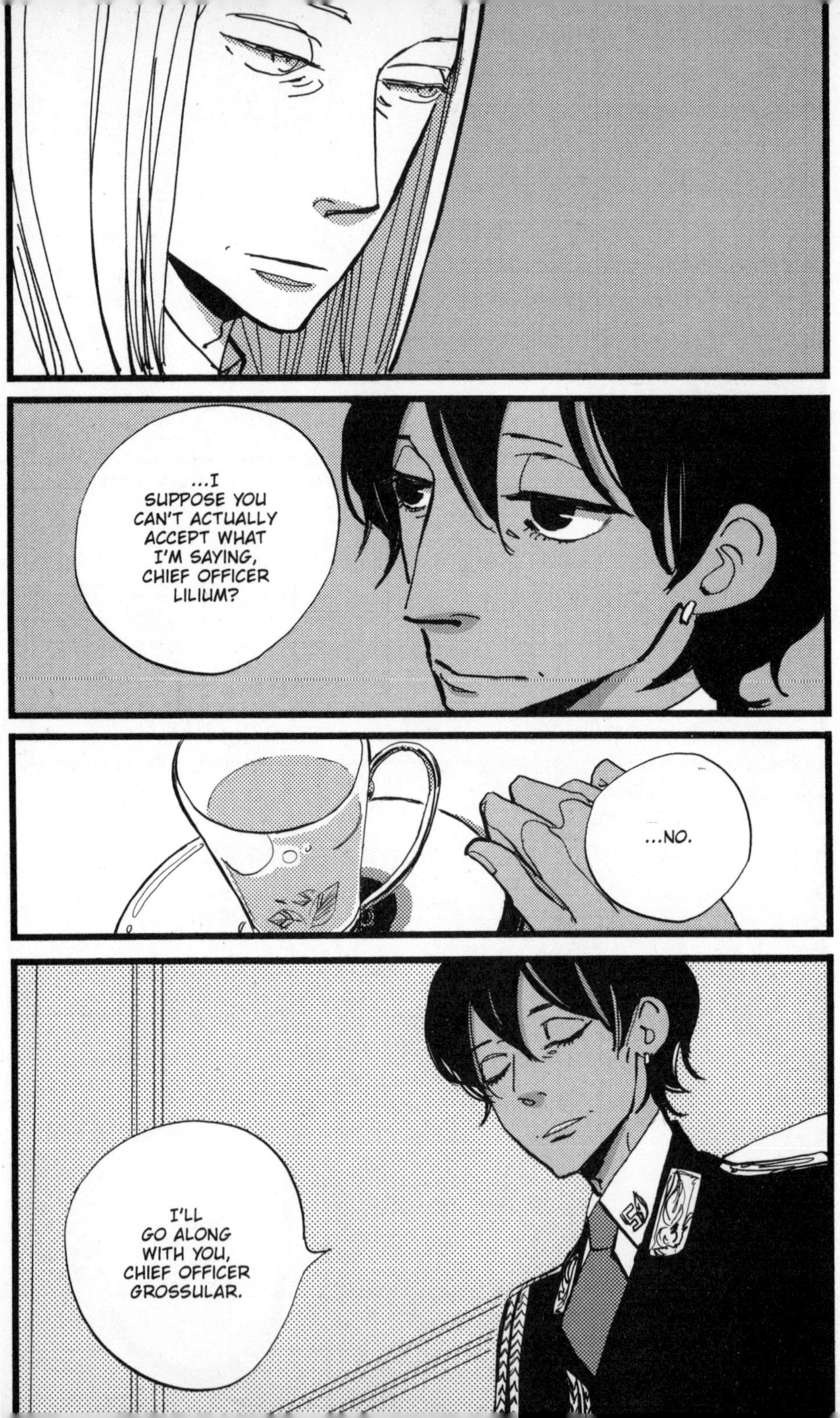
...I SUPPOSE YOU CAN'T ACTUALLY ACCEPT WHAT I'M SAYING, CHIEF OFFICER LILIUM?
...NO.
I'LL GO ALONG WITH YOU, CHIEF OFFICER GROSSULAR.

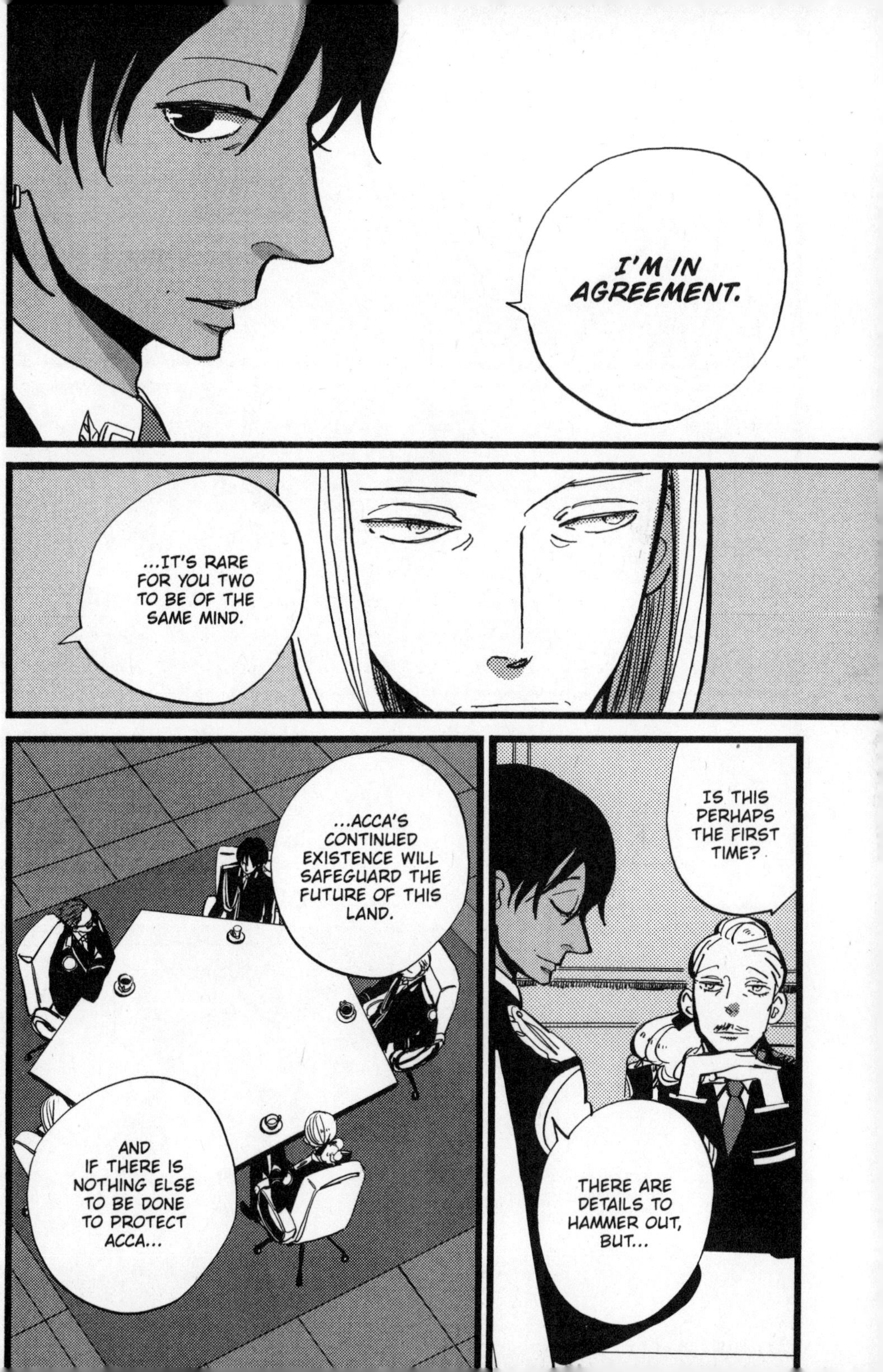
I'M IN AGREEMENT.
...IT'S RARE FOR YOU TWO TO BE OF THE SAME MIND.
IS THIS PERHAPS THE FIRST TIME?
THERE ARE DETAILS TO HAMMER OUT, BUT...
...ACCA'S CONTINUED EXISTENCE WILL SAFEGUARD THE FUTURE OF THIS LAND.
AND IF THERE IS NOTHING ELSE TO BE DONE TO PROTECT ACCA...

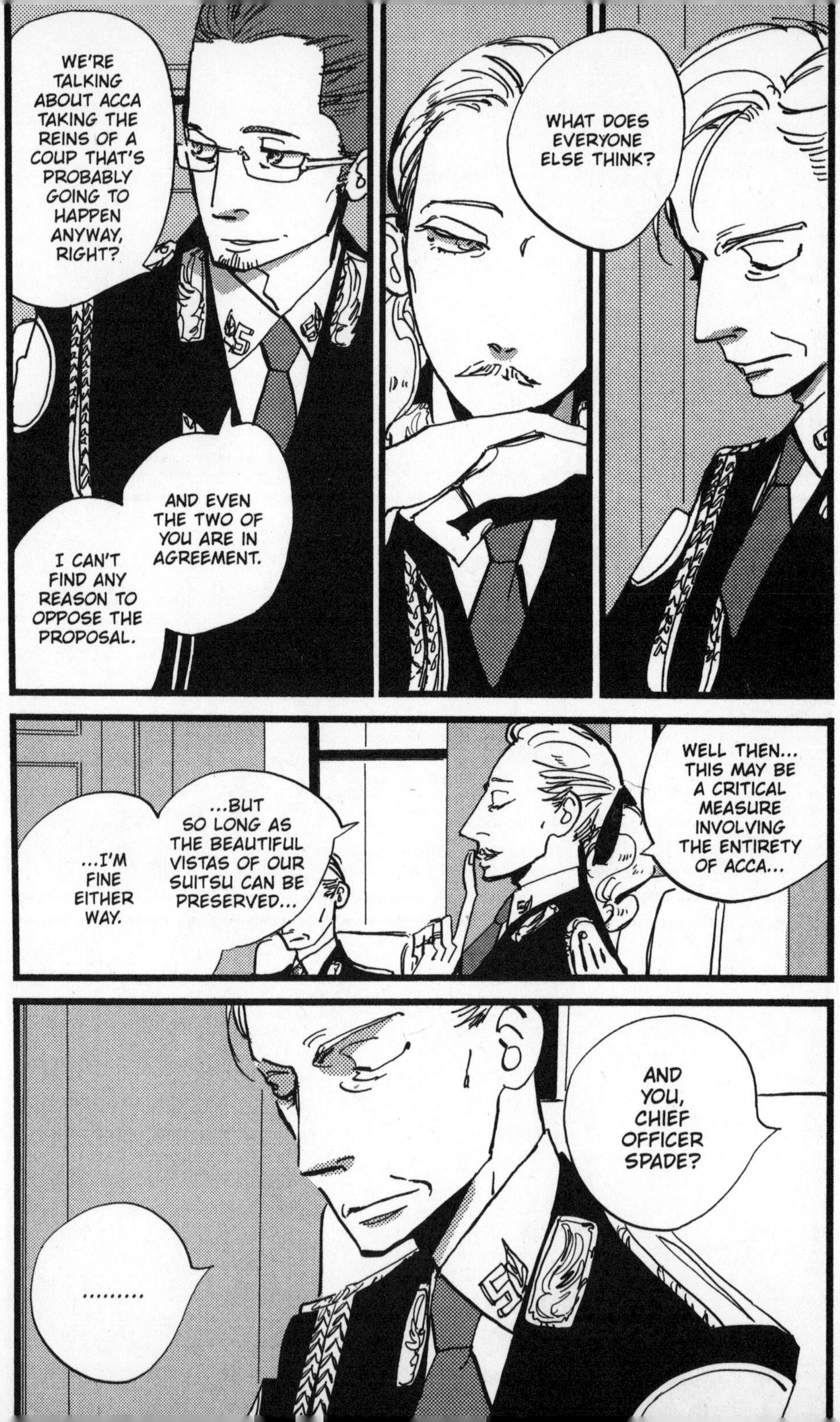
WHAT DOES EVERYONE ELSE THINK?
WE'RE TALKING ABOUT ACCA TAKING THE REINS OF A COUP THAT'S PROBABLY GOING TO HAPPEN ANYWAY, RIGHT?
AND EVEN THE TWO OF YOU ARE IN AGREEMENT.
I CAN'T FIND ANY REASON TO OPPOSE THE PROPOSAL.
WELL THEN... THIS MAY BE A CRITICAL MEASURE INVOLVING THE ENTIRETY OF ACCA...
...BUT SO LONG AS THE BEAUTIFUL VISTAS OF OUR SUITSU CAN BE PRESERVED...
...I'M FINE EITHER WAY.
AND YOU, CHIEF OFFICER SPADE?
....

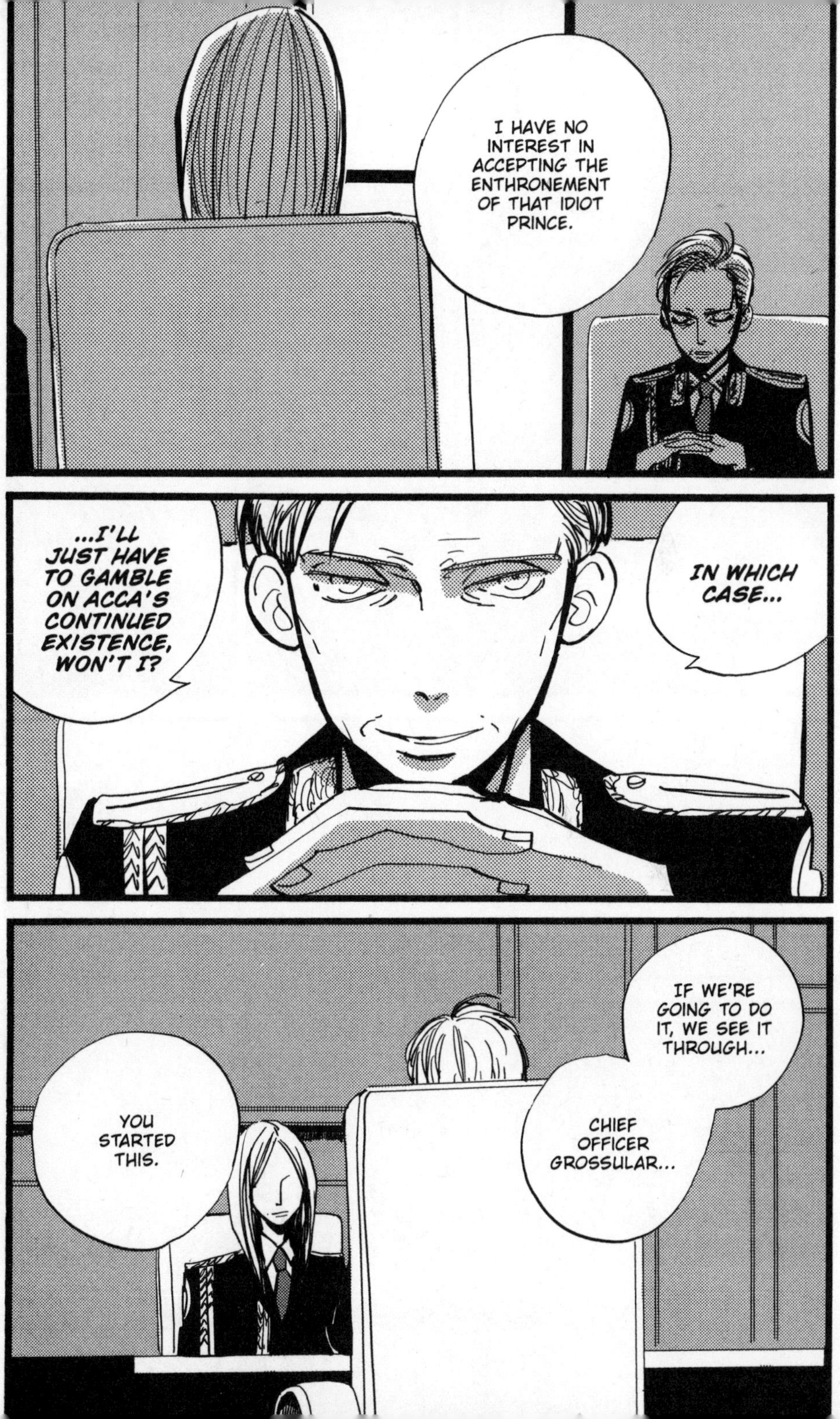
I HAVE NO INTEREST IN ACCEPTING THE ENTHRONEMENT OF THAT IDIOT PRINCE.
IN WHICH CASE...
...I'LL JUST HAVE TO GAMBLE ON ACCA'S CONTINUED EXISTENCE, WON'T I?
IF WE'RE GOING TO DO IT, WE SEE IT THROUGH...
CHIEF OFFICER GROSSULAR...
YOU STARTED THIS.

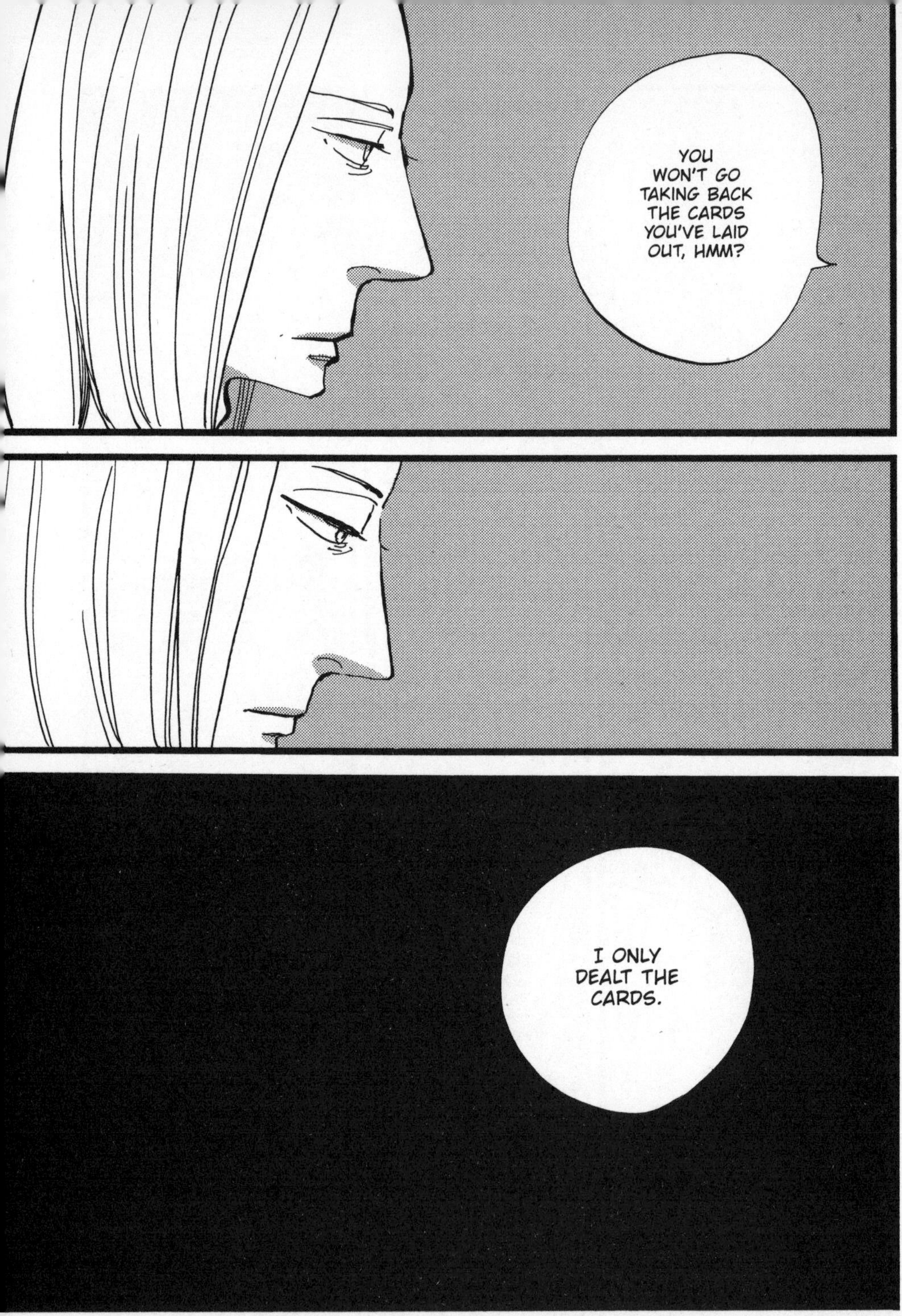
YOU WON'T GO TAKING BACK THE CARDS YOU'VE LAID OUT, HMM?
I ONLY DEALT THE CARDS.

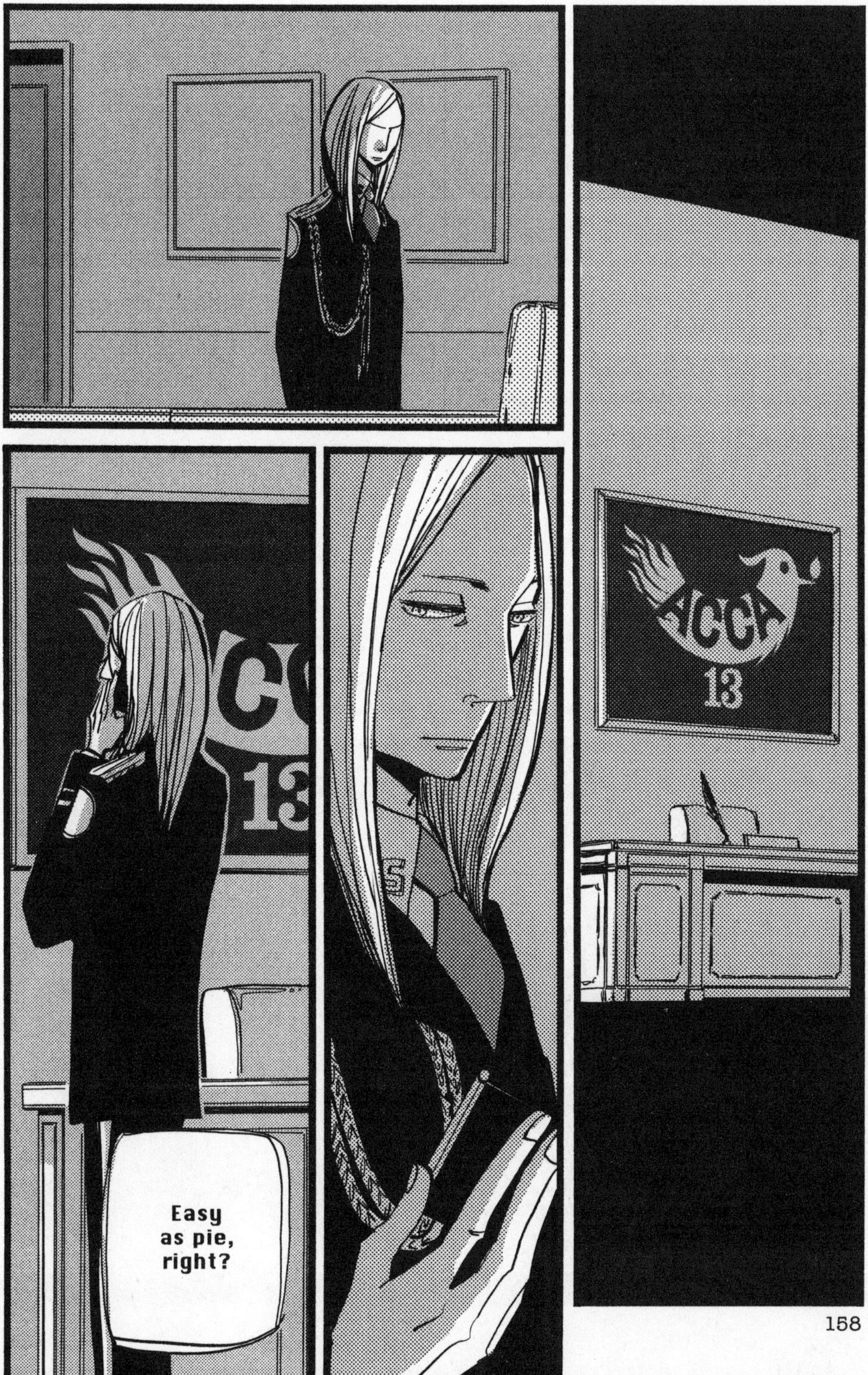
ACCA
13
Easy as pie, right?

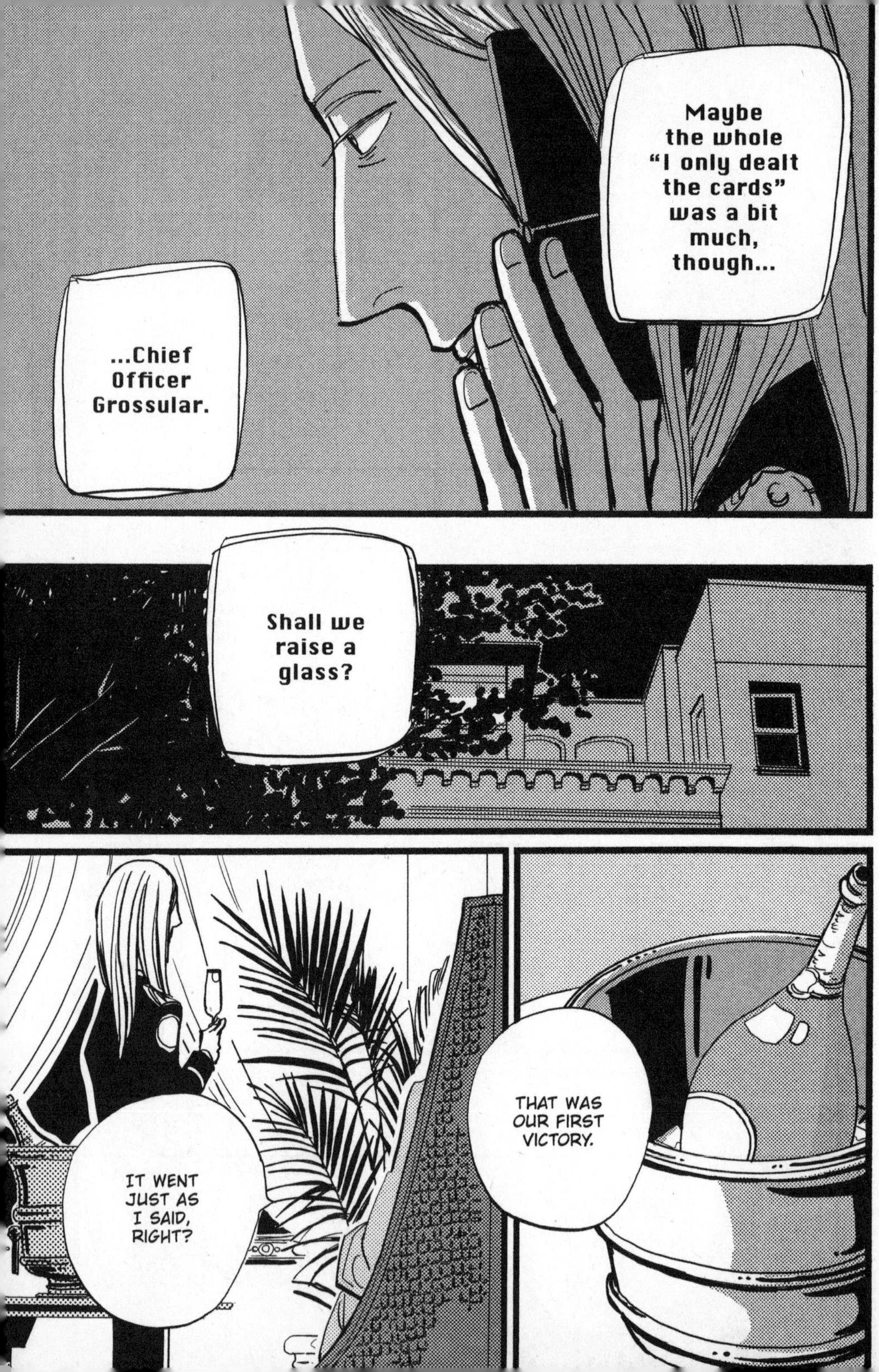
Maybe the whole "I only dealt the cards" was a bit much, though...
...Chief Officer Grossular.
Shall we raise a glass?
THAT WAS OUR FIRST VICTORY.
IT WENT JUST AS I SAID, RIGHT?

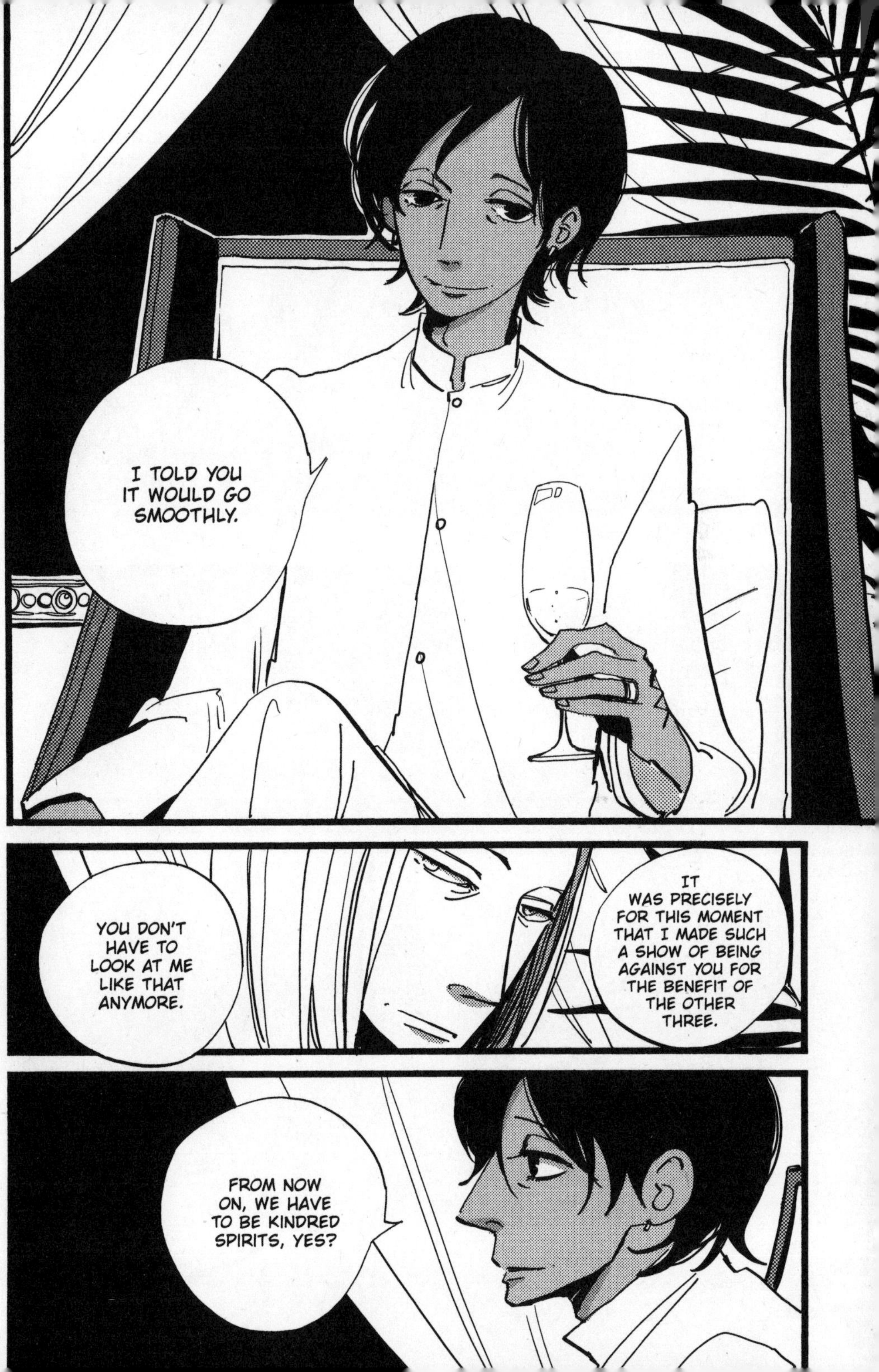
I TOLD YOU IT WOULD GO SMOOTHLY.
IT WAS PRECISELY FOR THIS MOMENT THAT I MADE SUCH A SHOW OF BEING AGAINST YOU FOR THE BENEFIT OF THE OTHER THREE.
YOU DON'T HAVE TO LOOK AT ME LIKE THAT ANYMORE.
FROM NOW ON, WE HAVE TO BE KINDRED SPIRITS, YES?

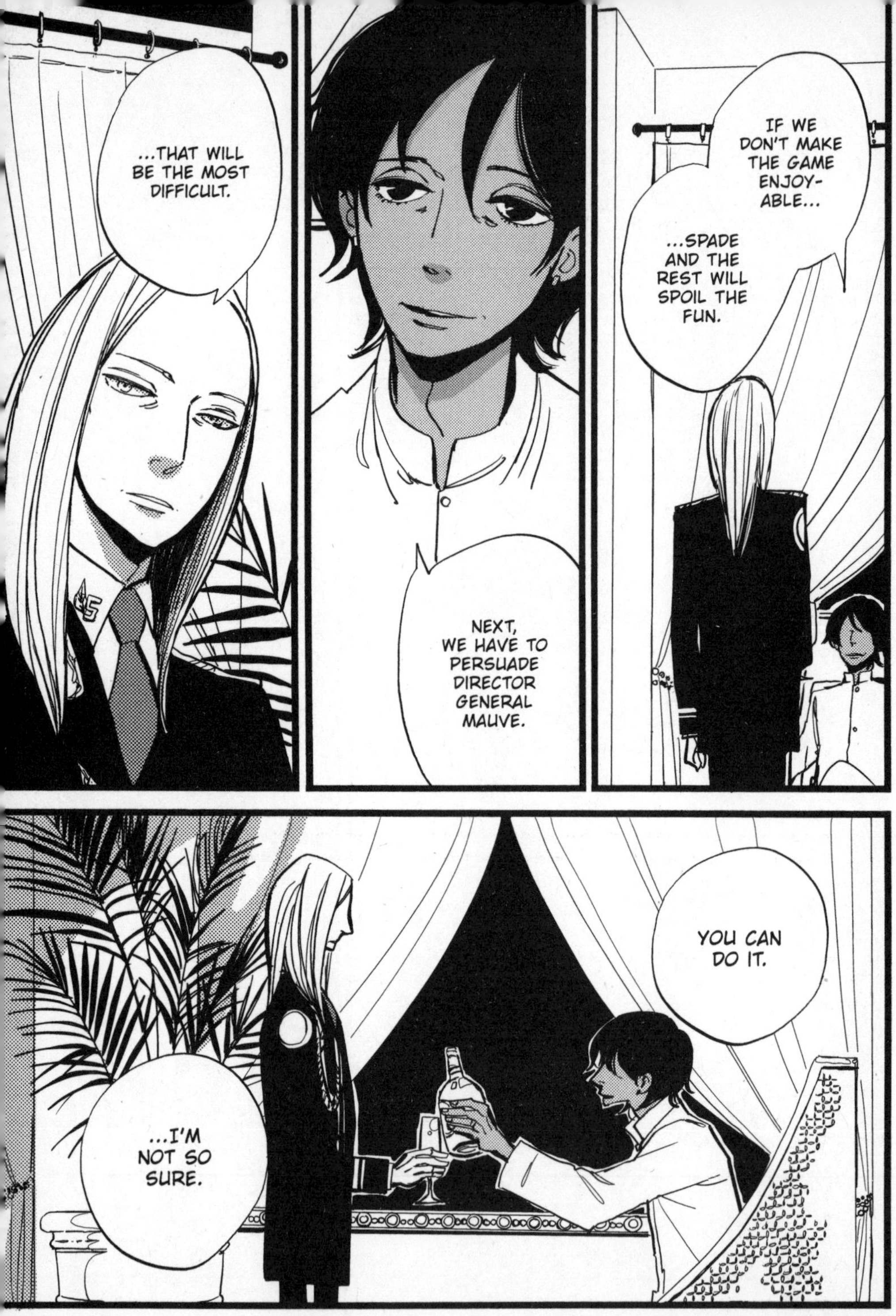
IF WE DON'T MAKE THE GAME ENJOY-ABLE...
...SPADE AND THE REST WILL SPOIL THE FUN.
NEXT, WE HAVE TO PERSUADE DIRECTOR GENERAL MAUVE.
...THAT WILL BE THE MOST DIFFICULT.
YOU CAN DO IT.
...I'M NOT SO SURE.

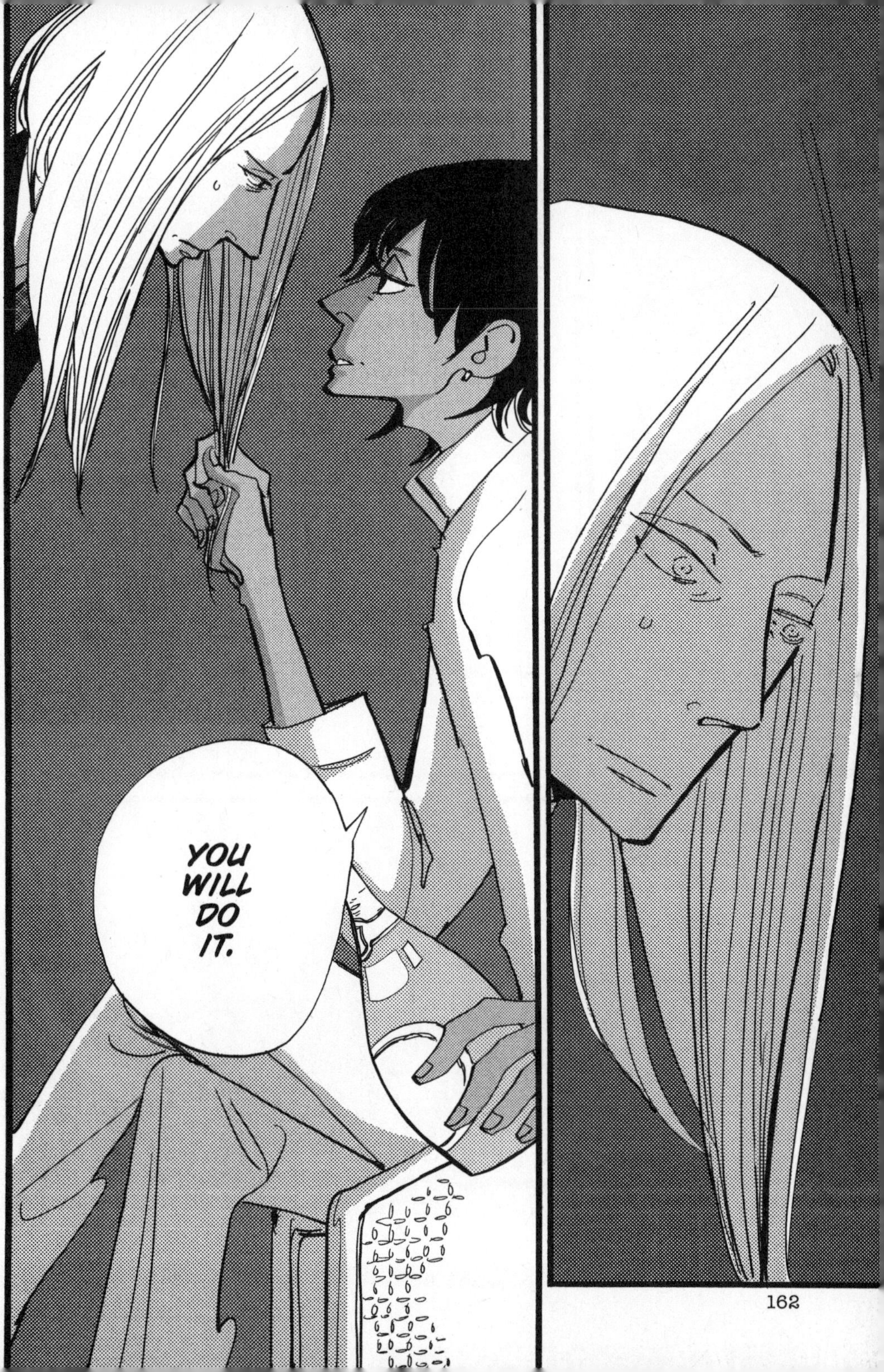
YOU WILL DO IT.

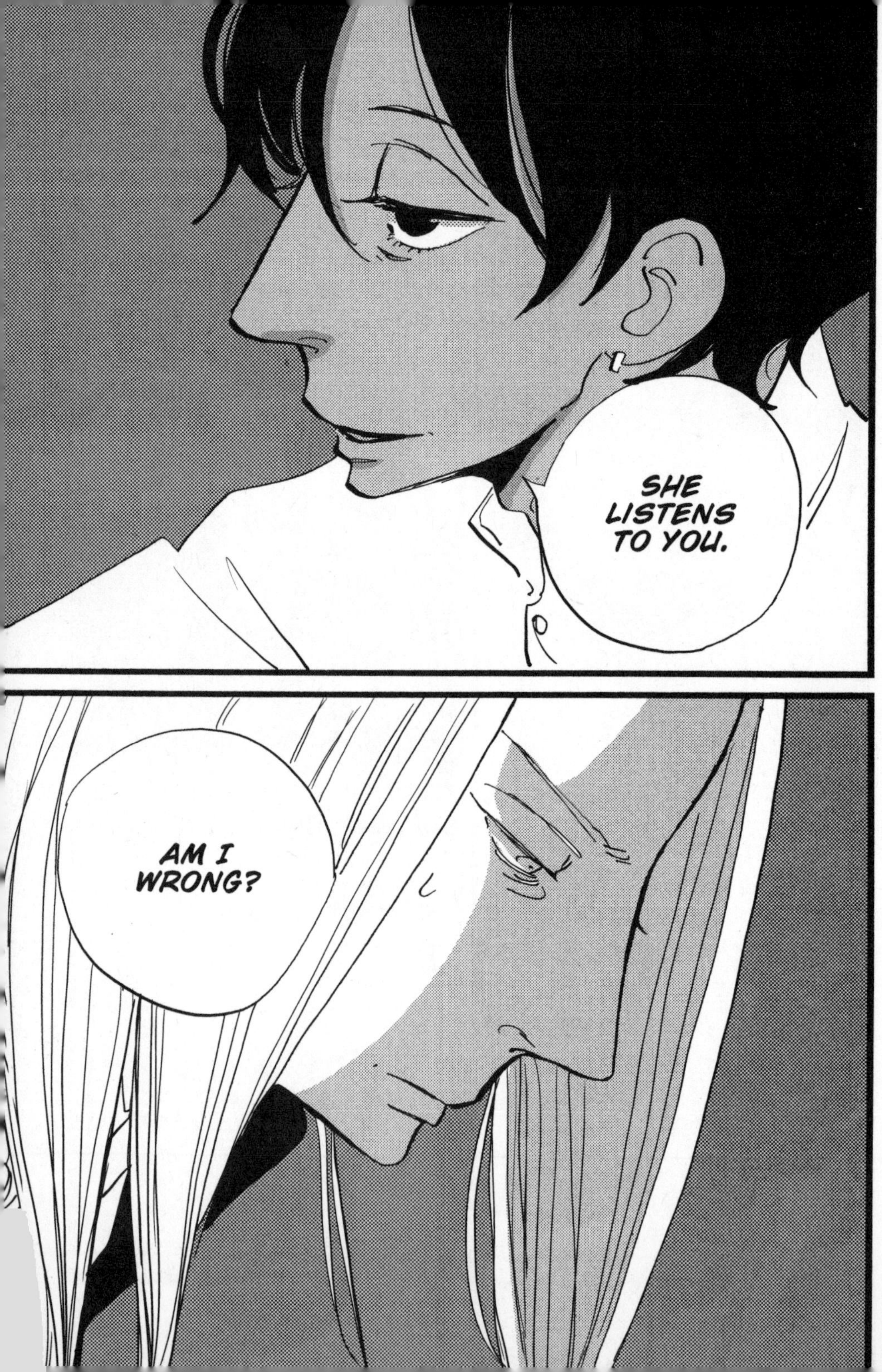
SHE LISTENS TO YOU.
AM I WRONG?

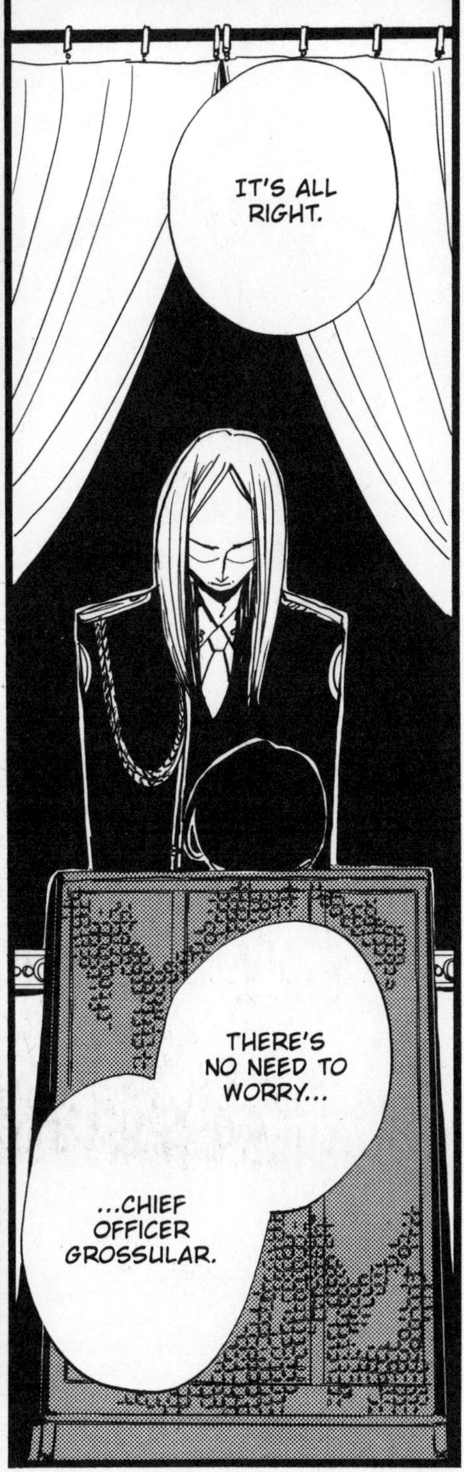
IT'S ALL RIGHT.
THERE'S NO NEED TO WORRY...
...CHIEF OFFICER GROSSULAR.
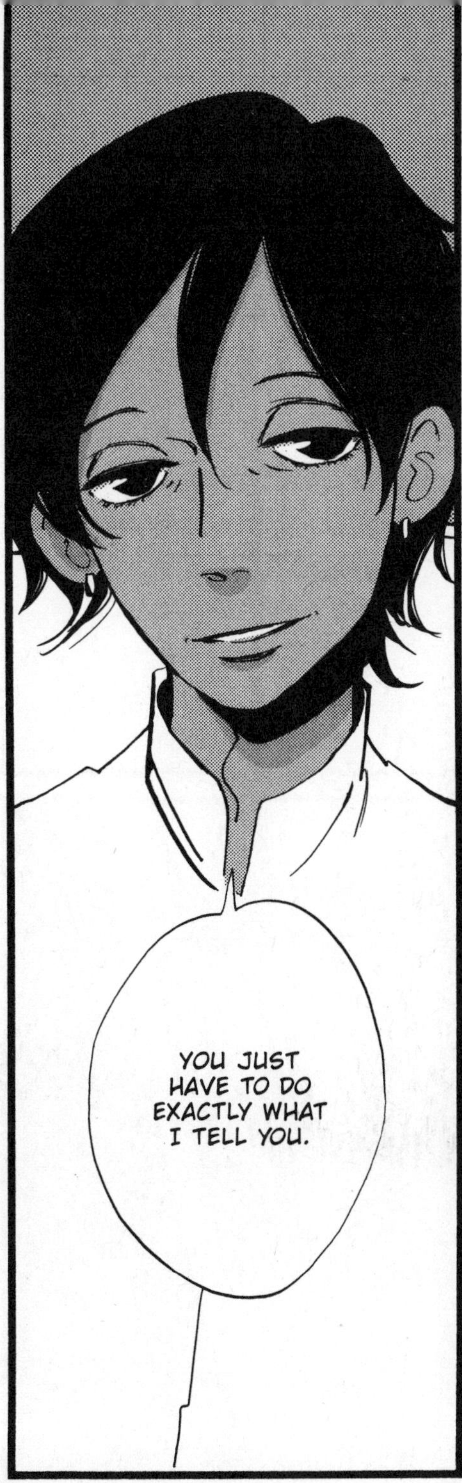
YOU JUST HAVE TO DO EXACTLY WHAT I TELL YOU.

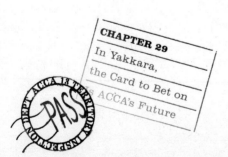

CHAPTER 29

In Yakkara,
the Card to Bet on
Is ACCA's Future

DEPT. ACCA 13 TERRITORY INSPECTION
PASS

ACCA Branch Uniforms | 11

Yakkara District

Many good-for-nothing types find their way to Yakkara with the aim of getting rich quick. ACCA branch agents wear wide-brimmed hats that hide their faces. They are strong individuals who more than compete on equal ground with these good-for-nothings.

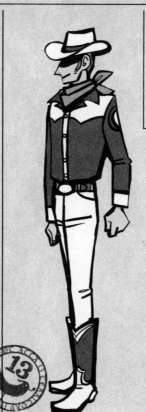

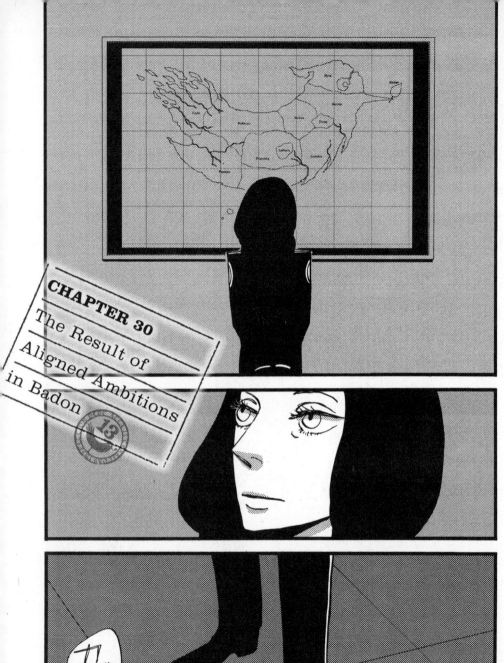

CHAPTER 30
The Result of Aligned Ambitions in Badon

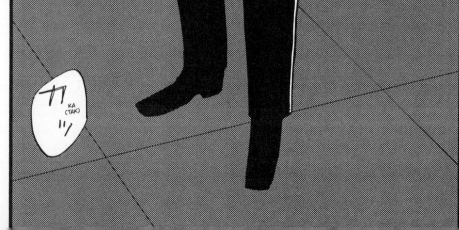

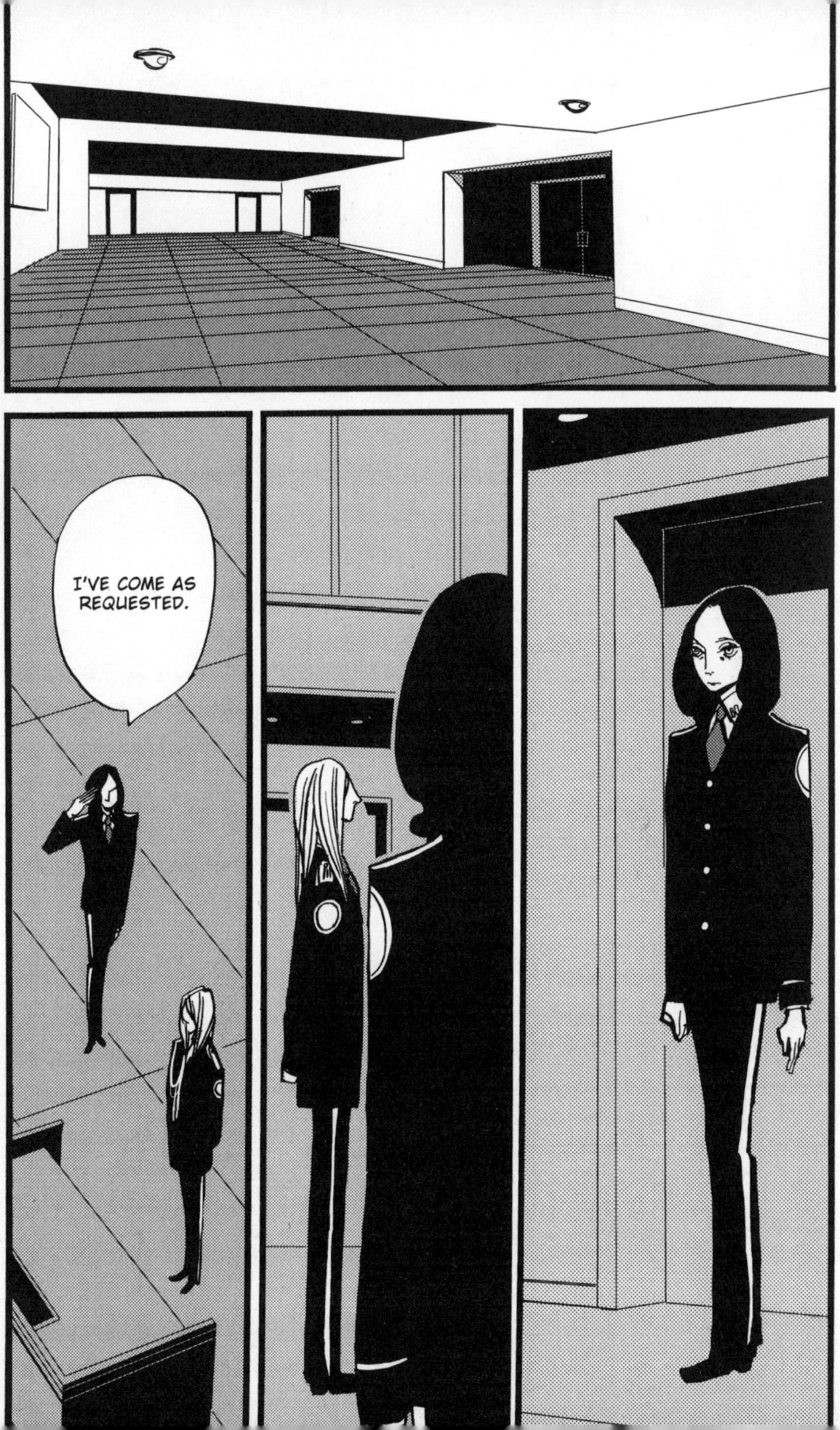
I'VE COME AS REQUESTED.

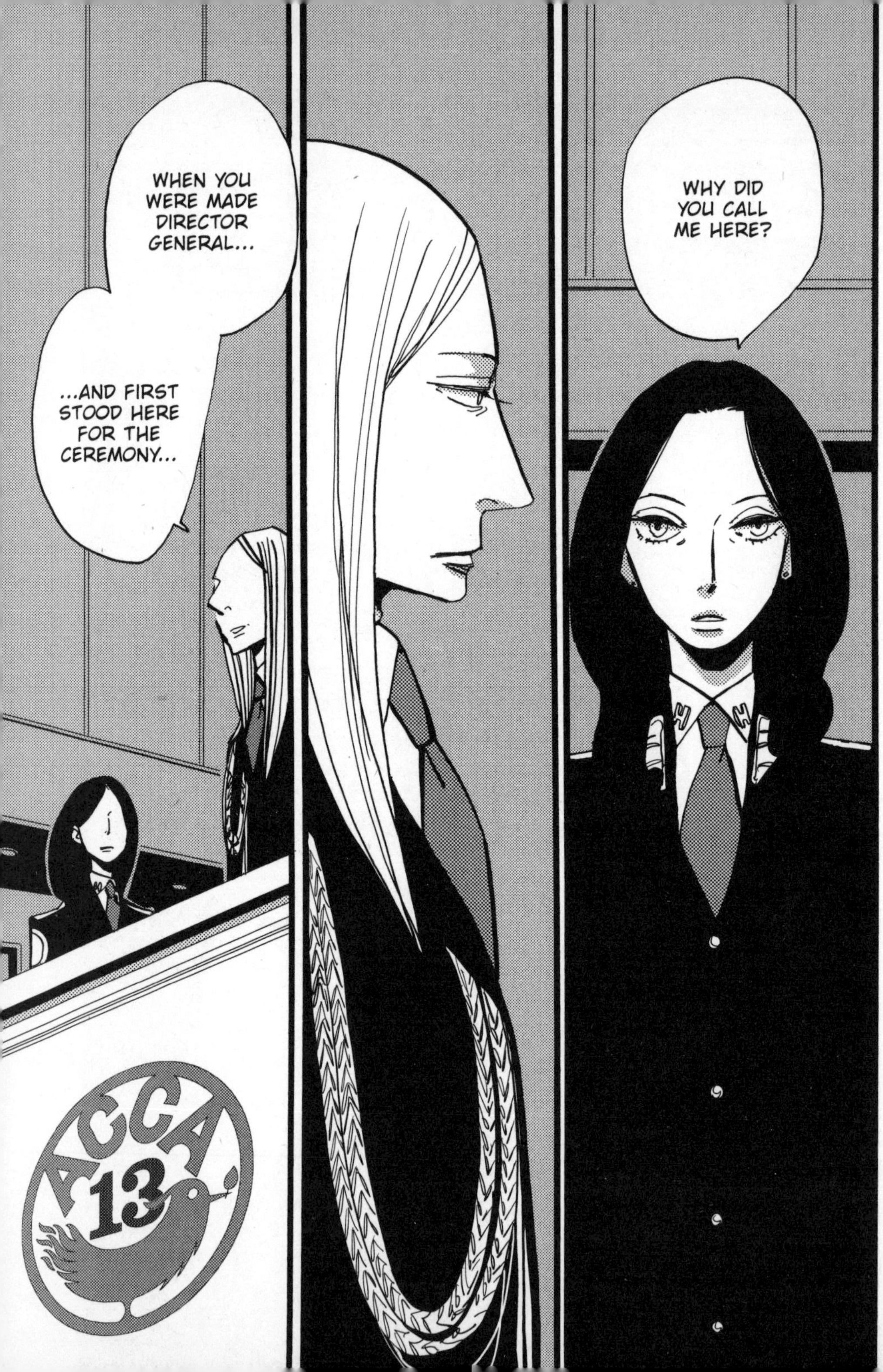
WHY DID YOU CALL ME HERE?
WHEN YOU WERE MADE DIRECTOR GENERAL...
...AND FIRST STOOD HERE FOR THE CEREMONY...
ACCA 13

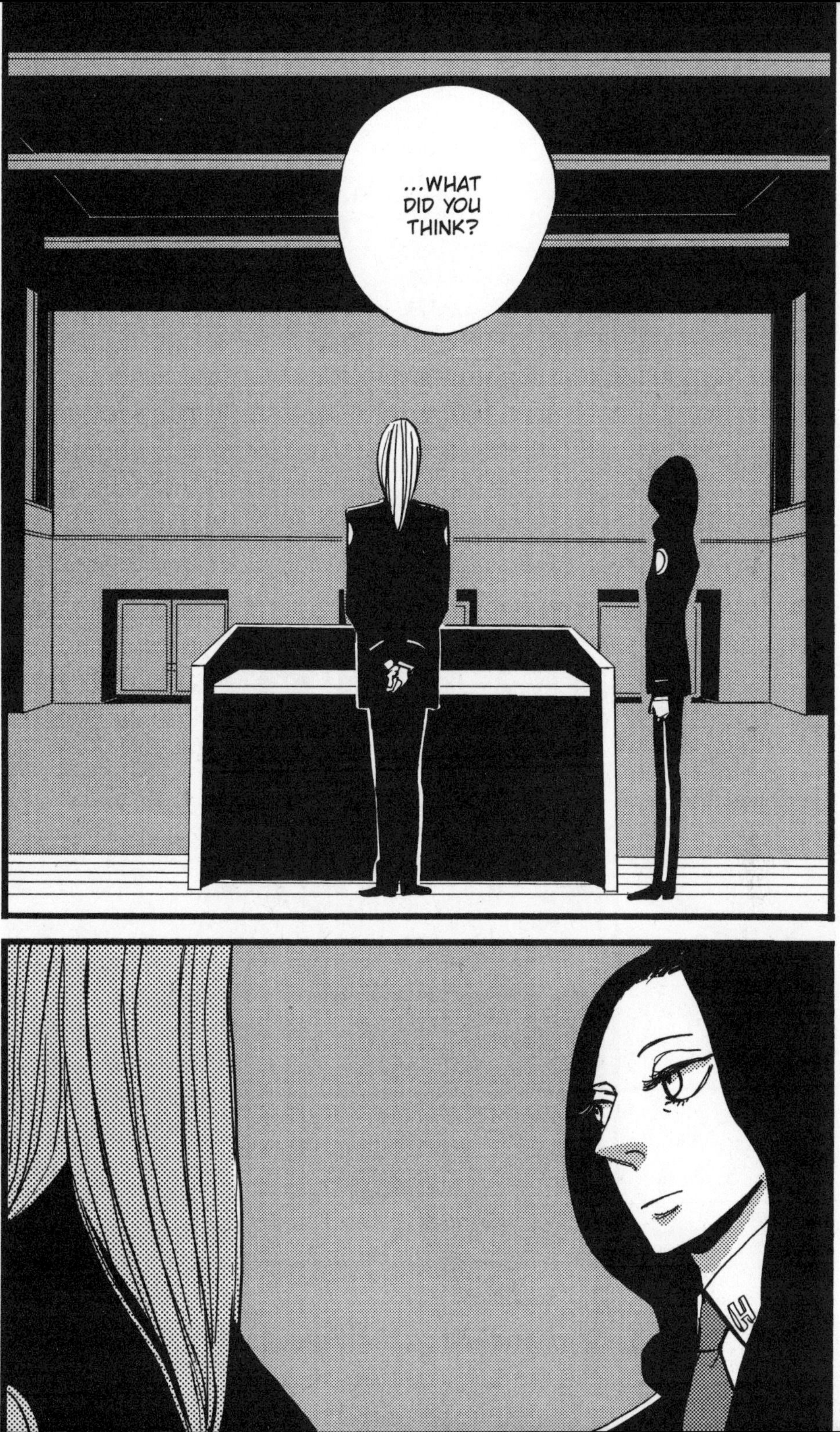
...WHAT DID YOU THINK?

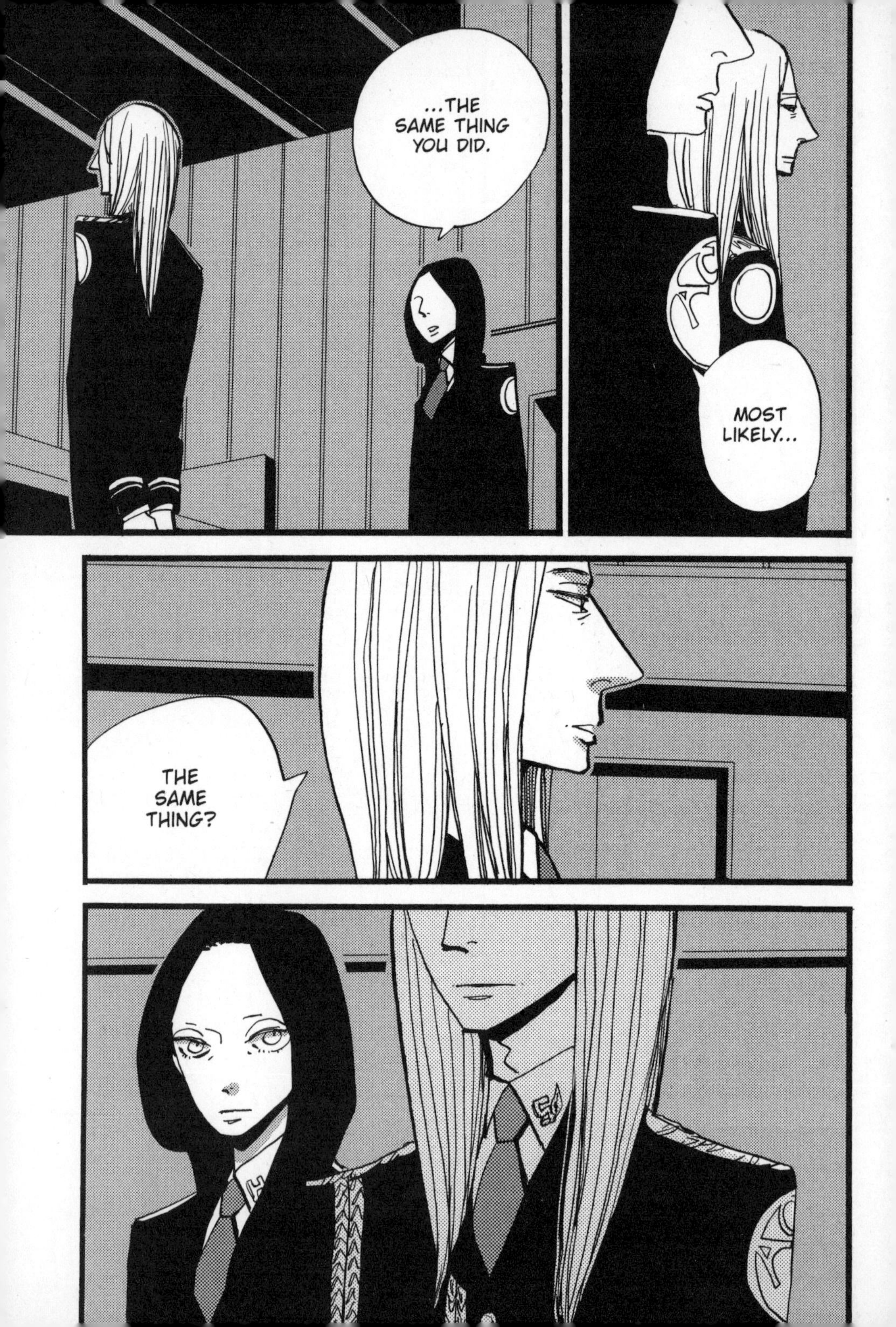
MOST LIKELY...
...THE SAME THING YOU DID.
THE SAME THING?

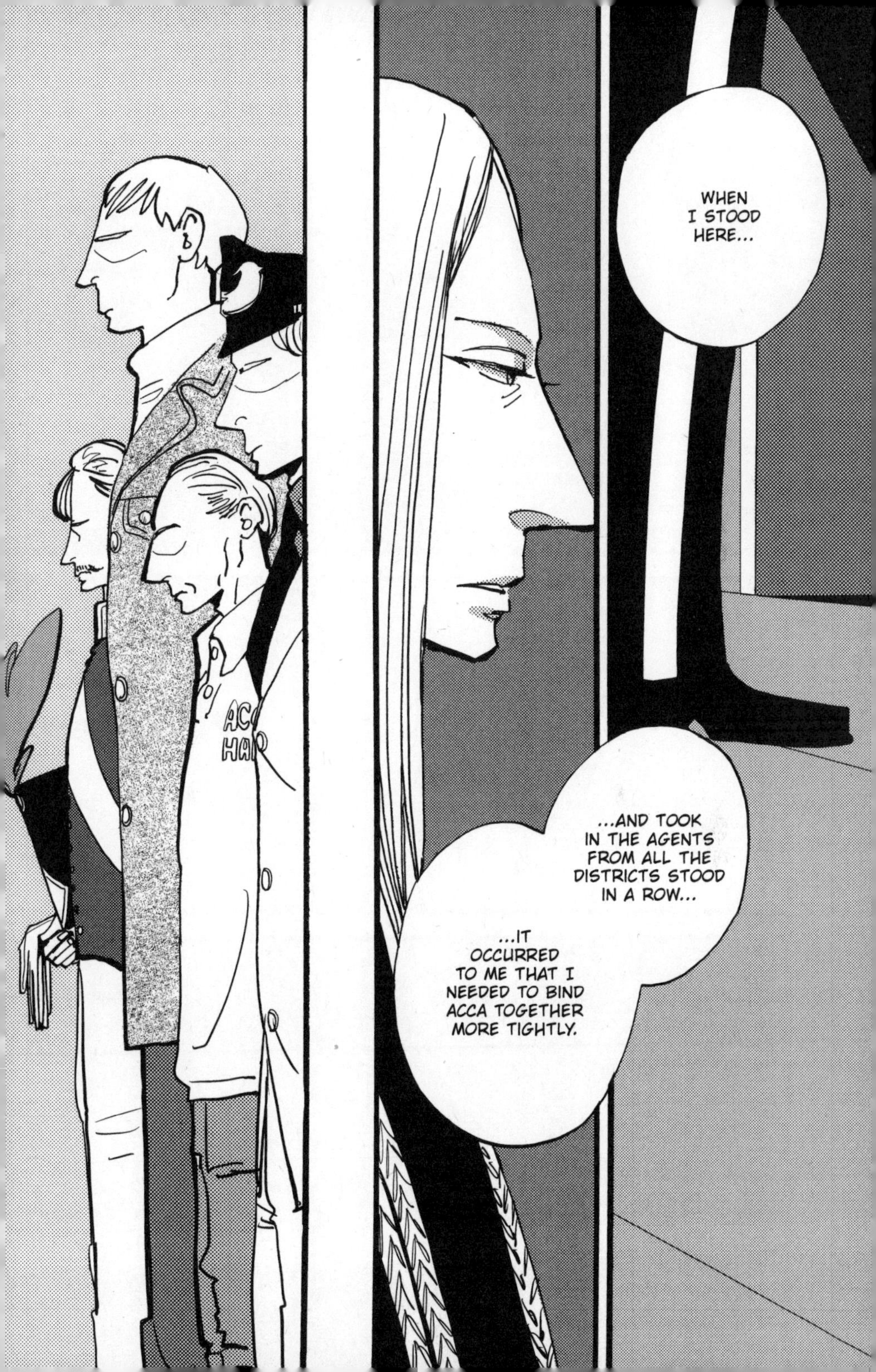
WHEN I STOOD HERE...
...AND TOOK IN THE AGENTS FROM ALL THE DISTRICTS STOOD IN A ROW...
...IT OCCURRED TO ME THAT I NEEDED TO BIND ACCA TOGETHER MORE TIGHTLY.

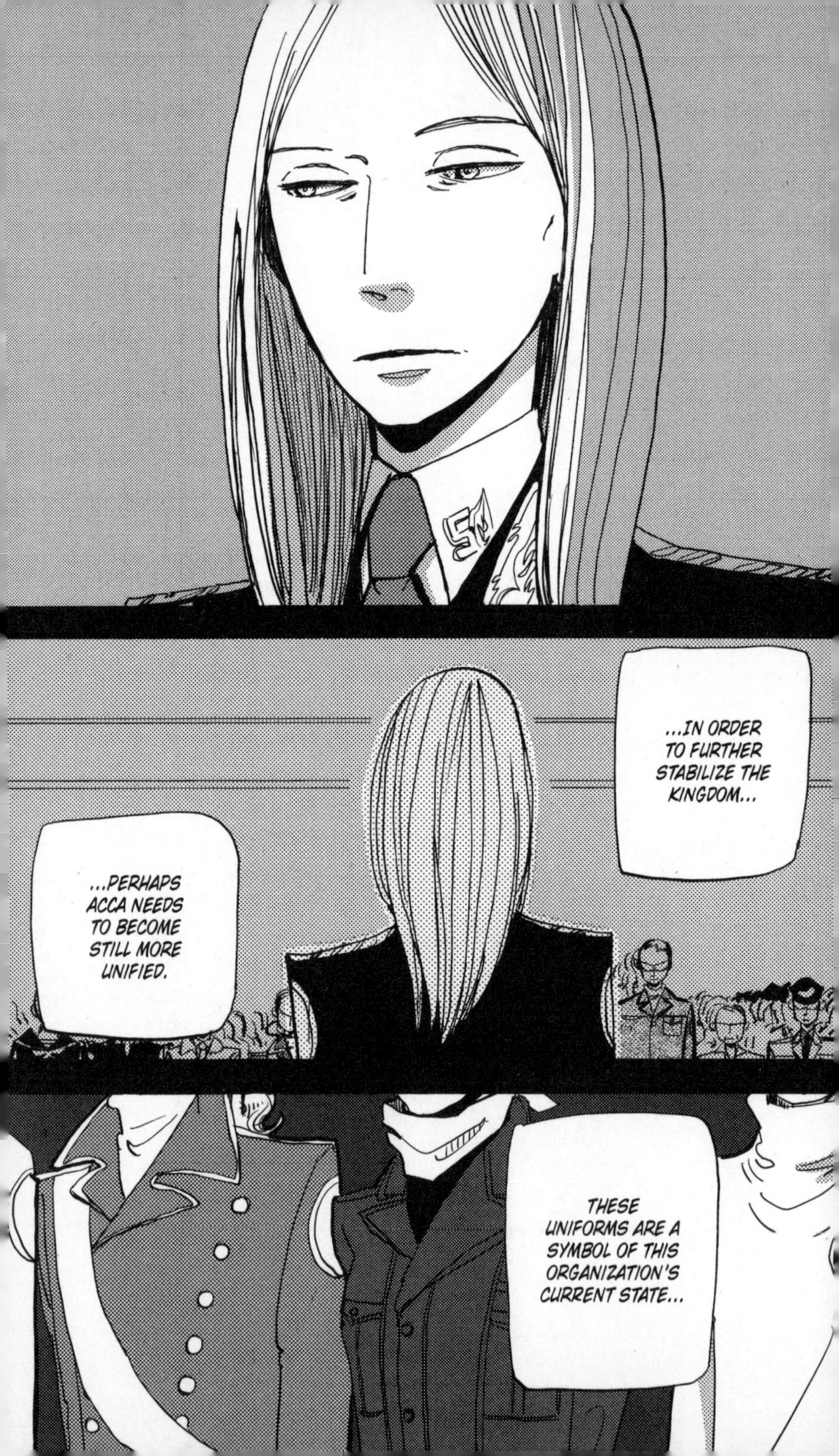
...IN ORDER TO FURTHER STABILIZE THE KINGDOM...
...PERHAPS ACCA NEEDS TO BECOME STILL MORE UNIFIED.
THESE UNIFORMS ARE A SYMBOL OF THIS ORGANIZATION'S CURRENT STATE...

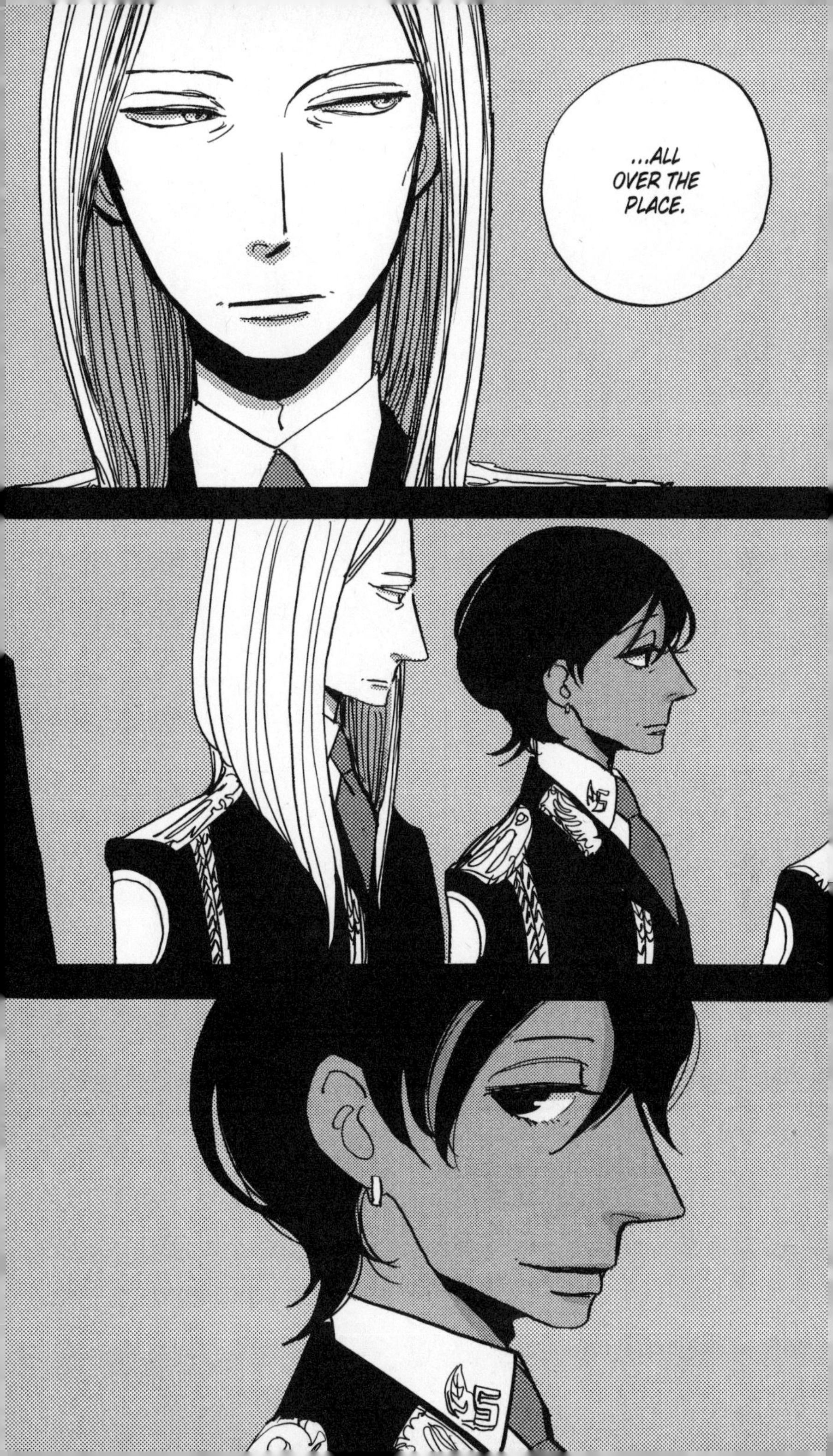
...ALL OVER THE PLACE.

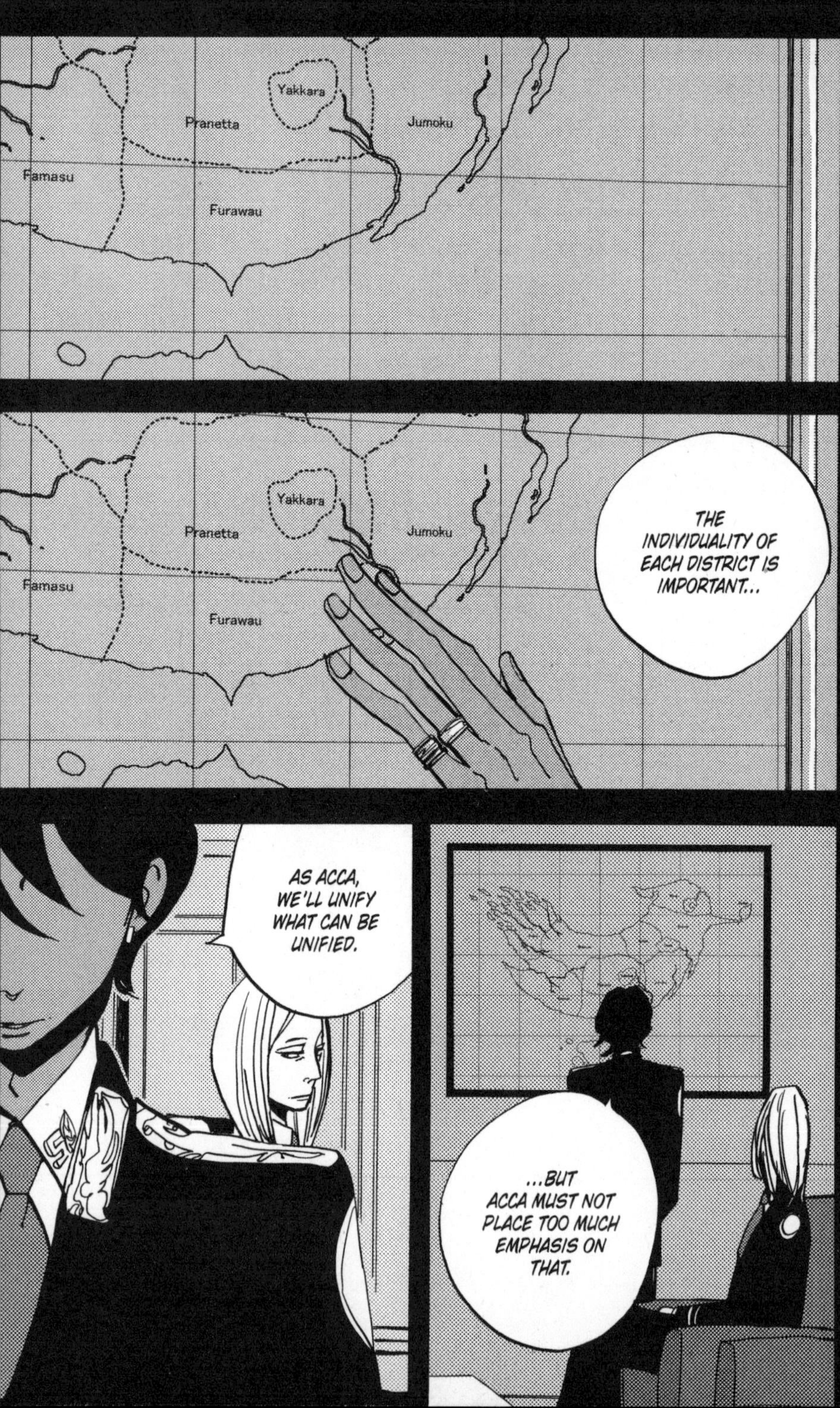
Yakkara
Pranetta
Jumoku
Famasu
Furawau
Yakkara
Pranetta
Jumoku
Famasu
Furawau
THE INDIVIDUALITY OF EACH DISTRICT IS IMPORTANT...
...BUT ACCA MUST NOT PLACE TOO MUCH EMPHASIS ON THAT.
AS ACCA, WE'LL UNIFY WHAT CAN BE UNIFIED.

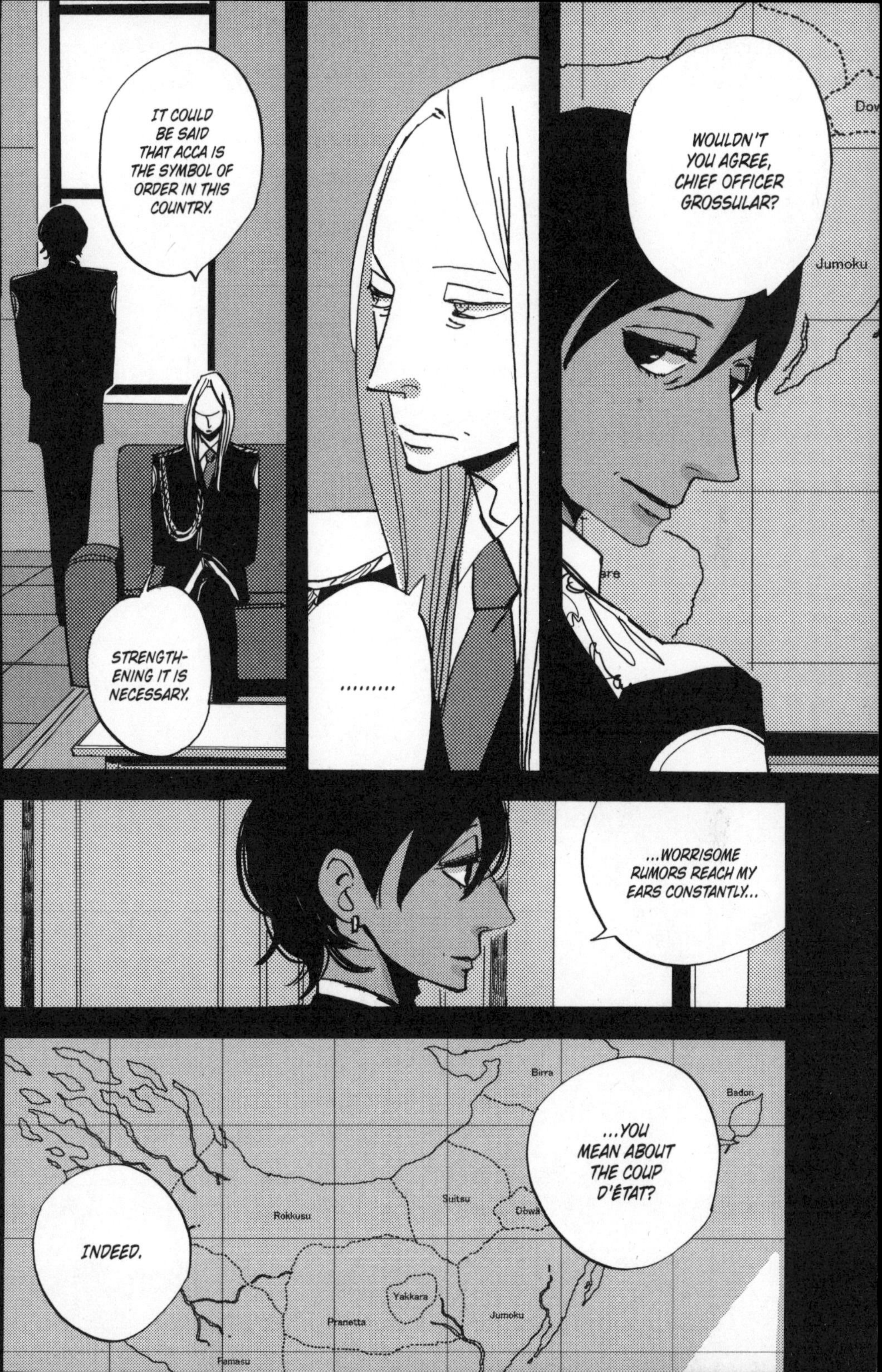
WOULDN'T YOU AGREE, CHIEF OFFICER GROSSULAR?
Jumoku
....
IT COULD BE SAID THAT ACCA IS THE SYMBOL OF ORDER IN THIS COUNTRY.
STRENGTH-ENING IT IS NECESSARY.
...WORRISOME RUMORS REACH MY EARS CONSTANTLY...
Birra
Badori
...YOU MEAN ABOUT THE COUP D'ÉTAT?
Suitsu
Dowa
Rokkusu
Yakkara
Jumoku
Pranetta
INDEED.

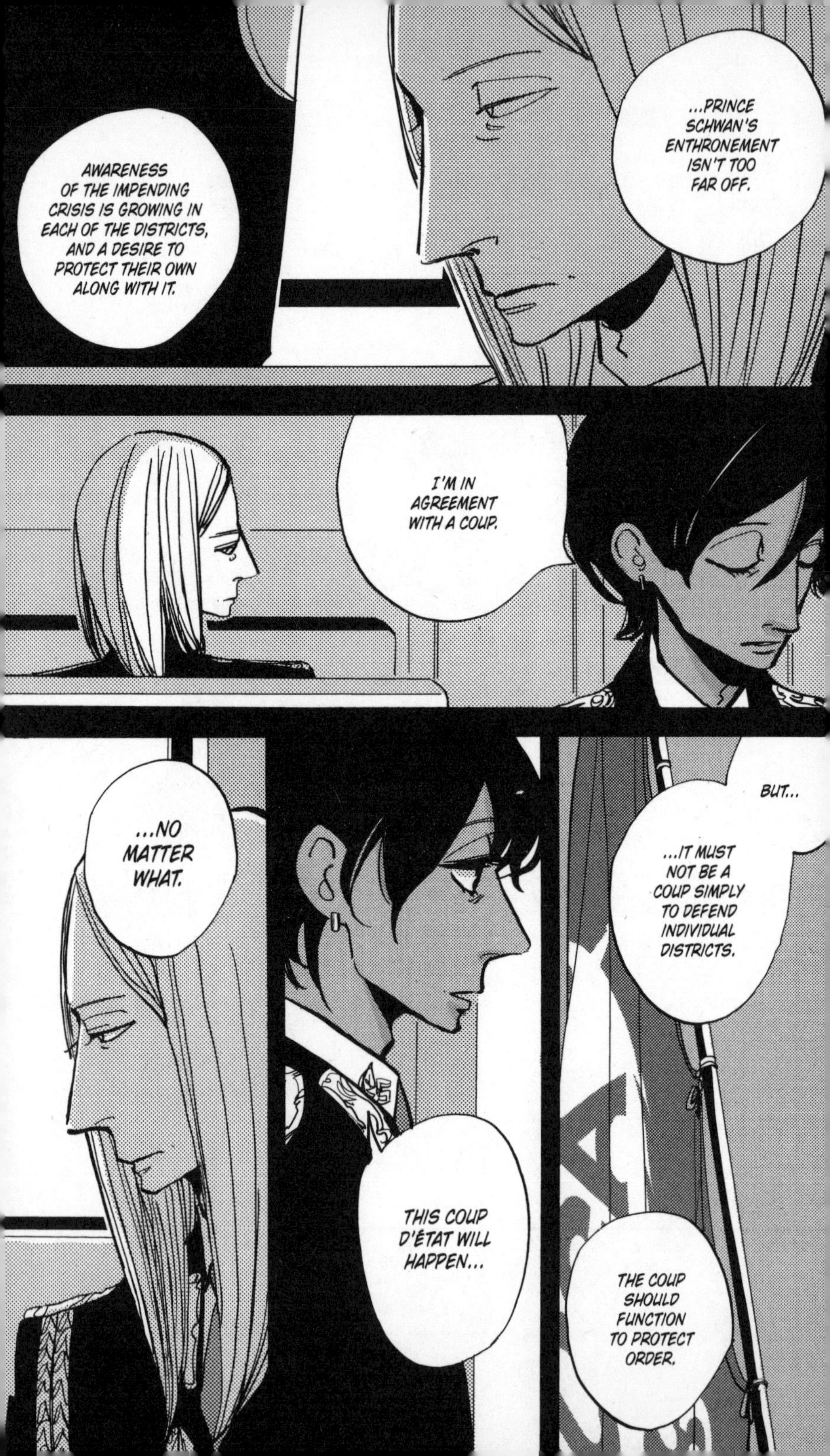
...PRINCE SCHWAN'S ENTHRONEMENT ISN'T TOO FAR OFF.
AWARENESS OF THE IMPENDING CRISIS IS GROWING IN EACH OF THE DISTRICTS, AND A DESIRE TO PROTECT THEIR OWN ALONG WITH IT.
I'M IN AGREEMENT WITH A COUP.
BUT...
...IT MUST NOT BE A COUP SIMPLY TO DEFEND INDIVIDUAL DISTRICTS.
THE COUP SHOULD FUNCTION TO PROTECT ORDER.
THIS COUP D'ÉTAT WILL HAPPEN...
...NO MATTER WHAT.

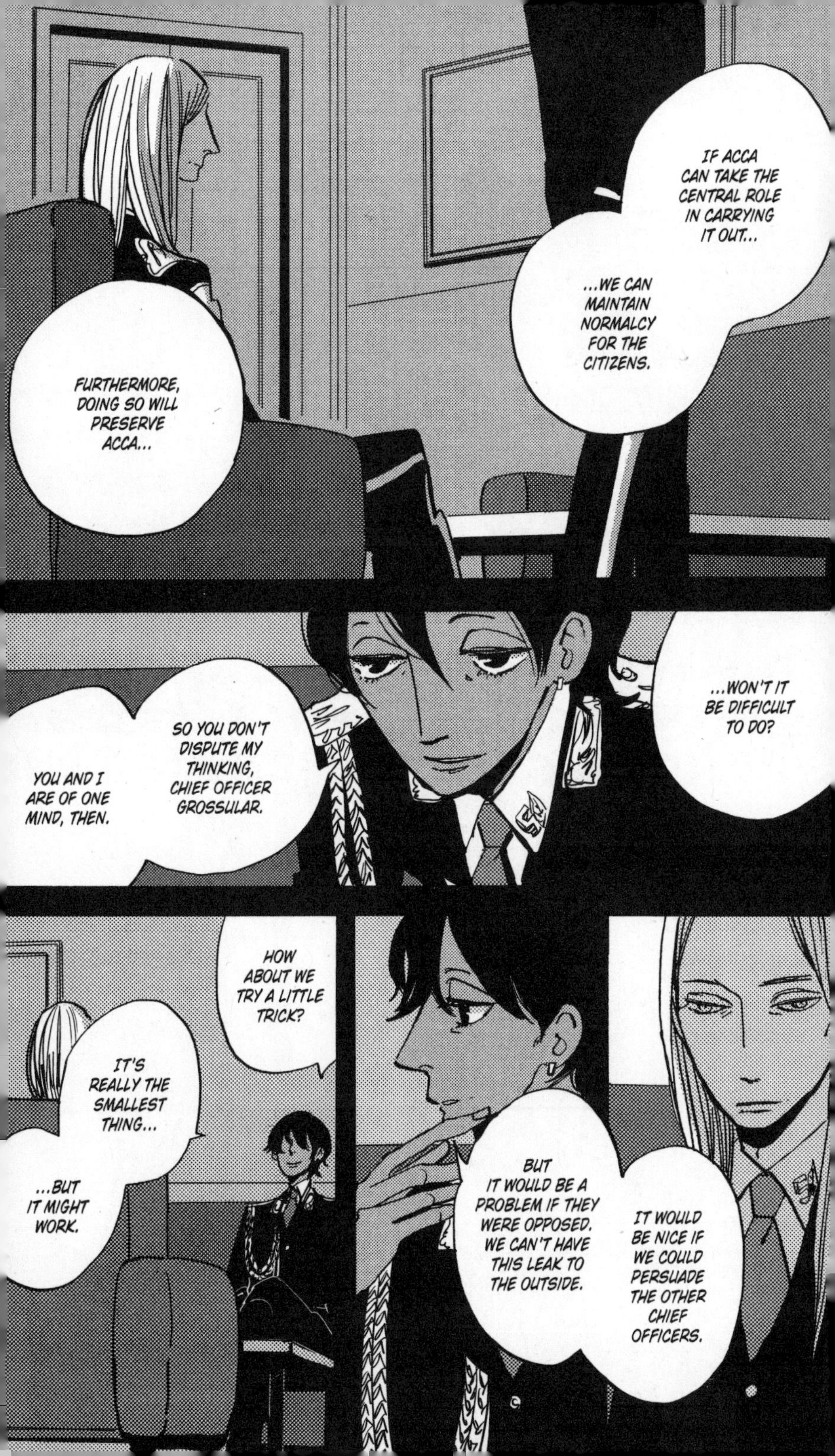
IF ACCA CAN TAKE THE CENTRAL ROLE IN CARRYING IT OUT...
...WE CAN MAINTAIN NORMALCY FOR THE CITIZENS.
FURTHERMORE, DOING SO WILL PRESERVE ACCA...
...WON'T IT BE DIFFICULT TO DO?
SO YOU DON'T DISPUTE MY THINKING, CHIEF OFFICER GROSSULAR.
YOU AND I ARE OF ONE MIND, THEN.
IT WOULD BE NICE IF WE COULD PERSUADE THE OTHER CHIEF OFFICERS.
BUT IT WOULD BE A PROBLEM IF THEY WERE OPPOSED. WE CAN'T HAVE THIS LEAK TO THE OUTSIDE.
HOW ABOUT WE TRY A LITTLE TRICK?
IT'S REALLY THE SMALLEST THING...
...BUT IT MIGHT WORK.

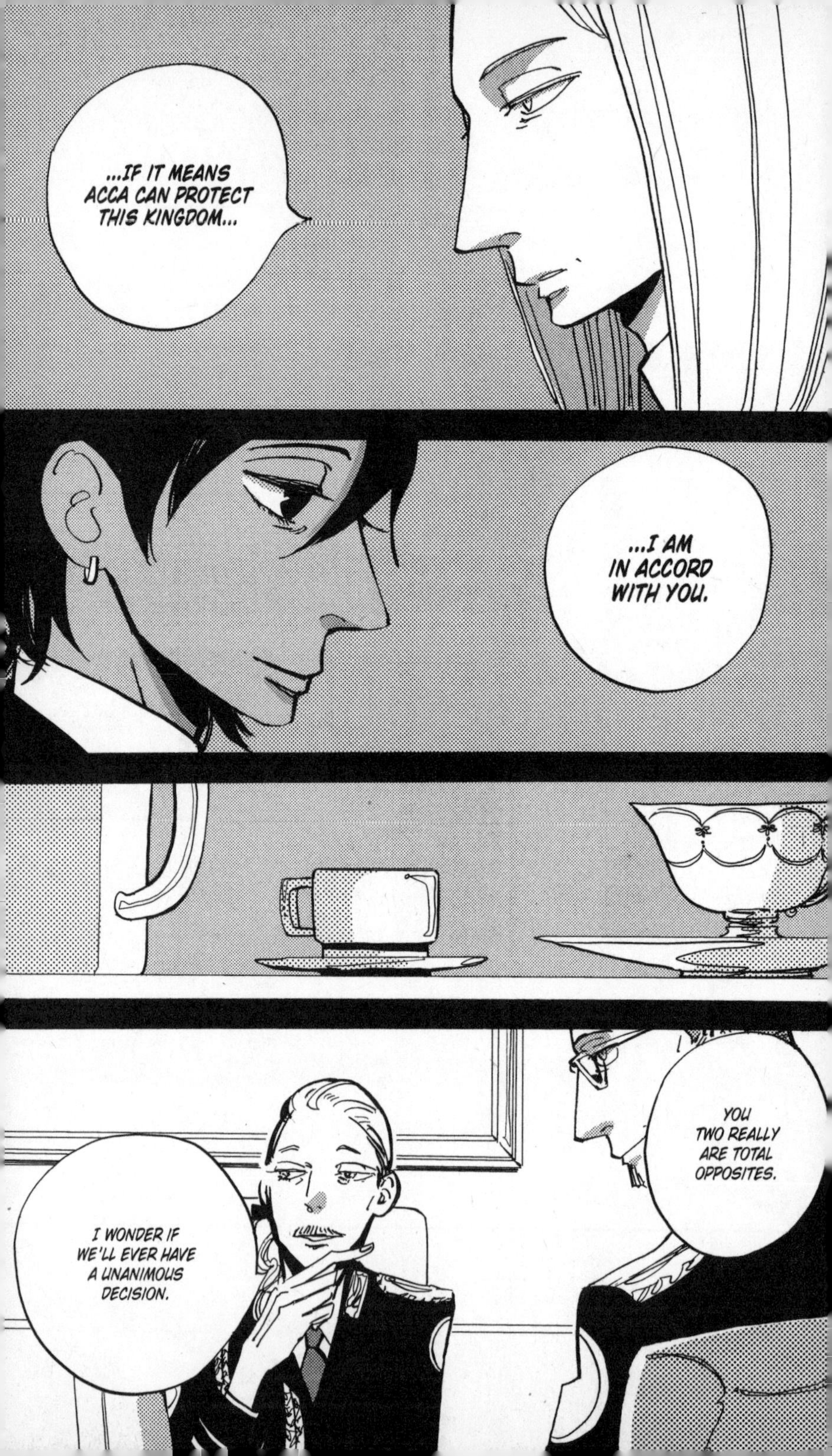
...IF IT MEANS ACCA CAN PROTECT THIS KINGDOM...
...I AM IN ACCORD WITH YOU.
YOU TWO REALLY ARE TOTAL OPPOSITES.
I WONDER IF WE'LL EVER HAVE A UNANIMOUS DECISION.

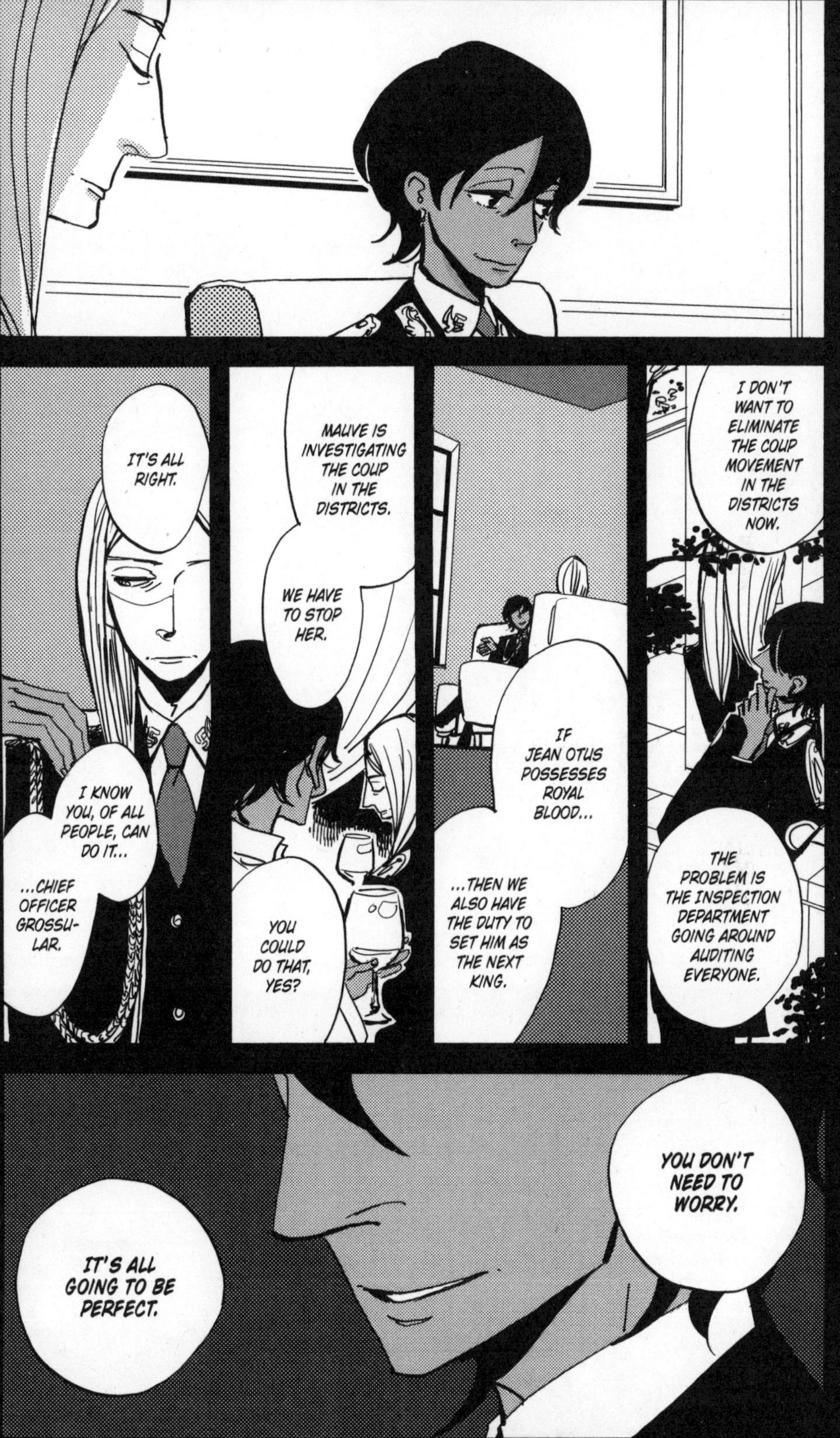
I DON'T WANT TO ELIMINATE THE COUP MOVEMENT IN THE DISTRICTS NOW.
THE PROBLEM IS THE INSPECTION DEPARTMENT GOING AROUND AUDITING EVERYONE.
IF JEAN OTUS POSSESSES ROYAL BLOOD...
...THEN WE ALSO HAVE THE DUTY TO SET HIM AS THE NEXT KING.
MAUVE IS INVESTIGATING THE COUP IN THE DISTRICTS.
WE HAVE TO STOP HER.
YOU COULD DO THAT, YES?
IT'S ALL RIGHT.
I KNOW YOU, OF ALL PEOPLE, CAN DO IT...
...CHIEF OFFICER GROSSULAR.
YOU DON'T NEED TO WORRY.
IT'S ALL GOING TO BE PERFECT.

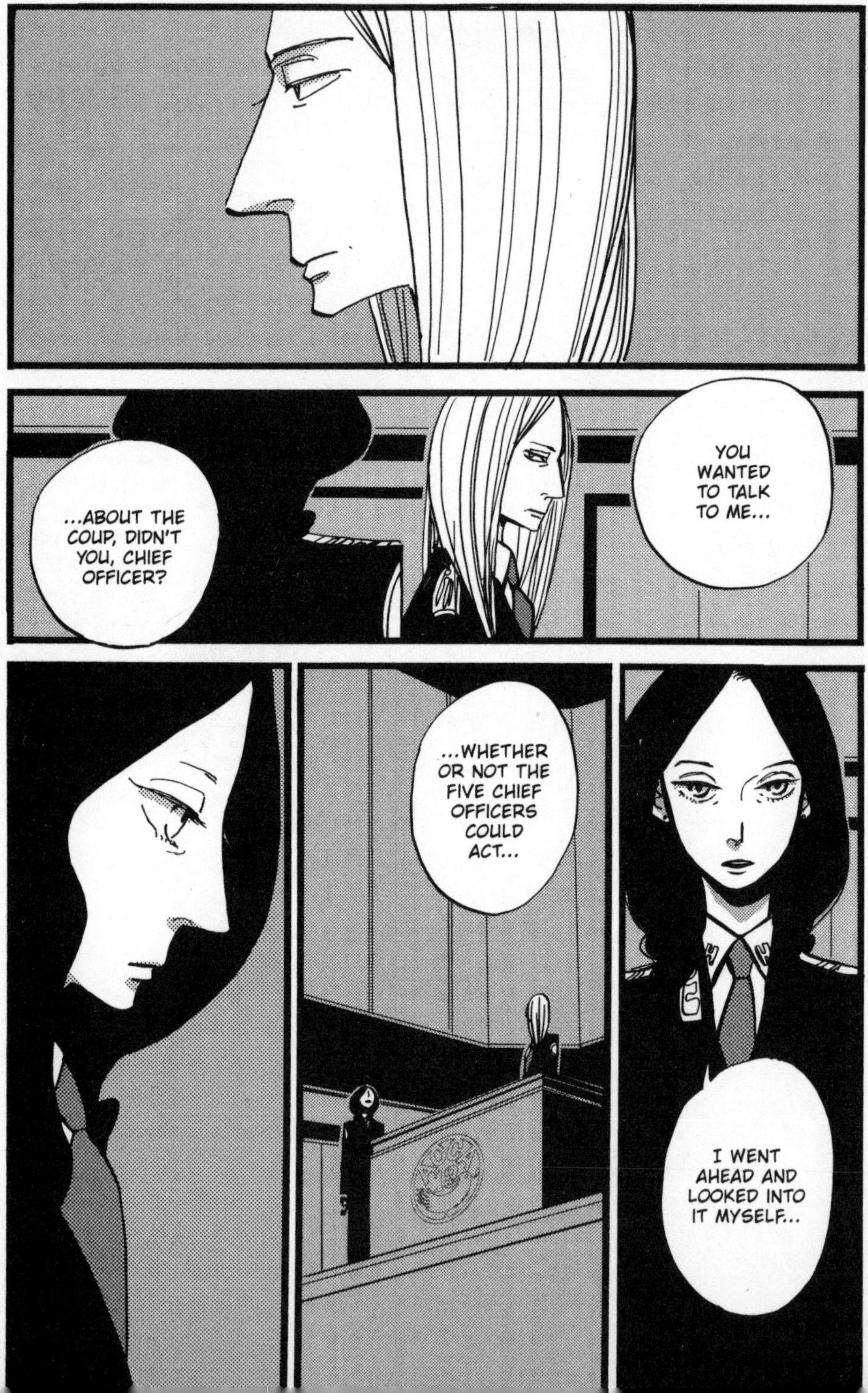
YOU WANTED TO TALK TO ME...
...ABOUT THE COUP, DIDN'T YOU, CHIEF OFFICER?
I WENT AHEAD AND LOOKED INTO IT MYSELF...
...WHETHER OR NOT THE FIVE CHIEF OFFICERS COULD ACT...

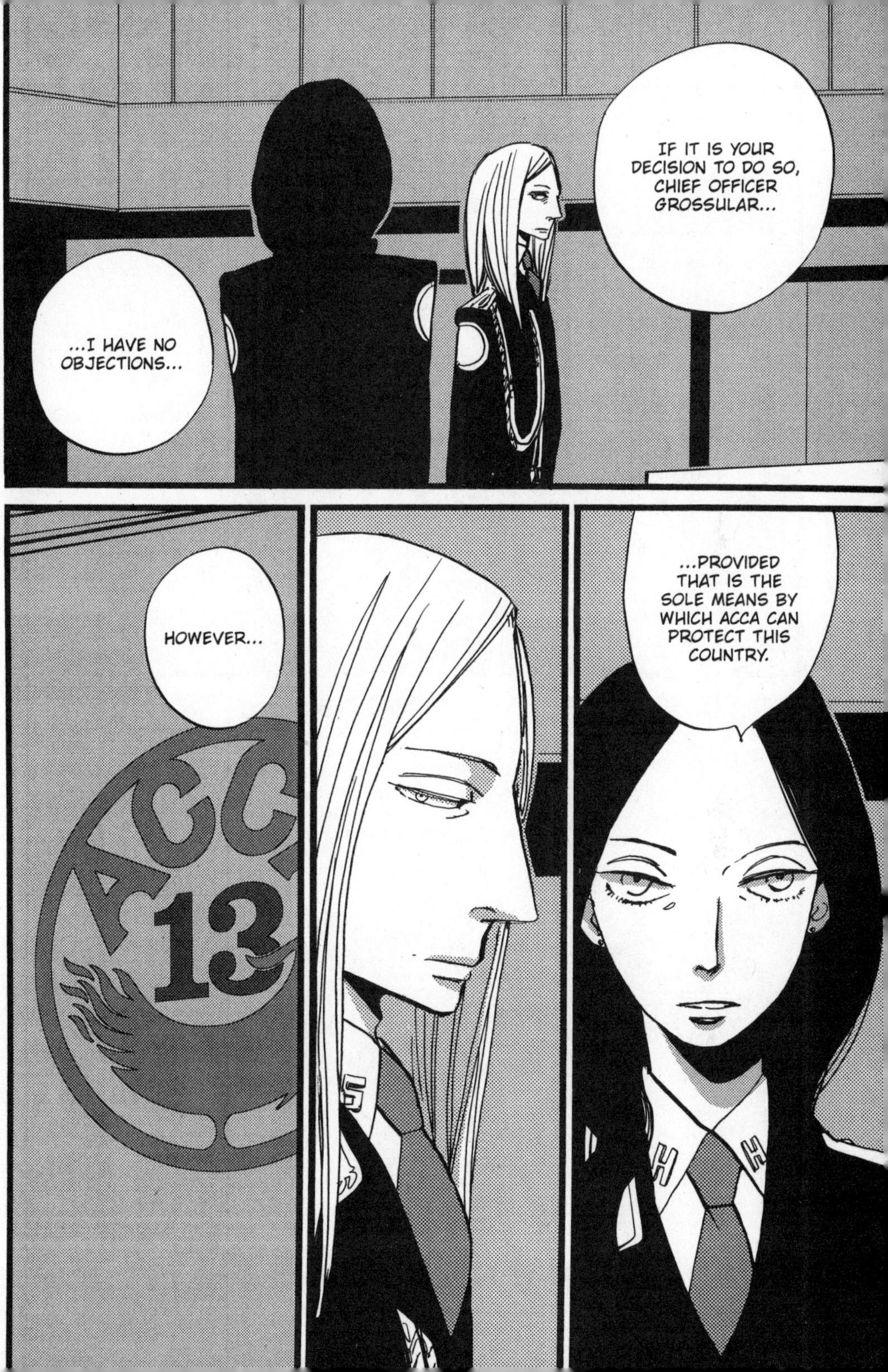
IF IT IS YOUR DECISION TO DO SO, CHIEF OFFICER GROSSULAR...
...I HAVE NO OBJECTIONS...
...PROVIDED THAT IS THE SOLE MEANS BY WHICH ACCA CAN PROTECT THIS COUNTRY.
HOWEVER...

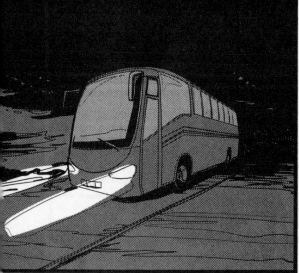

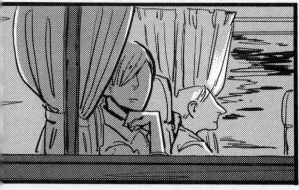

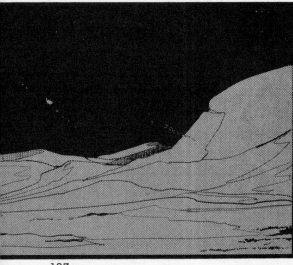

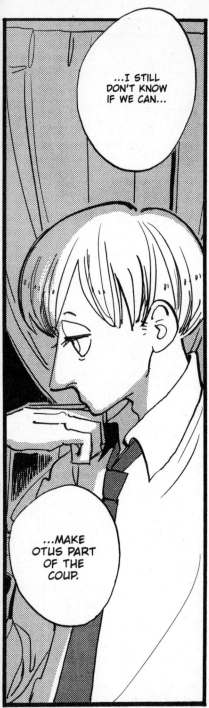

...I STILL DON'T KNOW IF WE CAN...

...MAKE OTUS PART OF THE COUP.

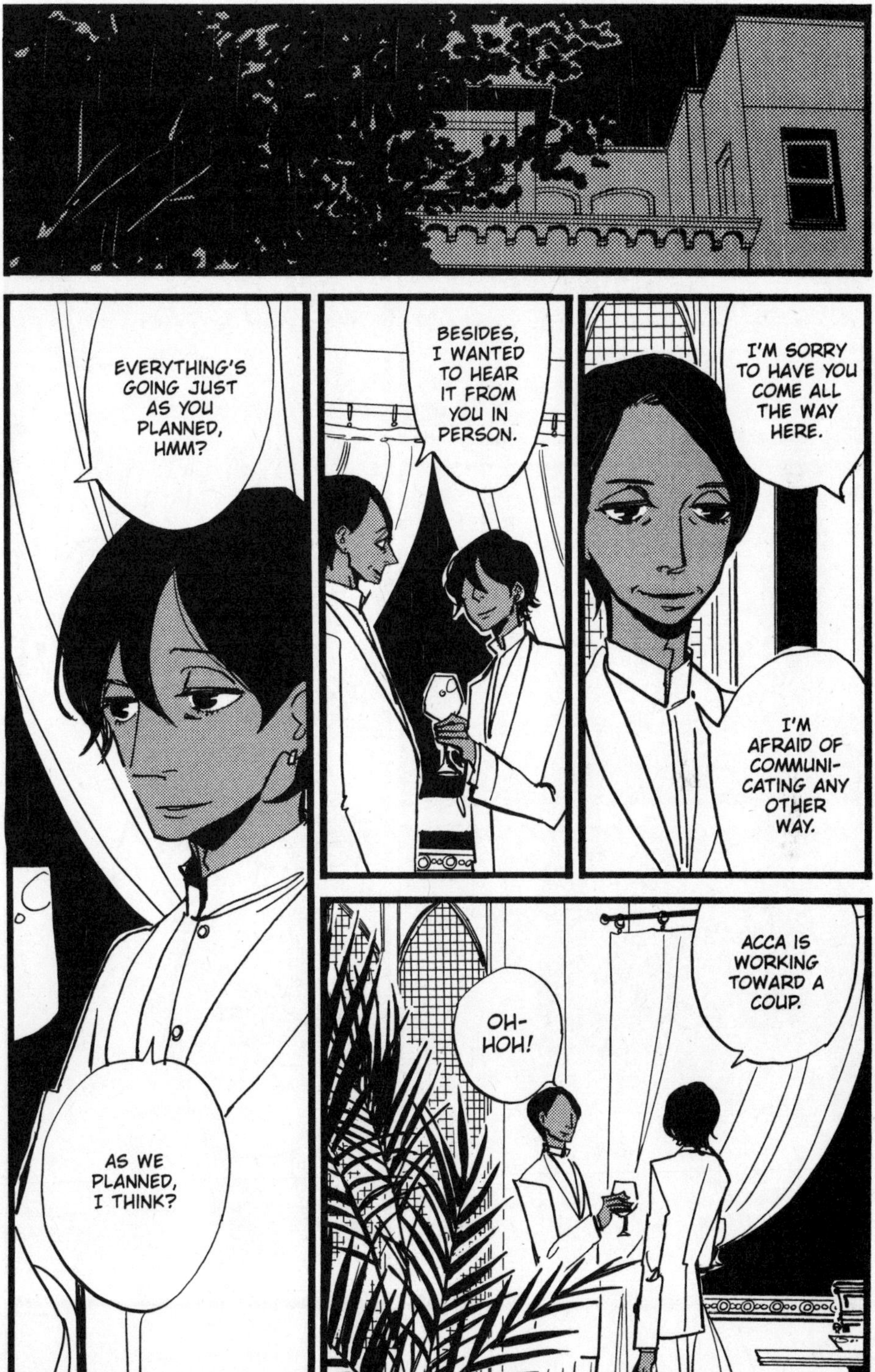
I'M SORRY TO HAVE YOU COME ALL THE WAY HERE.
I'M AFRAID OF COMMUNICATING ANY OTHER WAY.
BESIDES, I WANTED TO HEAR IT FROM YOU IN PERSON.
ACCA IS WORKING TOWARD A COUP.
OH-HOH!
EVERYTHING'S GOING JUST AS YOU PLANNED, HMM?
AS WE PLANNED, I THINK?

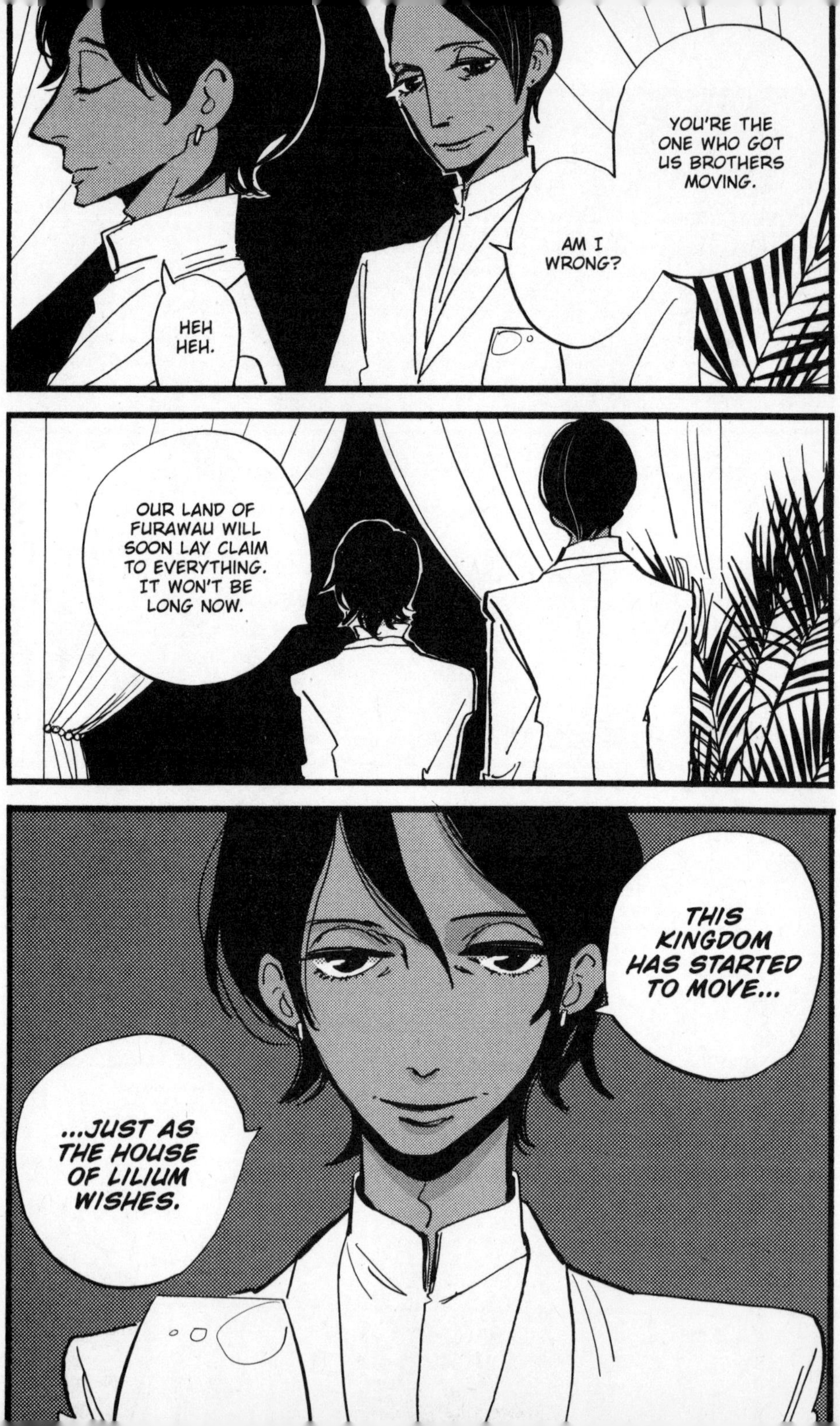
YOU'RE THE ONE WHO GOT US BROTHERS MOVING.
AM I WRONG?
HEH HEH.
OUR LAND OF FURAWAU WILL SOON LAY CLAIM TO EVERYTHING. IT WON'T BE LONG NOW.
THIS KINGDOM HAS STARTED TO MOVE...
...JUST AS THE HOUSE OF LILIUM WISHES.

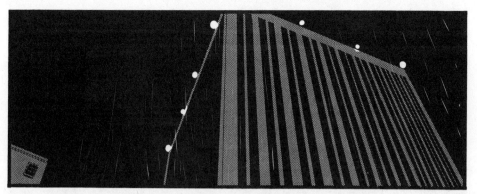

AN ASSORTMENT OF...
...HA! CHI! KU! MA! COOKIIIIES!
EEEEEE!
THIS ONE'S A BUTTER COOKIE!
DESSERT PARTY!
IT'S TOO BAD WE COULDN'T DO THE BARBE-CUE...
...BUT WE HAVE LOTS OF SWEETS! SO BE HAPPY!
HERE!
....
THANKS...

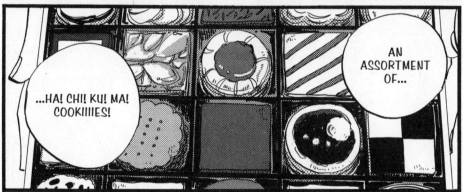

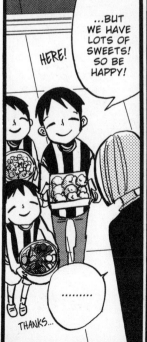

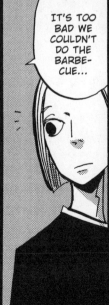

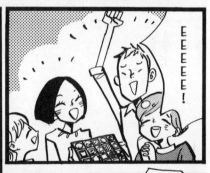

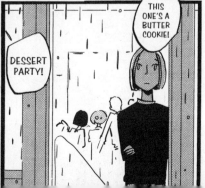

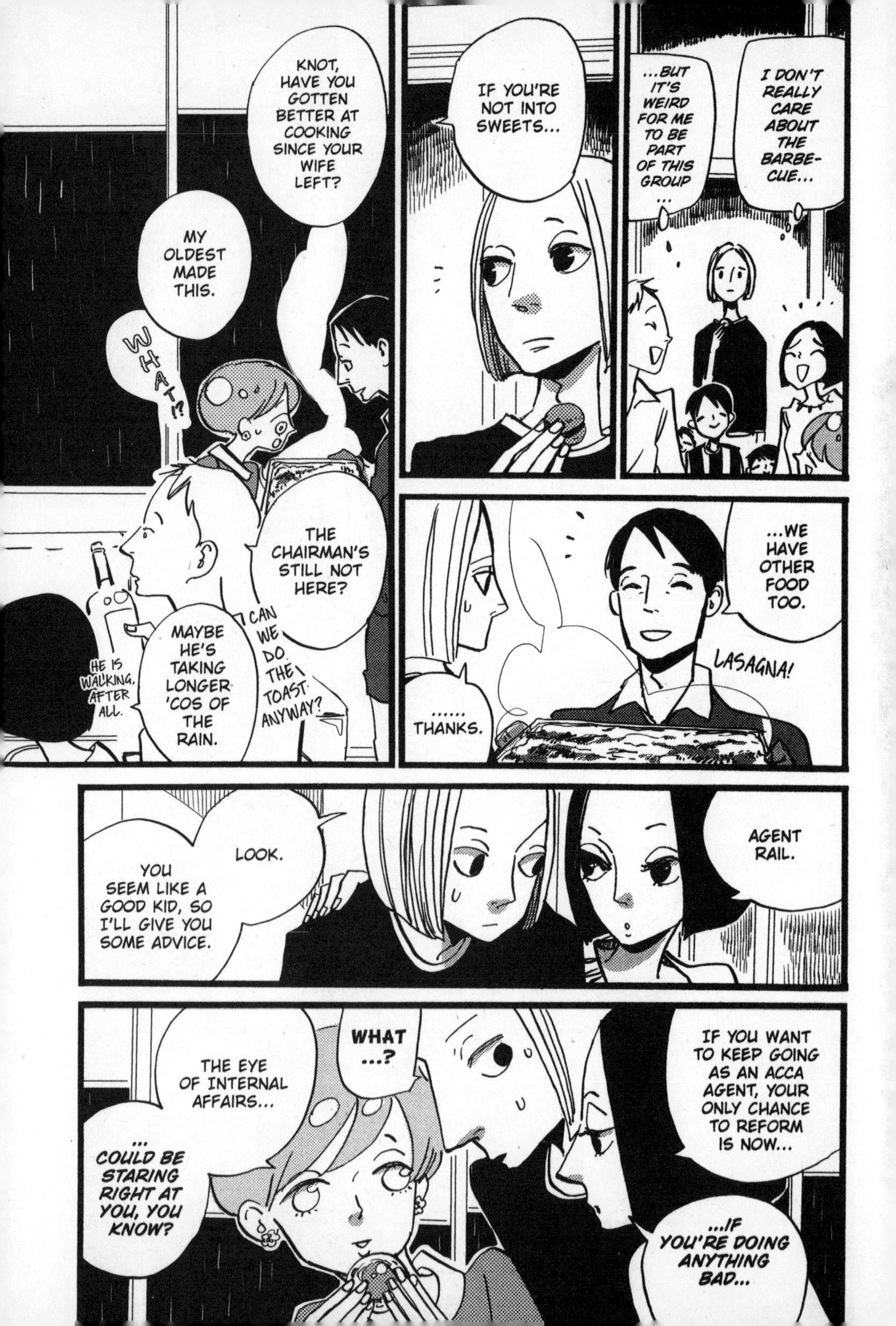
I DON'T REALLY CARE ABOUT THE BARBECUE...
...BUT IT'S WEIRD FOR ME TO BE PART OF THIS GROUP...
IF YOU'RE NOT INTO SWEETS...
...WE HAVE OTHER FOOD TOO.
LASAGNA!
......THANKS.
KNOT, HAVE YOU GOTTEN BETTER AT COOKING SINCE YOUR WIFE LEFT?
MY OLDEST MADE THIS.
WHAT!?
THE CHAIRMAN'S STILL NOT HERE?
CAN WE DO THE TOAST ANYWAY?
MAYBE HE'S TAKING LONGER 'COS OF THE RAIN.
HE IS WALKING, AFTER ALL.
AGENT RAIL.
LOOK.
YOU SEEM LIKE A GOOD KID, SO I'LL GIVE YOU SOME ADVICE.
IF YOU WANT TO KEEP GOING AS AN ACCA AGENT, YOUR ONLY CHANCE TO REFORM IS NOW...
...IF YOU'RE DOING ANYTHING BAD...
WHAT...?
THE EYE OF INTERNAL AFFAIRS...
...COULD BE STARING RIGHT AT YOU, YOU KNOW?

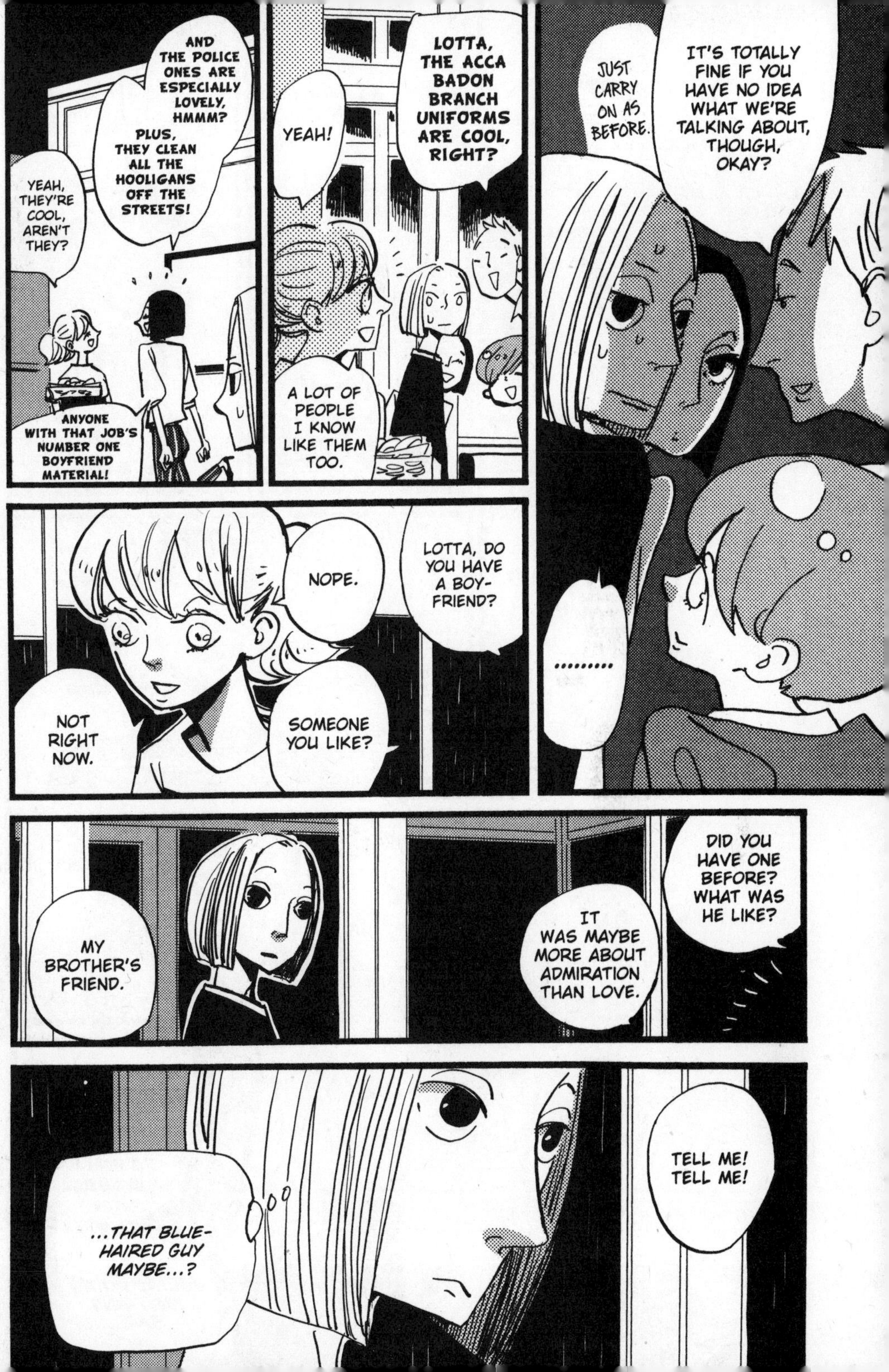
IT'S TOTALLY FINE IF YOU HAVE NO IDEA WHAT WE'RE TALKING ABOUT, THOUGH, OKAY?
JUST CARRY ON AS BEFORE.
....
LOTTA, THE ACCA BADON BRANCH UNIFORMS ARE COOL, RIGHT?
YEAH!
A LOT OF PEOPLE I KNOW LIKE THEM TOO.
AND THE POLICE ONES ARE ESPECIALLY LOVELY, HMMM?
PLUS, THEY CLEAN ALL THE HOOLIGANS OFF THE STREETS!
YEAH, THEY'RE COOL, AREN'T THEY?
ANYONE WITH THAT JOB'S NUMBER ONE BOYFRIEND MATERIAL!
LOTTA, DO YOU HAVE A BOY-FRIEND?
NOPE.
SOMEONE YOU LIKE?
NOT RIGHT NOW.
DID YOU HAVE ONE BEFORE? WHAT WAS HE LIKE?
IT WAS MAYBE MORE ABOUT ADMIRATION THAN LOVE.
MY BROTHER'S FRIEND.
TELL ME! TELL ME!
...THAT BLUE-HAIRED GUY MAYBE...?

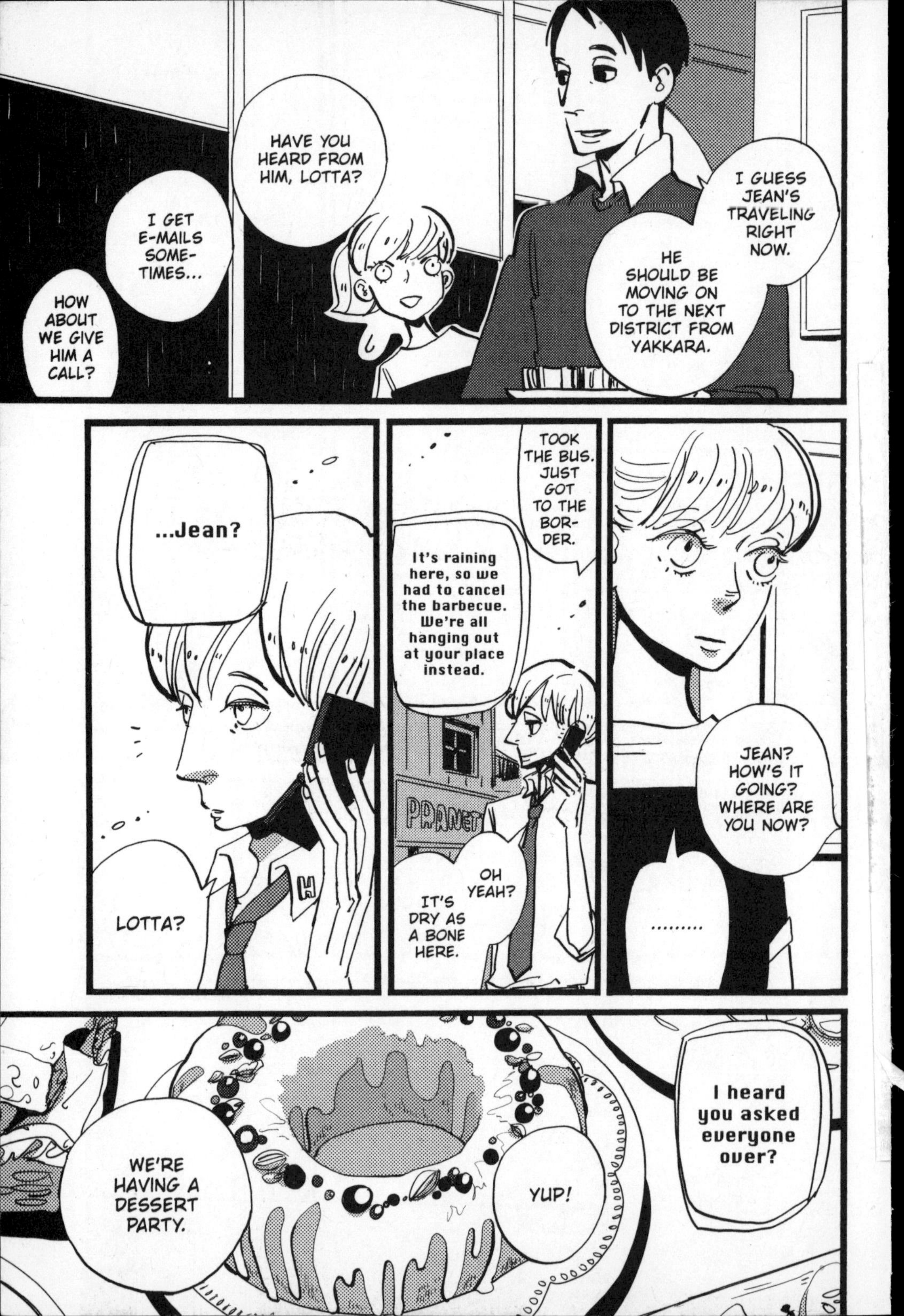
I GUESS JEAN'S TRAVELING RIGHT NOW.
HE SHOULD BE MOVING ON TO THE NEXT DISTRICT FROM YAKKARA.
HAVE YOU HEARD FROM HIM, LOTTA?
I GET E-MAILS SOME-TIMES...
HOW ABOUT WE GIVE HIM A CALL?
JEAN? HOW'S IT GOING? WHERE ARE YOU NOW?
....
TOOK THE BUS. JUST GOT TO THE BOR-DER.
It's raining here, so we had to cancel the barbecue. We're all hanging out at your place instead.
OH YEAH?
IT'S DRY AS A BONE HERE.
...Jean?
LOTTA?
I heard you asked everyone over?
YUP!
WE'RE HAVING A DESSERT PARTY.

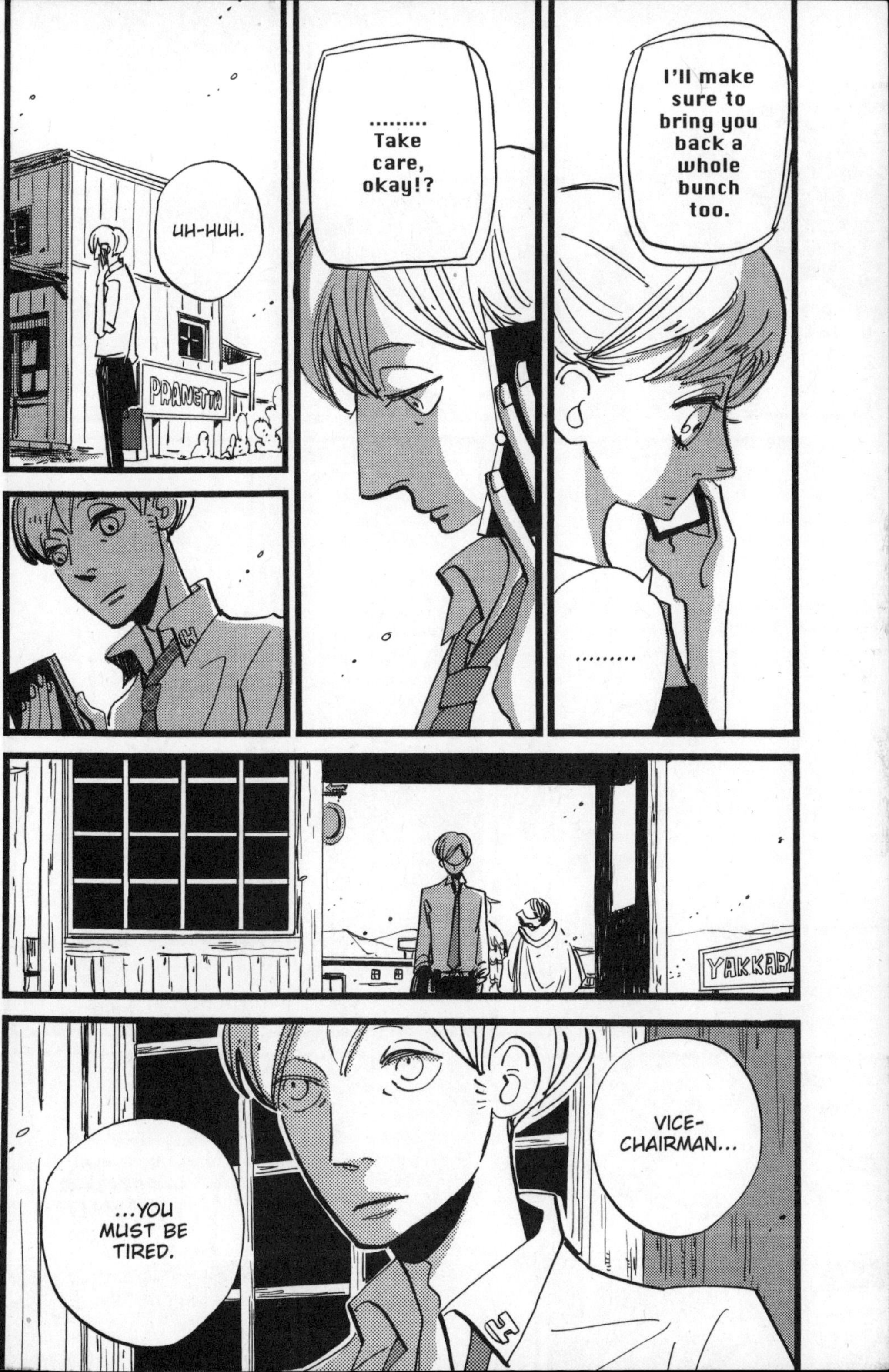
I'll make sure to bring you back a whole bunch too.
....
....
Take care, okay!?
UH-HUH.
PRANETTA
VICE-CHAIRMAN...
...YOU MUST BE TIRED.

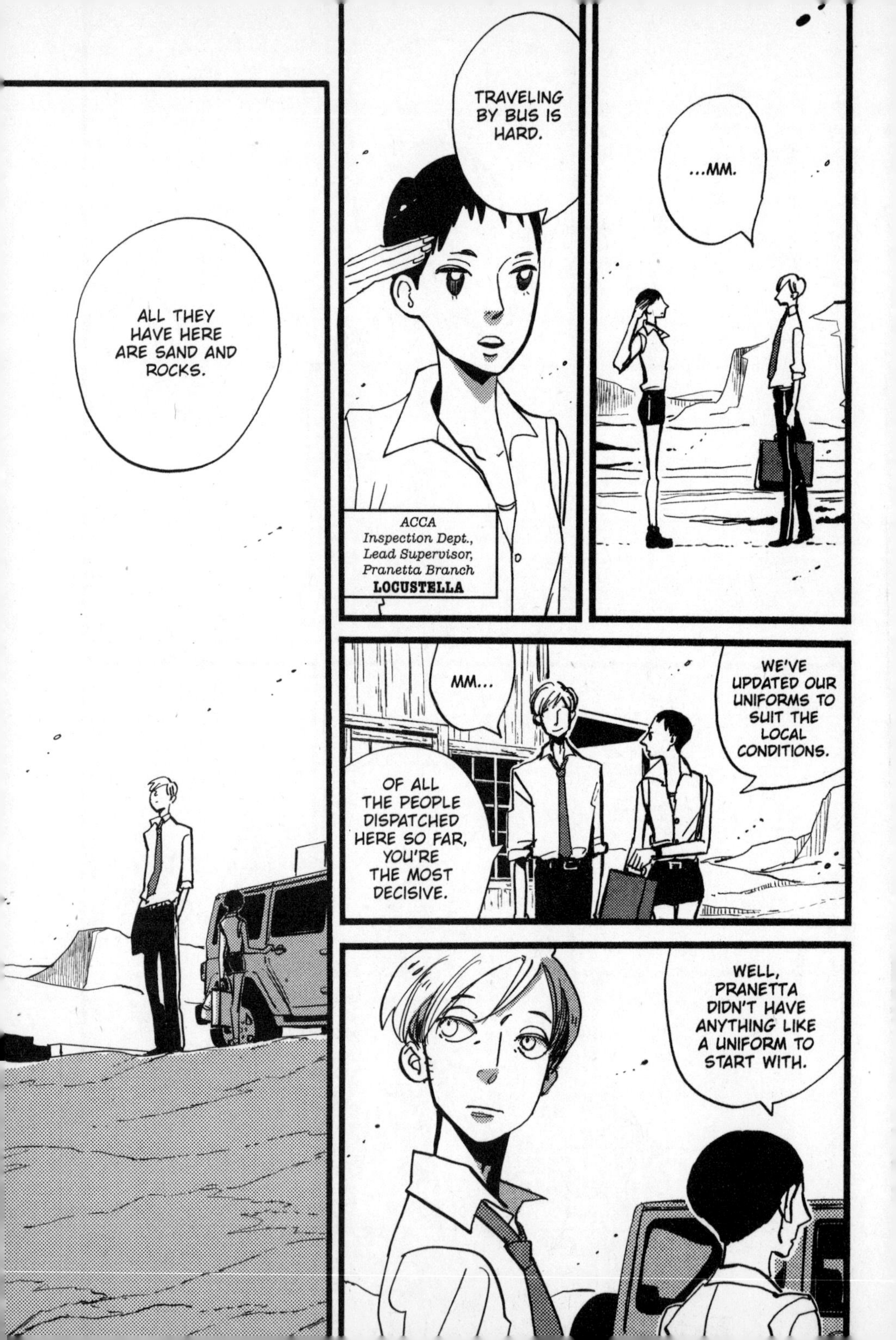
...MM.
TRAVELING BY BUS IS HARD.
ACCA Inspection Dept., Lead Supervisor, Pranetta Branch LOCUSTELLA
WE'VE UPDATED OUR UNIFORMS TO SUIT THE LOCAL CONDITIONS.
MM...
OF ALL THE PEOPLE DISPATCHED HERE SO FAR, YOU'RE THE MOST DECISIVE.
WELL, PRANETTA DIDN'T HAVE ANYTHING LIKE A UNIFORM TO START WITH.
ALL THEY HAVE HERE ARE SAND AND ROCKS.

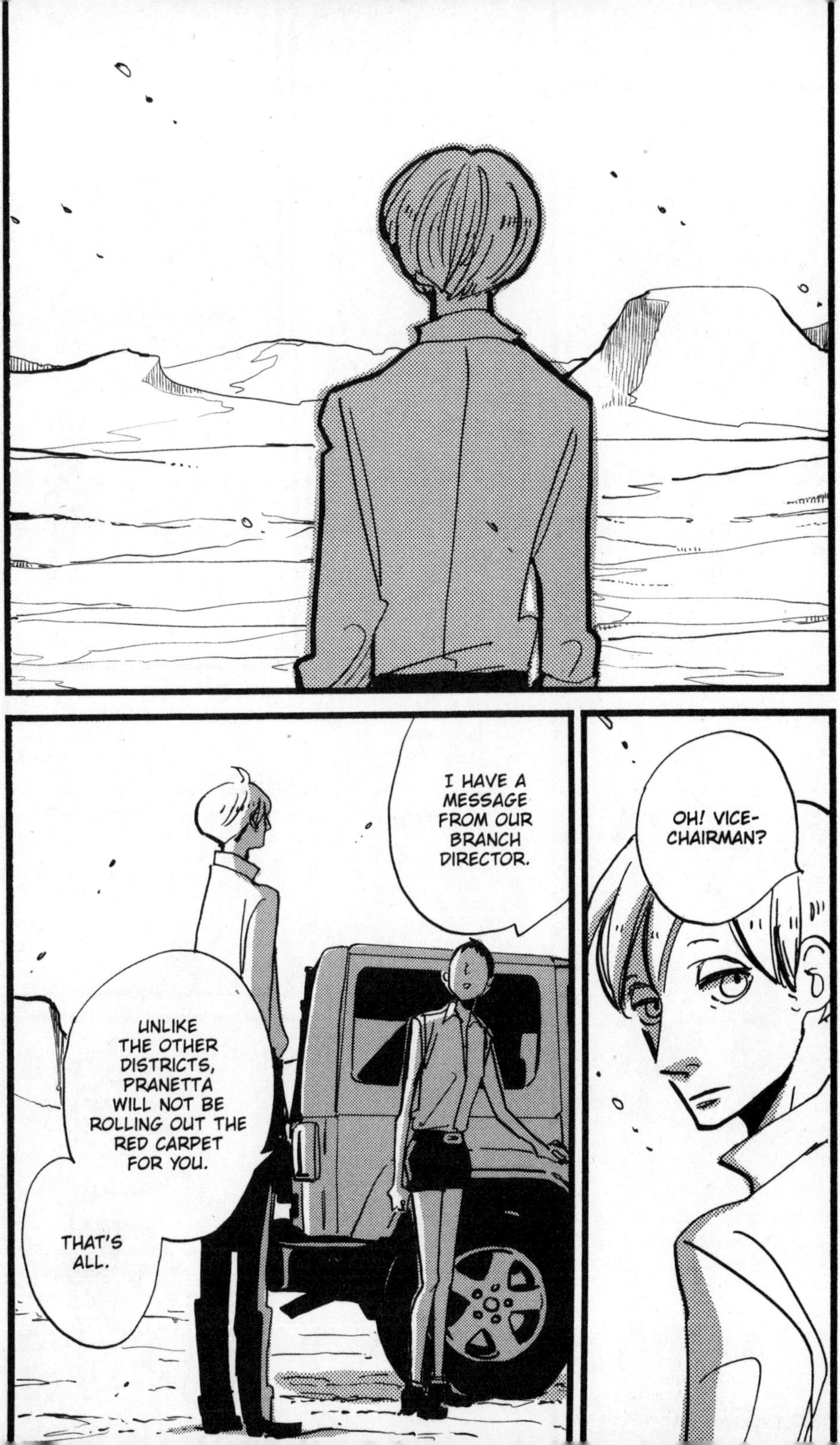
OH! VICE-CHAIRMAN?
I HAVE A MESSAGE FROM OUR BRANCH DIRECTOR.
UNLIKE THE OTHER DISTRICTS, PRANETTA WILL NOT BE ROLLING OUT THE RED CARPET FOR YOU.
THAT'S ALL.

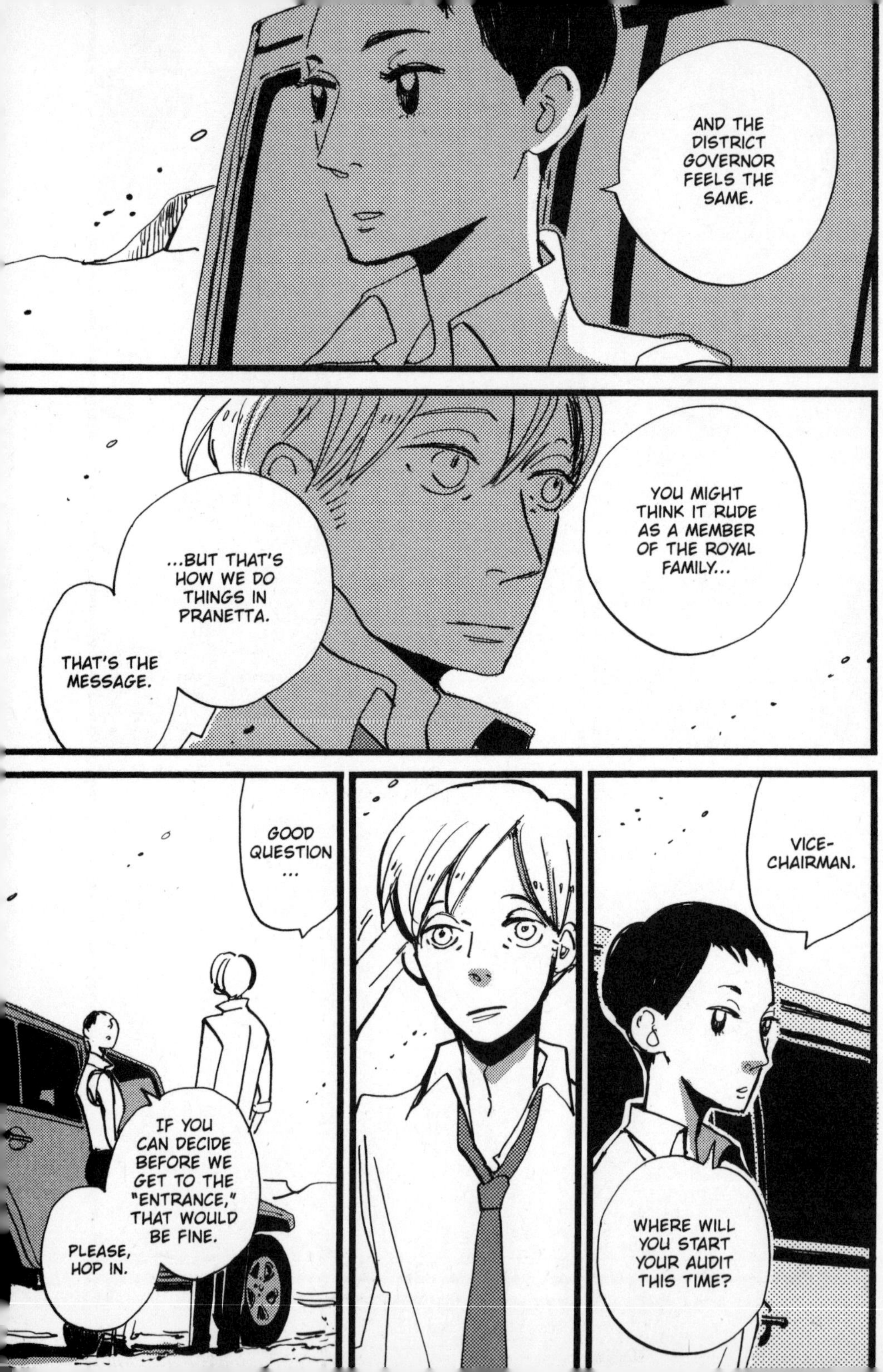
AND THE DISTRICT GOVERNOR FEELS THE SAME.
YOU MIGHT THINK IT RUDE AS A MEMBER OF THE ROYAL FAMILY...
...BUT THAT'S HOW WE DO THINGS IN PRANETTA.
THAT'S THE MESSAGE.
VICE-CHAIRMAN.
WHERE WILL YOU START YOUR AUDIT THIS TIME?
GOOD QUESTION ...
IF YOU CAN DECIDE BEFORE WE GET TO THE "ENTRANCE," THAT WOULD BE FINE.
PLEASE, HOP IN.

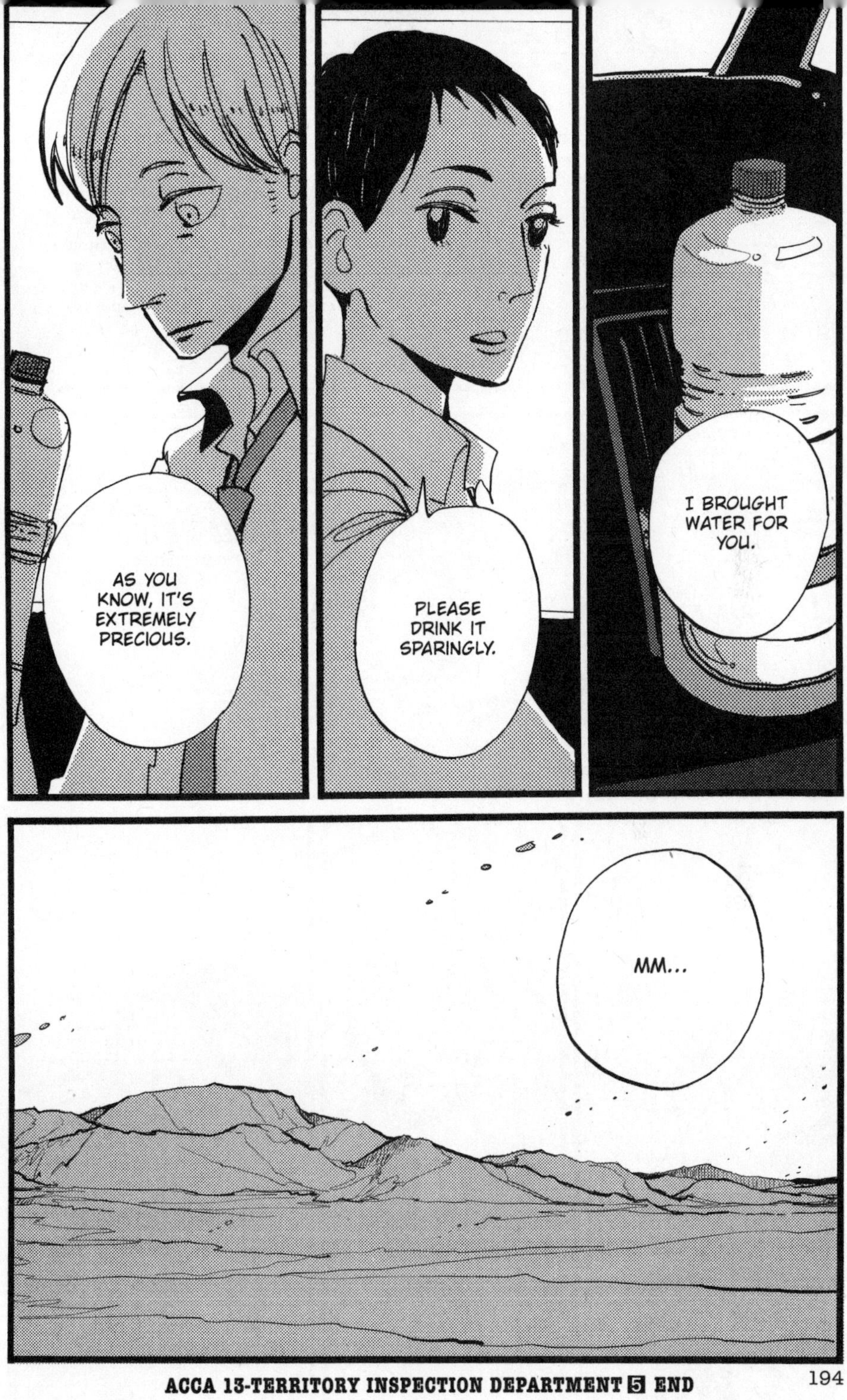
I BROUGHT WATER FOR YOU.
PLEASE DRINK IT SPARINGLY.
AS YOU KNOW, IT'S EXTREMELY PRECIOUS.
MM...

ACCA 13-TERRITORY INSPECTION DEPARTMENT 5 END

Kingdom of Dowa

Dowa, a kingdom with regional self-government, is divided into thirteen districts, with each district having its own unique culture.

ACCA is a massive unified organization, encompassing the police department, the fire department, and medical services, among others. The organization is managed by the branches in each district, with Headquarters in the capital performing the role of uniting the thirteen ACCA branches. The Inspection Department Jean belongs to has Headquarters agents stationed at each branch and also sends a supervisor to audit at irregular intervals in order to monitor the daily operations of the branches.

Birra
Badon
Korore
Dowa
Peshi
Suitsu
Rokkusu
Yakkara
Jumoku
Pranetta
Famasu
Furawau
Hare

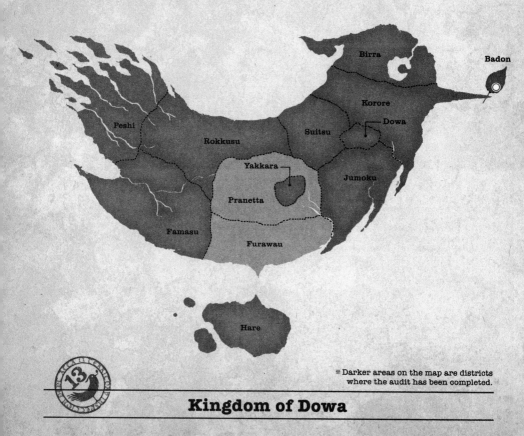

※ Darker areas on the map are districts where the audit has been completed.

Kingdom of Dowa

CHAPTER 30

The Result of Aligned Ambitions in Badon

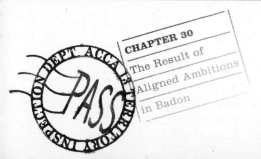

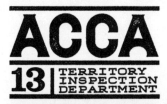

ACCA

13 | TERRITORY INSPECTION DEPARTMENT

NATSUME ONO

Translation:
Jocelyne Allen

Lettering:
Lys Blakeslee

ACCA JUSAN-KU KANSATSU-KA Volume 5 ©2016 Natsume Ono/ Square Enix Co., Ltd. First published in Japan in 2016 by Square Enix Co., Ltd. English translation rights arranged with Square Enix Co., Ltd. and Yen Press, LLC through Tuttle-Mori Agency, Inc.

English translation ©2018 by Square Enix Co., Ltd.

Yen Press
1290 Avenue of the Americas
New York, NY 10104

Visit us at yenpress.com
facebook.com/yenpress
twitter.com/yenpress
yenpress.tumblr.com
instagram.com/yenpress

First Yen Press Edition: November 2018

Yen Press is an imprint of Yen Press, LLC.
The Yen Press name and logo are trademarks of Yen Press, LLC.

The publisher is not responsible for websites (or their content) that are not owned by the publisher.

Library of Congress Control Number: 2017949545

ISBNs: 978-0-316-44682-2 (paperback)
978-0-316-44683-9 (ebook)

10 9 8 7 6 5 4 3 2 1

WOR

Printed in the United States of America